EUCOTAX Series on European Taxation

# International Exchange of Information and the Protection of Taxpayers

**EUCOTAX Series on European Taxation**

VOLUME 24



*The titles in this series are listed at the back of this volume.*

KLUWER LAW INTERNATIONAL

EUCOTAX Series on European Taxation

# International Exchange of Information and the Protection of Taxpayers

Tonny Schenk-Geers



Wolters Kluwer
Law & Business

AUSTIN BOSTON CHICAGO NEW YORK THE NETHERLANDS

*Published by:*
Kluwer Law International
PO Box 316
2400 AH Alphen aan den Rijn
The Netherlands
Website: www.kluwerlaw.com

*Sold and distributed in North, Central and South America by:*
Aspen Publishers, Inc.
7201 McKinney Circle
Frederick, MD 21704
United States of America
Email: customer.service@aspenpublishers.com

*Sold and distributed in all other countries by:*
Turpin Distribution Services Ltd.
Stratton Business Park
Pegasus Drive, Biggleswade
Bedfordshire SG18 8TQ
United Kingdom
Email: kluwerlaw@turpin-distribution.com

*Printed on acid-free paper.*

ISBN 978-90-411-3142-3



Printed in Great Britain.

# Table of Contents

**Preface** **xv**

**Chapter 1**
**Introduction and Problem Definition** **1**
1. Introduction 1
2. The Importance of International Exchange of Information in Tax Matters 2
3. Recent Points of View on Legal Protection in the International Exchange of Information 3
4. Problem Definition 6
5. The Dutch Situation 6
6. Structure of This Book 7

**Chapter 2**
**Backgrounds of Legal Protection** **9**
1. Introduction 9
2. From Law to Justice: The Development of the Constitutional State 11
   2.1. The Liberal Constitutional State 11
   2.2. The Democratic Constitutional State 12
   2.3. Law and Principles of Law 14
   2.4. 'The Right to Equal Concern and Respect' 17
3. The Relational Concept of Law 18
   3.1. Legal Relationships 19
   3.2. Symmetrical Legal Relationships 19
   3.3. Legal Relationships in Administrative Law 20
   3.4. Obligations of Citizens in Legal Relationships of Administrative Law 21

4. Legal Relationship in International Tax Matters 22
4.1. The Exchange of Information as a Legal Relationship in Tax Matters 23
5. Summary 25

**Chapter 3**
**Interpretation of Tax Treaties** **29**
1. Introduction 29
2. Nature and Objectives of Tax Treaties 31
3. Function of the Model Convention 33
4. Two Frameworks of International Law for the Interpretation of Tax Treaties: The Vienna Convention and the OECD Model Convention 33
4.1. The Need for a Uniform Interpretation of Treaties 34
4.2. Interpretation of Treaties According to Article 31 of the Vienna Convention 35
4.3. Interpretation of Tax Treaties: Article 3, Paragraph 2 of the OECD Model 37
4.4. Article 3, Paragraph 2 of the OECD Model Convention and the Exchange of Information 41
4.5. Conclusion 42
5. The Meaning of the OECD Commentary 43
5.1. Conclusion 47
6. Static or Dynamic Interpretation 48
6.1. Domestic Dynamics and the Interpretation of Treaties: an Area of Conflicts 49
6.2. Possible Solutions 53
6.3. International Dynamics and the Interpretation of Treaties 54
6.4. Evaluation of Dynamic Interpretation 57
6.5. Conclusion 59
7. Summary and Conclusions 60

**Chapter 4**
**Aspects of International Law and the Obligation Concerning the Exchange of Information** **63**
1. Introduction 63
2. Ethical Norms in International Law 65
2.1. Tax Treaty Law 67
2.2. Conclusion 73
3. Exchange of Information 'An Ongoing Process' 74
3.1. Recent Developments 75
3.2. Conclusion 77
4. Different Obligations Concerning the Exchange of Information: An Analysis 78

4.1. Obligatory Exchange 79
4.1.1. OECD Model Convention on Double Taxation 79
4.1.2. Obligatory Exchange in Other Rules 80
4.2. Relevance for Taxation 80
4.2.1. OECD Model Convention on Double Taxation: 'Such Information as Is Foreseeably Relevant' 80
4.2.2. Relevance for Taxation: Strasbourg Convention 82
4.2.3. Relevance for Taxation: Directive 77/799 82
4.2.4. Relevance for Taxation in Council Regulation 1798/2003 on VAT 83
4.2.5. Relevance for Taxation in the OECD Agreement 83
4.2.6. Conclusion 83
4.3. Objects of Exchange 83
4.3.1. Objective Scope of the OECD Model Convention 84
4.3.2. Objective Scope of Directive 77/799: Ranking of the Obligations Concerning the Exchange of Information 85
4.3.3. Objective Scope of Council Regulation 1798/2003 on VAT 88
4.3.4. Objective Scope of the Strasbourg Convention 89
4.3.5. Objective Scope of the OECD Agreement 89
4.3.6. Retroactive Implementation: All Regulations 90
4.3.7. Conclusion 92
4.4. Objectives for the Exchange: Extended and Narrow Exchange 94
4.4.1. OECD Model Convention 94
4.4.2. Narrow Exchange (Model Convention on Double Taxation) 95
4.4.3. Extended Exchange (Model Convention on Double Taxation) 97
4.4.4. Objectives of Exchange in Other Exchange of Information Rules 98
4.4.5. Conclusion 99
4.5. Methods of Exchange 99
4.5.1. Development and Compulsory Nature of the Exchange Methods (OECD Model Convention) 99
4.5.2. Development and Compulsory Nature of Methods in Other Regulations 100
4.5.3. Exchange upon Request 101
4.5.3.1. Conclusion for Exchange on Request 108
4.5.4. Simultaneous Auditing 108
4.5.4.1. OECD Model Convention, Directive 77/799, Strasbourg Convention, Council Regulation 1798/2003 108
4.5.4.2. Conclusions for Simultaneous Investigations 110

4.5.5. Attending Investigations Abroad 110
4.5.5.1. OECD Model Convention on Double Taxation, Strasbourg Convention, Directive 77/799, Council Regulation 1798/2003 on VAT 110
4.5.5.2. Attendance at Investigations Abroad: Strasbourg Convention 111
4.5.5.3. Attendance at Investigations Abroad: Commentary on OECD Model Convention on Double Taxation 112
4.5.5.4. Attendance at Investigations Abroad: Community Rules 113
4.5.5.5. Attendance at Investigations Abroad: OECD Agreement 113
4.5.5.6. Conclusion for Attendance at Foreign Investigations 114
4.5.6. Automatic Exchange 115
4.5.6.1. OECD Model Convention on Double Taxation 115
4.5.6.2. Automatic Exchange in the Strasbourg Convention and Directive 77/799 116
4.5.6.3. Automatic Information Exchange: Council Regulation 1798/2003 on VAT 117
4.5.6.4. Conclusion 118
4.5.7. Spontaneous Exchange 118
4.5.7.1. OECD Model Convention 118
4.5.7.2. Spontaneous Exchange in Directive 77/799 120
4.5.7.3. Spontaneous Exchange in Council Regulation 1798/2003 on VAT 121
4.5.7.4. Spontaneous Exchange in the Strasbourg Convention 122
4.5.7.5. Conclusion 122
4.6. Subjects of Exchange 122
4.6.1. Circle of Taxpayers/Subjects 123
4.6.1.1. OECD Model Convention on Double Taxation 123
4.6.1.2. Circle of Taxpayer/Subjects in Other Regulations 124
4.6.2. Competent Authorities/All Rules 125
4.6.2.1. Competent Authorities in the Strasbourg Convention 126
4.6.2.2. Competent Authorities in Council Regulation 1798/2003 on VAT 126
4.6.2.3. Conclusion 127
5. Summary and Conclusions 127

## Chapter 5
## Terms and Conditions Relating to the Exchange: Secrecy and Use 133

1. Introduction 133
2. Secrecy in the OECD Model Convention 134
   2.1. Secrecy According to the 1963 OECD Model Convention 135
      2.1.1. Absolute Duty of Secrecy 135
      2.1.2. Circle of Parties Entitled to the Information 136
   2.2. Secrecy According to the 1977-2005 Model Convention 137
      2.2.1. Relative Duty of Secrecy 138
      2.2.2. Circle of Parties Entitled to the Data 142
      2.2.3. Extension of the Use of the Data 144
      2.2.4. Conclusion 145
3. Secrecy Clauses in European Law: Directive 77/799 and Value Added Tax Regulation 145
   3.1. Secrecy in Council Directive 77/799 146
      3.1.1. Relative Secrecy 146
      3.1.2. Use of the Data: Collection, Prosecution, Forwarding, Use in Criminal Proceedings 146
      3.1.3. Conclusion 148
   3.2. Secrecy in Regulation 1798/2003 on VAT 148
      3.2.1. Relative Secrecy 148
      3.2.2. Use of the Data: Collection, Prosecution, Forwarding, Other Use (Criminal Proceedings) 149
      3.2.3. Conclusion 150
4. The Secrecy Clause in the Strasbourg Convention 151
   4.1. Relative Duty of Secrecy 151
   4.2. Use of the Data: Collection, Prosecution, Forwarding, Other Use (Criminal Proceedings) 151
      4.2.1. Conclusion 154
5. Secrecy in the OECD Model Agreement 154
   5.1. Absolute Duty of Secrecy 154
   5.2. Use of the Data 155
6. Summary and Conclusions 155

## Chapter 6
## Limitations to the Obligation to Exchange Information 159

1. Introduction 159
2. Obligations and Limitations 160
   2.1. Text of the Limiting Provisions 162
      2.1.1. Specific Provisions 163
3. Sovereignty of the Domestic Laws or Administrative Practice 165
   3.1. Sovereign Domestic Laws 166
      3.1.1. The Tax Authorities' Powers 166
      3.1.2. The Rights of Taxpayers (Model Convention, Other Regulations) 169

3.1.2.1. Rights in the Tax Audit Process 170
3.1.2.2. Rights of Information 170
3.1.2.3. Ban on Self-Incrimination 171
3.1.3. National Secrecy Laws, No Grounds for Exception (All Regulations) 171
3.1.4. Taxpayers' Rights in Other Regulations 172
3.2. Sovereign Administrative Practice 174
3.2.1. Definition: OECD Model Convention, Strasbourg Convention 174
3.2.1.1. 'Laws and Administrative Practice' 175
3.2.2. Sovereign Law and 'Administrative Practice' in Other Regulations 176
3.3.2.1. Strasbourg Convention 176
3.3.2.2. Directive 77/799 177
3.3.2.3. Regulation 1798/2003 on VAT 177
3.3.2.4. OECD Agreement 178
3.3.2.5. Conclusion 178
4. Reciprocity 178
4.1. Reciprocity in the Model Convention 179
4.2. Reciprocity in Other Regulations: Strasbourg Convention, Directive 77/799, Regulation 1798/2003 and OECD Agreement 183
4.2.1. Strasbourg Convention 183
4.2.2. Council Directive 77/799 184
4.2.3. Conclusion 184
5. Business or Professional Secret; '*Ordre Public*' 185
5.1. Definition of Business Secrecy 186
5.1.1. OECD Model Convention 186
5.2. Developments with Regard to Business Secrets 187
5.3. Business and Banking Secrecy 188
5.4. 'Solicitor's Privilege' 189
5.5. Business and Professional Secrecy in Other Regulations: Strasbourg Convention, Directive 77/799, Regulation 1798/2003, OECD Agreement 190
5.5.1. Strasbourg Convention 190
5.5.2. European Directive 77/799 191
5.5.3. Regulation 1798/2003 on VAT 192
5.5.4. OECD Agreement 192
5.5.5. Conclusion 193
5.6. Public Order (All Regulations) 193
5.6.1. Conclusion 194
6. Other Limitations 194
7. Summary and Conclusions 195

**Chapter 7**
**Interests of the Taxpayer** **199**

1. Introduction 199
2. (General) Position of Taxpayers in the Exchange of Information 201
   2.1. Conclusion 203
3. Position of the Taxpayer in the Present Rules on the International Exchange of Information 203
   3.1. OECD Model Convention 204
   3.2. OECD Agreement 205
   3.3. Strasbourg Convention 206
   3.4. European Rules on the International Exchange of Information 206
   3.5. Conclusion 207
4. Interests of the Taxpayer (in the Requested State) 208
   4.1. The Exhaustion Rule (The Principle of Subsidiarity) 209
      4.1.1. Conclusion 211
   4.2. The Importance of Secrecy 212
      4.2.1. Absolute Duty of Secrecy 212
      4.2.2. Relative Duty of Secrecy 214
      4.2.3. Solutions by Changes in the International Conventions 215
      4.2.4. Solutions for the States 217
      4.2.5. Conclusion 218
   4.3. Other Interests of Taxpayers 218
      4.3.1. Sovereignty of Domestic Legislation and Administrative Practice 219
         4.3.1.1. Conclusion 220
      4.3.2. Reciprocity 220
         4.3.2.1. Conclusion 222
      4.3.3. Commercial, Industrial, or Professional Secrets/Rights of Information 222
         4.3.3.1. Informational Rights 224
         4.3.3.2. Conclusion 226
      4.3.4. The Public Order/*Ordre Public* 226
         4.3.4.1. Conclusion 227
5. Position of Taxpayers in the Requesting (Receiving) State 228
   5.1. Exhaustion Rule in the Requesting State 228
   5.2. Secrecy Concerning the Received Information in the Requesting State 229
      5.2.1. OECD Model Convention, Convention on the Mutual Administrative Assistance in Tax Matters, OECD Agreement 229
      5.2.2. European Community Rules 231
      5.2.3. Conclusion 232
   5.3. Principles of Sovereignty and Reciprocity in the Requesting State 233
      5.3.1. Conclusion 233

6. Legal Duty Toward the Taxpayer in the Other State 234
7. Summary and Conclusions 235

**Chapter 8**
**Outlines for a System of Legal Protection** **239**
1 Introduction 239
2 Informational Interests of Citizens 241
2.1 Characteristics of Informational Law 242
2.2 Basic Principles of Data Processing and the Exchange of Information between States 244
2.2.1 Purpose Specification and Legitimacy Requirements 245
2.2.2 'Fair Processing' Requirement 245
3 Informational Legal Protection in the Collection of the Information 247
4 Informational Protection in the Privacy Directive 248
4.1 What Protection? 249
4.1.1 Direct Collection of Data 250
4.1.2 Collection of Data from Third Parties 252
4.1.3 Restrictions on the Rights to Information 253
4.1.4 Right to Object 254
4.1.5 Transfer to Third Countries 255
4.1.6 Conclusion 257
4.2 Who Is Being Protected? 258
4.2.1 Data Subject in the Privacy Directive 258
4.2.2 Data Subject in the Exchange of Information 259
4.2.3 Extension of the Term Data Subject? 261
4.2.4 Conclusion 264
5 Toward Data Processing Law with a Stronger Focus on Property 265
5.1 Informational Self-Determination 266
5.2 Information as Property 267
5.3 Protection through Other Sets of Standards 268
5.3.1 General Standards of Administrative Law 268
5.3.2 Protection via the Standard of Public Access to Government Information 271
5.3.3 Protection via the Doctrine of the Unlawful Government Act 272
5.3.3.1 Liability Due to Unlawful Disclosure 274
5.3.3.2 Shared Liability of States 275
5.3.3.3 Liability by Unlawful Use 275
5.3.4 Protection via European Law 276
5.3.4.1 Conclusion 278
6 Proposals for National Rules on the International Exchange of Information Between States 280
6.1 Notification of the Taxpayer 280
6.1.1 Proper Publicizing 280
6.1.2 Content of the Notification 281

6.1.3 Interested Party 281
6.1.4 Time of Notification 283
6.2 Objection and Appeal: Assessment Criteria 284
6.2.1 Objection and Appeal: Lawfulness 285
6.2.1.1 Guarantee of Confidentiality of the State Receiving Information 286
6.2.1.2 Objective and Subjective Scope of the Rules on the International Exchange of Information 286
6.2.2 Objection and Appeal: Reasonable Weighing of Interests 287
6.2.2.1 Standard of Exhaustion/Principle of Subsidiarity 287
6.2.2.2 The Argument of Sovereignty of Domestic Law 288
6.2.2.3 The Argument of Reciprocity 288
6.2.2.4 The Business Secret or Professional Privilege 288
6.2.2.5 The Argument of Public Order 289
6.2.2.6 Conclusion 290
6.3 Protection and the Methods of Exchange 290
7 Summary and Conclusions 291

**Chapter 9**
**Summary and Conclusions** **297**
1. The International Framework of the Exchange of Information 300
1.1. Ways to Protect Taxpayers in the International Exchange of Information 301
2. Interests of the Taxpayers 303
2.1. Ways to Protect Interests 305

**List of References** **309**

**Table of Cases** **319**

**Index** **323**

# Preface

This in-depth study examines the international exchange of information in tax matters from the viewpoint of the taxpayer. I became interested in the subject during my time at the Netherlands' Ministry of Finance and, later, the Netherlands Tax Service, at the time when international exchange of tax information was becoming increasingly more important.

The Dutch Parliament passed the Dutch Mutual Assistance in Tax Matters Act, aimed at implementation of international duty to exchange tax information, in 1986. This Act included protection for the position of the taxpayer in providing information to the tax administration. Implementation of this safeguard induced much discussion in the Dutch literature, as well as case law on the balancing of the interests of both the Dutch treaty partners and the taxpayers who provide information to the tax administration.

Some authors were of the opinion that the protection was too limited because it included only the person (taxpayer) in the information-supplying state, not the one in the requesting state, whose assessment was at stake. I did not agree with this view, and now, with time, experience, and considerable thought, I am presenting my view.

The investigation of this subject was, in itself, a great journey, leading me to the heights of philosophy in search for the answer to the question of what law is essentially about. It also involved scrutinizing and analysing the existing rules on international exchange of information. I had to determine whether it was possible to unite the two different obligations of countries exchanging information – toward their treaty partners and toward their taxpayers.

Finally, there were other fields of law to explore, to find norms and values suitable to serve as anchors for a system of information protection for taxpayers.

I certainly did not complete this study on my own. My *promotores*, of Tilburg University, Professors Richard Happé, Eric Kemmeren, and Hans Gribnau guided, encouraged, and supported me. I am grateful for, and miss, our expansive and interesting discussions and grateful as well that they welcomed me as a visiting investigator to their Fiscal Institute.

I also am greatly indebted to my employer, the Netherlands' Tax Administration, for allowing me the time to work on this study. I am thankful to Hans van Leijenhorst, of the Centre for the Development of Processes and Products, who encouraged me to begin the dissertation. This department sponsored the English translation of my dissertation and provided financial support for this book.

I am also grateful to my colleagues, who brought to my attention material they thought would be of relevance, making this study more complete than it would otherwise have been.

But, at the end of the day, what counted most was the support and patience of family and friends. I owe them most of all. This book is therefore dedicated to my husband, Peter, and my children, Guido and Miyana.

# Chapter 1
# Introduction and Problem Definition

## 1. INTRODUCTION

Generally speaking, the primary goal of human actions is to obtain as many chances and advantages as possible. This is by definition true for economic activities. Nonetheless, in all more complicated societies, citizens are under the obligation to pay taxes. This obligation is justified by the fact the individuals, in order to reach their goals, need a certain level of predictability, order, and safety that they themselves are not able to generate. This protection must be offered by the state community the citizens are part of, which in turn is entitled to coerce them to forfeit private means for the benefit of the collectivity. In modern rules of law, this coercion inter alia takes place by the creation of a tax liability by means of acts of parliament, and the execution of these acts in the imposition of taxes, which in its turn is ruled by procedural tax law. Of late, it has become clear that these purely national legislations and powers are no longer satisfactory when it comes to the implementation of a just and correct system of taxation.

The world has become a 'global village', in which the economies of the states become ever more closely intertwined. Parts of the world income or profits of taxpayers will increasingly find their origin in states other than their state of residence or will be strongly influenced by facts and circumstances abroad.

This leads to an ever-increasing need of states to obtain tax-related (counter) information from abroad.[1] However, basic premises of international law such as sovereignty and subsidiarity prevent states from operating independently within the jurisdiction of other states.

This problem, recognized in the 1920s, has been tackled by means of treaty law. In double taxation conventions, room was created for international

1. Counterintelligence is information that may either substantiate or falsify information provided by taxpayers to the tax authorities.

cooperation in tax matters through the exchange of information. The Model conventions on double taxation drawn up by the League of Nations, and later by the Organization for Economic Cooperation and Development (OECD), constituted a considerable contribution to this effort. The OECD models contained standard provisions in which contracting states were obligated to exchange information in tax matters, an obligation from which they could escape only in certain well-defined situations. Comparing different versions of the Model conventions, it becomes clear that over the years the exchange of information in tax matters has gained importance.

Within the European Community, too, the importance of international cooperation in tax matters was recognized. This was put into a special Directive, in which the term Mutual Assistance was used for the first time. The exchange of information in tax matters was extended by means of provisions concerning the actual participation of officials of the Member States in tax examinations abroad.[2] This development ultimately lead to the conclusion in 1988 of a multilateral assistance convention which was drawn up by the OECD and the Council of Europe in a joint effort, covering the entire field of assessment and collection of taxes.[3] Basically, this convention also covers local taxes and national insurance contributions. The Community customs treaties also contain provisions for multilateral assistance.

The scope of this book is limited to mutual assistance in matters of taxation. All forms of cooperation in the field of taxation eventually boil down to the exchange of information. Therefore, for the rest of this book I will use this term. In my view, the term 'mutual assistance' must be reserved for *all* forms and methods with which states can assist each other, including the service of official documents on behalf of other states and taking collection measures, including assessment prejudgment attachment and the independent operations of customs officials in bordering countries.

## 2. THE IMPORTANCE OF INTERNATIONAL EXCHANGE OF INFORMATION IN TAX MATTERS

Although not all states have pursued quite the same course of action, ideas on mutual exchange of information in tax matters keep developing. The great importance that is attached to is proven by the international discussion that took place not long ago concerning the so-called 'harmful tax competition'. An important issue in this discussion, both within the OECD and the European Union, was the emphasis

2. This happened for the first time in the Council Directive of 19 Dec. 1977 concerning mutual assistance of the competent authorities of the Member States in the field of direct taxation (77/799/EEC), which was extended several times later. This line was continued in the Council Regulation No. 1798/2003/EC of 7 Oct. 2003.
3. Joint Council of Europe/OECD Convention on mutual administrative assistance in tax matters of 25 Jan. 1988, concluded in Strasbourg.

that was placed on increased international transparency as a means to combat this phenomenon. The OECD Committee on Fiscal Affairs defined the lack of effective international exchange of information as one of the characteristics of tax havens.[4] It took the initiative for consultations with a number of 'committed jurisdictions' outside the OECD, to draw up a model convention on the exchange of information. After extended rounds of negotiation, this convention was eventually adopted in 2002.[5] Within the European Union, after years of laborious discussion, the matter of the exchange of information between Member States on savings deposits was clinched.[6] At the same time, the European Commission developed new legal instruments to improve the effectiveness of the method of cooperation, especially meant as a 'weapon' against the vast Value Added Tax (VAT) fraud.[7] In the meantime the European Court of Justice (ECJ) continuously stressed the importance of Directive 77/ 799 on Mutual Assistance between Member States as an instrument to combat tax fraud and tax evasion, menacing the full effect of the EC Treaty.

## 3. RECENT POINTS OF VIEW ON LEGAL PROTECTION IN THE INTERNATIONAL EXCHANGE OF INFORMATION

In recent years, as the importance attached to the international exchange of information increased, more attention has been drawn to the issue of legal protection of taxpayers within the framework of this form of cooperation in tax matters. This issue is substantially about the recognition of the fact that the exchange of information on tax matters between states is not possible without the cooperation of the taxpayers in the supplying state. The latter must provide the information, which is then exchanged by their state to other states. They run the risk that the data collected from them are incorrect or interpreted incorrectly by the other state, that their confidentiality is not properly respected in the other state, or the data are used unlawfully, and that thus the taxpayers' good name and reputation are jeopardized, as well as their economic interests.

In short, the international discussions at this point are about the following aspects: (a) about the quality of the warranty of secrecy of the receiving state, included in all regulations on the exchange of information, and (b) about the necessity, or at least the desirability, of a right of information for the supplier of

4. *Harmful Tax Competition: An Emerging Global Issue*, Paris: OECD, 1998.
5. OECD (<www.oecd.org>, 18 Apr. 2002). See also Barnard (2002) and McLure (2001), 338, 339.
6. It must be said, in fairness, that mainly the effectiveness of the Savings Tax Directive is a topic of discussion. Some states (and authors) deem a withholding tax on outgoing interest a more effective solution. See Tanzi/Zee (2000), who call the faith in the effectiveness of international exchange of information in this respect rather naïve.
7. COM(2000)214, of 28 Jan. 2000, and Proposal for a Regulation of the European Parliament and of the Council amending Regulation 218/92 on administrative cooperation in the field of indirect taxation (VAT), COM(2000)394 final.

the information exchanged, which would give him the possibility to have the lawfulness of the exchange of information reviewed and, if necessary, put up a defence against it.

Item (a) A lawsuit of a large American publishing company against the local tax authorities, concerning the disclosure of internationally agreed individual advance pricing agreements, in 1999 raised a good deal of dust in the communities involved with international cooperation in the field of economies and taxation. The publisher claimed the disclosure of a number of Mutual Agreement Procedures (MAPs) in which the American tax authorities had agreed with contracting states on the determination of the arm's length nature of certain intercompany prices. This implied an infringement of the confidentiality of data exchanged between states within the framework of exchange of information law, more specifically their mutual consultation procedures. The American tax authorities United States Internal Revenue Service (IRS) felt obligated to disclose these agreements in the United States, after having consulted the various contracting states.[8] Based on the secrecy clause in the exchange of information provisions in their conventions, they were bound to secrecy with regard to foreign intelligence in the MAPs, in the same way that they were bound to secrecy with regard to information of their national taxpayers. However, the IRS was now confronted *within* its own country with two conflicting civil interests: the fundamental right of confidentiality with regard to information supplied in tax matters on the one hand and the fundamental right of freedom of information on the other. The relation between these two, sometimes conflicting, fundamental rights was in this case complicated by the obligations under the treaties, which led to the question whether the IRS could be forced to disclose the correspondence exchanged by the contracting states during the preparation of the treaties.

The lawsuit triggered the question of which legal duty of the states had priority in case the freedom of information rule was invoked with regard to cross-border exchange of information: to protect the tax confidentiality of their own citizens or their obligations toward their contracting partner states.[9] The lawsuit gave rise to certain articles in the international professional journals, in which authors from various countries presented overviews of their domestic legislation on confidentiality restrictions in tax matters.[10] In the revision of Article 26 of the OECD Model convention of 2005 the Committee on Fiscal Affairs expressed its views on the

8. *BNA v. IRS*, Nos 96-376, 96-1473 Daily Tax Report for Executives, Bureau of National Affairs, 99.
9. The duty of states to provide public access to information has hitherto almost always been based on domestic legislation. The only exception is the European Union, where this duty was created at an international level, that is, Art. 255 of the Treaty of Amsterdam, with regard to administrative actions of European Community institutions. European citizens have the right of access to the documents concerning the decision-making processes of the European authorities. The 'Public Access regulation' was drawn up on 30 May 2001. The OECD does not have this kind of codification.
10. *International Transfer Pricing Journal* 7 nr. 1 (January 2000), nr. 2 (February 2000), nr. 3 (May/June 2000), nr. 4 (July/August 2000).

desired relationship between the international restrictions on confidentiality in tax matters and domestic legislation on this subject.[11]

Item (b) Moreover, in international professional journals the question recently arose what the right to 'informational self-determination', which in some countries is made explicit in domestic legislation, could mean for a taxpayer involved in the exchange of information in tax matters, the latter also being a form of data processing. The reason for the authors raising this question was the fact that especially the rules on the exchange of information as laid down in the OECD Model convention showed little concern regarding the legal position of the taxpayer or withholding agent involved. The text of the provision on the exchange of information in the Model convention lacks any reference to this subject, while the official Commentaries according to the authors never take a clear point of view on it. They all point to a connection with the current ideas about information as an asset, valuable in money, which can also be exploited commercially for those who are able to lay their hands on it. Thus the party supplying the information, or the party that is the subject of the information, can also be considered the *owner* of it, or the interested party, as is recognized in other OECD legal sources.[12] Therefore, according to some of these authors, the right of 'informational self-determination' should also apply to data exchanged between states.[13]

The same problem can be pointed out with regard to the Community exchange rules. The informational rights formulated in the 'Privacy Directive' [14] for natural persons subject to data processing within the European Union seem to apply only in part to the exchange of *tax* data between Member States.

In the Report of the European Commission of January 2000 on the evaluation of the European information exchange, this Commission expresses the view that certain forms of openness and legal protection in the exchange of information, as developed by some Member States, are not compatible with the increasing demand for efficiency in obtaining cross-border information,[15] because they would weaken the position of the Member States in the continuous battle against tax fraud. In the Council Regulation bringing together the two separate European acts on the exchange of information for VAT purposes, however, the Commission's viewpoint is toned down.[16] In the Dutch domestic law with regard to cross-border exchange of information, this viewpoint of the Commission led to an impoverishment of the legal protection against these government activities.

11. See Ch. 5 hereafter.
12. OECD Guidelines on the Protection of Privacy and Trans border Flow of Personal Data, Sep. 1981. See also Ch. 8.
13. See Calderon (2000). Also Schaumburg/Schlossmacher (2000). Other authors take a more moderate view, but do advocate a right of informational self-determination with regard to the supply of information.
14. Directive 95/46/EC of the Council of Europe of 24 Oct. 1995, OJEC L281.
15. Based on Art. 14 of the Regulation 92/218/EEC, the Member States must evaluate the effects of mutual assistance in tax matters on a regular basis.
16. The Directive and the Regulation were brought together in the Council Regulation 1798/2003/EC of 7 Oct. 2003, OJEU L264.

## 4. PROBLEM DEFINITION

In the previously mentioned cases and discussions, the main question is what the scope of legal protection should be with regard to cross-border information exchange practices, against the background of law formation in the more general field of informational self-determination that has developed both within the OECD community and the European Community.

For the taxpayers/interested parties, two interests are at stake: the confidentiality of information on the one hand and the disclosure of this information on the other.

From the American lawsuit on the cross-border exchange of information in tax matters it became clear that this question also came up with regard to the exchange of documents between states and that the exchanging state is forced to play a double role, that of a treaty partner in a contractual relationship with other treaty partners on the one hand and that of rule of law in the public law relationship with its citizens on the other.

The question about the proper relationship between the interests of the states and those of taxpayers/interested parties involved in cross-border exchange of information is relevant because of the prominent role that is bestowed on this instrument of international cooperation by the international bodies in looking after the interests of the states. The risk this involves is that aspects of legal protection are neglected in favour of aspects of efficiency of the regulatory framework.

The proper balance between both interests, in my view, can be found only in a more overall approach of law as a social principle of regulation, especially with regard to the relationship between the state and its citizens as it was developed in rules of law. By means of that legal-philosophical analysis, an assessment framework can then be developed to evaluate the existing rules on the exchange of information at this point.

In doing so, the answer can be found to the question of the *existence* of a legal duty for states to protect those involved in the international exchange of information in tax matters. If that answer is positive, it can be investigated whether within the existing positive law on the exchange of information compliance with such a legal duty would be possible and, if so, *which* interests it would have to protect. Finally, the question can be answered as to *how* that protection would be best realized.

## 5. THE DUTCH SITUATION

To the Dutch cross-border exchange of information, all this is of considerable importance. The Dutch economy is highly globalized, and therefore the need to obtain foreign information in tax matters is equally great. The Netherlands has entered into agreements with more than sixty states, based on different versions of the OECD Model convention, the Council Directive 77/799, and the multilateral

Treaty of Strasbourg. Dutch assistance, therefore, is an important aspect of the international policy on treaties.

The Dutch Act on international assistance with regard to the assessment of taxes (hereinafter called WIB),[17] contains rules regarding the legal protection of taxpayers. The latter has met with criticism in the national official journals (and also from the national ombudsman), for not going far enough. The legislator did in no way honour this criticism, on the contrary. In the course of time, the rule was mitigated, in the sense that the appeal period was shortened. The reason for this was embedded in the political desire to mitigate criticism from the international bodies on the incentives Dutch tax policy contained to 'seduce' companies to take domicile in the Netherlands, which in their eyes was far too favourable. This required compensation by means of increased transparency.[18] In this context, it was deemed proper to take measures that could lead to a more adequate and speedy exchange of information with other states.

In 2004 the right of appeal against the exchange of information for VAT purposes was even entirely abolished, as a consequence of the Dutch interpretation of Regulation No. 1798/2003/EC.[19]

Keeping this in mind, it is interesting to know how the national ideas about the relationship between the authorities and taxpayers will develop with regard to the so-called duties of cooperation and disclosure of information of taxpayers in tax matters. Another complicating factor is the relationship between the Dutch Freedom of Information Act (*Wet openbaarheid van bestuur*) and the tax confidentiality provision of Article 67, section 2 of the Dutch State Taxes Act (*Algemene wet inzake rijksbelastingen*), mainly when this is challenged in the context of cross-border exchange of information. The authorities must then balance not only two conflicting interests of citizens within a state,[20] but also the interests of the other state, which must be looked after in the best possible way based on treaty law.

## 6. STRUCTURE OF THIS BOOK

This book does not contain a comparative study of the way in which the legal protection of the taxpayers involved in the exchange of information is organized in the different states. It is about the questions that precede this topic, such as those laid out in section 4.

In finding the answers to those questions I propose to follow a course that will begin at the abstract level of legal-philosophical backgrounds of the idea of legal

17. Enacted 24 Apr. 1986, Stb. 249, last changed by Act of 15 Dec. 2005, Stb. 2005/683.
18. See the Report of the Primarolo Group within the European Union, V-N 2000/6.
19. Change of the WIB by Act of 14 Dec. 2001, Stb. 2001/641, and thereafter by Act of 24 Nov. 2004, Stb. 2004/618.
20. Like this emerges from the letters of the Secretary of State to Parliament of 13 Mar. 1998, nr. WJB 98/46, (published in V-N 1998/19.6) and of 20 Mar. 2001, nr. BOB 2000/01536 (V-N 2001/18.9).

protection in Chapter 2. This will be followed by a description and analysis of the international legal framework of cross-border exchange of information in four closely connected chapters. This will enable us to find the answer to the question as to what extent the existing international law on mutual assistance connects to the principles 'found' earlier. Because of the important role of the OECD Model convention, Chapter 3 will be dedicated to the nature of this Model convention and especially to the problems arising at its interpretation. Subsequently, the nature of the duty of states to exchange information as laid down in the OECD Model convention will be discussed, as well as those laid down in the OECD Agreement on Exchange of Information on Tax Matters, the Convention of Strasbourg, the European Directive 77/799, and the Regulation 1798/2003 (Chapter 4). The discussion will take place thematically, so that unnecessary iteration may be avoided and both the similarities and differences may be pointed out. The same method will be applied in Chapter 5 when discussing the conditions for the exchange of information. The subject of Chapter 6 is the boundaries and limitations of the duty to exchange information. There the margins will become visible within which states are able to balance their interests when performing their duty to exchange information. After this analysis of international legal duties of states, which largely determine the legitimacy of these government acts, in Chapter 7 the public law reality of cross-border exchange of information will be discussed. This will define the scope of the duty of care states should have with regard to the interests of taxpayers and answer the question whether it is possible to embed these in international law. Chapter 8 will be dedicated to a search for the best possible ways of concrete protection of taxpayers involved in these government actions. Various existing sets of standards will be looked into for this purpose.

I shall conclude with a summary, in which the relative connection of the conclusions from the preceding chapters will be presented.

# Chapter 2
# Backgrounds of Legal Protection

## 1. INTRODUCTION

Mutual administrative assistance in tax matters is the comprehensive set of measures that states can take to assist each other in the execution of their tax laws. Exchanging information is an essential part of it. The tax authorities require reliable data to issue their tax assessments, data that should be supplied by the taxpayers or withholding agents.[1] In almost any state, the national tax laws therefore contain obligations to supply information to tax authorities.

In modern society, information, also information regarding persons, is seen as an (immaterial) asset to the party to whom it is available.[2] The European Court for Human Rights (ECHR) holds the same view, and this is shared by the European Court of Justice (ECJ).[3] Between market parties, information creates the possibility to acquire a leading market position and to generate corporate income. However, with regard to personal information, the availability thereof to other parties than the person himself also involves risks, even (or even more so) if the other party is the State authorities.[4] This is certainly also true for the availability and exchange of tax information to other states by the administration as part of the international exchange of tax information. Those risks could occur by failure of the receiving State in meeting its obligation of secrecy by incorrect reproduction of the received data or unlawful use of them. This could cause material or immaterial damage to the party concerned.

---

1. For the sake of briefness, hereinafter referred to as 'the taxpayer'.
2. For information as a material asset, see Hartlief (1995), 129.
3. ECJ, 24 Jun. 1986, Jur. 1986, 1992 on information in documents of the Commission that might contain business secrets. Before taking a decision on disclosure of the documents, the presence of those business secrets must be established by decree.
4. See Blok (2002), 116.

The four examples given in the Introduction, the American lawsuit, the report of the European Commission, the international discussion on the law of informational self-determination, and the recently deteriorated legal protection of the taxpayer in Dutch legislation regarding the exchange of information, all concern interests of taxpayers involved in the non-disclosure or disclosure of tax information exchanged about them. The examples clearly show that the interests of the information-providing *taxpayers* do not as such run parallel with the interests states have in providing data to other contracting states as efficiently as possible, in compliance with the international obligations they entered into.

Within this framework, the following questions arise: how should the interests and risks of citizens and states be weighed against each other? What is the scope of the legal duty of administrations to protect their own citizens against the consequences of an agreement between them and other contracting states? Which interests prevail if conflicting civil interests are at stake?

A simple answer to these questions is by no means available. The alternatives in the examples can lead in different directions, depending on the chosen point of view. A general analysis of the concepts of justice and legal protection could help solve this dilemma. In this analysis, it is essential to explore the ideas regarding the relationship between the State and its citizens, as they were developed in the course of the twentieth century by important philosophers of law.

Therefore the paragraphs hereafter will dwell on the outlines of the development of the classical constitutional state with its rationalist, positivist concept of law toward the modern democratic constitutional state, which embraces the concept of justice as a set of legal principles that essentially refer to legal values concerning freedom and equality. This, if anything, enthusing concept of 'the individual as it appears to us in all its dignity',[5] that has an inalienable right to develop itself in freedom, gains depth only against the background of the factual circumstance that each individual for its existence depends on others. This notion gave rise to the assumption that justice also has an 'ethical' mission, that is, to relieve the tension between equality of human beings on the one hand and different factual circumstances on the other. This lead to the idea that (legal) persons have a duty of care in all relations they enter into and that this should especially be true in a relationship in which one party is stronger or more powerful than the other. In the legal relationship between citizens and the administration, the stronger party is the administration; this is also the case in the field of the exchange of tax data with other states. These presumptions and notions will be elaborated on and amplified in this chapter.

To find an answer to the question whether or not states exchanging information *can* actually fulfil their duty of care toward their taxpayers without coming into conflict with the good faith they owe their treaty partners, the existing international rules on the exchange of information must be analyzed. They will be discussed in the following four chapters.

5. Scheltens (1976).

## 2. FROM LAW TO JUSTICE: THE DEVELOPMENT OF THE CONSTITUTIONAL STATE

It is hardly possible to analyze the content of terms such as justice and legal protection without considering the historic '*Werdegang*' of these terms. Essential in this analysis if the concept of the constitutional state,[6] which was developed halfway through the seventeenth century and during the eighteenth century in the writings of philosophers such as Hobbes, Locke, and Rousseau.[7] These philosophers developed their ideas about the ideal form of administration against the background of the Ancien Régime in some European states, in which a strong central authority was deemed indispensable to create peace, order, and unity to the members of the society. The latter were subjects in a literal sense, without a proper political identity. The will of the absolute prince was the law, legitimized by the 'God-given rights of the sovereign'. Thus the sovereign was the source of justice and safety; he had a monopoly as to the use of force and the right to raise taxes. The social allocation of tasks, inherent to the class society, resulted in tax being levied exclusively from the so-called third class ('*le tiers état*'). Nobility and clergy were exempt from taxation.

### 2.1. The Liberal Constitutional State

During the seventeenth and eighteenth centuries, the inequality caused by these class privileges, together with the uncontrollability of the power executed by the sovereigns of centralist states, were important factors in the development of the idea of the liberal constitutional state.

The God-given power of the sovereign was demystified by Hobbes and Rousseau. Instead, they put forward a concept of the state as a 'social contract' between the prince and his subjects, in which both parties have rights and duties. Thus, in theory, the prince's subject evolved into a free and independent individual, only owing compliance to the authorities inasmuch as they protected its freedom. The individual became a legal subject, a bearer of rights. His freedom was defined as being 'shielded' from the influence of the administration and other individuals. This idea was formulated in the writings of Montesquieu and Kant. The latter formulated as the task of the law: to protect the greatest possible freedom that can still exist next to the freedom of other individuals '*zusammen bestehen kann*' (can coexist).[8] This necessarily led to the postulation of an equal right to freedom for all individuals. This freedom could be infringed only by statutory law.

6. For the development of the 'constitutional state' see D'Agostino (1995), but also Raz (1977), 177, and Crane (1996), and a number of other (text)books and publications in most of the modern languages of the world.
7. Thomas Hobbes; John Locke; Jean-Jacques Rousseau, see Gribnau (1998), Gribnau (1999), Happé (1996), D'Agostino (1995).
8. See Gribnau (1998, 1999); Happé (1996); D'Agostino (1995), Friedman (1977).

This 'principle of legality' and the formal concept of freedom are the two most characteristic aspects of the developing liberal constitutional state.[9] The law is the only source of justice. Justice and law are identical.

This inviolability of the law also became visible in the separation of powers (Trias Politica).[10] In this doctrine, worded by Montesquieu, the legislative power possessed no other than the *highest* authority: the binding assessment of general rules of law. The execution of these rules by the administration is bound by this legislation, as well as the courts, which will not be able to alter the law. They 'can moderate neither its force nor its rigor' said Montesquieu.[11] If anything, the classical interpretation of the Trias Politica focused on the *separation* of powers and the determination of their relevant hierarchy, whereas in the rise of the democratic constitutional state it is considered a system of common law formation, in which the three powers are complementing in a carefully kept balance.[12]

The liberal concept of justice put citizens and State apart from each other. The administration had the duty to safeguard the freedom and safety of its citizens, as well as to guarantee the continuity of the State as society. Therefore it also needed the law to levy taxes. If necessary, the administration had to enforce compliance with the laws by means of sanctions. That is where its task ended. The freedom, the autonomy of citizens, had to be left untouched as much as possible and could be infringed only by statutory law. This 'principle of legality' made the acts of the administration predictable and provided certainty for the citizens. However, although it is still one of the most essential principles of constitutional states, other principles have developed in the course of history having similar impact.[13]

## 2.2. The Democratic Constitutional State

During the course of the second half of the nineteenth century, the idea of the liberal 'night watch society' dwindled. The analytically oriented liberal philosophy led to an atomized concept of society, in which, according to Hegel '*Jeder sich Zweck (ist), alles Andere ist ihm nichts*'.[14] In combination with the economic interpretation of the classic liberal concept of freedom great social injustice had arisen. The strict binding of acts of the administration to the law proved no guarantee whatsoever for the realization of an existence worthy of human beings. As a reaction to the sometimes poignant consequences of that liberal concept of law, a more ethically coloured concept of law arose and a more active and emancipatory concept of freedom. Freedom was increasingly defined as the possibility

9. Happé (1996), 10.
10. Happé (1996), 12; Hirsch Ballin (1991), 71 e.v.
11. Montesquieu (1989), 163.
12. Gribnau (1999), 25 points out that this is only true for more 'simple' laws. For more complicated laws, according to Montesquieu the court has to search for '*l'esprit des lois*'.
13. Happé (1996), 9 and Gribnau (1999), describe this development of legal principles at large.
14. 'Everybody is an aim in himself, everything else has no meaning'. See the elaboration on Hegel's comment (Happé (1996)).

for citizens to develop themselves and to participate in the formation of the society they lived in.[15] Groups that were hitherto excluded from the political scene sought ways to enter it.[16] Democracy was embraced as the political framework in which the free legal subjects had to be able to participate in the debate about what the public interest is.[17]

At that point, the concept about the role of the state changed. It now had to play an active role in society to realize the new ideals of emancipation and equality. The result was a frequent and detailed administration interference. The task of the legislature evolved from 'codification into modification',[18] and thus it lost its monopoly, its 'sovereignty of the law'. The very detailed regulations required to reach the social targets of the legislature could no longer be 'dictated' in general rules.[19] This led to a retreat of the legislature in favour of local administrations, a retreat of statutory law in favour of orders in council and regulations. However, more striking is that, in fact, all these lawmakers inevitably made way for administrative bodies for various reasons.[20] The detailed demands made on administration necessarily led to a stratification of standards, especially in administrative law. The legislature contented itself with the creation of a 'mere' framework for administration acts, which needs to be filled in by further legislation and/or orders in council by local administrations.[21] This meant that eventually, the classical principle of legality, in which all administration powers must be based directly on the law, lost magnitude. Paradoxically, this retreat has hardly resulted in a decrease in number of rules and regulations enacted.[22]

This development intensified the call for general, abstract principles that could act as 'higher' legal standards for the various law forming bodies. For if a court 'delivers judgment' in the cases brought to it, and if the administration executes its powers of decision in a particular case, the process of lawmaking takes place exclusively by implementing general principles representing legal values supported by society and already presumed in its laws. Those principles should be present as 'leading ideas' in every statutory provision and decision and in every court ruling.[23] Those principles of law must be able to connect the notions of '*Sollen*' crystallized in existing law with the ever-changing circumstances in which the law must be executed. Thus the social outlook of the philosophy of

15. See Gribnau (1999).
16. See Gribnau (1999), 8-14.
17. In the beginning, democracy was conceived as the right of just the upper middle class (the '*tiers état*') to be involved in the political debate as a consequence of their growing contribution to the wealth of the States.
18. Koopmans (1970).
19. Gribnau (1998), sees already in Montesquieu's writings a denial of the 'commanding' structure of the classical constitutional state-concept. He stresses the necessity for the legislative to take into account the factual circumstances en de needs of society.
20. van Wijk (1959). Also see Gribnau (1998), 163 e.v., for this development in the Netherlands. See also Happé (1996), 73, e.v., and van Wijk/Konijnenbelt/Van Male (2002), 135.
21. van Wijk/Konijnenbelt/van Male (2002), 149 e.v.
22. Gribnau (1998), 165, calls this process the 'paradoxale retreat of the legislature'.
23. Scholten (1935), 1980.

law, described earlier, gradually changed into a focus on the ethical-normative aspects of law. This perspective is described hereafter in more detail.

## 2.3. Law and Principles of Law

In the classical constitutional state, developed on the foundations of the nineteenth century liberal philosophy, law was seen as a set of rules designed to regulate the execution of state power. There was no law outside these tangible rules. This concept was especially held by the early English 'positivists' like Hobbes and Bentham. They considered law as an existing complex of do's and don'ts, crystallized in a legal system that was construed logically, and that rendered a certain predictability to rules juxtaposed to acts. Therefore they deemed it applicable to the behaviour of human beings.[24] Positivism is a closed circuit, in the sense that the validity of a legal standard is exclusively based on another legal standard creating authority, and not on a moral standard or value. Positivist were preoccupied with the separation of the church and the state, and between the state and the individual, 'to keep distinct the demands of conscience and the demands of the state'.[25] The legalist concept of law in positivism served to create predictability and legal certainty for the citizens, but lacked a moral dimension. Once, this aloofness of the state concerning morality was the beginning of freedom for its legal subjects. It is still the political perspective for states facing irreconcilable political ideologies, in which the execution of power is of poor democratic quality. However, in the democratized societies emerging in the twentieth century in the Western world, ideas and opinions were increasingly formed in an open and public debate. There it was less necessary to consider the law as a protection against ideological claims of the party in power.[26] In this climate, a less 'value-free' and less mechanical concept of law was able to develop.

A representative of this new concept is Herbert Hart, who in the sixties of the last century gave positivism a more internalized character. According to Hart, the constitutional state does not merely exist outside its legal subjects, as a command that must be obeyed. The rules must be practiced by its legal subjects in a true sense, which means that they are accepted by them. As mentioned before, the acceptability of these rules depends on their coming into effect. The internal aspect of acceptance is shown in the way in which citizens and 'officials' reject deviations from the rule.[27] The legal force of the rules is exclusively based on the acceptance

24. See Foqué (1998), 1. He mentions especially Hobbes, Bentham, Austin.
25. Guest (1992), 12.
26. Guest (1992), 14.
27. Foqué 1998, MacCormick/Hart, 1981, 103-120.

of the rules by the officials as standards for their law forming activities.[28] That is the 'rule of recognition'.[29]

This acceptance by the community of legal subjects and by officials can itself not be based on a rule, however. Therefore also Hart's mitigated positivism cannot explain the *existence* and meaning of law, nor can it be a guideline to cases for which positive law does not provide.

A counter-movement arose. Law was increasingly seen as a set of principles and basically as an ethical phenomenon: an instrument to regulate human interactions. Law thus finds its meaning in the realization of the idea of justice, which eventually leads back to 'the dignity of each individual person'.[30]

In the Netherlands, for example Scholten and Scheltens defended this notion.[31] In the Anglo-Saxon literature on the philosophy of law, this ethical concept is especially represented by Dworkin. The heart of the notion of 'integrity' as used by Dworkin is the moral dimension of law. He does not consider law as something 'that is simply out there', but as a set of principles of law,[32] based on a substrate of moral principles. Those are 'standards that (are) to be observed ( . . . ) because it is a requirement of justice or fairness or some other dimension of morality'.[33] If anything, law is determined by these legal principles. They are that abstract, and at the same time they are that constantly present in the ideas of society about what is right and proper, that they can be guidelines in the ever-changing circumstances in which legal practice takes place.

At the formation of *new* law, the various legal principles are balanced in the democratic process of legislative procedure. This more or less warrants the rationality of the process.[34] Because the legislature is bound by the law as well, it has to keep the focus on these principles of law in the law forming process, to avoid the risk that rules of law would be regarded too much as instruments for social and economic goals outside law. Although justice must be aimed at certain goals to be *meaningful*, legal values such as legal certainty and equality must not be sacrificed for that purpose.[35] Social goals, however justified in themselves, cannot be our only guide to determine what law is. Dworkin sums this up in his thesis: 'Law is

---

28. Also see Foqué's reference to Taylor, in which he analyzes following a rule as a 'dialogical practice'. The latter also steps aside of the closed system of the positivistic concept of law, in a 'psychological' sense, but is not judging along moral standards.
29. Hart (1961), 97-107, and Guest (1992), 30-31. Also Hirsch Ballin (1991b), 57.
30. Hirsch Ballin (1991a), 6.
31. See Hirsch Ballin (1991a), 5.
32. See Dworkin (1977). However, he is not a real philosopher of natural law in the true sense. To Dworkin, law is a human phenomenon, and therefore subject to social changes, although the core values are universal.
33. Dworkin (1986), 438.
34. Gribnau (1998), 53, 68.
35. De Bruin (1991). See also Niessen (1996), who deems it acceptable to use tax legislation for other aims then strict fiscal ones, as long as interference with the private lives of citizens is limited. Moreover, there must be a visible link for them between the aims and the means.

about rights, politics is about goals'. In a just society, the legal values must be implicit in all goals: 'Rights trump goals'.[36]

When it comes to *existing* law, reflection based on principles is necessary as well. In society, law is never found in its pure form, but gets different contents during the process of law formation. It is an interpretative phenomenon, meaning that in every concrete situation the rule must be reinterpreted. According to Dworkin this should take place 'in the best possible sense', and that is the 'moral sense'.[37] This perception also determines the altered concept of the task of the court in the process of law formation.[38] For the positivist, the court has discretionary powers. In the so-called 'hard cases', for which existing law does not provide a rule, the court must determine a new rule, that fits in with the existing legal practice and with the expectations legal subjects have attached to it. That new rule of law will then, based on its 'constitutional' roots and by means of acceptance by legal practitioners, in its turn become part of law.

Dworkin keeps his distance from this conventionalist 'protected-expectations' approach. In his opinion, it is too focused on the further development of judicial customary law, which in the 'hard cases' will offer either no solution or an unjust one. The task of the judge is to find the most ideal meaning (the sense) of the rule of law he is bound to interpret. He will have to regard that rule as (perhaps imperfect) an expression of the standards and values of society.[39] In the 'hard cases', where existing law does not bring a solution, he must decide 'within the ample platform of the law, and thus also of the general principles of law – sometimes pointing in different directions – in which fundamental opinions are embedded'. By balancing the principles of law, the judge 'finds' 'the one true answer.[40] Thus the judge is able to offer a certain counterbalance against the administration, with its often unilaterally defined powers. Principles of law have a dimension that rules of law have not: that of weight and importance.[41]

Other modern philosophers of law also choose this approach,[42] which parallels the way in which the judges themselves experience their task. Court decisions must fit within this set of rules and principles of law and intuitions that are already crystallized in legal practice (Dworkin's dimension of fit), and they must be able to morally justify the existing legal practice (dimension of justification).[43]

36. Dworkin (1977).
37. Dworkin (1986), Guest (1992).
38. The importance Dworkin attaches to the judge in the continuing process of law formation is shown in his 'creation' of the super judge Hercules, whom he puts on the stage to describe that lawmaking process in a heuristic way.
39. Dworkin (1986).
40. Brouwer (1991) does not agree with Dworkin's idea that the ethical conception of law would always lead to 'the one just answer'. According to him this cannot be proved, only defended.
41. See Soeteman (1991, 1992), 774. Also Cf. Happé (1996), 77ff., From the outcomes of the balancing process concerning the legal principles in court cases he deduces priority-rules.
42. See Gribnau (1998), 33, who sums up Dutch authors, and Guest (1992), who gives an overview of international literature.
43. Dworkin (1985), 158 and Dworkin (1986), 90; Soeteman (1992).

Finding rules that fit into the set of 'current' principles in society gives justice its coherence. The combination of the dimensions, 'fit' and 'justification' Dworkin calls 'integrity'.

The most important justification for the existence of a rule, or of law in general, is that it creates a framework for the realization of 'a kind of equality among citizens'.[44] Each rule of law to be formed should be the best possible effect of this (abstract) principle of equality.

## 2.4. 'The Right to Equal Concern and Respect'

The ideal of equality, although an essential characteristic of the democratic idea, is not undisputed in its political effect. In some political circles the fear exists that too great an emphasis on equality could have a devastating effect on society. In their opinion the more talented members of society who in pursuit of their individual goals could stimulate social phenomena such as science, art, trade, and techniques, in an egalitarian society would only be frustrated. The ideal of equality would thus rather cause a 'levelling down' than a 'levelling up' of those members.[45] Fuller also points out that a unilateral pursuit of factual equality as leading principle in society would imply the risk of a utilitarian concept of law. Law would then be used as an instrument to obtain a maximum public interest for a maximum number of individuals, where it really should serve the realization of the idea of justice.[46] Dworkin, too, rejects this utilitarian concept. According to him, the power of numbers should have no effect on law, because it offers no explanation to question whether a decision or rule of law is good in itself, or 'why there is anything to regret when a disaster kills thousands though it improves the situation of a few'.[47] In his view the answer to the question what law is, can be found only on a higher level of abstraction. The point is 'to show to others the concern to which human beings at least are entitled'.[48] Thus equality should not be regarded as factual equality, and not even as the right to equal treatment. It is much more the right of all individuals to be regarded as a purpose in itself, not as an instrument for the goals of another.[49] Equality then concerns equal opportunities for all individuals to gain access to the means with which they can develop themselves. The 'equality' to which individuals are entitled consists in the fundamental right to 'equal concern and respect'.[50]

---

44. Dworkin (1986), 96.
45. Raz (1986), Dworkin (1981), 181.
46. (Fuller) 1977.
47. Dworkin (1981), 181. Also see Soeteman (1991) and Guest (1991).
48. *Ibid.*
49. Guest 1992 mentions Anglo-Saxon publications on this theme as from the seventies of the last century.
50. Dworkin (1977).

## 3. THE RELATIONAL CONCEPT OF LAW

The description of the ideal of the democratic constitutional state given in the previous section shows that this fits in a concept of society that is no longer (primarily) characterized by vertical relationships. The perspective of the modern philosophers of law is not so much the dichotomy of ruler versus subject (the vertical point of view), but rather the interaction between the legal subjects, in which the legal values of society must be realized.[51] Thus law is not merely a means to regulate power, but an instrument to regulate interpersonal relationships, to such an extent that all parties are able to realize their own goals as much as possible. The latter supposes freedom of the legal subject to create its own existence. However, this can be realized only within the framework of interdependent human relationships, in such a way that the other person is not degraded to the status of an object, but by recognizing him as a person that 'appears to him in all his dignity', as Scheltens so inspiringly describes this principle of equality.[52] The tension between these interdependencies, which happens to be the 'condition humaine' for every human being and the pursuit of maximum self-realization for all, requires an ordering principle in which these interdependencies can be interpreted thus, that the goals of one individual do not a priori play second fiddle to those of the others.[53] Leading principles in this field are the above-mentioned 'basic values' of freedom and equality. Thus we touch the intrinsic, moral value of law, that cannot be bargained with, not even when the focus on those legal values would minimize the influence of the administration.[54]

At a political level, this concept of law became manifest in the increasing interaction between the cornerstones of the separation of powers (Trias Politica) and the ever-increasing interference by the administration. As a result of the growing complexity of society from the first decades of the twentieth century onward, the latter finds itself increasingly faced with the task to 'fill in' the contents of statutory laws. In this interaction among the legislature, the administration, and the judiciary principles of law provide balance and coherence. These principles of law penetrate the different branches of law, in their quality as guardians of all relationships people are able to have. In civil law so-called 'open standards' are formulated, such as due care, reasonableness, and fairness. These concern the way in which legal subjects should take each other's interests into account, and they assume a mutual duty of care of (legal) persons. Although this duty does not imply that the interests of others should be given priority over one's own interests, it does mean that those interests must be weighed in the decision-making process. Thus the ideal of the autonomy of the legal subject is toned down in favour of a profile of the individual as a social being having a certain responsibility toward others. Parallel to that development, general principles of proper administration are

51. Glastra van Loon (1958), 514-521.
52. Scheltens (1976), 85-105.
53. Dworkin's right to 'equal concern and respect'.
54. Hirsch Ballin (1991), 21 e.v.

being formulated for the benefit of the relationship between administration and citizens. This development can be observed in most Western states.[55]

The fact that the most prominent legal values, such as freedom and equality, are mainly aimed at the personal emancipation of each individual requires an active participation of the members of that society in the realization of those values. Because law should offer protection to all, it must be rooted in the standards and values resulting from the process of orientation of that entire, ever-evolving society.[56] Thus, being a legal subject in this concept implies the obligation of active citizenship, expressing itself in a certain duty of compliance of citizens with the targets of the administration.[57]

## 3.1. Legal Relationships

Legal values can never be found as such; they should be given concrete form in the acts and decisions of law-forming bodies, resulting from concrete relationships between individuals. In the interactions, in which the individuals realize their goals, freedom becomes 'organized' by law, in a continuous, time-bound process.[58] Thus, those interactions are *legal relationships.* This is true for relationships between citizens as much as for those existing between the citizens and the administration, because the latter is not to be considered as standing above the law, but is bound to it, (the principle of legality). So we can conclude that the relational concept of law serves to reach a better understanding of the reality of law. It shows us that every time the legal subject claims its freedom to realize its targets, it will encounter the freedom of others. Law is the instrument to balance its interests against those of others. How the balance between these interests must be found is determined by the mutual positions within legal relationships. These vary in different branches of law, such as civil law and administrative law, including tax law.

## 3.2. Symmetrical Legal Relationships

The literature on the philosophy of law distinguishes between symmetrical and asymmetrical legal relationships, depending on the mutual position of the parties. In civil law, legal relationships are by nature symmetrical because both legal subjects can enter the relationship freely and at will, so they are established by consensus. In principle, the parties are autonomous *therein* (within the boundaries of the law). However, the consequence of their mutual interdependence is that they react to each other's actions, and that expectations about the other party's

55. Koopmans (1986). Zie ook Barents/Brinkhorst (1996) and de Moor-van Vugt (1987), Crane (1996).
56. See Gribnau (1998), 26.
57. Foque (1998), 10.
58. Hirsch Ballin (1991a), 7.

behaviour intertwine. Those expectations are based on standards such as equality, reasonableness, and due care. This gives rise to a legal duty to have regard for each other's interests.

It must be kept in mind, however, that also in civil law, factually asymmetrical situations can occur in cases in which the two legal subjects do not possess the same knowledge and expertise, although their position is formally an equal one. This discrepancy can lead to a very unequal realization of otherwise equal rights. During the past century, on the basis of this factual asymmetry, law became a more socially oriented phenomenon, in which the freedom of the 'stronger' legal subject was limited in favour of the weaker. This resulted in an increasing number of mandatory rules of law to protect that weaker party, and the development of open standards such as 'reasonableness and fairness' in civil law. Thus in the Netherlands as well as other constitutional states it was recognized that relationships in civil law were often in fact vertical.[59]

### 3.3. Legal Relationships in Administrative Law

The notion that the parties in a legal relationship mutually influence each other's actions can (for civil law) already be found in the writings of the nineteenth-century German scholar Savigny.

In administrative law, this mutual influence can also be observed in legal relationships between citizens and their administration. In the Netherlands, this concept of law can be found in the Memorandum of Reply to the General Administrative Law Act.[60] However, the parties, although legally equivalent at an abstract level, are in fact not equal. The power of self-realization that determines the content of a legal relationship in administrative law is conferred to the administration, because it has the authority to impose obligations on the citizens.

A citizen is not free to enter into this legal relationship or not, he cannot change roles, like in civil law he can (at least theoretically) take turns in being buyer or seller, for example, and he is dependent on the decisions the administration makes. The principles of law should 'repair' this legal asymmetry as much as possible. For according to the principle of the constitutional state, citizens are bearers of the right of individual self-realization, of which freedom and equality are the most fundamental elements. It is the duty of the administration to protect these rights as much as possible. The *freedom* of citizens is protected because the limitation of their rights (by imposing obligations) can take place only by way of statutory law, after a democratic debate about the public interest. In legal relationships the right to equality (understood as he right of a person to be treated as an equal),[61]

59. Compare the principle of 'Treu und Glauben' developed in German and Swiss law, which was of great influence on the development of 'open standards' such as reasonableness and fairness in Dutch civil law, but especially in administrative law.
60. Kamerstukken II 1988/89, 21 221, nr. 3 (MvT), 12.
61. See Dworkin (1977).

must be realized through the duty to respect the interests of the other party, resting especially on the administration. As the most powerful party it must yield something of its position. The administration must take into account the interests of the citizens as they themselves define these and must grant them the right to serve these interests.[62] The citizens cannot be obligated to take up the cause of the public interest to the extent the administration does.[63] The standards of sound administration that must be taken into account in the relationship with citizens are laid down in positive law, but can also be found in unwritten general principles of sound administration, which in most constitutional states were developed in case law and thus became of common knowledge. sometimes stronger than written law.[64]

## 3.4. Obligations of Citizens in Legal Relationships of Administrative Law

In the mutual, interdependent relationship between the state and its citizens, the latter, too, has obligations. In a constitutional state, these obligations of citizens must be written in statutory laws or derived from them. The law creates certainty and predictability for individuals and protects them against arbitrariness in a situation in which they are the weaker parties. For individuals, it is the basis for their trust in justice and thus it serves the public interest, which in society is defined democratically.[65] It is the task of the administration to realize this interest through its administrative actions, but it cannot succeed in doing so without the cooperation of its citizens, especially by means of communication and the supply of information. The legal obligations of citizens are therefore especially focused on these elements. Based on the principle of legality, unwritten obligations can hardly be imposed on citizens. There is no pendant of the general principles of sound administration for citizens. However, this does not imply that they would not be subject to extrastatutory standards. Their behaviour too is subjected to standards developed on the basis of expectations existing in society on the proper behaviour and due care of parties in legal relationships. However, citizens cannot be held *responsible* for the accomplishment of the targets of the administration. Thus an interested party cannot be expected to supply information on tax matters voluntarily to help the tax authorities reach their targets.[66] It could be said that citizens have 'conditional' obligations. If a citizen does not fulfil these obligations and this

62. Gribnau (2007).
63. Happé (1996), 75, 76.
64. See van Wijk/Konijnenbelt/van Male (2002), 346, for some cases in Dutch case law, and 11 for some international literature. See also Koopmans (1986), and de Moor-van Vugt (1987), Crane (1996).
65. See Hirsch Ballin (1991), 193, for an overview of the role of the principle of legality in several European countries.
66. Happé (1999).

must be deemed as serious negligence on his part, the court could be led not to allow the citizen's appeal to the protective effect of principles of sound administration. Of course. the court, against the background of the given asymmetrical nature of this legal relationship, would have to adopt a reticent attitude here.[67] The existence of unwritten obligations on the part of citizens should only be assumed inasmuch as they are made known, that is to say, inasmuch as they can be deemed to be rooted in the concepts of society on justice and injustice.[68] An example is the informational duty of citizens. The citizen as the weakest party in the legal relationship with the government is not to be held responsible for the execution of the measures of the latter. The duty of compliance of taxpayers must therefore be limited by the principles of good administration. If the statutory provision does not provide for that, the court is not allowed to supplement the statutory legal duty of citizens without further ado. It will rather apply the principles of proportionality and/or fair play, (or the principle of the most obvious party) to the conduct of the administration, as in this a-symmetrical legal relationship the latter carries the bulk of the responsibility for the realization of equality.

## 4. LEGAL RELATIONSHIP IN INTERNATIONAL TAX MATTERS

The topic of this book is legal protection in the exchange of tax-related information. As we have seen above, the exchange of information between states also supposes the existence of a legal relationship between an administration and a taxpayer, as the data for the other state will be collected from the taxpayer. Therefore, I wish to briefly discuss legal relationships in tax matters, thus providing an answer to the question to what extent states, in the specific situation in which they exchange tax data with their partners in the convention, have the duty to offer their taxpayers legal protection. The legal relationship in tax matters is one of administrative law, and thus in nature a-symmetrical. The tax authorities eventually assess the statutory tax liability of the individual legal subject (although in many cases after having contacted him). The administrative body largely depends on the cooperation of its legal subjects (taxpayers), who must provide the necessary information. Thus, in every legal system tax laws will contain provisions on the obligations of taxpayers concerning cooperation, administration, retention and information.[69] In *constitutional states*, compliance will always more or less have to be warranted by the attribution of executive auditing powers to tax officials. In most states, they comprise the power to requisition (the inspection of) documents, copies, the power to enter industrial premises, whereas information about the taxpayer himself and about third parties can be collected. All modern

67. Gribnau (1998), 223.
68. Nieuwenhuis (1999).
69. For an overview of the position of taxpayers in Western states, see the OECD Report on 'Taxpayers' Rights and Obligations (1990), 12.

states have created obligations concerning retention of the administrations of companies, and have expressed requirements as to transparency. States having a system of withholding tax (income in wages, interest, dividends paid), obligate certain individuals or legal persons to keep their accounts in a way that will suit the tax authorities in the assessment of tax liabilities of third parties. Within the European Union, specific demands are also made regarding the recording of transactions for the levying of VAT, and taxpayers are obligated to record these transactions in a strictly prescribed way. For the benefit of the tax administration, legal subjects are thus faced with administrative costs for which no immediately identifiable consideration exists. From the 1990 OECD-report on 'Taxpayers' Rights and Obligations' it appeared that these powers of the tax authorities were seen as (very) interfering by a majority of taxpayers. The justification for that interference is the public interest, which in constitutional states is defined democratically, and the realization of which is attributed to the administration. However, citizens are, in as far as the general standards on what is proper permit them to do, free to pursue their own interests. The size of their playing field is determined by law. The way citizens perceive the principle of equality differs from that of the administration. To citizens, equality means that they are allowed certain 'selfishness in pursuing their interests and those of their loved ones, provided that they respect the interest of others'. To the administration, equality means that all legal subjects must be treated with 'equal concern and respect'.[70] The principle of legality, and standards of proper behaviour, such as the principles of sound administration, must warrant a sound execution of power, including a proportional weighing of interests.

The specific written standards regulating the legal relationship between the administration and its citizens will differ from state to state. They are to be considered solutions to the conflict between the public interest and individual interests, common to all constitutional states. The contents of these standards are determined by their background, dependent as they are on the nature and the history of societies.[71] The unwritten standards, the principles of law, exceed these backgrounds and are similar in all states. Thus, in this thesis, it is not so much the question whether states do or do not know rules on legal protection in the international exchange of information, but whether states in general should know these rules and how they should affect treaties and guidelines. Only then will we be able to answer the question of what requirements legal protection should meet.

## 4.1. The Exchange of Information as a Legal Relationship in Tax Matters

In the international exchange of information, the legal relationship between the state and its taxpayers is complicated by the fact that it is embedded in the legal

70. Happé (1996), 48, 75-76.
71. Bentley (1998), gives an overview of the rights and duties of taxpayers in respect of tax audits in many countries.

relationship of international law between that state with its tax convention partner to whom it promised to help look after its tax interests. In practice, especially the legal duty toward the other state has hitherto determined the contents of the international law on the exchange of information. In the following chapters of this study it will become clear that hitherto the states have paid little attention to the 'moral' question of the duty to provide legal protection. Yet it was pointed out in the introduction that in the everyday practice of the international exchange of information, questions arose on this subject. So choices will have to be made regarding the relationship between the legal duty of a state to supply information and the interests of the taxpayer involved in this exchange. For the answer to the question of what that relationship should look like, we must take a closer look at the specific legal relationship that comes into existence when states intend to exchange information with their tax convention partners.[72]

To do so, the exchange of information upon request will be taken as a starting point, as the most logical example. Without anticipating too much in regard to the following chapters it can be deemed of common knowledge that treaty partners who have agreed on this can mutually request the exchange of information for the benefit of their own tax levying. The data requested must be collected in the requested state: from files or data files that have been 'filled' either through the compliance of tax withholding agents, or directly from audits of individual taxpayers. For the requested state, this information is available only on the basis of its legal relationship with its taxpayers, which for the latter implies a statutory obligation to cooperate in the assessment of their tax liabilities or those of third parties. Provided that the statutory power of the administration to compel disclosure of information from taxpayers *includes* the foreign tax interest, these third parties may also be registered abroad. In fact, the latter will often be the case.

As we saw before, between these taxpayers and their administration a mutual duty of care exists, and because of the asymmetrical nature of this particular legal relationship the greater part of it can be deemed to lie on the state. Assuming that the requested (constitutional) state already applies written and unwritten standards regarding compliance, the question remains whether the international exchange of information justifies a more specific legal protection.

Thus, in case in the requested state an enquiry must be made into an individual taxpayer, the number of situations in which he will be obligated to cooperate will be extended. Besides that, as the information collected from him, which therefore partly refers to him, is passed on to *another state*, he runs a greater risk than in situations in which he must provide information on third parties for *national* tax levying. The data disappear from the jurisdiction of his own state, which can no longer be held responsible for secrecy and proper use of the data. In my opinion, both elements – the existence of a legal relationship between the state and the supplier of information, and the greater risk the latter runs that his data are wrongfully disclosed or used – create the obligation for states to bring about

72. Also see Schenk-Geers (2006), 98.

legal protection against these acts of the administration. This legal protection will have to be focused on the informational interests of taxpayers and must at least contain a duty for the *requested* tax authorities to inform the taxpayer it collected the data from, because the latter has an interest to know that information about him was disclosed elsewhere and the purport of the data concerned. Moreover, he must be able to verify whether the exchange takes place in a lawful manner and with sufficient care. Therefore, as a minimum, the data concerned, the receiving state, and the purpose of the exchange must be disclosed. To make a weighing of those interests possible and enforceable, a defence facility must be created. In this matter, the same question arises as was discussed in the Introduction of this book in the case of the American lawsuit, that is, how sometimes conflicting civil rights such as those of information and secrecy relate to each other, as well as how they relate to obligations under a treaty.

In my view, in case the requested state collects the data from the tax authority's paper and digital files, the administration has the same duty of care. Those files exist as a consequence of the duty of taxpayers to provide information as laid down in the law. Even if they are under no obligation to cooperate more than their due in any particular case, in my view, the interest they have in the lawfulness of the exchange of 'their' data to another state needs protection. How this protection must be implemented will depend on the nature of the exchange. However, this concept must be checked against the concept on which other instruments of informational legal protection are based, such as the European Privacy Directive.[73] Maybe this example of informational legal protection can be a source of inspiration for the creation of rules for the protection of the position of the taxpayer involved in the international exchange of information, as well as in the formation of an opinion on 'informational self-determination' as it was enshrined in the statutory laws of some states during the last decades of the last century.

However, in the first place, we must look at the international framework for the exchange of tax-related information to verify whether it creates possibilities for states to fulfil their legal duties under public law and, if so, to what extent.

## 5. SUMMARY

1. The notion of legal protection is inextricably linked with the notion of the relationship between the state and its citizens.

During the period of the European Ancien Régime legal protection of citizens hardly existed. The sovereign had absolute power, and his subjects were not considered as independent carriers of rights.

As a reaction to the arbitrary acts of these administrations in the eighteenth century, the idea of the liberal constitutional state arose. The sovereign and his

73. Directive 95/46 EC on the protection of individuals with regard to the processing of personal data and on the free movement of such data, *Official Journal of the European Communities* L281, 23 Nov. 1995, 31.

subject were, rather, considered as parties to a contract, both having rights as well as duties. The sovereign's subjects evolved (in theory) to free and autonomous legal subjects. The central authority was to leave this freedom intact as much as possible, so that the individual could realize its own targets. Law was the instrument to regulate power, and in that concept of law, legislation was pivotal. The separation of the legislature from the executive and the judiciary sealed its incontestability, to which the executive and the judiciary had to yield. Law and justice were identical. This ideal of the free and autonomous individual inspired large groups of citizens to participate in the decision-making process of states, thus being able to pursue their interests. This gave rise to criticism on the aloofness of the liberal state that did not protect the weak, and did not bring about justice.

2. The so-called democratic constitutional state that evolved as a reaction to the liberal constitutional state took a greater responsibility for the emancipation of its subjects. This resulted in a more detailed interference of the State in the development of society and a less unbiased, more ethical concept of law. In this process the law lost its central position to the principles of law. These common notions about what is just and proper between people provide leading principles and coherence to the law formation process by the legislature, the courts, and the administration, and in constantly changing circumstances they 'crystallize' in legislation, regulations, and court decisions time and again.

3. Moreover, society was increasingly considered as a system of mutual relationships between people who need other people for the realization of their goals. Thus the autonomy of the legal subject was put into perspective. Law was seen as an intersubjective phenomenon – as an 'instrument' to coordinate mutual dependencies between individuals.

4. This must take place within a concrete legal relationship: a relationship between legal subjects governed by law. This 'interactive' perspective gave more depth to the legal value of equality, formulated by Dworkin as 'the right of the individual to be treated as equal'. This led to the recognition and wording of a mutual duty of care for both parties in a legal relationship, whether it be in civil law or in administrative law.

5. Especially in administrative law (including tax law) legal relationships, the positions of the legal subjects are not equal. The administration has a superior position, which can be justified only by the necessity to pursue the public interest as defined democratically. The principle of equality then implies that the legal relationship in administrative law creates a heavier duty of care for the administration. This means that it must take into account the principle of proportionality when it puts an administrative burden to its citizens (taxpayers), and that it must weigh the interests of the other party in a reasonable manner.

6. Tax data that are to be exchanged on the basis of international agreements must be obtained with the cooperation of the taxpayers. This assumes the existence of a legal relationship in tax matters, with an inherent duty of care for the administration. As the risks of taxpayers as suppliers of data are of an informational nature, that duty of care must be created by means of a notification of the requested state of the fact that data will be exchanged, the nature of the data to be exchanged

and the state that will receive those data. Besides that, information supplying the taxpayer must also be offered the possibility to defend himself if the exchange is incorrect and/or unjustified. Examples of this already exist in the rules on privacy and data protection that evolved as from the seventies of the last century. All this will naturally have to fit in the international legal relationship of the requested state with its partner in the convention, because the actions of the administration are based on this relationship.

Chapter 3

# Interpretation of Tax Treaties

## 1. INTRODUCTION

In Chapter 1, it became clear that for tax-treaty partners cross-border exchange of information is an important instrument for the assessment of the national tax liability of taxpayers. The increasing globalization of their economies has led states to the conclusion that international agreements in this field are a dire necessity. We have then seen that the exchange of information can take place only because the supplying state can gather these data from its taxpayers or tax withholding agents (for the sake of brevity hereinafter to be called taxpayers). From this conclusion, the question arose as to what the position of the taxpayer must be in this international legal relationship between states, dominated as this is by *their* fiscal and economic interests.

To find the answer to this question, we have explored the abstract field of legal philosophy. There we found the basic concept of the inalienable dignity of each individual and the right of freedom and personal development, as this was postulated as a fundamental right from the end of the eighteenth century onward. However, it turned out that for each individual it is possible to realize this right only in relationships with other individuals and that not every individual is equally equipped to do so. It appeared that in solving the conflict between his pursuit of autonomy on the one hand and his dependence of other individuals, a leading principle was needed, that could organize human interrelationships in such a way that this freedom and personal development would be within everyone's reach. Thus the leading principle proved to be the principle of equality, which within this context does not refer to actual equal treatment for all, but to the much wider norm, formulated by Dworkin, of 'equal concern and respect'. The parties in a legal relationship must treat each other *as equals*. The burden of that responsibility rests heavier on the party that has the strongest position. The latter has as a duty of care regarding the interests of the other party. In the legal relationship between citizens and the state, that duty of care lies with the state. This is of course also true for fiscal legal relationships under which the state gathers information from taxpayers to fulfil its obligation toward a contracting state. In its actions, it must take the interests of the latter into account as well.

This conclusion triggered the question of whether or not the international obligation of states to exchange information in tax matters offers them a possibility to fulfil their duty of care as well. To find an answer, this international obligation must be further scrutinized, which will take place in Chapters 4-6 of this book. As the origin and focal point of this obligation is embedded in tax-treaty law, it is sensible to first discuss the problems regarding interpretation in this chapter.[1]

These tax treaties were nearly all concluded based on the Model Convention drawn up by the Organization for Economic Cooperation and Development (OECD). The Model convention also served as a source of inspiration for the multilateral Convention of Strasbourg of 1988 as a joint product of the OECD and the Council of Europe and the European obligations to exchange information, such as the Council Directive 77/799 and the Council Regulation 1798/2003 on VAT. They were all at least partly based on these Model texts.[2] The most recent initiative of the OECD to this day in this field was the establishment of the Agreement on Exchange of Information on Tax Matters with certain former tax havens.[3]

All treaties are governed by a duty of loyalty toward contracting parties and the resulting obligation to reach a common viewpoint if doubts arise about the meaning of a provision of the treaty concerned. The problems that may arise in this effort will be discussed hereafter.

---

1. Meanwhile, tax treaties, usually based directly or indirectly on the OECD Model convention, form an almost global network, and their number is still increasing.
2. EU Directive of 19 Dec. 1977, concerning the mutual assistance by the competent authorities of the Member States in the field of direct taxes, PbEU 1977, L 336:
   - EU Directive of 6 Dec. 1979, no. 1070/79, PbEU 1979, L 331.
   - EU Directive of 25 Feb. 1992, no. 92/12, PbEU 1992, L 76 also for individual excise duties.
   - Directive 2003/93/EU of the Council of the European Union of 7 Oct. 2003, concerning the mutual assistance by the competent authorities of the Member States in the field of direct and indirect taxes, PbEU L 264; see also V-N 2003/58.24.
   - Council Regulation (EU) 1798/2003, of 7 Oct. 2003, concerning the administrative collaboration in the field of taxation of added value and repeal of the Council Regulation (EU) 218/92, PbEU 2003, L264/1. (Hereafter called Council Regulation 1798/2003); see also V-N 2003/57.23.
   - Regulation (EU) 1925/2004 from the Commission, of 29 Oct. 2004, to arrange further implementation regulations for certain stipulations of the Council Regulation (EU) 1798/2003 concerning the administrative collaboration in the field of taxation of added value, PbEU L 331 (hereafter called Implementation Council Regulation).
   - Multilaral Convention of the Council of Europe and the OECD on mutual administrative assistance in tax matters, 25 Jan. 1988 in Strasbourg.
3. See <www.oecd.org>. Also Barnard (2002).

## 2. NATURE AND OBJECTIVES OF TAX TREATIES

In the relational concept of law as described in the previous chapter, a treaty may best be compared with a common law contractual relationship.[4] The state, pre-eminently a subject of international law,[5] is free to enter into this relationship. States are inclined to enter into such a relationship if they feel it will further their goals. The result of this interdependence is that in this legal relationship they must respect each other's interests. In the beginning, treaties were especially seen by the states as a means to safeguard their own, sometimes only recently obtained, sovereign powers. They mainly contained rules on coexistence, and the better part of them was aimed at the demarcation of this autonomy. In the second half of the nineteenth century, however, the states became increasingly aware of their international interdependence. As a result, mutual obligations of means were added in an effort to safeguard domestic interests.[6]

Tax treaties spring from the need to avoid double taxation in situations in which taxpayers engage in cross-border economic activities. This danger of double taxation originates amongst others from the fact that states in principle deem themselves entitled to tax the incomes of their residents (residence principle) or subjects (nationality principle), while at the same time they also intend to tax the activities and incomes of non-residents. Based on the country-of-origin principle this taxation can be justified by assuming that the revenues of the activities of those non-residents could be achieved only because the state offered certain facilities, for example, the presence of minerals, an adequate infrastructure or a professionally skilled population. Another reason for levying taxes is that the source of income of the non-resident lies within the territory of the state (the source principle). Taxing the income of residents generated outside their 'own' state is by no means prohibited by the international principle of territoriality. States have an inalienable right to levy taxes, embedded both in their constitutions and in international law.[7] In principle, this right is operative within minimal territorial boundaries, but the international rules on this subject are so vague that within the international context, in the end, it is in fact the sovereign states themselves that determine the scope of their power to levy taxes.[8] Therefore an international ban on double taxation does not exist.[9] As a result, double taxation can be prevented only by either a unilateral legal policy of prevention in which in certain cases an exemption or deduction of taxes is granted, or through an international agreement, by which

4. Schaumburg (1998), para. 3.3 describes the treaty as a 'Willenseinigung zwischen Volkerrechtssubjekten, deren Gegenstand die Begründung oder Änderung völkerrechtlicher Rechte und Pflichten ist'.
5. Kooijmans (2000), 20.
6. *Ibid.*, 3.
7. Vogel (2003), Einleitung, Rz. 7. Schaumburg (1998), Teil 1, para. 2.7, speaks of the 'Universalprinzip'.
8. Within this international context, economic and political interdependences will naturally play a role.
9. Schaumburg (1998), paras 2.7 and 3.14, and Vogel (2003), Einleitung, Rz. 14.

states either mutually divide their taxing rights or limit their national powers to levy taxes.[10]

Thus, in my view, tax treaties contain elements of delineation of obligations as well as elements of cooperation. They mutually delineate their powers to levy taxes because for a sound development of their economies, the states are interdependent. Relinquishing their sovereign right to levy taxes in certain cases is the price that must be paid to keep the balance.[11] However, treaties also contain obligations to cooperate, which imply that on certain occasions, efforts have to be made that exclusively serve the interests of the contracting party. The obligation to exchange information in tax matters is an example of the latter.

The treaty obligations concern the interests of the states themselves and those of their citizens. They are completely embedded in the fiscal legal relationship the states and their citizens have entered into. Therefore it goes without saying that the states, also in the actual execution of their tax treaties, are bound to legal principles, such as legal certainty, protection of the freedom and integrity of the individual, and equality, which are already embedded in their domestic tax laws.[12]

The problems states experience in providing for the prevention of double taxation, tax avoidance and tax fraud are largely similar. Therefore, since the Great War, efforts are being made in the Western world to standardize tax treaties by means of models. The scope of this book leaves me no room to dwell on this matter.

In 1963, the OECD developed a Model based on the OECD Convention, which actually served as a format for the participating states in concluding their bilateral tax treaties.[13] In that Model convention, the mutual assistance in tax matters was inserted in the convention itself (Article 26 of the Model); it was not laid down in a separate Model convention, as was the case in the models of the League of Nations. The OECD Model convention is accompanied by an official Commentary.

In 1977 a revised version was published, reflecting the experiences of the states with the increasing globalization of their economic systems. Since 1992, the Model convention and the Commentary are continually adjusted to either the fiscal and economic or tax law developments and published in a loose-leaf edition.[14] The consequences of this choice for the interpretation of the existing treaty net will be dealt with later in this Chapter.

---

10. The term 'double taxation' covers a variety of many specific situations and problems, which are continually analyzed and categorized in the international professional journals. A description of this complex matter lies beyond the scope of this study. See Kemmeren (2001), 12 e.v., with international references.
11. Cf. also Vogel (2003), Rz. 16 and Bunders/Overgaauw (2000), 27-32.
12. Cf. Ch. 2, Backgrounds of legal protection, for a more thorough discussion of this topic.
13. Vogel (2003), Einleitung Rz. 17 ff. with references to international literature, and Bunders/ Overgaauw (2000).
14. Cf. Vogel's review in 2000.

## 3. FUNCTION OF THE MODEL CONVENTION

The general view is that the Model convention in its nature is not legally binding.[15] Article 5 of the 1960 OECD Convention offers the possibility to take decisions and issue recommendations to the Member States. The Model convention must be seen as a recommendation to conclude tax treaties as much as possible according to the established wording.[16] According to the Introduction of the Commentary, it is the specific tax treaties, 'signed by Member Countries, which, unlike the Model, are legally binding international instruments'.[17] In spite of the important exemplary function of the Model convention, each individual convention must be considered autonomous. States will deviate from its text in accordance with their needs and those of their treaty partners. They are inclined to repeat those deviations in subsequent conventions, either based on the fact that their own specific interests are thus served best, or because of the fact that new treaty partners demand the same provisions as their predecessors, if these are considered favourable (the so-called parallel treaties).[18]

## 4. TWO FRAMEWORKS OF INTERNATIONAL LAW FOR THE INTERPRETATION OF TAX TREATIES: THE VIENNA CONVENTION AND THE OECD MODEL CONVENTION

International law springs from different sources: customary practices of states to act in a certain way,[19] international legal principles ('*allgemeine Rechtsgrundsätze der Kulturvölker, die sich aus dem innerstaatlichen Recht der Staaten entnehmen und auf international Sachverhälte übertragen lassen*'[20]) and treaties. According

15. Anders: Engelen (2004), 425 e.v. See also para. 3.6.1.
16. Tieskens (1999), considers these recommendations more binding than authors generally do, especially the fact that their wordings are agreed on after ample deliberation, and that states have the possibility to make their position clear in reservations and observations, and implies in his view that these recommendations are meant to have some binding power. See also Engelen in his dissertation. Those states that have not inserted a 'reservation' in the Model convention or an 'observation' in the Model commentary, or other wordings in their specific treaties, in his view are bound to the Model convention and the Commentary. This is because of the requirement of the Vienna Convention that states must execute their treaties in 'good faith'.
17. OECD Commentary, 1977-2001, Introduction, para. 29.
18. Vogel (2003), Einleitung, Rz. 140.
19. According to case law of the International Court of Justice, a custom can be considered as law only if the actions undertaken have taken place during a longer period of time and apparent to other parties, and if this practice arises from the opinion of the state that it *must* act in this way for reasons of decency (de opinio juris sive necessitatis). See Engelen (2004) *(diss.)*, 12.
20. (Basic principles of law of civilized peoples that can be transferred to international situations.) Schaumburg (1998), 315. Among these legal principles are also general rules of law, such as the rule that younger provisions supersede older ones, and that special provisions supersede general ones, as well as general principles of law, such as 'der Grundsatz von Treu und Glauben', reasonableness and fairness.

to its nature, the law of treaties is mainly written law.[21] Since the Second World War, it has increasingly made ground to international customary law, as its written form offers more possibilities to reflect and 'control' the increasing complexity of inter-State relationships.[22] In the second half of the last century, international customary law was laid down in a number of 'codification treaties' under the guidance of the International Law Commission (ILC) of the United Nations.[23] During this period, the 1969 Vienna Convention on the law of treaties was also drawn up. This will be discussed in more detail further on.

### 4.1. The Need for a Uniform Interpretation of Treaties

For a practical application of treaty rules there must be clarity on the terms that are used in it, both at the time of conclusion of the treaty and in all kinds of future unforeseen cases. Treaties are concluded between equivalent sovereign states and there is no 'higher instance' having authority over the contracting partners.[24] Therefore the interpretation of international agreements within states is not only referred to national judges who will apply rules of interpretation that are current in their legal system, as well as internationally accepted,[25] but is also taking place at an official level with the 'mutual agreement' procedures based on Article 25, first and third paragraphs of the Model convention. In this procedure, the extent in which interpretation is bound by the literal meaning of the text of the treaty provisions is very important.

In the early literature, the opinion prevailed that interpretation of treaties must be based exclusively on their wording; because states could be deemed to have waived their sovereignty only inasmuch as this could be gathered unequivocally from the text of the agreement.[26] This is explainable from the emphasis that in many domestic law systems was put on the text of Acts of Parliament since the inception of the classic rule of law. For it was only on those Acts of Parliament that the legitimacy of supposedly necessary infringements of the freedom and property rights of the individual could be based. According to the Dutch Constitution as well, taxes may be levied only by statutory force.[27]

Although the initial awe of the law attached a strong binding force to the *text* of the law, as from the sixties of the last century this positivist approach became the subject of criticism (cf. paragraph 2.2.2.). In the interpretation of laws, which

21. See Kooijmans (2000), 12 and Engelen (2004), 19.
22. Engelen points out that an agreement between states can be called a treaty only if it shows the intention of the parties to be bound.
23. An important motor for this codification is the ILC of the United Nations, also because in this codification newer insights are also incorporated. See Kooijmans (2000), 12.
24. Although for the solution of certain disputes states can submit to the International Court of Justice in The Hague. Kooijmans (2000), 118 e.v.
25. van Soest (1996).
26. Cf. also Vogel (2000), Einleitung, Rz. 102, 106.
27. Article 104 of the Dutch Constitution.

increasingly contained 'open standards', besides the wording of the law and general legal principles, the intention of the legislator must serve as a guideline as well. In doing so, it is not necessary to dogmatically follow the statements of the historic legislator. In certain cases, social circumstances also can play a role in the interpretation of the law. This development also occurred in the application and interpretation of the tax treaties.[28]

The interpretation of treaty terms was generally codified for the first time in the Vienna Convention of 23 May 1969 on the Law of Treaties, as part of all international rules concerning treaties. This convention can (at least partly) be considered as the codification of a number of hitherto unwritten rules on what was considered reasonable between treaty partners, or should be considered so.[29] The starting point is the rule that treaties must be performed in good faith (Article 26 of the Vienna Convention) and do not bind parties in relation to any act or fact that took place or any situation that ceased to exist before the date of the entry into force of the treaty, unless a different intention appears from the treaty or is otherwise established (Article 28 of the Vienna Convention).

## 4.2. Interpretation of Treaties According to Article 31 of the Vienna Convention

The requirement of good faith also returns in Article 31, first paragraph of the Vienna Convention: the text of the treaty must be interpreted in good faith in accordance with the ordinary meaning of the terms of the treaty in their context and in the light of its object and purpose. Thus the importance of the text of the treaty is confirmed. Interpretation of a treaty does not imply an 'investigation *ab initio* into the intentions of the parties' and must not lead to states reading in the treaties what they do not say, says the Explanatory Memorandum.[30] The 'meaning of the text', however, is the only point of departure of the interpretation.[31] This needs not necessarily be the ordinary meaning. If an internationally accepted legal meaning of a term exists, or if a term has a specific professional scope, such as tax law, then that must be the guideline.[32] The 'ordinary meaning' can, of course, be jointly replaced by the parties by a 'special meaning' (Article 31, paragraph 4 of the Vienna Convention).

---

28. Cf. Vogel/Prokisch (1993), 57, 58.
29. See Engelen (2004). He points out that the process of drafting the Vienna Convention by the International Law Commission (ILC) of the United Nations, was not only that of codification of unwritten customary law, but certainly also a discussion about which method of interpretation should prevail; the grammatical or de teleological method.
30. Explanatory Memorandum to the 1969 Vienna Convention, Art. 31, para. 11.
31. *Ibid.*, Introduction, para. 9.
32. Vogel (2003), Einleitung, Rz. 108. Also Pijl (1997), 540. He concludes from Art. 31, lid 4 Vienna Convention that the specific meaning is in fact more important, that is, the meaning of a term on the moment of the concluding of the treaty. This is conflicting with the dynamic interpretation favoured and recommended by the Committee of Fiscal Affairs.

According to Article 31, paragraph 1 of the Vienna Convention, apart from the meaning of the text, especially the 'object and purpose' of a treaty determine the meaning of its terms.[33] Therefore states must look for what binds them, rather than for what keeps them apart, and they must choose the interpretation that leads to the desired purpose.

This provision creates a barrier against interpretation methods that are too artificial, which at a later state could favour the interest of one party to the treaty over that of another. That would imply a breach of the good faith the partners to a treaty must observe toward each other.[34] 'Object and purpose of the agreement' can be found in the context (the description of the purpose and/or the preamble and the treaty as a whole), where the term 'purpose' must not be understood as a subjective intention of the parties to the treaty, but as the objectifiable purpose of the treaty.[35]

Not only the preamble and annexes to a treaty are part of the context, but also that which happened *between parties* at the time of the conclusion of the treaty: the agreement on the treaty at the time of conclusion and the deeds drawn up at this occasion by one or more parties and that are recognized by third parties as relevant to the treaty. Parliamentary documents in the individual states, such as Explanatory Memoranda, going with the concept treaties in the ratification process, do not form part of the context in the sense of the Vienna Convention. Generally accepted international legal rules, however, do form part of the context, as well as subsequent agreements between the parties on the interpretation and/or application of the treaty, or any subsequent practice between the parties in the application of the treaty. Thus the scope of the term 'object and purpose' is not fully determined by the '*travaux préparatoires*', but is also determined by what has happened between the contracting parties since the time of conclusion. This is of importance for the interpretation of the tax treaties, which are subject to changes from several directions. I shall return to this subject in paragraph 3.6. Meanwhile, it must be kept in mind that the term 'context' in tax treaties is generally more broadly interpreted than its equivalent in the Vienna Convention.

Supplementary means of interpretation (Article 32 of the Vienna Convention) can confirm the result of the application of Article 31 or offer help in cases in which the meaning cannot be established unequivocally or clearly through Article 31 or would lead to a result that is unreasonable or absurd. Supplementary means of interpretation may be drawn from the '*travaux-préparatoires*', inasmuch as common viewpoints are expressed. Under the Vienna Convention, only what

33. In professional literature, the meaning of 'the terms of the treaty' was looked into. There are authors who assume that a word merely derives its meaning from the intentions of its user. There is also a discussion going on about the function of the word as a carrier of conceptual content, or rather as a sign. This is of importance in relation to the question whether national legal fictions are to be 'incorporated' in the interpretation of treaties. See Pijl (1997), 543.
34. Vogel/Prokisch (1993), 61 report that most states are indeed of the opinion that in the interpretation of treaties, the interests of *both* parties to the treaty must be taken into account. They speak of 'the postulate of a neutral interpretation'.
35. Vogel (2003), Einleitung, Rz. 109.

happened *between the parties* is part of the context, so the question arises whether texts drawn up during the formation of multilateral treaties (such as the OECD Model convention) are also part of the context for new states, because the newcomers were not present during the written preparatory rounds.[36]

In my view, this question must be answered in the positive. Joining a multilateral treaty, as well as the choice to base a tax treaty on the OECD Model, happens voluntarily and thus in agreement with the solutions and insights incorporated in the multilateral treaty. If a state is not willing to commit itself to a viewpoint that has already been taken, it must be able to do so, for example by, inserting a 'reservation' in the text of the treaty or an 'observation' in the Explanatory Memorandum, as is made possible in the OECD Model convention.

## 4.3. Interpretation of Tax Treaties: Article 3, Paragraph 2 of the OECD Model

In tax treaties, too, an unequivocal definition of the relevant terms is of course of paramount importance. Therefore, in the various articles of the OECD Models, many definitions are worded. The massive scope of the application of the tax treaties, which moreover takes place between large numbers of different states, leads to the situation that not all terms in the Model convention can be defined. Besides, it must be kept in mind that a treaty must form a bridge between the various tax systems of the contracting states. It is therefore important that the states are given a certain margin for the interpretation of treaty terms.[37] The interpretation provision of the Model convention itself therefore recommends that for the interpretation of terms not defined, states base themselves on the meaning of those terms in their domestic laws.[38]

Article 3, paragraph 2, of the OECD Model convention reads as follows: (authentic italics)

> As regards the application of the Convention *at any time* by a Contracting State any term not defined therein shall, unless the context otherwise requires, have the meaning that it *has at that time* under the law of that state *for the purposes* of the taxes for which the convention applies, *any meaning under the applicable tax laws of that State prevailing over a meaning given to the term under the other laws of that State.*

36. Vogel (2003), Einleitung, Rz. 109. In his view, the wording of Art. 31 is meant as a protection for Member States entering multilateral treaties at a later stage and that are therefore not bound to the *travaux préparatoires*.
37. Vogel/Prokisch (1993), 55.
38. See van Raad (2001), 212, where he sums up all kinds of undefined terms that occur in the Model convention.

The connection that is made between the applicable law of the State and the treaty term gives rise to questions in the application of the separate treaties. These questions concern:

- the relation between Article 3, paragraph 2 of the OECD Model convention and Article 31 of the Vienna convention;
- the question of which domestic law should be leading for the interpretation;
- the question how the multiple changes in the domestic tax law affect the interpretation of the tax treaties.

In my view, the relation between Article 3, paragraph 2 of the OECD Model convention and the Vienna Convention must be considered as the relation between a *lex specialis* and a *lex generalis*, as laid down in Article 31 of the Vienna Convention. For tax treaties, the 'ordinary meaning' described therein must be found in the domestic laws of the parties to the treaty. Thus, in the interpretation of tax treaties, the provision in the OECD Model convention has supremacy, but it must be applied in accordance with the Vienna Convention.[39] Based on the Model convention, national meanings are valid only as far as the context does not require something else. I have already mentioned above that according to some authors, the context in the tax treaties must be interpreted more broadly than is the case in the Vienna Convention. In their 'General Report' of the 1993 IFA Congress, Vogel and Prokisch mention various concepts of the interpretation rule of the Model convention and of the term 'context'. Roughly speaking, they distinguish between authors who think that a joint interpretation must be reached 'by any means possible', putting the context as the first element to be examined, whereas others prefer the examination of domestic terms.[40] In these approaches, a different concept of the scope of the term 'context' plays a role, the latter itself not being unequivocally delineated. In my view, from the wording of the provision the conclusion must be drawn that to determine the meaning of a treaty term that is not defined, the context must be examined first, before the domestic meanings are addressed.[41] As far as I can see, this may be concluded from the Vienna Convention, which obligates the

39. Cf. e.g., Vogel/Prokisch (1993), 77, as well as Ault (1994), who considers Art. 3, para. 2 of the OECD Model convention as a specification of the possibility for the states to establish a 'special meaning', if the ordinary meaning does not clarify the subject. Different from van Raad (1984), 159 e.v. He is not so sure about the meaning of the Vienna Convention for tax treaties: after all, the OECD Model convention has its specific interpretation rule.
40. Vogel/Prokisch (1993), Rz. 81. Cf. Heinrich/Moritz (2000), 143 and onward. They criticize the Austrian concept of the role of the treaty context. In their view, this was wrongly left out of consideration in the change of the Austrian domestic laws concerning the remuneration of foreign professors. In their view, this has resulted in a 'treaty-override' effect.
41. Vogel/Prokisch (1993), 64, are even of the opinion that the 'common interpretation requirement' can actually put aside the reference to the domestic law in Art. 3, para. 2 of the OECD Model convention. In their view, the latter does not have 'unconditional priority' in any way. A joint interpretation based on the objectives of the treaty is preferred.

states to interpretations 'in good faith', therefore to the furtherance of 'Entscheidungsharmonie' in the interpretation, which must be the purpose of it.[42] An investigation into the context will bring to light the joint purpose of a tax treaty sooner than the focus on domestic meanings: the prevention of double taxation in a certain case.[43] In practice, this 'ranking order' must not be conceived all too rigidly, for that matter.[44] Not every meaning arising from the context must be given priority over the domestic meaning. The best method seems to establish both meanings and to balance them against each other, against the background of the purpose of the treaty.[45] A broad concept of the term 'context' according to British example, of which the '*travaux préparatoires*' of a provision forms part, could facilitate a common interpretation.[46] This principle of 'common interpretation' is adhered to in many countries.[47] According to the – report of the 1993 IFA Congress, national judges also look for references in each other's rulings or in those of third states. This practice could be improved by a better availability of the case law of national judges in other states.[48] An extension of the provision on the exchange of information in the OECD Model convention would be worth considering to this purpose.

On the basis of Article 3, paragraph 3 of the Model convention, if treaty terms are not defined, the national meanings of a certain expression may be explored. A motivation for this solution is that in the prevention of double taxation, the terminology of the state applying the treaty should be adhered to as much as possible because its tax administration and judiciary are most familiar with it.[49] Moreover, in this manner the sovereignty of the states would be best respected.[50] It seems to me that the position of the taxpayer is also of importance. His frame of thought, too, is determined by the national body of legal definitions.

42. The Dutch Supreme Court has also occasionally taken the Vienna Convention as a guideline for the interpretation of an undefined term in a tax treaty. In this case the meaning of the term 'temporary' in Art. 10 of the tax treaty between Germany and the Netherlands. In its rulings of 29 Sep. 1999, BNB 2000/16 and 2000/17 the Dutch Supreme Court first interpreted the text grammatically, then placed it against the background of the purpose of the provision, also examining the ordinary meaning of the word '*vorübergehend*' or 'temporary' in the texts of the treaty.
43. Also see van Raad (1984, 1996), 1413, who asks the question 'whether the context *always* prevails or that this is only in cases of *essential* differences with domestic law in a state'.
44. Pijl (1995), 1254, has a different opinion. In his view Art. 3, para. 2, OECD Model convention is not only a reference to the domestic legal system, but a also a 'prescription' to first take into account the specific definition of a term in the treaty, then searching for its national (domestic) meaning, and at last for the context of the term.
45. van Raad (1984), 161.
46. Vogel/Prokisch (1993), 82.
47. Vogel (2003), Einleitung, Rz.114, refers to a number of international examples of case law in which this is shown.
48. Vogel/Prokisch (1993), 64 and 84, and van Raad (1996), both complain about the difficulty of access of foreign case law.
49. Vogel (2003), Einleitung Rz. 106.
50. Vogel/Prokisch (1993), 77.

However, when domestic laws serve as a point of reference, the states face various problems, which can be summarized as follows:

- What must happen if states diverge in their qualification of certain income?
- What if in a national legal system terms can have more than one meaning?
- What is right by law if the meaning of a national legal term has changed in the course of time?

The first question, which qualification must prevail in case national interpretations diverge, has been the topic of discussion up to now. Article 3, paragraph 2 of the OECD Model convention mentions the national meaning that it has *at that time* under the law of the state applying the treaty. With regard to the so-called 'lex fori' rule, in literature the question was raised whether or not both the state of residence and the source state can be considered to apply the treaty. Avery Jones gives a strict interpretation of the term 'to apply': if on the basis of a tax treaty, a state limits or waives its right to levy taxes in a certain case, then the law of that state prevails.[51] However, this approach is not adhered to by all authors. I refer to my above remark on the advantages of an autonomous interpretation, against the background of the context of the treaty.[52]

In the 2000 version of the OECD Commentary, this problem is 'solved' in the advantage of the source state.[53] Articles 23a and 23b of the Model Convention must be understood thus, that the state of residence steps down if the source state has correctly qualified the treaty under its domestic rules of law. According to Vogel, in that case, there is no more cause for double taxation to arise.[54] But authors are not unanimous in this either. The Netherlands and Switzerland have inserted an 'observation' in the previously mentioned notes in the OECD Commentary, reserving the right to choose a different method of interpretation, depending on the circumstances of the case and the relationship with the partner to the treaty.

The second question concerned the problem that was caused in the application of Article 3, paragraph 2 of the OECD Model convention by the fact that in a legal system, a certain term can have various contents. This question was answered as well. In 1995, Article 3, paragraph 2 of the Model convention was changed in the sense that the meaning of an undefined treaty term must be drawn from the domestic meaning of that term in the state applying the treaty, in which the meaning in *the tax laws prevails over other meanings.* Thus a much clearer picture has emerged, although the final word in this matter has not yet been spoken.[55] A related problem is whether domestic legal fictions, or the fiscal interpretation of facts that

51. Also van Raad (1984), 164 and Avery Jones (1984), 14.
52. Cf. Vogel/Prokisch (1993), 78.
53. OECD Commentary, 2000, Art. 23, para. 32.4.
54. Cf. Vogel (2000).
55. Cf. Vogel (1997). He points out that the added n. 13. 1 to the Commentary to Art. 3, para. 2 of the Model convention yet again leaves room for discretion. Also, within tax laws, a term can be substantiated in more than one way.

in certain countries are considered to be tax abuse, determine the interpretation of the treaty as 'national meaning' in the sense of Article 3, paragraph 2 of the OECD Model convention as well. The position of the interpretation provision under the Chapter 'General Definitions' in the Model convention gives Vogel and Prokisch reason to conclude that such an application does not concur with the tenor of the provision. It would cause too much uncertainty.[56] Until 2003, the OECD Commentary reflected the lack of international consensus concerning the acceptance or the existence of a general anti-abuse principle in the law of treaties.[57] I am of the opinion that in this field, restraint must be exercised, because in the words of Happé[58] the legal fictions in themselves are already at odds with the equality principle and are (or at least should be) tested more strictly in court. In treaty situations, where the intentions of *two* contracting states constitute the frame of reference, this will be all the more necessary. The *fraus legis* doctrine can be applied only if it shows from the context of the treaty that the parties have actually intended to apply it. However, a fixed allowance or deduction can maintain its meaning, because it refers to only the extent of a taxable income.[59]

The third question concerned the most important problem with regard to the role of the national meanings in the interpretation of treaties. It is closely related to the changeability of domestic tax laws. Theoretically, domestic law changes can influence the interpretation of existing treaties. The scope of that influence depends on the answer to the question of whether the interpretation of the treaty should take place either under domestic law applicable at the time the parties *entered* into the treaty or under the law applicable at the time of the *application* of the treaty. This leads us to a discussion on static versus dynamic interpretation, which also plays a role in a wider context. This question will be dealt with in paragraph 3.6.

## 4.4. Article 3, Paragraph 2 of the OECD Model Convention and the Exchange of Information

Article 26 of the Model convention (the provision on the exchange of information) also contains terms the meaning of which states should find in their domestic laws. Although the content of this article is to be thoroughly discussed in the Chapter 4, I wish for this moment to point out the term 'necessary'. The object of the exchange of information in the wording of Article 26 is 'Such information as is *necessary*'. At first, the term was not defined. The Dutch State Taxes Act (Article 47), however, contains only a duty of taxpayers to provide information that 'may be

56. Vogel/Prokisch (1993), 79.
57. OECD Commentary, 1977-2005, Art. 1, para. 24. In Dutch literature, several concepts were defended, from the application of so-called legal fictions in the interpretation of the treaty. (See Pijl (WFR 1995/6164, 1254)), to the opposite concept that legal fictions are not valid in treaty situations (De Bont (2001) and van Weeghel (2002)).
58. Happé (2002).
59. See Burgers in her annotation of the verdict of the Dutch Supreme Court 3 Dec. 2004, BNB 2005/92.

*relevant*' for taxation. At this point also Schaumburg finds a discrepancy in the German tax legislation,[60] and this turned out to exist in many countries. In 2005, when the text of the OECD Model convention was reviewed, the term 'necessary' was replaced by the term 'foreseeably relevant'.[61] Terms such as 'prosecution' in the definition of the purpose of the exchange, or 'the normal course of the administration' can, however, have different meanings in every state, whereas terms such as 'trade, business, industrial and professional secrets' are certainly not always defined in the (tax) laws of the states.

Problems concerning the qualification of revenue categories can present themselves if one of the contracting states defines a certain income in such a way that, in the view of the other state, it can no longer be qualified as one of 'the taxes covered by the treaty' and on which on the basis of Article 26 information can be exchanged. In the Netherlands, the question arose whether after a change of the tax system in 2001 and especially concerning the flat-rate tax on imputed return on investment, which at the time was newly introduced. Some authors found that this tax would not fit in the existing tax treaties.[62] Recent changes in the substance of Article 26 of the Model convention have to a large extent solved this problem for later treaties.[63] The question whether subsequent changes can influence an existing treaty, in other words, whether existing treaties must be interpreted dynamically, shall be dealt with in paragraph 3.6.

## 4.5. Conclusion

The desirability of one Model convention to model various fiscal relationships between states implies the desirability of a uniform interpretation of treaties. Article 3, paragraph 2 of the OECD Model convention contains its terms of reference. Also of great importance is the more generally defined Article 31 of the Vienna Convention, which contains a rule of interpretation for all treaties.

Article 31 of the Vienna convention provides as a fundamental rule that treaties must be interpreted in good faith, in accordance with the ordinary meaning of the terms used in the treaty in their context and in light of the object and purpose of the treaty. In this respect, the 'ordinary meaning' also can be found in special laws if necessary or may be substantiated jointly by the states. 'Object and purpose' must be interpreted from the context, which includes the treaty's preamble and annexes, but also its *travaux préparatoires*, as well as documents drawn up by both parties or drawn up by one party and accepted by the other. In the provision

60. Schaumburg (1998), para. 19.36.
61. From the 1990 survey 'Taxpayers' Rights and Obligations' by the OECD Committee of Fiscal Affairs, it became clear that several states had problems with the term 'necessary'.
62. See Feskens/Engelen (1999), 1505.
63. The 2000 version of Art. 26 of the OECD Model convention no longer limits the exchange of information to 'taxes covered by the Convention', but has a much wider scope, i.e., 'taxes of every kind or description'.

elements of both grammatical and teleological interpretation methods can be recognized. Especially the reference to the 'object and purpose' of the treaty is intended to further a joint interpretation. The fact that subsequent agreements or practices between parties concerning the application of the treaty also can be deemed part of the context certainly renders the provision a dynamic element.

For the 'ordinary meaning' of the terms in a tax treaty, article 3, paragraph 2 of the OECD Model convention refers to the meaning these terms have in the domestic laws of the states, at the time of the application of the treaty provision, unless the context otherwise requires.

The question remained as to which element should be leading in the interpretation of treaties: either domestic laws or the context. In the latest concept, more emphasis is put on the joint purpose of the treaty and on the requirement of 'common interpretation'. The indication of domestic laws as a frame of reference triggers the question of which state's domestic law should be leading at the interpretation and which domestic law should be consulted. The Commentary has settled the first dispute by 'stipulating' that the state of residence withdraws if the source state has correctly qualified the income under its domestic tax laws. The answer to the last question is found in an amendment of Article 3, paragraph 2 of the OECD Model convention: the meaning of a term in the *tax* law of a state has priority over other meanings, if any. That does not yet answer the question of whether fictions and fixed sums or anti-abuse provisions in the domestic law can be carried over into treaty situations. Because they are often unclear to the other state, their application in treaty situations should be allowed only if it becomes clear from the context that this was actually intended by the parties.

## 5. THE MEANING OF THE OECD COMMENTARY

In paragraphs 29 and 35 of its Introduction, the OECD Commentary emphasizes its own role in the interpretation of treaties. It dwells on the general acceptation the Commentary enjoys in the application of treaties by a variety of tax administrations, taxpayers, and courts of appeal,[64] as it is deemed 'to reflect the consensus of the OECD Member Countries as to the proper interpretation of existing provisions and their application to specific situations'.[65]

In the literature, the important role of the Commentary is indeed generally acknowledged as 'treasury' for the interpretation by the judicature of the Member States. In the words of Vogel, it already has significance from the '*Grundsatz der Entscheidungsharmonie, die deren Berucksichtigung geböte*'.[66] However, the authors are less unanimous about the answer to the question of what is the binding

64. OECD Commentary, 2000, Introduction, paras 29.1-29.3.
65. *Ibid.*, Introduction, para. 35.
66. (The basic axiom that the courts in the different countries should try to decide in harmony with the international law.) Vogel (2003), Einleitung, Rz. 123 e.v. The author gives a survey of both its advocates and adversaries. An important adversary is Avery Jones (1984a).

force of the Commentary.[67] An '*abgeschwächte Verpflichtung*'[68] for states to follow the Commentary is about the most positive definition of its power. Some authors (including Dutch) consider the connection between the Commentary and any specific tax treaty too lose to consider the Commentary as agreed 'in connection with the conclusion of the treaty', as Article 31, paragraph 2 the Vienna Convention requires. Because the Commentary already exists when a specific tax treaty is entered into, the parties involved, in their opinion would not consider it to be part of the context of a treaty.[69]

This concept seems artificial to me, for it is the explicit will of the OECD states to shape their tax treaties after a common and jointly developed model. Their negotiations on specific tax treaties will therefore take place against the background of the current OECD Model and Commentary. This means that the existing ideas and concepts laid down in the Commentary will be explicitly scrutinized by the newcomers. This will generally lead to the acceptance of these opinions. If not, the newcomer can insert an 'observation' on certain provisions of the Commentary. Therefore, in my view, the OECD Commentary must be considered as part of the context of the tax treaties. So, I think that the OECD Commentary is to be considered as a part of the context of the specific convention between two countries. This view is shared by van Raad, Avery Jones,[70] Lang and Ward.[71] The Commentary can be 'built in' the system of Articles 31 and 32 of the Vienna Convention by inserting it in Article 32 of the Convention, as one of the 'supplementary means of interpretation' that may be consulted to confirm the meaning of treaty terms found elsewhere or to retrieve the 'special meaning' states have attached to the treaty terms (if the latter has not become clear by other means).[72] Except as the reflection of a consensus between states that came about in the course of time, the Commentary may also be seen as the reflection of a treaty practice that has developed in time.[73] Thus the contents of Article 31, paragraph 3 of the Vienna Convention can be considered part of the context of a treaty.[74]

If the Commentary as 'indicator' of the intentions of the contracting parties is part of the context of a tax treaty, this implies that in principle, the Commentary can bind the states in their interpretation of the treaty. This is however only if they have

---

67. Tieskens (1999) gives a usable review of the different positions of authors in the course of history of the Model Convention.
68. Vogel (2003), Einleitung, Rz. 126. Reimer (1999) mentions the year-long German opposition against too strong a role of the Commentary, also in German case law.
69. See also for a survey of international literature Lang (1997) and Vogel (2003), Einleitung, Rz. 124.
70. van Raad (1984), Avery Jones (2002), Lang (1997) and Ward (2006).
71. However, both authors have their doubts about the 'validity' of a provision of the Commentary that was subsequently altered for the interpretation of an 'earlier' treaty.
72. Ault (1994). See also Wattel/Marres (2003), 227.
73. However, cf. Ward (2006), who is of the opinion that the Commentary changes too quickly for that.
74. Heinrich/Moritz (2000) and Pijl (1997), 545.

not included an observation, and if the provision of the treaty is identical to the provision in the Model convention.[75]

The Dutch author Engelen goes farthest in this respect:[76] He does not, as many other authors do, consider the Commentary as 'soft law', but as directly binding on the basis of the good faith that in the Vienna Convention is required of the contracting parties.[77] The definition of good faith in treaty relations includes the international principles of acquiescence and estoppel, both protecting the justified expectations of the contracting parties. In analogy of the 1962 ruling of the International Court of Justice on a border conflict between Thailand and Cambodia, Engelen deems the OECD Commentary, although not binding in itself, binding for the states that did not include observations at the drafting of the Commentary, or made reservations at the conclusion of their bilateral agreement.[78] In his view, OECD Members who have not included such a reservation can be deemed to endorse Article 5, section b of the founding treaty of the OECD, on the basis of which the Commentary should be considered as the expression of the joint viewpoint of those OECD Members.[79] This is all the more so because in 1997 the OECD Council explicitly stated its viewpoint on the interpretation of treaties. It was then recommended that the dynamic interpretation of the Model convention be adopted in the future. In spite of the fact that the Commentary, according to its wording, was not meant to be binding, states that have not made use of this occasion to clarify their position are not allowed to change that position toward their partners in treaty, the author claims. Therefore to those states, the Commentary is directly binding.

From an international law angle, Engelen's vision is rather extreme. However, the merits of this vision lie in the fact that the author assigns a central meaning to the justified expectations of the other party to the treaty. Thus he creates a more morally based concept of law, in which honesty, reliability, and responsibility for the contracting party are paramount,[80] and he implicitly makes it clear that also in horizontal and symmetrical legal relationships such as those of international law, the parties are under the obligation to treat each other 'as equals'.[81]

Ward, however, has a different starting point.[82] According to him, the Articles 31 and 32 of the Vienna Convention were certainly not intended by the ICL as the

---

75. See Wattel/Marres (2003), 227. In their opinion. these are the conditions under which the Dutch High Court takes into account the OECD Commentary as context of a tax treaty. Cf. Vogel (2003), Einleitung, Rz. 123 e.v.
76. Engelen (2004).
77. In his view, the ruling of the Dutch Supreme Court of 2 Sep. 1992, BNB 1992/379, that the Commentary is of great importance for the interpretation of the treaty provision at stake, does not go far enough.
78. Engelen (2006), 105.
79. Also see Tieskens (1999), who sums up seven arguments why text and Commentary of the Model convention must be considered as binding.
80. Engelen (2004), 122.
81. Cf. para. 2.1.4. In my view, this concept is also influenced by the fact that in Dutch administrative law, created expectations of citizens are to be respected, a principle that in Dutch case law regularly has supremacy over strict compliance. See Happé (1996), 109 e.v.
82. Ward (2006), 97 onward.

only frame of interpretation for treaties. In these articles, he finds only a limited significance for the interpretation of tax treaties. In his view, these should be interpreted by reference to Article 3, paragraph 2, of the OECD Model convention. The requirement of good faith, and the principles of acquiescence and estoppel linked to it, he claims to be valid only if the parties actually entered into an *obligation*. However, the view of the joint OECD Member States establishing the Commentary under the supervision of the Committee of Fiscal Affairs is a different one, but the Commentary cannot be seen as a codification of developed customary law either.[83] In the view of the author, the Commentary does form part of the context of the tax treaties, because the intentions of the parties are shown in it. Ward (and other authors, too) in fact limit the term context to the Commentary as it existed *at the time of drafting* of the tax treaty. The question remains as to how to deal with changes in the Commentary that were made after the conclusion of the tax treaty valid between the parties. That question will be dealt with in the next paragraph.

The reservations of some authors with regard to the Commentary is also inspired by its 'undemocratic' nature.[84] It is said to be only 'the writings of government officials', 'the interest of which should not be overrated'.[85] It is also considered paradoxical that a non-binding Commentary takes a viewpoint on its own status, namely its 'non-bindingness'.

It is undeniably true that the drafting of the Commentary easily evades democratic control. The provisions of the Model convention itself are regularly submitted to the parliaments of the states, inasmuch as they are inserted in the separate tax treaties. This is not true for the Commentary, at least not directly. In the Netherlands, the Explanatory Notes to the separate treaties regularly refer to the Model convention and the Commentary. In such an event, a parliament may assume that the OECD Commentary has had a substantial effect on their wordings. Thus parliaments can express their opinion on their contents and application. At that stage, parliaments cannot be said to be of influence on the drafting of the Commentary. Austria has tried to solve this-dispute by the explicit agreement in a number of recent tax treaties that the OECD Commentary will be leading for the interpretation of those treaties.[86]

In 2001 the role of the (changing) OECD Commentary was the subject of a joint conference of the International Fiscal Association and the OECD. There, the conclusion was that the Commentary is definitely of importance, but that its

83. Moreover, in Ward's opinion, protection of expectations created by a state is due only when the other state will suffer damage as a result of the indistinct utterance of its treaty's partner.
84. Also see Becker (1982), who considered the spontaneous and automatic exchange of information on the basis of German tax treaties illegal because these methods were not included in the text of the treaty obligation itself, but only in the OECD Model Commentary. In his view the breach of the domestic tax secret, a condition for the cross-border exchange, can be based on only a genuine treaty obligation, recognizable for all citizens.
85. Juch (1999), 115 e.v.
86. Lang (1997) strongly criticizes this solution. In his view, it is based on neither international law nor the Austrian Constitution.

influence on the interpretation of treaties depended on the measure of change and the underlying cause.[87] Within the OECD, the legal status of the Commentary in international law is now being closely examined.[88]

In Dutch case law, the Commentary plays a role as well. In this respect, Vogel mentions a ruling of the Dutch Supreme Court as early as 1976.[89]

## 5.1. Conclusion

In accordance with Article 5 of the OECD Treaty, the Committee of Fiscal Affairs considers the Commentary to be the reflection of the train of thought of the OECD Member States on the Model convention, which is not binding. Its meaning in the interpretation of treaties is, according to some authors, open to question because it did not come into effect in relation to the conclusion of the separate treaties between parties and therefore, according to the definition of Article 31 of the Vienna Convention, does not form part of the context of such a treaty. This concept seems artificial to me. States concluding a tax treaty after the example of the OECD Model convention by this also accept the Commentary as frame of reference, at least inasmuch as they did not have an 'observation' inserted.

The Commentary can be the source of information on the intentions of the parties. It can be used to achieve a joined interpretation. It can also be considered as one of the supplementary means of interpretation to find the 'special meaning' of a term in a treaty or as the reflection of a developed practice (between OECD Member States) and thus be included in the term 'context' in the sense of the Vienna convention. Engelen, however, holds the view that the Commentary is binding without further ado because of the fact that the existence and the status of it are laid down in Article 5 of the OECD Convention, which also creates the possibility for states to make known their deviating positions by means of 'observations'.

Engelen is of the opinion that the latter is an obligation resulting from the requirement of good faith. Parties are not allowed to suppress their position with respect to the Model convention and the Commentary, because in doing so they

87. Avery Jones (2002; an account of the IFA San Fransisco Conference). He thinks that a subsequent version of the Commentary does indeed influence existing treaties.
88. Vogel (2000a).
89. Cf. Dutch Supreme Court ruling HR 2 Sep. 1992, BNB1992/379. The OECD Commentary on Art. 10, para. 5 of the 1963 Model convention is considered to be of great importance for the interpretation of the Irish-Dutch treaty. Arguments for this ruling were that the article in the treaty was an exact copy of the related article in the Model convention and that from the rest of the treaty, including the Explanatory Note to Parliament, it became clear that the contracting states based themselves on the OECD Model convention as much as possible. HR 9 Sept., BNB 1999/267 not only refers to the Commentary at the time the treaty was concluded, but also to subsequent versions of the Commentary. Another line of thought was picked in Supreme Court Ruling 21 Feb. 2003, BNB 2003/178, V-N 2003/13.9) with regard to the 183-day period of the Dutch-Nigerian treaty (The subsequent change in the Commentary could not influence the treaty because it was obviously deviant from the text of the Model Convention).

could betray the confidence of the other contracting party. In my opinion, the merit of his view is that with the relationship of international law, which is symmetrical by nature, a moral element of reliability and responsibility is introduced, which may further the cooperation between the states.

Ward denies the Commentary's direct binding force because of the fact that the Commentary itself declares to be non-binding. In his view, in that case good faith cannot play a role. However, he does consider the Commentary a part of the context of the separate treaties at the time of their conclusion.

I consider the adjective 'undemocratic' for the Commentary somewhat understandable. The foreseeability and transparency with regard to the positions taken requires efforts by the separate states. However, basically for OECD Member States, the Commentary can be considered as resulting from the OECD Convention the states have bound themselves to in a democratic way and that Article 5 recommends the states to jointly draft and maintain the Commentary.

For a better legal basis in the national legal systems, the tax authorities should explicitly refer to the Commentary in the ratification files. Apart from that, however, they should inform their parliaments regularly on the subjects placed on the agendas of the working parties of the Committee of Fiscal Affairs and the positions they are considering to take with regard to those subjects.

## 6. STATIC OR DYNAMIC INTERPRETATION

The interpretation of international treaties is complicated by the dynamics of tax law, which occurs in two areas. On the one hand, there are the constantly changing tax laws of the various states that, by way of the interpretation rule of the Model convention, can be of influence on the application of tax treaties. On the other hand, the application of treaties is strongly influenced by the train of thought being maintained by the Committee of Fiscal Affairs in the tax 'working parties' of the OECD. This regularly leads to changes in the text of the Model convention itself or more often in the related Commentary, while the separate tax treaties that were modelled after previous model versions of course continue to exist. The information provision, as well, has been extended continually in the various versions of the Model convention.

These developments in international and national tax law take place at a pace that differs from that which determines the drafting and review of the tax treaties. This triggers the question of whether ongoing national and international developments in tax law should be reflected in the interpretation of – sometimes long-existing – treaties. In other words, should those treaties be interpreted dynamically, or should they be interpreted in accordance with the contents of the terms at the time of conclusion: the static interpretation. It is of course the concept of law in general that defines the choice between these methods. The modern concept of law as a living and dynamic concept, where the development of legal values in society is of more importance than the existence of legal rules as such, will result in a dynamic interpretation of treaty terms. The static method of interpretation is more linked to a positivist concept of law, in which its meaning can be found only in the (analysis of the) legal rule itself.

Article 31 of the Vienna Convention does not explicitly advocate a static or a dynamic method of interpretation. In my view, however, it does contain dynamic elements, because subsequent agreements or subsequent practices between states in relation to the application of treaties shall also be taken into account.[90]

## 6.1. Domestic Dynamics and the Interpretation of Treaties: an Area of Conflicts

Of the changes occurring in different areas of tax law, those in the domestic tax laws of the separate states are the most complicating in the application of treaties. As on the basis of Article 3, paragraph 2 of the Model convention, they can be a relevant factor for the interpretation of undefined terms in tax treaties. Changes in those domestic laws will influence the interpretation of these treaties, too. The Committee of Fiscal Affairs has struggled to find the answer to the question of how to reach a balance between guaranteeing of a certain amount of 'firm ground' in the commitment between states on the one hand and doing justice to changing insights on tax levying on the other, as the latter develop both nationally and internationally.

The influence of national changes on the law of tax treaties is complicated. Apart from the question of which element should tip the balance in the interpretation of undefined treaty terms, Article 3, paragraph 2 of the OECD Model convention leads us to conclude, at any rate, that the national meanings of the terms as well as the context are of importance.[91]

Domestic tax laws can, however, be changed, and that is what happens continually. If this takes place in the source state *after* a tax treaty was concluded, for the interpretation of that treaty, two solutions are possible. In the 'static method' of interpretation the domestic law at the time of conclusion of the treaty is used as a guideline, in the 'dynamic method' the interpretation is determined by the meaning it has today.

Seen from the angle of the states, both methods have disadvantages. In the dynamic method the application of the treaty is subject to changes, because changes in domestic laws can alter the interpretation of treaty terms *a postiori*. There is the risk that their treaty partner, in spite of the general adage that '*pacta servanda sunt*',[92] and in spite of the prohibition to do so, will change its domestic law in such a way that the effect of the treaty, which it considers to be negative, is mitigated.[93] It is also possible that legislative changes are realized that simply do

90. Vienna Convention, Art. 31, para. 3.
91. Cf. para. 4.4.2 for the various concepts on the relationship of domestic law and context in the interpretation of treaties.
92. The principle of law that is the basis of Art. 26 of the Vienna Convention.
93. Cf. para. 11 of the OECD Commentary.

not take into account the implications for the application of the already existing treaty. Static interpretation would solve this problem, but the method involves important drawbacks.

Until 1982, the dynamic method of interpretation was the international standard. The law at the moment of the treaty application served as a frame of reference for the interpretation of treaties. After a high-profile case in Canada in 1982 (the so-called Melford case), in which the Canadian High Court ruled that the law valid at the time the treaty was concluded prevailed, an extensive discussion arose within the doctrine. The case was especially thoroughly discussed during the 1985 congress of the International Fiscal Association.[94] A large number of authors defended the concept of dynamic treaty interpretation, based on the argument that tax treaties are always concluded with a view to the future and that states therefore, in taking domestic laws as a frame of reference in the interpretation of treaties (the *lex-fori* clause) already allow for future changes in their domestic laws.[95] It was also considered practically unfeasible to search for the meaning of terms in all sorts of obsolete domestic laws.[96] In 1992, the Committee of Fiscal Affairs also adopted the 'ambulatory approach'. This choice was laid down in the Commentary and argued from the necessity to apply the treaty 'in a convenient and practical way over time', in which 'reference to outdated concepts should be avoided'.[97] In 1995 the dynamic interpretation method was also embedded in the *text* of Article 3, paragraph 2, of the Model convention. For the application of the treaty '*at any time*' undefined terms will have the meaning valid *at that time* 'under the law of that State'.

The Commentary points out that this could trigger the risk that a state 'should make a Convention partially inoperative by amending afterward in its domestic law the scope of terms not defined in the Convention'.[98] This 'treaty override' is at odds with the requirement of good faith between treaty partners.[99] Therefore it is internationally detested. The Committee of Fiscal Affairs claims it possible to mitigate the risk of eroding the treaties through domestic law changes by emphasizing in the Commentary that the context of the treaty, which on the basis of Article 3, paragraph 2, can tone down the role of the national terms in the

94. Cf. the 1985 IFA Bulletin, containing the summary of Seminar b of that congress.
    Cf. also Langbein (1987), 4, etc. The author discusses the Melford-case and the German concept of the relation between domestic and international law.
95. For a survey of the literature, cf. Vogel (2003), Einleitung Rz. 186. Also Vogel (1997). The author also mentions advocates of the static method, like Lang (1997) and Wattel/Marres (2003), 222.
96. The fact that this still happens is shown from Vogel's explanation of a recent ruling of the Austrian *Verwaltungsgerichtshof*, in which the High Court reverted to the 1974 meaning of the term '*unselbständige Arbeit*' for the interpretation of the Arts 14 and 15 of the Swiss-Austrian Treaty.
97. OECD Commentary, Art. 3(2), para. 13.
98. *Ibid.*, Art. 3(2), para. 13.
99. Vogel (2003), Einleitung, Rz. 194-195 and Schaumburg (1998), para. 3.2, 27 and the survey presented there of mainly German literature on treaty override, for which especially the United States was criticized by the professional journals.

interpretation ('unless the context otherwise requires') is especially determined 'by the *intentions* of the Contracting States *when signing the Convention*'.[100]

However justified in itself it may be in the interpretation of treaties to take into account the joint purpose of the treaty; this does not necessarily imply that that purpose should be drawn from the historic moment of 'signing the convention'. This would lead to the reintroduction of a historicizing, static interpretation method. Rejecting 'outdated concepts' on the one hand and returning to the intentions at the time of conclusion of the treaty on the other does not make the viewpoint any clearer. In my view, van Raad justly criticizes this ambiguity.[101]

Although Article 27 of the Vienna Convention does not allow states to invoke a domestic law to avoid fulfilment of a treaty obligation, this in fact could occur. The only sanctions international law contains are the temporary suspension and the definite denunciation of a treaty. The latter can of course work only as a last resort.[102] More constructive solutions would be starting talks to reach a joint solution and applying to the competent court in one of the states.

Depending on the place international law has in the Constitution of a state, the court *can* reverse a law that is in contravention of a (direct) treaty provision. This can take place in so-called monistic systems, in which international law is considered higher ranking than domestic law.[103] In its review for compliance, the court will have to interpret not only domestic law, but also the treaty itself.[104] In doing so, the court, on the basis of Article 3, paragraph 2, will have to form an opinion about what must be understood by the intentions of the parties, which, however, do not necessarily need to be those from the past.[105]

Because of the fact that domestic laws can be tested against international law, in a monistic constitutional system attention ideally will be paid to the implications related to international law when drafting new legislation or changing laws. In states having a so-called dualistic constitutional system, in which international law and domestic law are considered to be two separate, equivalent areas of law, it is not possible to test domestic laws against a treaty. In such a system, international

100. OECD Commentary, Art. 3, para. 12.

101. van Raad (1992). Cf. also van der Bruggen (2003), who is of the opinion that the 'domestic renvoi' in Art. 3, para. 2, OECD Model convention cannot be considered as a '*lex specialis*' with respect to the Vienna Convention. Fundamental notions such as 'good faith' and other principles of international law would thus recede into the background. Art. 3(2) OECD Model is only a method to detect the 'ordinary meaning' of a term in a tax treaty. 'Unless the Context requires' in his opinions basically means 'unless the Vienna Convention requires'.

102. As provided for in Art. 60 of the Vienna Convention.

103. See Kooijmans (2000), 74 e.v.

104. Avery Jones (2001) also dwells on the double loyalty the court has in the interpretation of treaties: toward the citizens of his state and toward the treaty partner. He does not think domestic court proceedings are a suitable way to defend the interests of states.

105. Cf. the ruling of the Dutch Court den Bosch, 6 Sep. 2001, V-N 2001/56.8, concerning the legal fiction about the remuneration of directors/owners of companies that were to be treated as 'wages'. The court ruled that this later 'legal fiction' could not apply against the background of the Belgian-Netherlands Tax treaty concluded in 1970, because at that time parties could not be considered to have had the intention to do so in cross-border situations.

law can become valid only by transformation into domestic law.[106] Subsequently, this domestic law is embedded in the normal ranking order, in which the younger law has priority over the older one and the law governing a specific subject matter has priority over the law governing general matters. If the change of legislation conflicts with the existing treaty, the purpose of the parties at the time of the treaty was concluded may well be found in the parties' early intentions, (as recommended in the Model convention). The younger law, however, will always have priority, unless in that law system, the provisions of the international treaties are always considered to be '*lex specialis*'.[107]

This search for earlier intentions and meanings will have to take place within the framework of the 'mutual agreement procedure' in Article 25, third paragraph of the Model convention. As only an obligation of means is created, in the opinion of most authors it does not give any warranty.[108] Moreover, it seems open to question to what extent the states are bound to the results of a 'mutual agreement'. These are entered into merely on an executive level, without the intervention of the legislature and therefore without democratic control.[109] The OECD Model convention cannot render binding decisions about the way in which the separate states bind themselves to treaty obligations. This depends on the Constitutions of the states involved,[110] in which sometimes a 'mutual agreement' is required between the competent authorities, published in certain official government organs.[111]

Engelen's opinion is a different one. From his concept that the recommendations of the OECD Convention concerning the Model convention and the Commentary are binding inasmuch as the states have not explicitly taken a different position, mutual agreements between them must be considered binding, as they result from Article 25, third paragraph, which was apparently (tacitly) accepted by both parties. In doing so, the obligation to abide by the agreement that was reached between them was born. In recent treaties between the Netherlands and the United States and Belgium, The Netherlands has added to the treaty protocols that mutual agreements between them can be binding.[112]

---

106. See Kooijmans (1996), 83 e.v.
107. In some states having a dualistic system, a change of legislation can override a treaty, but only if the intention to do so is clearly indicated in the drafting. Cf. Langbein (1987), about the Melford case and the situation in Germany.
108. Article 25, para. 3 of the OECD Model convention reads: 'The competent authorities of the Contracting States shall *endeavour* to resolve (...).'
109. Runge (1997) would consider it a step forward if the mutual agreements could overrule the court decisions, at any rate, until there would be a general obligation for the OECD Member States to engage in arbitration procedures, or even better an 'International Tax Court' would be established. This obligation will indeed be inserted in the 2006 proposal on the review of Art. 25 of the Model convention.
110. Cf. Vogel (2003), Rz. 136.
111. Cf. Heinrich/Moritz (2000), for the situation in Austria, and Reimer (1999) for Germany; for the Netherlands cf. Dutch High Court HR 19 Sep. 1999, BNB 2000/16, V-N 1999/469.
112. Protocol 1, item 3 to Art. 28 of the new Belgian-Dutch treaty for the prevention of double taxation. It becomes clear from the joint explanation per article that the Mutual Agreement will have to remain within the context of the treaty and should be published by both countries.

The question of whether these agreements could also be binding for the taxpayers depends on national Constitutions and will if necessary be decided by the court. To increase the democratic content of these mutual agreements, Engelen suggests that the responsible government member be obligated to announce the intention to enter into these agreements to parliament, so that an explicit approval procedure may eventually be requested.[113] However, in practice this is complicated.

## 6.2. Possible Solutions

In drafting paragraph 12 of the Commentary to Article 3 of the Model convention, in my view, the Committee of Fiscal Affairs disregarded the choice states make in their legal systems regarding the ranking order of domestic and international law. As I see it, the Commentary unjustly calls the wording of Article 3, paragraph 2, of the OECD Model a 'satisfactory balance' between efficient (dynamic) treaty application and monitoring the commitment of the states to their arrangements by returning to the *original* intentions).[114] Treaty eroding is an existing risk between treaty partners, but an adequate solution for it cannot be found by way of this somewhat *historicizing* interpretation of the objectives. In monistic states this might work, if applied or confirmed by the court, but especially in those states the risk that treaty eroding laws are drafted is hardly existent. In dualistic systems, where this danger is greater, in my opinion, falling back on the intentions of the parties during the conclusion of the treaty cannot result in a situation in which a younger law must give way to an older one (the existing treaty).

Only if a treaty is interpreted on the basis of its context and if the 'intentions of the Contracting States', are not treated as the individual and historical intentions of the parties,[115] but rather as the object viable purpose of the treaty, the possibility exists to include continuing insights within (inter)national tax law in their interpretation.[116]

States can solve this kind of treaty-override problem by announcing the unilateral termination of the treaty to the other contracting party.[117] Additionally, the ILC of the United Nations is developing the so-called 'Draft Articles' with regard to the liability of states breaching their international obligations. According to some, these may also play a role in holding a state liable that is in breach of its

113. Cf. Engelen (2004), 431 e.v.
114. Otherwise: Vogel (1997), who quotes the term 'a satisfactory balance' in para. 13 of the Commentary with approval.
115. Pijl (1995) calls this 'subjective' intentions.
116. Cf. Dworkin (1985), where he defends the dynamic and 'construing' interpretation in general. In his view, falling back on the original intentions of the legislature is not the best method of finding law. The latter fails to notice that law is an evolving phenomenon and that the original legislature has not been able to foresee future events. Those who apply the law (such as courts) have a duty to construe an intention. However, the construed intention must fit into the legal system (the dimension of fit). Cf. Soeteman & Dworkin (1992).
117. Article 60, third paragraph of the Vienna Convention.

duty to prevent double taxation or imputation.[118] (In this connection I also find possibilities with regard to the duty of a state to secrecy of data obtained in the exchange of information). The international rules on liability and interpretation should be applied by a supranational court of appeal, such as the International Court of Justice, a World Tax Court, or a body as already proposed in the models of the League of Nations. Until now, this idea has been rejected because the states fear their sovereignty to crumble. Maybe an independent panel of experts that could solve questions regarding the interpretation of treaties could bring this problem closer to a solution.

In my view, the most adequate solution is for the Committee of Fiscal Affairs to mitigate the role of domestic laws in the interpretation of treaties[119] and to include more (and more clear) definitions and rules of interpretation in the various treaty provisions.[120] In any case, the insertion of an obligation for the states to submit to arbitration in Article 25 OECD Model convention is a step in the right direction.[121] This could at the same time improve the up to now weak legal position of taxpayers.[122]

### 6.3. International Dynamics and the Interpretation of Treaties

Not only domestic laws are subject tot change. The Model convention and the Commentary itself also change. They are screened every 6 months on a permanent basis by the various working parties of the OECD. From 1963 until the adjustment in 2005, several versions of the Model convention and the Commentary were adopted.[123] Sometimes a change in a treaty provision is indicated only in the Commentary, although this should actually be done in the treaty provision itself, a practice that in my opinion is much to be criticized.[124]

118. van der Bruggen (2001), refers to *Analytical Guide to the Work of the International Law Commission 1949-1997* (New York: United Nations, 1998), 226-256.
119. Vogel/Prokisch (1993), together with the 'national reporters' reach this conclusion at the IFA Conference in their General Report.
120. van Raad (2001); also suggested by Tillinghast (2002).
121. Cf. e.g., Runge (1997) and the German policy to insert an arbitration clause in tax treaties. In the Netherlands the same policy has been applied from the 1990s. Tillinghast (2002), about the efforts of the International Chamber of Commerce and the Business and Industries Advisory Committee of the OECD to get this item on the agenda of the Committee of Fiscal Affairs, which in 2007 proved to be successful. Cf. also Owens (2006), 1057.
122. Taxpayers do not have any warranty in international law that states will start a mutual agreement procedure on request, let alone a warranty with regard to reaching any results.
123. In 2001 the Committee of Fiscal Affairs decided to take a proactive approach by publishing a concept version of the Model convention. Cf. Vogel (2001). This approach may be helpful to bring about conflicting opinions at an early stage and thus prevent interpretation problems at a later stage.
124. van Brunschot (2005) and van Raad in his annotation of the ruling of Dutch Supreme Court HR 1996/108, where he refers to the 'bad habit' of the Committee of Fiscal Affairs to make alterations in the Commentary, and not in the Model convention itself.

Parliaments can express their opinions about changes in the text of the Model provisions during the approval procedure accompanying the ratification of a treaty. Of course, they can refer to the (changed) Commentary, but this is merely an inspection *a posteriori* (Cf. section 5).

As the separate bilateral treaties concluded on the basis of the Model convention 'live' much longer than the Model convention, within the area of international law, various 'circles of velocities' exist. All this gives rise to the question as to what extent the revised text of the Model convention and the Commentary can be deemed applicable in the interpretation of the treaties concluded under an 'old' model.

For those cases, too, the Committee of Fiscal Affairs has propagated dynamic interpretation from the first adjustment of the Model convention and the Commentary in 1977. The existing treaties must be interpreted in the spirit of the new commentaries, even if they should not (yet) contain the 'more precise wordings' of the new Model text.[125]

In 1992, it was decided that the Model convention and the Commentary must be adjusted regularly to do justice to the continuing changes in society as reflected in the discussions within the tax working parties of the OECD. That decision was accompanied by a recommendation of dynamic interpretation of treaties.[126] In accordance with paragraph 35 of the Introduction, the latest Model text, or the latest Commentary can be relevant only for the interpretation of van previous treaty texts if the latter cannot be considered 'different in substance' with regard to the older texts. Then the interpretation should take place by the static method. It should be kept in mind of course that the term 'different in substance' also is subject to interpretation.[127]

Ward differentiates between changes of the OECD Commentary meaning *an extension* of certain existing concepts, and so-called 'gap-filling' changes that render a direct adjustment of the Model convention superfluous.[128] The last category must be taken due note of by the states, as is the case with changes being presented as the recording of an existing practice.[129]

125. OECD Commentary, 1977-2005, General Remarks, para. 30.
126. *Ibid.*, Introduction, para. 33.
127. An important discussion in this respect was whether the 1977 Commentary (which contained the voluntary exchange of information) influenced the types of information exchange in treaties concluded after the 1963 Model: Daniels (1987), 16. Also van Raad/Milders (1988), 58 and forward. They are in favour of the statistic method of interpretation of the 1963 Commentary. However, in Dutch case law the highest court of Administrative Law (Council of State) was mostly in favour of the dynamic method. See ARRvS 30 Nov. 1990, R01.88.3427, Infobulletin 1993/237 en ARRvS, 24 Jul. 1991, V-N 1991/5.
128. Ward (2006).
129. Indeed, the Committee of Fiscal Affairs seems to apply these changes to establish a *desired* practice, rather than to record an existing one. One example in the cross-border exchange of information is the priority 'recorded' in the Commentary in 2005 of the international obligation to secrecy over the national 'freedom of information legislation' (OECD Commentary, Art. 26, para. 12). Cf. Ch. 5, s. 2.2.

In all these cases, the choice of the Committee of Fiscal Affairs for dynamic interpretation has not met with general approval. The opponents militate against it because they consider the changes as a dynamics that is partly created by the Committee itself or because of the 'non-legal status' of the Model convention and the Commentary. The idea is that erosion of treaties can take place not only as a result of legislative changes by the states, but also as a result of the continuous evolution of the Model convention and the Commentary.[130] In my view, this is correct. As a result of the 'ongoing process' of change and adjustment as envisaged by the Committee of Fiscal Affairs, the discrepancy between the separate treaty texts and the Commentary can become too prominent, and this will not further its practicability. The changes in the deliberations on treaty provisions should be included in the Model text itself as much as possible,[131] or else uncertainty will arise for both citizens and states.[132] The extent of commitment of the treaty partners to the Commentary will not always be clear. Because the Commentary itself declares to be not binding and may thus be experienced as a noncommittal explanatory memorandum, states will not always go through the trouble of making reservations.[133]

A dynamic interpretation of a treaty in which the latest developments are leading can also influence the position of the taxpayers. This can be compared to the interpretation of domestic law texts by the court. There too, social developments can have an impact and historical statements of the legislature do not always dogmatically have to be followed.[134] The legal certainty in itself is not yet at stake, provided that the court carefully protects and balances the interests of the citizens.

In the end, it is the court that must decide whether or not a change has a 'substantial' nature and thus whether or not dynamic interpretation is allowed.

---

130. Lang (1997), criticizes the impact that the choice of the Committee of Fiscal Affairs for dynamic interpretation has had. This was caused by the fact that Austria had officially adopted the dynamic interpretation method in 1995, although in his view there was no legal basis for it, neither in the Commentary, which as we know is not binding, nor in (Austrian) case law. Engelen/Pötgens (2000a), reject the dynamic application of the Commentary because of the low juridical status of it. Alterations that were not submitted to democratic debate cannot be considered reflecting the intentions of the states. Cf. also Wattel/Marres (2003). Later versions of the Commentary in their opinion can just be implied in the '*complementary* means of interpretation', mentioned in the Vienna Convention, and under the condition that they do not concern essential elements.
131. Ault (1994), 145.
132. An example from the Commentary concerning the provision on the exchange of information is the 2005 change in which a priority rule is established for the international secrecy provision over the national 'freedom of information' Act. This change should have been included in the text of the treaty (cf. Ch. 5, s. 2.2.1). In my view, this is also true for the change in the secrecy clause from an absolute to a relative wording. Cf. Ch. 5.
133. Cf. Avery Jones (2002; a survey of the San Fransisco IFA Conference), in which the conclusion was drawn that a later version of the Commentary will influence existing treaties, but that this depends on the extent of the change and its cause. Engelen, however, takes the stand that modifications in the Commentary are binding when no reservation has been made.
134. van Soest (1961).

Wattel proposes to consider a post-treaty change of the OECD Commentary a country (in this case the Netherlands) has agreed to as a policy stand of the government organ, which the court can take into account to reach a decision, although it is not decisive (the so-called resolution doctrine).[135]

Engelen takes a different stand here too. From his concept on the binding nature of the Commentary he claims that dynamic interpretation is basically mandatory.[136] However that may be, a discussion on his ideas will at any rate increase awareness of the tax authorities of the states about the importance of their attitude in the tax working parties of the OECD Committee of Fiscal Affairs and of the consequences a passive attitude could possibly have there. I shall return to this subject later in this study with regard to the cross-border exchange of information.

## 6.4. Evaluation of Dynamic Interpretation

Not extending the effect of the latest insights from the international discussion would mean that new texts in the Model convention and the Commentary would apply only as a guideline for future treaties and that new developments could break through only by means of a review of an already existing agreement. In view of the politically sensitive and labour-intensive nature of treaty negotiations, it does not seem likely that the states intended this. A certain amount of flexibility with regard to the changing circumstances should be built into the application of the treaties. Even Wisselink's proposal of a *published* exchange of documents on the interpretation of a treaty when changes have occurred can already bring about the necessity of labour-intensive international negotiations.[137] Of course this '*hinein-interpretieren*' must be limited to clarifications in the texts and should not concern fundamental changes. However, also under this condition, the dynamic interpretation of treaties has consequences for the legal certainty of the citizen, especially with regard to the foreseeability of standards.

In view of the fact that legal certainty may be jeopardized by this ongoing further development of the Model convention and the Commentary, I am of the opinion that the programme of the Committee of Fiscal Affairs must be scrutinized at this point.

In my view, these deliberations would benefit from more reflection, to exceed the sometimes unilateral attention for political hot issues with respect to enforcement aspects. The Committee of Fiscal Affairs would have to show more activity in

135. The so-called 'resolution model'. Cf. his conclusion at BNB 2003/178. See also Burgers c.s. (2005), 59-60. Different: Engelen.

136. Apart from the recommendation of para. 33 in the 1992-version of the Model convention he also refers to the 1997 Recommendation of the OECD Council to follow the change of the Commentary. If states have not opposed against it, the author claims they are obligated to use dynamic interpretation. See also the review on Engelen's dissertation in WFR 2005/6644 by Burgers.

137. Wisselink (1996), 75. The OECD Commentary, Introduction, para. 35, recommends that states initiate an exchange of documents, but does not recommend on publishing these.

obtaining expertise in the field of international law during the preparatory phase of viewpoints. The efforts made by the Committee of Fiscal Affairs during the change of the century to partly lift the veil of secrecy around internal decision making within the OECD, were a good starting point, as well as the publication of concept versions of the Model convention since 1992 (also on the Internet).[138] Furthermore, says Vogel, expert members of the international corporate sector are asked for their advice and commentary.[139] The consultation process however is not always totally transparent for the members of the working parties of the Committee of Fiscal Affairs. More direct contact and discussion with the members of the so-called Technical Advisory Groups could improve the quality of the decision making. This would probably lead to more reservations in the drafting of the texts of the Model convention and the Commentary, but would further clarity between the states and therefore also between the latter and their citizens.

In addition to this furtherance of the quality of the deliberations its accessibility should be increased. Vogel rightly points out the '*defizitäre Veröffentlichtspraxis*' of the OECD, which does not even have an official organ to publish its decisions.[140] Of course, the Internet can offer new possibilities here.

In addition to that, the separate states should, for the sake of their citizens, reflect on ways to present important proposals of change for the Model convention to their parliaments as early as the opinion formulating process, for example, within the framework of an integrated discussion of the tax-treaty policy. Engelen's proposal to submit intended mutual agreements to parliament can certainly further the democratic quality of treaty application. A substantive parliamentary discussion could lead to a more transparent and balanced point of view on important matters concerning international law that bring about obligations for the citizens.

All of this is also of importance for the cross-border exchange of information. To citizens, an extension of the obligation to exchange information in the Model convention or the Commentary that is reflected in the application of an 'old' treaty can lead to extended powers of the tax authorities to claim information and to an increase of their informational risks. Whether such a change should have an impact depends in this case, too, on whether it concerns a clarification or a substantive change. I shall return to this topic in the following chapters when necessary. The undeniable importance of a flexible and effective application of treaties, in which new insights and developments are reflected, can thus also lead to an increase of the original burden of the citizen. In my view, the latter should at any rate be compensated within the legal relationship of the exchanging state and its citizens by careful balancing their interests. Why and how this will take place will be described in the following chapters.

As will become clear hereafter, the obligation to provide information in the Model convention and the Commentary has been extended since the original

138. Juch (1999), 115 e.v.
139. Vogel (2001).
140. Vogel (2003), Einleitung, Rz. 128.

version of the Model convention. The darker purpose of it was the fight against fraud and tax avoidance. That goal will be harder to reach in a static interpretation. In my view, if it concerns an extension of the states' obligation of means or the methods of information exchange, both of which can be considered as clarifications, the provision must be interpreted dynamically.

However, in case the partners to a treaty have deviated from the currently valid Model text, the information provision should be applied strictly.[141] In those cases, it must be assumed that states had the explicit intention to give their cooperation a more limited scope than is usual at that time.

## 6.5. Conclusion

Within the law of tax treaties, both exogenous and endogenous dynamics exist.

The first type of dynamics arose because the domestic laws of the states, which partly determine the contents of treaty terms, change more rapidly than the treaties themselves. This brings about the question of whether today the terms of the treaty must be explained on the basis of the law as it was worded at the time the treaty was concluded (the static method) or on the basis of the meaning of the present wording of the law (the dynamic method). The first method offers legal certainty for citizens and treaty partners, but often causes problems in the practical implementation of the treaty. The second method has a drawback in the sense that it can considerably change the contents of the treaty and can even undermine its goals. The Committee of Fiscal Affairs has eventually opted for the interpretation of terms on the basis of the law as it was worded at the time of application of the treaty (dynamic interpretation), inasmuch as its context does not require otherwise. In looking for that context, the starting point is the intentions of the parties 'when signing de convention', which introduces a static element. In my view, a better solution would be to mitigate the role of domestic laws as a criterion for the interpretation (which implies that more terms in the treaty itself will have to be defined) and not to understand the term 'intentions' as 'historical' intentions, but as the objectiviable purpose of the treaty. If administrative consultations do not lead to a solution, an arbitration committee or an international court of justice should be able to make a decision.

The endogenous dynamics is brought about by the Committee of Fiscal Affairs itself, aiming at an ongoing development and adjustment of the Model convention. According to the Committee of Fiscal Affairs, in this connection existing treaties also should be interpreted in the sense of the current Commentary. In my view, this is acceptable. Without dynamic interpretation, treaty application would not be feasible in changing times. In any case, care must be taken that changes and

141. Daniels (1987), 20. Cf. Docclo (1999), 318, about the Belgian practice of concluding treaties containing a provision on the exchange of information, which is more limited than the OECD Model.

supplements do not deviate too much from the original Model texts, and that real changes are inserted in the text of the Model convention itself.

## 7. SUMMARY AND CONCLUSIONS

1. The development of cross-border exchange of information is directly related to that of the treaties for the prevention of double taxation. In 1963, the OECD Committee of Fiscal Affairs established a Model convention for the prevention of double taxation, in which standard measures are specified with regard to the allocation of powers of taxation between the states. In Article 26, the duty to exchange information is discussed. The OECD Model convention is to be considered as a set of recommendations for the states for the design and application of their tax treaties. It is accompanied by an official Commentary.

2. In 1969, the international law of treaties was codified in the Vienna Convention. This also contained an instruction for interpretation. The treaties must be interpreted in good faith and in accordance with the ordinary meaning of the terms of the treaty in their context and within the light of the object and purpose of the treaty. The text of the treaty must be the basis for its interpretation. The object and purpose of the treaty are to be found in the context. Parts of this context are the documents drawn up in connection with the drafting of a treaty and as such are recognized by both contracting parties, as well as subsequent agreements and practices. The interpretation can be confirmed by supplemental means of interpretation, such as preparatory documents.

3. It is laid down in Article 3, paragraph 2 of the OECD Model convention that for *tax treaties*, the treaty terms that are undefined must be interpreted in accordance with the meaning the term has in the state applying the treaty, unless the context requires otherwise. In the literature there is a difference of opinion on the question of whether the context of a separate treaty also includes the official Commentary, because this was not drawn up in connection with this separate treaty. Moreover, the critics point out that the Commentary is written by officials, without ratification in Parliament, and therefore cannot be binding. In my view, other international authors rightly endorse the definition in the Commentary itself concerning its role in international case law. New OECD Member States, or non-members of the OECD who wish to draft their tax treaty on the basis of the OECD framework, may not have been part of the preceding deliberations, but, as their position in treaty negotiations clearly shows, are well aware of them. If they do not agree with a specific element of the Model convention or the Commentary, they must make this clear in their separate treaties. During the deliberations in the Working Parties, OECD states and aspiring members also have the possibility to insert a 'reservation' in the Model Convention or an 'observation' on the Commentary, to make their position clear to the other states.

4. Because of the massive character of the application of tax treaties, taking place between all kinds of countries, it is not feasible to define conclusively all the terms of those treaties. The reference in Article 3, paragraph 2 of the Model

convention to the national meanings of the terms in the state that applies it, however, has given rise to a permanent discussion. In the end, the Committee of Fiscal Affairs has given precedence to the qualification of income of the source state for the purpose of the interpretation of a treaty. Some authors, however, take a different view.

5. National meanings can change, and therefore the meaning of a treaty provision can be subject to erosion. Falling back on the meaning it had under 'old' domestic laws is often not feasible. Moreover, current circumstances and insights are insufficiently taken into consideration. In its effort to find a balance between the risk for treaty erosion on the one hand and a too-rigid and therefore impractical concept of the law of treaties on the other hand, the Committee of Fiscal Affairs has chosen a somewhat dualistic approach. In the first place, *current* national meanings determine the interpretation, but when taking the context into consideration, the intentions of the parties 'when signing the Convention' must be taken into account. Thus a historical aspect is reintroduced, ignoring the fact that the Constitutions of some states do not contain a clause stating that domestic laws that are contradictory to international law may be rendered inoperative by a court of law. In those states, international and domestic law are of equal ranking and in accordance with general principles laws covering specific subjects override general laws, and current laws override previous ones. In this situation, finding a conjunction with a historizing approach of the context is difficult.

6. It would be better to base the interpretation of treaty terms on the intentions of the parties as such, without the historical overtones. The role of the national meanings in interpretation should also be mitigated. Furthermore, it would help if interpretation issues could (or should) be submitted to a court of arbitration that can render binding decisions. The legal position of the taxpayer should also be improved with respect to the current mutual agreement procedure. The latter does not entitle taxpayers to results, and, moreover, it is far from certain whether an agreement made by officials and not discussed in Parliament will always be binding to the states.

7. Furthermore, in the ongoing monitoring process of the OECD tax working parties, the Model convention and the Commentary are regularly adjusted in accordance with the economic and tax law developments. These dynamics also lead to a different cycle of existence of the Model texts and the Commentary than that of the tax treaties. This friction leads to the question of whether these dynamics must be reflected in the interpretation of already existing treaties.

8. The Committee of Fiscal Affairs is of the opinion that existing treaties must be interpreted in accordance with the current versions of the Model and the Commentary, except in case the current version deviates too much from the original meaning and can no longer be construed as a *clarification* of the meaning of the Model convention, but has become a *modification.* In this respect, the international community must guard against substantive modifications being presented as a 'mere' review of the Commentary, because they wrongfully lack any democratic substantiation. The question remains, of course, what a substantive modification actually is.

9. Based on the concept that the law of treaties, too, is a dynamic phenomenon, and that its purpose is the ongoing realization of legal values embedded in international society, in my view the dynamic interpretation of treaties cannot be seen as an unlawful infringement of the position of the citizens of the states. However, in their interpretation of treaties, states do have a duty to take into account the interests of their citizens, including legal certainty.

Chapter 4

# Aspects of International Law and the Obligation Concerning the Exchange of Information

## 1. INTRODUCTION

In the first part of this study, I defined from a general legal philosophy point of view the supplying of fiscal information to other states as a government action concerning the taxpayer from whom it has to collect the information. I perceived this government acting as embedded in a legal relationship that should be subject to the rule of law principles of legality and equality. That this government action occurs within a contractual relation with treaty partners, consisting of mutual obligations, makes both the public law and the international law action more complicated.

To answer the main question of this book about the relationship between international legal duties of the states toward their treaty partners and the legal duties toward their citizens, it is essential to examine this international law framework first. The state's public law duty implies that in the asymmetrical legal relationship with the taxpayer, it is obliged to consider the taxpayers' interests carefully. The state is the strongest party after all.[1] Only after a thorough analysis of the international exchange law will it become clear whether the international law aligns with the nature of this public law relationship. Can the international law relationship be defined solely in 'horizontal' terms such as sovereignty and reciprocity, or have ethical norms such as respect and solicitude of the weaker parties been developed in international law also?

1. Gribnau/Meussen (2002).

In this chapter, the first of three, I shall try to examine the 'compatibility' of both legal systems by considering the fiscal treaty law from this general 'ethical' perspective, and I shall examine the international exchange law itself, as it has developed in the different regulations in that field. In this chapter the objectives and the substantive scope of the exchange obligation will be explored, in Chapter 5 the conditions for the exchange of information, and in Chapter 6 the restrictions on the obligations. The aim is to understand which interests the information-exchanging state defends and considers as a party to the contract. In a subsequent chapter the extent to which the state can also be a protector of its citizens' interests will then be explored.

The international law framework of the international exchange of information already covers many treaty relationships, embedded in different legal sources of international exchange of information law.

In global terms, the bilateral tax treaties, modelled on the example of the Organization for Economic Cooperation and Development (OECD) Model convention on double taxation (OECD Model Convention) form the most commonly occurring legal framework within which information exchange can take place. A general outline of the problems encountered with the implementation of this treaty law was presented in the previous chapter. In addition, in 1988, in Strasbourg, the OECD and the Council of Europe jointly concluded for the Member States of both communities a specific Multilateral Treaty for Mutual Administrative Assistance (Strasbourg Convention). It owes its name to the fact that it covers more than just the exchange of information; there are other measures that states are required to take on behalf of the taxation of other states.[2] In 2002, the OECD, in the context of the fight against 'harmful tax competition', was the initiator of the establishment of a separate Agreement on Exchange of Information on Tax Matters for non-OECD states that had confirmed their 'commitment' to the OECD (OECD Agreement).[3]

The European Economic Community[4] also created several separate legal instruments for the mutual administrative assistance between the Member States. In 1977, Council Directive 77/799/EC (hereinafter Directive 77/799) was published, which established an exchange obligation between the Member States in the area of direct and later also indirect taxes.[5] In 1992, when the physical customs

2. Examples include assistance with collection of tax arrears and the serving of documents.
3. Agreement on Exchange of Information on Tax Matters, Paris 2002, <www.oecd.org>. Established in collaboration between OECD states with 'committed jurisdictions': Aruba, Bermuda, Bahrain, Cayman Islands, Cyprus, Isle of Man, Mauritius, the Netherlands, Antilles, the Seychelles, and San Marino. See also Barnard (2002). See Easson (2004) and Oberson (2003).
4. Since 1993 termed the European Union.
5. Directive 77/799/EEU of the Council, dated 19 Dec. 1977, concerning the mutual assistance of the competent authorities of the Member States in the areas of direct and indirect taxes, revised most recently by the Directive of 7 Oct. 2003, 2003/93/EU, concerning the exclusion of indirect taxes from the obligation to provide mutual assistance and the extension of the obligations to cover levying insurance premiums, and the Directive of 21 Apr. 2004, 2004/56/EU, concerning the improvement and modernization of the procedures, particularly concerning simultaneous auditing, the confidentiality clause, and the obligation to assist with the notification of fiscal deeds and decisions from other states.

borders in the European Community disappeared, the assistance directive was supplemented by Council Regulation (European Union) 218/92, concerning the automatic exchange of value added tax (VAT) data on intra-community transactions.[6] This was in turn recently replaced by Council Regulation 1798/2003 (hereafter referred to as 'Regulation 1798/2003 on VAT'). Finally, the European Savings Directive was established, which aims to stimulate flows of information, but refers to Directive 77/799 for the exchange law itself.[7]

Although they all have individual accents because of their different origins, the different exchange of information rules are strongly influenced by each other and thus highly comparable in a number of aspects. To prevent unnecessary repetition, I shall discuss them according to theme, where the differences will be highlighted while searching for similarities. I shall always first discuss the information provision from the Model convention, because, especially in the first period of its development, it greatly influenced the Strasbourg Convention and Directive 77/799/EEC. Council Regulation 1798/2003 will always then be considered next. Finally, if appropriate,[8] the Model Agreement on the Exchange of Information in Tax Matters will be discussed.

## 2. ETHICAL NORMS IN INTERNATIONAL LAW

The question posed previously concerning the existence of a concept of 'duty of care' for weaker parties in international law can be more or less answered affirmatively in my opinion. As in the modern concept of the law in general, since the 1960s an adjustment has become evident in international law also toward a more ethical concept of the law. Treaty law is no longer considered an organizing of the intercourse between sovereign states in this interpretation, but is developing into a law of cooperation, with a focus on achieving mutual objectives.[9] Thus it continues to develop into a tool to establish a global legal order based on justice and determined by the universal values of mankind.[10] This 'socialization' of international law is manifested most meaningfully in the creation of the specific 'human rights treaties', such as the Charter of the United Nations and the International Covenant on Civil and Political Rights (ICCPR).[11] Legal values concerning the freedom and equality of individuals, and the associated norms for government actions toward

6. Council Regulation (EU) 218/1992, dated 27 Jan. 1992, PB L 24/1.
7. Directive 2003/48/EU of the Council dated 3 Jun. 2003 concerning taxation on income from savings in the form of payment of interest, PbEU L 157.
8. The Model Agreement will not be considered under all of the themes. It concerns only exchange upon request.
9. Kooijmans (2000), 3.
10. See Hirsch Ballin (2000), with literature references. Also Bentley (1998), 1, see the 'human rights viewpoint' as the starting point for the development of 'taxpayers' rights' in national laws and in treaties.
11. International Covenant on Civil and Political Rights, New York, 19 Dec. 1966, Trb. 1969, 100.

their citizens, are thus raised in that case to a communal guideline for states.[12] From the second half of the last century, such a system of values has arisen for the mutual evaluation of the national law of states. In this way international law has contributed to the development of the national state as a constitutional state.[13]

This development has also occurred in Community law. It is striking that general law principles occupy such an essential position in the legal order of a primarily economically defined collaboration like the European Community. This can be seen, for example, in Article 6 of the EU treaty, which forbids discrimination of citizens based on nationality, and in the task given to the Court of Justice (in Article 220 of the Treaty of Europe) to respect 'the law' when applying and explaining the Treaty. This open legal concept requires the Court to take account of other legislation than that incorporated in the Treaty.[14] The Court has fulfilled this task in several decisions in which the scope for political policy-making of all Community institutes is defined by the treaties forming the foundation of the Community, with the aim of guaranteeing the fundamental human rights.[15] When choosing which basic rights should be protected, the Court bases its decisions on the EU treaty, on the international human rights treaties created by the Community itself, especially the European Convention for the Protection of Human Rights (ECHR),[16] and the European Social Charter,[17] as well as on the constitutional institutions of the Member States. Under the basic rights recognized by the Court are the non-discrimination principle; protection of property; right to privacy; freedom of religion, of association, and of speech; right to equal pay for men and women; and right to a fair trial.[18] The position of the fundamental rights in the Community has been confirmed by the official Declaration of the Fundamental Rights and Freedoms in the European Parliament Resolution of 12 April 1989. This explicitly expressed that the values and norms of the Universal Declaration of Human Rights and of the European Convention on Human Rights deserved protection by Community legislation.[19]

This, however, does not mean that equal attention is paid to the legal position of the citizen in *all* areas of Community law, or even *sufficient* attention. The continuous changes in society force the Member States to modify the law

12. One example of this is the 'list of requirements' that the European Union presents to candidate states seeking potential membership in the Union, which primarily concerns the way in which human rights are respected.
13. For the influence of especially the ICCPR law on the formation of the substantive principle of equality in tax law, see Happé (1990, 1996), 99. See also Geppaart (1994), in which he distinguishes between the positive effect of that treaty (as source of inspiration when designing laws) and the negative effect: the subsequent revision of legal rules based on Court decisions.
14. See Barents/Brinkhorst (1996), 48 ff.
15. ECJ C29/69 (Stauder). See Jans (1999), 147, see also Lenaerts (1991).
16. Treaty of 4 Nov. 1950.
17. Because of the lack of a Bill of Rights in Community law, the Court uses 'general legal principles' in this matter. See Jans (1999), 149.
18. For examples of decisions, see Barents/Brinkhorst (1996), 71 ff.
19. Lenaerts (1991).

continuously in this respect. This task sometimes seems difficult to fulfil, as we shall see in Chapter 7.

## 2.1. Tax Treaty Law

Around the world a large number of tax treaties are modelled on the OECD Model convention, the large majority of which also contain an exchange of information provision; thus it is primarily important to examine the extent to which the concepts of solicitude and respect for weaker parties are expressed in this Tax treaty law as well.

In this field of law the development of an ethical-normative interpretation of the law is less well manifested than in the general treaty law.[20] But it has certainly had an influence. Vogel described the international discussion conducted in the 1960s about which principle should be decisive when assigning the taxation rights of states over the cross-border activities of their subjects. Should the taxation right be based on the nationality or the place of residence of a person, so that the country of residence in principle levies tax on all income generated (the universality principle), or on the economic link between the income and the state in which it is generated (the territoriality principle)?[21] In this strongly economically oriented discussion, the Latin-American fiscal science favoured the territoriality principle, which should lead to more justice between the states.[22] Musgrave agreed with this. He introduced the term 'equity' as a keyword in his study of how to organize the government finances to lead to a 'just or equitable distribution' of the national welfare.[23] Equity is a moral term, ultimately referring to the acceptance of the existence of an inalienable right of individuals to *'equal concern and respect'*, as Dworkin formulates it.[24] It is not so much a term set in stone, but rather a moral ordering principle, a guideline that can be followed through all the 'layers' of that law, from the most abstract legal principle to the most concrete legal rule, and that must be 'recognizable' through a process of 'constructive interpretation' in practice. This leads to cohesion of the law: Dworkin's 'integrity of law'.[25]

Richard and Peggy Musgrave applied the term 'inter nation-equity' to the question of which criteria to use between states to harmonize imbalances in their 'national gain' caused by the cross-border activities of their citizens.[26]

20. In any case Schaumburg is not convinced of this. Schaumburg (1998), 1-3. He reports the discussion conducted in the (German) literature about the question of what international tax law is and which norms support it. He feels it involves a collection of rules concerned with cross-border cases, but with no underlying general system of norms concerning the relationships between the states.
21. Vogel (2003), Introduction, Rz. 12.
22. *Ibid.*
23. Vogel (1988) calls his contribution to the Symposium Taxation and Operations Abroad, 1960: Criteria for Foreign Tax Credit. See also Musgrave/Musgrave (1989), 82 ff.
24. Dworkin (1985), 181. See also Soeteman/Cliteur/Loth (1992). See also Vogel (1988), 393.
25. See Dworkin (1985), 52, 176 and 225.
26. Musgrave/Musgrave (1972), 63.

To promote fair wealth distribution, they developed a model of variable tariffs for tax withheld at source for treaty relationships between poor, capital-importing states on the one hand and rich, capital-exporting states on the other. The tariff system it contains was related to the difference in wealth between the states, and it was arranged to reduce these differences.[27]

This more ethical approach to international tax law is not yet generally accepted in tax treaties, at least with reference to the distribution of taxation rights between the states, as the continuing discussion proves.[28] The term is also part of the discussion concerning the 'harmful tax competition', in which the international community struggles with the question of to what extent states can be held *responsible* for the economic consequences they inflict on other states through the creation and maintenance of competing tax legislation.[29]

To answer the question of whether this approach did develop into the international norm concerning the obligation of states to treat their citizens 'as equals', we must examine more closely the OECD Model convention (as biotope in which the exchange law came to maturity).

Van der Bruggen distinguishes the following fiscal treaty obligations in the OECD Model convention:

- the obligation to prevent double taxation according to the methods in Article 19,[30] or Article 23A; or 23B, and to withdraw (as source state) in reference to the taxation rights on dividends (Article 10, Model convention), interest (Article 11, Model convention), and royalties (Article 12, Model convention);
- the obligation to carry out a 'mutual agreement' procedure with their treaty partner at a citizen's request (Article 25);
- the obligation to treat citizens of other states on a comparable fiscal footing as its own residents (Article 24);[31]
- the obligation to exchange information (Article 26).[32]

The first two obligations concern a certain parallelism between the interests of the states and those of the taxpayers and thus an implicit interest in their position.[33] It is

27. Thus, according to Vogel the allocation of taxation rights to the source state would do more to fulfil the requirement of 'inter-nation equity' than a worldwide taxation imposed by a state on the basis of the territoriality principle; Vogel (1988).
28. See e.g., Kemmeren (2001).
29. See the OECD report Towards a Level Playing Field, from the OECD Global Forum, a comparative study about the collection and exchange of information in eighty countries. The aim given is the development of higher standards between states 'in a manner that is fair, equitable and permits fair competition between all countries, large and small'. See also Hay (2006).
30. Article 19 contains a special regulation to prevent double taxation of civil servants.
31. Bentley (1998), 13, calls this stipulation the sole example of more attention being paid to the rights of taxpayers that he can find in the OECD tax treaties.
32. van der Bruggen (2001), 124.
33. Also the memorandum 'International fiscal (treaty) law', Parliamentary paper II 1997/1998, 25 087, no. 4, 31 states the interests of the business community when concluding a treaty, even if only for the protection offered by the anti-discrimination stipulation.

certainly in the taxpayers' interest that their state in certain cases waives its taxation rights over cross-border income, and it is not unusual for (the political parties of) enterprising citizens to raise the possibility of a tax treaty with their states.[34] The *obligation* for states to start mutual consultations, upon a taxpayer's request,[35] is of course also in the taxpayer's interest. In the case of conflicts about application of the treaty, access to a judge is guaranteed for taxpayers in national states (assuming that the OECD states are constitutional states), but that is not a solution for differences of opinion *between* the states. After all, a national law can support an obligation for a state to plead the taxpayer's case with the treaty partner, but cannot arrange that the treaty partner is prepared to enter into that discussion. The obligation to do so can be established only in a treaty. This was acknowledged in Article 25, first paragraph, Model convention. With this provision, the citizen can actively request that attention be paid to his/her interests in his/her country of residence or in the country of citizenship.[36] This shows, as does the fact that states must initiate a mutual agreement procedure in situations in which the ban on discrimination is being violated,[37] that Article 25 was also written for the protection of citizens, not just for conflict management between states.[38]

These provisions in Article 25, and indeed the anti-discrimination provision itself, produce at least some 'visibility' for the taxpayers' interests. But let us not exaggerate its effect. In the literature the imperfections of Article 25 have been a focus of attention. It leaves open the possibility for states to keep certain national legal issues outside the procedures, which does happen repeatedly.[39] It does not give the citizen a right to a procedure; whether one is instituted is left to the discretion of his/her state.[40] The interpretation of the competence differs per

---

34. McLure (2001) names the benefits that states acquire with the restriction of their fiscal sovereignty: security for investors, guarantee of equal treatment for their citizens, being able to obtain fiscal information, of which the first two certainly are also important for taxpayers.
35. If the request for the judgment of one's own state is reasonable. See OECD Model convention, Art. 25, first and second paragraph, in connection with OECD Commentary, 1977-2005, Art. 25, para. 2. It mentions the problems of the taxpayers, which 'the competent authorities *shall* endeavour to solve'. However, there is no obligation to achieve a *result*. (By the way, the Committee on Fiscal Affairs has since presented a proposal to include the obligation that the states must subject an unsolved issue to arbitration at the request of a taxpayer. See Owens (2006), 1057).
36. In addition, the stipulation serves to solve by discussion the problems that the states experience when explaining or implementing the treaty. However, they are not *obliged,* but *invited* to do so, OECD Commentary, 1977-2003, Art. 25, para. 3.
37. OECD Model Convention, Art. 25, para. 1 refers to Art. 24. OECD Commentary, 1977-2005, Art. 25, paras 2 and 6. It obliges states to enter into a mutual dialogue when taxpayers in their opinion are not treated in agreement with the convention.
38. In the same sense van der Bruggen (2001), 13.
39. Owens (2006), 1057, reported on the discussion in the Committee on Fiscal Affairs about improvement of the mutual agreement procedure. See also the report 'Improving the Process for Resolving International Tax Disputes', <www.oecd.org/ctp>.
40. See also Bricker (1998), Velthuizen (2002), 435 and Bakker (2003).

state.[41] Also according to the treaty the citizen has no right to a result: the states must only *try* to find a solution.[42] And if there *is* a solution, the extent to which the state is bound to it depends on the national law.[43] Moreover, the citizen cannot exert a personal input regarding this provision. The procedure is conducted between states. The requirements that the treaty puts on this relationship (like the necessity to 'offset' the potential effect of a certain case against other agreements) can supersede the taxpayers' interests. Thus these provisions of the OECD Model convention (except for the anti-discrimination provision) do not lead to a *clear* norm for the protection of the taxpayers' position.

That aspect is rather surprising, because although these treaty obligations primarily aim to create a bond between states, they work on two levels, like all provisions of a tax treaty: between two states *and* between states and their citizens.[44]

What is the situation like for the obligation to exchange information in Article 26, Model convention?

This obligation has its own place in the entirety of treaty obligations. It derives from the tension between the increase of cross-border income in many states and the principle of formal territoriality in international law. The latter forbids states from conducting tax inspections in another state without the latter's permission. So, for the proper implementation of the treaty provisions and of their national laws, they are dependent to a great extent on each other's willingness to provide information.[45] The possibility of obtaining foreign information is considered one of the 'benefits' for which states conclude tax treaties,[46] although the positive effect is certainly not the same for all states.[47] Although the exchange of

---

41. Calderon (2001) also feels that as a result of the treaty, states have a legal obligation to start a mutual agreement procedure if a taxpayer requests one. A judge must be able to enforce this. He named a few states (e.g., Spain) in which the regulation is found in the national law. The Netherlands has not yet adopted an obligation to start a mutual agreement procedure. See also HR 10 Dec. 2004, 38 317, BNB 195/05.
42. See Owens (2006) for the Committee on Fiscal Affairs proposals to incorporate in a new article paragraph the obligation to take unsolved cases to an arbitration committee, if the taxpayer requests this.
43. See the Dutch Supreme Court (HR) ruling of 19 Sep. 1999, BNB 2000/16. The court denied the legal force of the agreement because it had not been properly published, with the possible context 'lack of democratic approval' of mutual agreements. Therefore they can be binding on taxpayers only when published correctly. See van Brunschot (2005) and Ellis (2005), 11. See also Engelen (2004), 425 ff. and Engelen/Pötgens (2000), 53 ff.
44. See Avery-Jones (2001), who likewise points out (in the context of the interpretation of treaties) that a tax treaty acts on two levels.
45. See Vogel (2003), Introduction, Rz. 16, with further (mainly German) literature references, and Schaumberg (1998), para. 19.26. See also Schaumburg/Schlossmacher (2000), 522; J. Malherbe 1991, General Report Barcelona Conference on Protection of Confidential Information in Tax Matters (hereafter Barcelona report), 48.
46. Along with security for their investors, and fiscal equality for their subjects in the other state, McLure (2001), 330.
47. For the various political-economic arguments states can use to exercise or avoid exchange of fiscal information, see Keen/Ligthart (2006), 81-110. Also further economic literature listed there.

information may not 'serve only the national interests of the treaty states', as Vogel states,[48] it does *principally* serve the interests of the states.[49] This becomes stronger in proportion to the extent that the exchange of information is used as an instrument to counteract tax evasion.[50] It is this function in particular that is being emphasized since the revision of the information provision in 1977, as we shall see.[51]

That the exchange of information is definitely considered the exclusive concern of states by the Committee on Fiscal Affairs of the OECD, is apparent from the fact that proper observance of the information provision obligation is not included in either Article 25, Model convention or the Commentary as a possible reason for taxpayers to request a mutual agreement procedure.[52]

What is said above about the exclusive concern of the states, expressed in the OECD law on the subject, is less true for the Community rules on exchange of information. The European Court of Justice repeatedly confirmed that the Directive 77/799 is mainly adopted to combat tax evasion and tax avoidance,[53] one of the 'important general interests', which under circumstances could justify a violation of the 'freedoms' of the European Convention.[54] In a series of judgments

---

48. Vogel (2003), Art. 26, Rz. 4, 1983. Schaumburg (1998), para. 19.46 points out that the provision of information is important not only for the receiving treaty partner, but also for the providing state, given the principle of reciprocity.
49. It is possible to imagine cases where the result of the exchange of information could be favourable for the taxpayer. Also, the existence of the possibility to exchange information as such could stop his/her state from imposing demands concerning the furnishing of evidence. See e.g., Case C-250/95 (*Futura*), in which Luxembourg was not permitted to demand submission of accounting conducted internally by a non-resident corporation to support its claim of loss adjustment. Luxembourg was allowed to request information from the state where the corporation was established. This decision is also important for the interpretation of the so-called exhaustion rule (see Ch. 4, s. 4.5.3). See also ECJ Case C-1/93 (*Halliburton*), about the refusal of the national reorganization exemption by the Netherlands for the transfer of real estate from a German to a Dutch daughter company of Halliburton BV. The Dutch tax authorities could have asked Germany questions about the equivalence of the foreign legal form on the basis of the European Directive 77/799, according to the Court.
50. OECD Commentary, 1977, Introduction, para. 8, calls the increased possibilities to evade paying tax one of the reasons to revise the Model convention. See also OECD Commentary, 1977-2005, Art. 1, paras 7-26, in which both 'tax evasion' and 'tax avoidance' are given as issues to be addressed. See also Schaumburg (1998), para. 19.27, 1304 and 19.46, 1314.
51. In its report, Improving Access to Bank Information for Tax Purposes: The 2003 Progress Report, the Committee on Fiscal Affairs provides a definition of the term 'tax fraud': 'intentional violation of a legal requirement concerning the accurate reporting, determination, or collection of tax'. This includes, e.g., not submitting tax returns, not fulfilling administrative obligations, and providing false information. All OECD members except Switzerland and Luxembourg agree with this definition.
52. The procedure does apply to '*taxation* not in accordance with the provisions of the Convention'.
53. See Opinion of the Advocate general Alber for Case 420/48 *W-N*, and Opinion of Advocate General Mazák in Case C-451/05 *Elisa*. Also Case C-150/4 *Commission-Denmark* at para. 52.
54. Case C-451/05 *Elisa* at paras 80–81, where the Court submits that: 'It is admittedly clear from the case-law of the Court that the prevention of tax evasion is an overriding requirement of general interest capable of justifying a restriction on freedom of movement.' Thus the freedom of capital could be hampered by the condition by France that the legal persons having their seat in a country that did *not* conclude a treaty with an obligation to exchange information, could not

the Court expresses that Member States do not have to violate these freedoms because in the Directive 77/799 they have an instrument to combat this tax evasion and tax fraud.[55] Thus the exchange of information can protect the interests of the European citizens as well. Moreover, Member States may not invoke the existence itself of an obligation to exchange information as a *general* condition for granting these freedoms to residents and non-resident legal persons alike. The Member States have to enable the taxpayer in their state to produce proof that they deserve the application of the rule.[56]

Recently, the exchange obligation has gained in importance as an instrument for the states within the OECD law because of the battle stirred up by the Committee on Fiscal Affairs against so-called 'harmful tax competition'.[57]

From the first report on this topic, the 'international transparency and exchange of information' has been considered the standard for the manner in which states should relate to each other.[58] Thus, the observance of the exchange obligation has evolved from a means in the hands of the states to promote their interests into the very litmus test to assess if a state has *any* notion of standards of international law.[59] This development also became apparent within the European Community, where some states have made the *existence* of an obligation to exchange tax information into a condition for equal treatment of legal persons who have their effective centre of management in another state, like became clear in the *Elisa* case.[60] These norms of international transparency and exchange of information, as the OECD advocated them, have been widely criticized, and justly so in my opinion. The unequal standards it created in this context for OECD

---

benefit from the 3% taxation rule on the commercial value of immovable properties. See also and Case C-150/04 *Commission v. Denmark* at para. 51 and the case law there cited).

55. See for instance C-383/05 *Talotta,* (2007) Case C-422/01 *Skandia and Ramstedt* (2003) ECR I-6817, at para. 42.
56. Case C-451/05 *Elisa* at para. 91. See also Case C-478/98 *Commission v. Belgium*, para. 45; and Case C-334/02 *Commission v. France* at para. 27; Case C-196/4 *Cadbury-Schweppes* at para. 50.
57. OECD Report: Harmful Tax Competition, An Emerging Global Issue, 1998, para. 16.
58. OECD Report: Harmful Tax Competition, An Emerging Global Issue, 1998, paras. 52, 62, and 64-68.
59. Regarding the international law norms of the OECD as evident in the Harmful Tax Competition Report, many noticed points of contention. Pires 2001 considers the idea of 'harmful tax competition' as overly concerned with the interests of developed countries. He is a proponent of the inclusion of a solidarity component in the evaluation of states' tax systems. Also, Makhlouf (2000) feels that the damaging nature of tax competition is overemphasized by the developed countries, while it can be healthy for companies and states and offer them opportunities.
60. Case C-451/05 *Elisa*. France applies a 3% tax on the commercial value of immovable property for legal persons established in France. For companies who have their effective centre of management elsewhere the 3% rule is only applied when they are established in a country that has concluded a conventional provision on mutual administrative assistance (and on discrimination). The Court, however, did not agree with that general condition. The foreign taxpayers invoking the advantageous rule have to be enabled to prove that they 'deserve' it and that they are not engaged in fraud or evasion schemes.

members and non-OECD members,[61] and the lack of respect and consideration for small and poorer states evident in its campaign, hardly reflect a moral concept of the law in which the focus lies on 'equal concern and respect' for all participants in a legal relationship.[62]

Against this background, the question of the suitability of the existing 'exchange of information law' to enable states to observe their *public* law duties as well is ever more important. That is certainly true when considering that the information to be exchanged is to be collected within the fiscal legal relationship between the supplying states and their taxpayers, with the taxpayer having the weaker position of power. The equality required within all legal relationships demands that in such an asymmetrical legal relationship, his interests should be carefully considered by the state. This especially applies because this instrument as such does not serve any of the interest, of this taxpayer, unlike with the other treaty obligations.[63] The other reason is that the Committee on Fiscal Affairs is increasingly considering the exchange of information as a weapon in the struggle against damaging tax competition between the states and against the increased 'sophistication' of tax fraud.

## 2.2. Conclusion

From these general considerations of the way in which the obligations of the states in the OECD Model convention are formulated, we can infer that the tendency evident in the 1970s toward a more social interpretation of international law has not penetrated far in the Model convention. Especially in the OECD discussion about 'harmful tax competition', there seems to be little consideration for the position of the weaker states. This lack of attention to concepts such as respect for the position of the economically weaker parties bodes ill for the weaker party being treated with respect in international exchange law, namely, the taxpayers who have to provide the information to be exchanged. This scepticism is supported by the role reserved for exchange law in the earlier-mentioned campaign in upholding the existing inequality between states.

61. See e.g., also the remark by Wright (1998), 461 about the velvet gloves with which Switzerland and Luxembourg were treated, 'in return for not sinking the whole report'.
62. See Easson (2004), 1037 ff., who lists a number of critics of the OECD initiative.
63. Schaumburg (1998), para. 9.45 speaks about a 'field of conflict'. Indeed, a taxpayer could have a direct interest in the exchange of information if it concerns his own obligation to pay tax. That could be the case if the information is exchanged to promote the correct implementation of the treaty. In other cases that interest could be indirect at best, because of the 'level playing field' created for all taxpayers when the tax laws are strictly upheld.

## 3. EXCHANGE OF INFORMATION 'AN ONGOING PROCESS'

Closer analysis of the various obligations concerning the exchange of information will reveal that we are not talking about a static phenomenon. Exchange of information was already being considered in the antebellum period in the so-called League of Nations models preceding the OECD Model convention.[64] Subsequently, the topic was incorporated in the first version of the Model convention on double taxation (from 1963) and thereafter regularly revised.[65]

The first modification of the exchange of information provision in the Model convention on double taxation was made in 1977. Reasons for this, given by the Committee on Fiscal Affairs, included the experiences with the Draft Convention of 1963, the changing tax systems in the Western world, and the increasing globalization in the economies of affiliated countries.[66] By expanding the subjective scope of the obligation, information about non-residents of the treaty states became subject to obligatory exchange. In addition, the confidentiality clause was revised. The modifications were presented by the Committee on Fiscal Affairs as a *clarification* of the first version 'by change in the wording of the Article and its Commentary without altering its effects'. This meant that the exchange of information provision in the tax treaties from before 1977 would largely have to be interpreted dynamically on recommendation of the Committee on Fiscal Affairs.[67]

Although it is an understandable attempt to bridge the differences between the international dynamic of the Model convention and the often long-standing separate tax treaties, this manner of presenting the modifications is somewhat contentious in some cases, as we shall see later. This applies especially when the earlier treaty text and the later commentaries grow too far apart. This risk became greater after 1991, when the increased sophistication of the methods of tax evasion[68] formed a stimulus for the Committee to develop the Model convention in an ongoing process.[69] Since 1992, changes have been made in the exchange of information provision, especially in the Commentary, with some regularity, leading to a continuous expansion of the exchange obligation. In Chapter 3 it was apparent that the Committee on Fiscal Affairs actions were not always transparent for the public

---

64. For the prior history, see van Raad/Milders (1988), 58 and Wisselink (1996), 23.
65. There are still treaty relationships that are modelled on the original version. The last review I am familiar with, the OECD report Tax Information Exchange between OECD Member Countries, A Survey of Current Practices, 1994, lists 40.
66. OECD Commentary, 1977, Introduction, para. 7.
67. *Ibid.*, para. 33. In note 34 this method was also imposed for the modifications done after 1977. For a discussion of this method of interpretation, see s. 6.
68. OECD Commentary, 1992, Introduction, para. 8.
69. *Ibid.*, para. 9. The Commentary has been regularly revised since 1992, with the changes being indicated as footnotes in the different subsequent texts. When referring to notes from the Commentary, I followed the numbering of the most recent Commentary (version 2005).

and for the countries' Parliaments, which increased the criticism of the Commentary's role.[70] Vogel talks in this context about a 'deficient publication style'.[71]

The European exchange law was also subject to revision, but to a lesser extent. The Directive 77/799,[72] produced in 1977 and amended repeatedly, closely resembled the OECD law, but in some respects had a wider scope. The revision of the directive in 1979 originally affected only the objective scope: the addition of indirect taxes[73] and certain excise duties.[74]

The realization of the Strasbourg Convention in 1988, a co-production of the OECD and the Council of the European Communities, brought integration of legislation concerning taxation and collection assistance. It thus makes a significant contribution to the development of a vision of what mutual administrative collaboration between states should be. Many elements of that Treaty have over time been incorporated in the OECD Model convention, and later also in Community law.

## 3.1. Recent Developments

In the first decade of the twenty-first century the exchange of information law in both communities was substantially revised, and in both cases the intensification of the fight against increasing tax fraud was the argument.

In the European exchange law the objective scope of Directive 77/799 by means of Directive 2003/93 was shrunk to just direct taxes (and insurance tax),[75] to bring all exchange of VAT data under the new Council Regulation 1798/2003.[76] This replaced the Council Regulation 218/92 EU, which had regulated the information exchange about intra-community transactions since the disappearance of the physical customs borders within the former Community. This replacement had become necessary in the eyes of the European Commission: the

70. See s. 5.
71. Vogel (2003), Rz. 128. He expresses his amazement that the OECD does not have an official organ to inform the public. The custom followed since 2001 of publishing draft versions of the Model convention, on the Internet also, is definitely an improvement.
72. EU Directive of 19 Dec. 1977, concerning the mutual assistance by the competent authorities of the Member States in the field of direct taxes, PbEU 1977, L 336.
73. EU Directive of 6 Dec. 1979, no. 1070/79, PbEU 1979, L 331.
74. EU Directive of 25 Feb. 1992, no. 92/12, PbEU 1992, L 76 also for individual excise duties. I have not considered the Council Regulation (EU) 218/219, of 27 Jan. 1992, concerning the automatic exchange of information in the field of indirect taxes, PbEU L 24/1, because of its specialist scope (intra-community transactions) and also because of the fact that it has already been rescinded as a separate council regulation.
75. Directive 2003/93/EU of the Council of the European Union of 7 Oct. 2003, concerning the mutual assistance by the competent authorities of the Member States in the field of direct and indirect taxes, PbEU L 264, see also V-N 2003/58.24.
76. Council Regulation (EU) 1798/2003, of 7 Oct. 2003, concerning the administrative collaboration in the field of taxation of added value and repeal of the Council Regulation (EU) 218/92, PbEU 2003, L264/1 (hereinafter Council Regulation 1798/2003). See also V-N 2003/57.23.

mutual assistance for VAT based on two separate regulations was inadequate, too bureaucratic, too heavy, and thus ineffective.[77]

In 2004, the Implementation Regulation EU 1925/2004 appeared, as an instrument to realize the obligation from the VAT Regulation to establish automatic information exchange in certain cases.[78] There was also Directive 2004/56/EU,[79] which contained more detailed rules for the implementation of the amended Directive 77/799. Council Regulation (EU) 2073/2004 established mutual assistance in the field of excise duties.[80] The Savings Directive[81] refers to Directive 77/799 as the sole source of exchange law concerning direct taxes, without the restrictions on the exchange of information obligation, which are specified in Article 8 of Directive 77/799. They were declared inapplicable in the Savings Directive.[82]

In my opinion, a countervailing development is apparent in the case law of the European Court of Justice. It continuously stressed the importance of the Directive 77/799 as an instrument to combat tax fraud and evasion, which makes it unnecessary (and thus unlawful) for Member States to create anti-abuse legislation with a discriminatory effect,[83] but at the same time did not accept that rights of individual taxpayers to prove their integrity were put aside. Member States are not allowed to make the mere existence of an exchange of information provision in their tax treaty to a general condition for equal treatment of foreign taxpayers.[84] This is even so in their relationship with Member States having limited information-gathering powers, which through Article 8, 1 of the Directive also limits their obligation to exchange information.[85]

Article 26 of the OECD Model Convention was radically revised in 2006.[86] According to the Committee on Fiscal Affairs, the stimulus for the revision was the realization in 2002 of the Model Agreement on Exchange of Information on Tax Matters, in collaboration between the Global Forum Group of the OECD and several 'committed jurisdictions'. They thus escaped from being placed on the

77. See the Preamble to Council Regulation (EU) 1798/2003, remarks 10-14.
78. Regulation (EU) 1925/2004 from the Commission, of 29 Oct. 2004, to arrange further implementation regulations for certain stipulations of the Council Regulation (EU) 1798/2003 concerning the administrative collaboration in the field of taxation of added value, PbEU L 331 (hereinafter Implementation Council Regulation).
79. EEU Directive from the Council of 21 Apr. 2004 to revise 77/799EEU concerning the mutual assistance by the competent Member States in the fields of direct taxes and certain excise taxes and duties on insurance premiums, PbEU L 127. See also V-N 2004/49.4
80. Council Regulation (EU) 2073/2004, of 16 Nov. 2004 concerning the administrative cooperation in the field of excise taxes, PbEU L359.
81. Council Directive 2003/48/EU of 3 Jun. 2003 concerning taxation on income from savings in the form of interest payments, PbEU L 157.
82. See Art. 9, para. 3, Savings Interest Rate Directive.
83. Like the French legislation inducing the Elisa Case.
84. See for instance Case C-418/07 *Papillon* (2008) at paras 54 and 55, and case law cited there. Also Case C-451/05 *Elisa* (2008) and Case C-383/05 *Talotta* (2007) at 29 and 34 and case law cited there.
85. Case C-451/05 *Elisa*, and case law cited there.
86. Published on the OECD website <www.oecd.org>.

blacklist of tax paradises associated with the Harmful Tax Competition report.[87] The Agreement was criticized because higher demands were placed on the transparency of these 'jurisdictions' and their legislation and financial services than on the OECD states active in the same financial markets.[88] In addition, the report 'Improving Access to Bank Information for Tax Purposes'[89] was also important, similarly related to the discussion on 'harmful tax competition'.[90]

The revision meant that the first paragraph of Article 26 was split into two, to highlight the condition of confidentiality better (in a separate paragraph). That is an improvement.[91] Also, the second paragraph of Article 26, containing the exceptions to the obligation, was supplemented with two new paragraphs. This addition, too, is a clarification, according to the Committee on Fiscal Affairs.[92] I would agree with that.

## 3.2. Conclusion

The development of the exchange of information obligation extends from the OECD Model convention in the different versions to the European exchange law (Directive77/799) and converges in the Strasbourg Convention realized jointly by both international communities. The development of the OECD Model convention was considered an ongoing task by the Committee on Fiscal Affairs. It carries, however, the risk that the text and the Commentary to the Model convention will harmonize less with the separate tax treaties concluded by the states. The development continues in the direction of increasingly greater commitment by the OECD states to fight tax fraud and tax evasion. This vision was also imposed on the former tax paradises ('committed jurisdictions') in the Model Agreement for information exchange on Tax Matters.

At the start of the twenty-first century, a rearrangement took place in the community fiscal exchange law, allowing the development of separate legislation for taxation assistance in the field of direct taxes and VAT: Directive 77/799 for the direct taxes and Council Regulation 1798/2003 Council Regulation 1798/2003 for VAT, and 2004/2004 on excises.

87. According to the Introduction, the Model Agreement aims to promote the international fiscal collaboration between states through information exchange. There are two versions, a multilateral and a bilateral, whose contents hardly differ. McLure (2005), 90, comments rightly about this instrument that the strongest 'weapon' of the 'committed jurisdictions', namely a low taxation rate, is left unaffected.
88. Hay (2006) reports that 80% of the 'offshore services' are performed from powerful centres in OECD states (London, New York, Tokyo), and that the small 'tax paradises' are being dealt with too heavy-handedly, especially considering the success of some states in their resistance to the Savings Interest Rate Directive.
89. OECD 2000 <www.oecd.org/taxation>.
90. OECD Commentary, 1977-2005, Art. 26, para. 4.
91. The change to the contents of the clause will be discussed later.
92. OECD Commentary, 1977-2005, Art. 26, para. 4.1.

## 4. DIFFERENT OBLIGATIONS CONCERNING THE EXCHANGE OF INFORMATION: AN ANALYSIS

In the earlier discussion, it seemed that the obligations in the OECD Model convention on double taxation affected only legal relationships between states, without making the taxpayer's role obvious. For the 'distribution rules' of the Model convention, that impression is deceptive, because they also are in the fiscal interest of taxpayers in the various states.

For the information exchange obligation, this invisibility is a fact, especially for the taxpayer who has to *provide* the information for exchange between the states.

Now the moment has come for an analysis of the obligations concerning the exchange of information as such. Several remarks in advance could help to orient our thoughts. The exchange of information takes place between a providing and a receiving state. The obligation to provide information is not absolute. Along with a description of the scope and conditions of the obligation, all exchange legislation contains grounds that states can use to get out of the obligation.

We must consider that the exchange of information clauses in the different rules as they currently exist definitely do not aim to forbid greater exchange between states. The state addressed has, in *international* law terms, the *possibility* to do more in a particular case than what is minimally required of it.[93] For example, it can supply information that requires more effort to obtain than it would normally exert for its own taxation according to its own legislation, or for which there no reciprocity exists. As the requesting state, however, it does not have the *right* to demand the same from its treaty partner.[94] The discretionary margin the treaty obligation gives the state should be 'filled' in its national law by legislation. This gives the taxpaying supplier of the information reassurance of how his/her state will interpret its exchange obligation in concrete situations. The taxpayer's position depends on the role (providing or receiving) that his/her state has in a concrete situation.

The thematic analysis utilizes as *guiding principles* the elements of Article 26 OECD Model convention 1977-2005 (the information provision). Part 1 reads as follows:

> 1- The competent authorities of the Contracting States shall exchange such information as is foreseeable relevant[95] for carrying out the provisions of this

93. See also OECD Commentary, 1977-2004, Art. 26, para. 5.2. Vogel 2003, Art. 26, para. 17, 1987 and para. 63, 1999 mentions the existence of the voluntary exchange, the so-called '*ex gratia*' or 'accommodating information', the implementation of which is precisely specified in German law.
94. That is specified unambiguously by the third paragraph of Art. 26 (new). See Ch. 6 for more details.
95. Until 2004 this was 'necessary'.

Convention or[96] to the administration or enforcement[97] of the domestic laws[98] concerning taxes of every kind and description imposed on behalf of the Contracting States, or of their political subdivisions or local authorities[99] insofar as the taxation hereunder is not contrary to the Convention. The exchange of information is not restricted by Article 1 and 2.[100]
2- Any information received under paragraph 1[101] by a Contracting State shall be treated as secret in the same manner as information obtained under the domestic laws of that State and shall be disclosed only to persons or authorities (including courts and administrative bodies) concerned with[102] the assessment or collection of, the enforcement or prosecution in respect of, or the determination of appeals in relation to, the taxes referred to in paragraph 1 or the oversight of the above.[103] Such persons or authorities shall use the information only for such purposes. They may disclose the information in public court proceedings or in judicial decisions.

## 4.1. Obligatory Exchange

### 4.1.1. OECD Model Convention on Double Taxation

From the choice of words in Article 26: 'the competent authorities *shall* exchange', it can be understood that in Article 26 OECD Model convention the intention is to establish an *obligation* between the treaty states. It is based on the fact that the essential foreign information can be obtained only with the assistance of another sovereign state and that only the existence of an international obligation can 'overrule' the national fiscal confidentiality provisions.[104] Commentary 1963 uses the term 'compulsory exchange of information'.[105] The Article covers all possible exchange options between states and thus also applies to information exchanged in the context of a mutual agreement procedure as mentioned in Article 25. After all, the function of that Article is nothing other than requiring the states to mutually solve the various problems that could arise when implementing the treaty. The sole

96. In 1963 this was *and.*
97. Added in the revision of 2004.
98. Until 2000 there was an insertion: *of the Contracting States.*
99. Until 2000 this said: *covered by the Convention.*
100. Reference to Art. 2 was added in 2000.
101. Added in 2004.
102. Replaced in 1995 by: *involved in.*
103. Added in 2004.
104. Vogel (2003), Art. 26, Rz. 3, 1983. See also Malherbe (1991), 60.
105. OECD Commentary, 1963, Art. 26, para. 5 reads 'obligation to furnish information'. OECD report Tax Information Exchange between OECD Member Countries, Paris 1994, mentions 'the binding character of the commitment to exchange information'. See also Wisselink (1996), 39.

competence created (in paragraph 4 of that Article) applies to certain civil servants designated by the states who can contact each other directly, bypassing the diplomatic channels. Article 25 thus does not establish a framework for the exchange of tax information on individuals. When this exchange is required in the opinion of the authorities involved in the consultation procedures, they should fulfil the demands and conditions of the exchange of information provision, of which especially the requirement of confidentiality is important.[106] This was reconfirmed in the 2005 revision of the information provision, in which the Commentary on Article 25 was modified.[107]

### 4.1.2. Obligatory Exchange in Other Rules

The first complete sentence in Article 1 of Directive 77/799, which remained unchanged in the most recent revision, reads: 'The competent authorities of the Member States provide each other ( . . . ) with all information.' This also indicates that the original intention was to establish an obligation, as in Article 1 of the Strasbourg Convention: 'The parties provide each other ( . . . ) with administrative assistance in fiscal affairs.' Council Regulation 1798/2003 states in Article 5, 'Upon request of the requesting authority the petitioned authority provides the regulations specified in Article 1 ( . . . ).'

The OECD Agreement formulates it in Article 5 as follows: 'The competent authority of the requested Party shall provide upon request of information.'

## 4.2. Relevance for Taxation

### 4.2.1. OECD Model Convention on Double Taxation: 'Such Information as Is Foreseeably Relevant'[108]

Until 2005 Article 26 of the OECD model contained the term '*necessary*'. This term was defined neither in the treaty provision nor in the Commentary, and therefore according to Article 3, second paragraph of the Model convention, has to be defined on the basis of the *national* definitions from the fiscal legislation of the states involved, unless the context requires otherwise (see section 3.4.4). For the information-supplying state, the important legislation is the one regulating the gathering of information from the taxpayers by the tax authorities. However, not all of the *domestic* tax laws in the various states use the term 'necessary' or something

106. That applies also to the information that could be exchanged in the discussion that should come to a definitive allocation of profit in the case of Art. 9, second paragraph of the Model convention. See also Vogel (2003), Art. 26, Rz. 7 and Rz. 51.
107. OECD Commentary, 1977-2005, Art. 25, para. 4.
108. Terminology used in version 2005.

equivalent.[109] The terminology of the treaty caused friction with these domestic laws of the states,[110] which had formulated the information obligations of their taxpayers in their own way.

Once it became apparent that 'control and search powers' of the tax administrations in all countries investigated in the OECD report: Taxpayers' Rights and Obligations[111] were intended to obtaining 'all *relevant* information', and because this was already acknowledged in the Commentary 2000,[112] the term 'necessary' was replaced in 2005 by 'foreseeably relevant'. The intention of the change is to create as broad a range of implementation as possible for the provision on one hand and to clarify on the other hand that there definitely must be a link to taxation with regard to the individual taxpayer, including the *fiscal* prosecution implementation.[113]

Paragraph 4.1 of Commentary 2005 qualified this change as a clarification of the treaty provision.[114] From the OECD's viewpoint, the earlier versions of Article 26 could therefore be interpreted dynamically on this point. I feel this is correct: the term 'necessary' as a condition for the obligation to exchange data is, if taken literally, actually unfeasible in the treaty relationship between two states, which forms the context in which the reading of this undefined treaty term should be made.[115] This context forms an argument for reading the term 'necessary' as an *assumed* relevance for assessing tax. In that sense we can state that its replacement by the term 'foreseeably relevant' in the Model convention is indeed a *clarification* of a connotation present from the beginning and that can thus be read with retroactive effect in the earlier treaties.

After all, the *necessity* for the requested information for the national taxation of the requesting state can be assessed only by that state. The requested (supplying) state, given the relation of good faith between the treaty partners, must ultimately rely on what the requesting state reports about it.[116] A marginal review, which I

109. The Netherlands 'General law on governmental taxes' specifies only that the information, to be collected, must be potentially '*important*' for (national) taxation, such as the Mutual Assistance on the Levying of Taxes Act, of 24 Apr. 1986, *Law Gazette* 249, latest revision in Act of 15 Dec. 2005, *Law Gazette* 683.
110. See e.g., Schaumburg/Schlossmacher (2000), who in proper German tradition divide the term 'necessary' into the terms 'suitability' (meaning an efficiency criterion), 'necessity' (referring to proportionality) and 'reasonableness' (an argument of considerations against the taxpayer's interests). See also Wisselink (1996), 133 and 134.
111. Taxpayers' Rights and Obligations, OECD 1990, 11. See also Bentley (1998), 44 ff.
112. OECD Commentary, 1977-2002, Art. 26, para. 5.
113. *Ibid.*, para. 5: 'Contracting States are not at liberty to engage in fishing expeditions.' Implementation for prosecution purposes is possible as long as the rights of suspects and witnesses are not infringed.
114. The intention was to link up with the new Model Agreement on Exchange of Information.
115. See Art. 3, para. 2, OECD Model Convention.
116. It is generally assumed that a state can trust the other state to make a proper assessment of the relevance of the requested data for the national legislation in the requesting state. See Vogel (2003), Art. 26, Rz. 12. In Dutch jurisprudence, the highest administrative court judge ruled in 1995 in a similar case that the Netherlands can trust the statement of the requesting state about the existence of relevance for taxation. See Dutch Council of State ruling of 7 Jul. 1995, Infobulletin 1995/19.

feel the supplying state is required to do because of his duty of care toward its taxpayer, can in its nature only concern a reasonable justification of the assumption of the *relevance* of the requested data.[117]

This applies even more so to the spontaneous information exchange, when the initiative lies with the supplying state. There, too, the term 'necessary' cannot be explained as other than a reference to the *assumed* interest in assessing tax (as was clear in Directive 77/799 and the Strasbourg Convention from the beginning).

The 2005 version of the Commentary specifies that not only 'taxpayer-specific information' can be exchanged, but also other sensitive information such as risk-analyses, methods of increasing compliance, fraud, and evasion patterns.[118] This information also falls under the confidentiality rule of the *new* second paragraph of Article 26 (see section 5.2).

### 4.2.2. Relevance for Taxation: Strasbourg Convention

Article 4 of the Strasbourg Convention also requires the parties to exchange information that 'can be anticipated to be important for' (a number of taxes TSG), after which it stresses once more that information that 'is unlikely to be important ( . . . )' must not be exchanged. This is as close as we are going to get to the term 'foreseeably relevant', I feel. Thus, it is surprising that the Committee on Fiscal Affairs, which was involved in the establishment of this provision, took until 2005 to insert this formulation.

### 4.2.3. Relevance for Taxation: Directive 77/799

The first sentence in Article 1, first paragraph of Directive 77/799, states in a manner unchanged since its commencement that the competent authorities of the Member States provide each other with all information 'that *could* be *useful* for the correct settlement of the tax debt'. This terminology provided the necessary room, long before a solution was presented for this in the Model convention, for states to decide on its relevance after receipt of the data, and the observance of the exchange obligation is not burdened with a judgment of its indispensability before its receipt.

117. The obligation to check derives from the state's legal duty towards its citizens to act lawfully, and thus examine as carefully as possible if the conditions for the exchange obligation, including a justified assumption of relevance, are present in a particular case. An independent investigation in the other state is not possible, and internationally also inappropriate. A marginal check is thus sufficient according to the Netherlands highest administrative court judge. Regarding the spontaneous provision of information, all exchange regulations have (in the meantime) objectified the requirement of interest in assessing tax by naming situations in which spontaneous provision is mandatory.

118. OECD Commentary, 1997-2005, Art. 26, para. 5.1.

### 4.2.4. Relevance for Taxation in Council Regulation 1798/2003 on VAT

Article 1 of the Regulation does not formulate a separate demand for interest in assessing tax. It simply talks of 'rules and procedures that enable the Member States to work together and mutually *exchange all information* for purposes of correct VAT taxation'. This continues in Article 5 for the exchange upon request: 'the petitioned authority *provides* (. . .) *the data specified in Article 1*', and similarly in Article 19, for spontaneous exchange. Article 17 makes automatic exchange compulsory in several, clearly specified cases.[119] This format gives the states less room for a review of the importance of the request, even a marginal one, or of something found in its own administration. This clearly shows the pragmatic basis on which this Regulation was conceived.

### 4.2.5. Relevance for Taxation in the OECD Agreement

Article 1 of the Model Agreement also requires only that the interest in assessing tax must be '*foreseeably relevant*' to provide the requested information. According to Note 3 of the Commentary, its intention is to create as wide a scope as possible for the obligation, while ensuring at the same time that states use the regulation only when it can serve a potential fiscal interest.

### 4.2.6. Conclusion

The choice of the undefined term 'necessary' in the OECD Model conventions before 2000 is unfortunate: it carries the risk for differences in interpretation between states, and it cannot refer to anything other than an assumed or reasonably assumable relevance of the requested information by the requested state. Given the parties' aim to establish as broad an information obligation as possible, the term 'foreseeably relevant' gives more room for lending assistance. The new term can be considered a clarification of the former term and thus implies the obligation for states to apply it to earlier versions of the OECD Model convention.

In the other exchange regulations, only an assumed or surmised relevance for taxation is required.

## 4.3. Objects of Exchange

The objective scope of the obligations concerning the exchange of information (the types of taxes referred to) is determined separately for each regulation.

---

119. For a more precise explanation of the terms 'automatic' and 'spontaneous' exchange, see ss 4.5.6 and 4.5.7.

### 4.3.1. Objective Scope of the OECD Model Convention

Regarding the obligations concerning the exchange of information in tax treaties modelled after the OECD Model convention, there is an evident development from an objective scope following the treaty framework to a more autonomously determined scope.

The 1963 version of the Model convention restricted the obligation to exchange to 'Information(-) concerning taxes covered by this Convention, insofar as the taxation there under is in accordance with this Convention.'

Thus the exchange of information was kept within the framework of Article 2 of the Model convention.[120] This covers the taxes on the total income, the total capital, or parts of it, including benefits obtained from the conveyance of personal property or real estate. Article 2, third paragraph, demands that the national taxes falling under these categories must be listed explicitly in the separate tax treaties. Based on Article 2, paragraph 4, later taxes of the same type also fall under the Model convention.[121] It is not necessary to comply with requests concerning other taxes, or taxes that are not consonant with the treaty.[122] States are permitted to specify a broader objective in their own taxation treaty.[123] Information that could be important only for the levying of taxes *not* covered in the treaty (for example, sales taxes, inheritance, and gift tax) was left out of the exchange obligation until 2000. In that year the objective scope of the obligation was expanded to 'Information (. . .) concerning *taxes of every kind and description*', even when imposed on the regional or local level.[124] This is in line with the expansion of the range of implementation of assistance as already incorporated in the Strasbourg Convention.

The possibilities offered by Article 26 are not restrictive, according to the Commentary.[125] Other international instruments for mutual fiscal assistance existing between states (for example, the Strasbourg Convention alongside a tax treaty) also can be used. Only customs taxation falls under specific treaties. The link between the exchange of information obligation and the tax treaty can be maintained only under the condition that the (national) levying of taxes for which the information is requested may not conflict ('not be contrary') with the treaty.[126] Examples of such taxation include a tax introduced after the conclusion of the treaty with a 'treaty-override' effect or tax legislation that would lead to

---

120. OECD Commentary, 1963, Art. 26, para. 3.
121. *Ibid.*, Art. 2, para. 3.
122. *Ibid.*, Art. 26, para. 5. As an example, the request regarding tax on capital is given.
123. E.g., if they want to use the exchange of information provision also for specific anti-misuse stipulations, see OECD Commentary, 1963, Art. 26, para. 6.
124. In OECD Commentary, 1977-2005, para. 10.1, the earlier example of the exclusion of 'sales tax' from the exchange obligation was also removed.
125. OECD Commentary, 1977-2005, Art. 26, para. 5.2.
126. *Ibid.*, Art. 26, para. 5.

discrimination.[127] The Commentary also acknowledges that the most recent expansion of the objective scope of Article 26 could cause problems for some states.[128] Those states could limit the obligation to the taxes specified in their treaty.[129] I conclude from this that the Committee on Fiscal Affairs rightly considers this large expansion not as a clarification but as a substantial change.[130] The gap between the expanded obligation and the 'old' model provision from 1977 is too great to be closed simply by a dynamic interpretation. That certainly applies to states that have incorporated a 'narrow' exchange clause in their tax treaties (see section 4.4.4).

### 4.3.2. Objective Scope of Directive 77/799: Ranking of the Obligations Concerning the Exchange of Information

Article 1 Directive 77/799 reads as follows:

> General provisions
>
> 1. In accordance with the provisions of this Directive the competent authorities of the Member States shall exchange any information that may enable them to effect a correct assessment of taxes of income and on capital.
> 2. There shall be regarded as taxes on income and on capital, irrespective of the manner in which they are levied, all taxes imposed on total income, on total capital, or on elements of income and capital, including taxes on gains from the disposal of movable or immovable property, taxes on the amounts of wages or salaries paid by enterprises, as well as taxes on capital appreciation and insurance premiums referred to in the sixth indent of Article 3 of Council Directive 76/308/EEC.
> 3. The taxes referred to in paragraph 2 are at present [–follows an enumeration of the taxes of all Member States]
> 4. Paragraph 1 shall also apply to any identical or similar taxes imposed subsequently, whether in addition or in place of the taxes listed in paragraph 3. The competent authorities of the Member States shall inform one another and the Commission of the date of entry into force of such taxes.

This list is deemed not to be exhaustive,[131] and 'from the principle of uniform interpretation of Community law it can be derived that the name given to a particular tax under national cannot be regarded as significant for the purpose

127. See also Vogel 2003, Art. 26, Rz. 40.
128. OECD Commentary, 1977-2005, Art. 26, para. 10.1.
129. *Ibid.*, Art. 26, para. 10.1. The Netherlands used the 'old' text of Art. 26, e.g., in the treaty concluded with Belgium in 2001.
130. OECD Commentary, Art. 26, para. 4 qualified most of the changes in 1977 as clarifications. This was not the case for the change in 2000.
131. Cf. Case C-451/05 *Elisa*. The Court concluded: 'It follows unambiguously from Art. 1(3) of Directive 77/799 that the list of taxes and duties specified in that article is not exhaustive.'

of determining whether that tax should be considered a tax within the meaning of article 1'.[132]

Along with this Directive, for European OECD states obligations to exchange information can derive from Article 26 OECD Model convention and Council Regulation 1798/2003. States can also be a party in the Strasbourg Convention. A convergence of several obligations concerning the exchange of information will occur most often for the European Member States that want to exchange information referring to direct taxes, because almost all of them concluded tax treaties after the OECD model as well. Whenever the obligations are not identical, because, for example, a restricted treaty obligation exists along with Directive 77/799 and/or the Strasbourg Convention, the question arises of which international law obligation takes precedence.

Article 26 OECD Model convention does not forbid basing the exchange between the states on other legal rules.

My earlier comment about the rationale for the exchange obligation is important here. It lies in the creation of a legal basis allowing the states to override their national confidentiality legislation. It sets only a few unavoidable conditions: the assumption of a relevance for taxation in the supplying state and the confidentiality of the information received in the recipient state. It formulates a *minimum position* concerning the scope of the obligation and leaves the states free to make greater efforts if they choose to do so.[133] This results in a neutral position for Article 26 of the Model convention compared with other obligations concerning the exchange of information. In 2005, the Commentary also established that unmistakeably: 'possibilities (...) provided by Article 26 *do not limit, nor are they limited by* those contained in other existing international agreements or arrangements between the Contracting States (...)'.[134] This means that in a convergence of two regulations allowing the exchange of information, the one with the widest scope can be chosen.[135]

Article 27, paragraph 1 Strasbourg Convention, has the same wording, although a choice must be made.[136] The EU Member States are in addition according to Article 27, paragraph 2 *obliged* to apply the provisions of the Community law.

132. ECJ C-451/05 *Elisa*, 11 Oct. 2008, Opinion of Advocate General Mazák. Cf. also Case C-314/85, *Photo – Frost* 1987 and C-11/70 *Internationale Handelsgesellschaft.*
133. See also Vogel (2003), Art. 26, para. 17, 1987 and para. 63, 1999 (these are not years, but numbers of the paragraphs in the volume of Vogel. and Wattel (1988), 566 ff. They state that 'the state does not act outside the treaty obligation if it (despite the "readily available" clause of an exchange of information provision TSG), collects the information anyway and provides it'.
134. OECD Commentary, 1977-2005, Art. 26, para. 5.2. The Commentary refers to the earlier para. 11.2, which was less clear.
135. van Raad (1987) stated that in such cases the widest-ranging regulation is *applicable*, which seemed to imply something obvious or an obligation. I feel, however, that this refers to a discretionary competence of the treaty partners.
136. See Strasbourg Convention, Explanatory Report, Art. 27, para. 256. The states may choose the most effective obligation, but they *do* have to choose.

Article 11 of Directive 77/799 specifies that *wider-ranging* obligations, based on other regulations are not restricted by this directive. The term 'wider-ranging' must be considered in terms of the objective of the exchange regulations: Supplying as much information as possible means here too that the broadest possibility can be chosen. Given the special nature of Community law, this term 'more broadly' refers to information *not* covered by Community law.[137] The provision does not provide clarity in cases in which the *treaty* obligation to exchange information is *more restricted* and thus probably benefits the citizen more, for example, if a bilateral treaty between two European Member States only makes the exchange of 'readily available' information mandatory, whereas this restriction is not accepted in the European Directive.

I am of the opinion that the ranking between treaty law and Community law is determined *for the Member States* by the European Court of Justice,[138] which has the exclusive competence to interpret the Community law.[139]

The Court has established in a continuous line of jurisprudence that the Community law forms its own legal order (van Gendt and Loos decision); that the states have limited their own sovereignty within it (Costa-Enel decision);[140] that this devolution is irrevocable (Simmenthal decision);[141] that thus the Community law takes precedence over treaty relationships between Member States;[142] and that Article 234 of the EU Treaty concerning existing treaties with third countries means that the Member States are obliged to renegotiate those treaties in the spirit of the EU law. According to the Court, this means that the Community law must be fully applicable to existing relationships between Member States.[143] If this were not so, Member States would be able in mutual agreements to revert to a restricted bilateral regulation that could undermine the objective of the relevant Community law. This would run counter to the injunction of Community loyalty in Article 5 of the EU Treaty.[144] After all, decisions of Member States to apply a *restricted* provision from a *tax treaty* would mean that the Community law could not fully be applied.[145] This conclusion agrees with Article 11 of Directive 77/799, which only gives way to *broader* provisions in international law. The precedence of

137. Also, see the Opinion of Advocate General Mazák in the Case C-451/05 *Elisa*.
138. The Member States voluntarily agreed to the EU Treaty, and thus accepted the existence of the Community legal order and the jurisdiction of the European Court of Justice. This does not apply to non-Member States, such as the United States.
139. Vogel (2003), Art. 26, Rz. 69, Heithuis (1993), 1650, and Wisselink (1996), 320.
140. ECJ, C-26/62, *Van Gendt and Loos* and C-6/64, *Costa-Enel*. See for a description Lauwaars (1997), 36.
141. ECJ, C-106/77, *Simmenthal*.
142. See ECJ C-495/03, *Intermodal Transports*.
143. ECJ, C-235/87, *Matteucci*. The states are obliged to support each other when ensuring the implementation of Community law.
144. ECJ C-170/05, *Denkavit*, at para. 53. De Graaf (2004), 252 thinks this is a real risk, for instance for the (planned) Pension Directive. The Netherlands would have to revise tax treaties that conflict with the Directive. Cf. also Kemmeren (2001), 233-234.
145. In the same sense, also Heithuis (1993) and Vogel (2003), Art. 26, Rz. 69, and Wisselink (1996), 320.

Community law applies regardless of the position of the national legal rule in the legal order of the states, also with regard to the constitutional laws.[146] This means that regardless of the 'bilateral' nature of the information provision, a Community legal rule takes precedence.

This precedence for Community law was established by the European Court in general terms. 'It derives like an innate characteristic from the special nature of the Community, rooted in the autonomic legal order', according to Lauwaars.[147]

The only significant discrepancy between Article 26 of the Model convention since 1977 and Directive 77/799 concerns the issue of confidentiality. Directive 77/799 Article 7, paragraph 2, gives the requested state the right to refuse information if the requesting state does not promise to implement the stricter confidentiality standard of this supplying state itself (see section 5.2). The rule of precedence given previously puts the Directive 77/799 first. Moreover, in this case a taxpayer will definitely not turn to a judge so quickly to demand implementation of the *treaty* obligation, because it offers less protection.

Convergence also can exist between an exchange of information obligation from a tax treaty and an obligation in the Strasbourg Convention. This situation is clearly regulated in Article 27, in the first paragraph of that treaty. It stipulates that other obligations concerning the exchange of information are not restricted by the Treaty. The Explanatory Report explains that 'in any particular situation the most effective instruments can be used'.[148] However, states must make a clear choice in each situation, because 'each instrument is self-contained, having its own characteristics'.[149] Article 27, paragraph 2, Strasbourg Convention makes an exception for the Member States of the European Community. They are obliged to follow the Community regulations.[150]

### 4.3.3. Objective Scope of Council Regulation 1798/2003 on VAT

According to Article 1, the objective scope of the regulation covers 'the tax on added value (VAT) on deliveries of goods, provision of services, intra-community purchases of goods and import of goods'.

This also includes the exchange of data about VAT on services supplied electronically (so-called e-commerce) and any associated information.[151] Exchange concerning intra-community transactions and the registration and

146. See Barents/Brinkhorst (1996), 66 ff.
147. Lauwaars (1997), 38 See also Heithuis (1993), 1650.
148. Strasbourg Convention, Explanatory Report, Art. 27, para. 257. The reference to other regulations must, according to para. 258, be stated very generally: all exchange of information provisions from bilateral treaties, the obligations the Scandinavian countries and the Benelux have taken on together, also in the field of collection assistance.
149. Strasbourg Convention, Explanatory Report, Art. 27, para. 257.
150. From the Explanatory Report, Art. 27, para. 259 it appears that this rule of precedence was formulated at the request of the European Community.
151. For implementation of the regulation as agreed in Art. 26*quater* of Directive 77/388.

tax returns for e-commerce activities takes place through communal electronic networks.

### 4.3.4. Objective Scope of the Strasbourg Convention

Article 2 of the Strasbourg Convention contains a comprehensive list of taxes:

(a) direct taxes on income, profit, and the capital gains tax levied by the central government;
(b) the same taxes levied by national units, and obligatory premiums for social security,[152] and administrative fines;[153]
(c) indirect taxes: inheritance and gift taxes, general and specific consumer taxes applied to certain goods, 'and all other taxes'.

Aside from the first group of taxes, which belong to the *minimum obligation*, states can make a reservation for the other groups of taxes on the basis of Article 30. The Netherlands made a reservation for the indirect taxes and for taxes levied by sub-national authorities when the treaty went into effect in 1996.[154] The reservation concerning indirect taxes was abolished in a letter from the Finance State Secretary in 2001.[155]

### 4.3.5. Objective Scope of the OECD Agreement

As already stated, the OECD Agreement has two versions: a multilateral and a bilateral one.

The objective scope is only described in the *multilateral* version of Article 3, first paragraph. It lists the following taxes for which exchange is mandatory:

- taxes on income or profit, definitely including according to Note 8 of the Commentary the gains from the conveyance of personal property and real estate;
- tax on capital;
- wealth tax; and
- taxes on estates and gifts. This can be expanded to include indirect taxes if the states choose to do so.

On the basis of Article 3, second paragraph of the multilateral version, taxes imposed by regional or local authorities can also be selected.

152. Strasbourg Convention, Art. 2, para. 1(b), jo. Explanatory Report, Art. 2, para. 24-36. According to Art. 3, the definition stipulation, the mandatory social security premiums are considered 'taxes'.
153. Explanatory Report, Art. 3, para. 41. The interpretation of the undefined term 'fine' should accord with the national legislation of the states involved.
154. Act of 26 Jun. 1996, *Law Gazette* 382, hereafter called the Sanctioning Act.
155. Letter from the Finance State Secretary, containing a request for tacit ratification, session 2001-2002, 127 595 (R 1675), no. 194 and 1. Also V-N 2001/10.8.

The bilateral version of Article 3, paragraph 1 does not contain any specific categories. The choice of categories from the multilateral version is left to the states: one or more of the four listed above or just the indirect tax.[156] The data in the obligatory minimum category must, however, be provided if the other state specifies that category in the treaty. The obligation does not have to be reciprocal therefore. Especially this last clause makes it clear that the Agreement was the result of a difficult negotiation process between the Global Forum of the OECD on the one hand, which wanted a multilateral standard for the exchange of information accepted, and the 'committed jurisdictions' on the other. The 'commitment' of the 'jurisdictions' to the bilateral version was clearly not enthusiastic either.[157]

That became evident in Article 3, paragraph 3 of the multilateral version and Article 2 of the bilateral one.[158] They contain a provision found in all tax treaties specifying that new taxes similar to older ones, but established after a treaty comes into force, are also subject to it. Given the cycle of existence of a treaty that is longer than the national laws of the states, this prevents the necessity of treaty revision whenever a national tax law in one of the states is replaced by a law with another name but the same character. Departing from this standard provision, mention is made in the OECD Agreement not only about *similar*, but also *identical* taxes established after the Agreement comes into force, which would thus fall under the obligation. It seems that the OECD countries feared that states would attempt to evade the obligations, simply by giving a tax specified in the Agreement another name.

### 4.3.6. Retroactive Implementation: All Regulations

Another element determining the objective scope of the exchange obligation is the period in which exchange is permitted, calculated from the moment of concluding the treaty. This was stated explicitly for the first time in the 2005 Commentary on Article 26 of the OECD Model convention.[159] Article 28 of the Model convention does not consider this element, nor does the Strasbourg Convention or the European exchange regulations, where one would expect it to be dealt with.[160] The question considered in the OECD Commentary is whether the exchange of information provision can also apply to fiscal years preceding the date on which the treaty entered into force. The 2005 Commentary reveals that nothing in the Model convention forbids the exchange of already existing data, as long as the provision takes place after the treaty came into force.[161] The Netherlands incorporated

156. OECD Agreement, Commentary, para. 9.
157. McLure (2005), 90, ascertains that this 'victory in the battle against tax – evasion' could be less substantial than appears at first sight. The treaty negotiations will be difficult, and in addition the low taxation rate, which is the most important 'asset' for most of the 'committed jurisdictions', remained untouched.
158. See for the negotiation phase Barnard (2002), 1043.
159. OECD Commentary, 1977-2005, Art. 26, para. 10.3.
160. Because it exclusively concerns the exchange of information.
161. OECD Commentary, 1977-2005, Art. 26, para. 10.3.

stipulations concerning the assistance in its treaties with Canada and Belgium with retroactive effect.[162]

This text deserves closer analysis. The issue of the admissibility of a retroactive implementation is important for the determination of the legality of a regulation or of an agreement between states. Its context is the principle that parties in a legal relationship may not be falsified in the expectations (the trust) with which they entered it. For an international law relationship this principle is established in Article 28 of the Treaty of Vienna, which states that stipulations of one treaty party are not binding 'on a deed or event preceding the date on which this treaty took effect, *unless another intention is apparent* from the treaty or in another manner' (italics TSG). This suggests that retroactive implementation is not always by definition unlawful, but that the parties must have considered in advance to what extent the implementation can be necessary.

Retroactive implementation in fiscalibus exists when an event that occurred before a law came into effect is taxed according to the new law.[163]

What are the exceptional situations in which retroactive implementation can be considered admissible? According to the European Court of Justice, in response to prejudicial questions from the Netherlands, there must be a fear of the occurrence of 'considerable notification effects, or the risk of extensive improper use or misuse of an existing law'. This concerned the legitimacy of the retroactive implementation when modifying the VAT-exemption system for real estate. The Court considered the retroactive implementation admissible in this case because it would prevent implementation of large-scale constructions to reduce the VAT burden during the legislation procedure, which the amendment act was trying to avoid. The condition, however, was added that the legitimate trust of the parties involved must be properly taken into account and the legal security ensured by an explicit and comprehensible statement about it addressed to the parties involved.[164]

The conclusion seems justified that the interest of the individual's legal security should be protected by not allowing laws to have retroactive effect on earlier situations, unless that interest consists solely of maintaining (longer than strictly necessary) possibilities for improper use or misuse of existing laws or regulations. In that case the law or the regulation must be modified according to the principle of legality, but retroactive effect to earlier situations is permitted if this retroactive implementation from the new regulation seems to be sufficient.

In my opinion, this generally acceptable view must also apply to the exchange of data. States must be able to switch to it to give the stipulation retroactive effect from its establishment or revision when they ascertain that their taxpayers are deliberately misusing in some way the lack of an exchange of information provision in their mutual relationship (for example, by withholding obligatory fiscal information from their own treasury). The fiscal position of the taxpayers

162. Treaty with Canada, Art. 27, added at the Second Revision Protocol of 1997, with retroactive effect for ten years, and Treaty with Belgium of 2001, Art. 33, para. 4.

163. Ellis (1995).

164. ECJ 26 Apr. 2005, C-376/02, *Stichting Goed Wonen v. State Secretary of Finance*.

does not change by doing so, and the interest of legal security applies in that case only to allowing the possibility of misuse to continue to exist: an interest of taxpayers that I feel should not be protected.

That is the importance of paragraph 10.3 of the OECD Commentary 2005. 'Information that existed before the entry into force of the Convention' can be requested and provided if '*the assistance* with respect to this information is *provided* after the Convention has entered into force' (italics TSG). This is in agreement with the legality principle, which prescribes that government actions that affect the legal position of its citizens (such as the provision of information to other states) should derive from the law. This also means that the intended retroactive implementation must be explicitly specified in the treaty text.[165]

How far back the states can extend the retroactive effect depends on their national legislation concerning post-clearance recovery and retention periods.

The argumentation concerning the retroactive implementation in the exchange of information given earlier should be required to apply even more so, in my opinion, to the Community information exchange. Directive 77/799 has no separate stipulation about entry into force, which depends, of course, on the date of implementation in the different states. The admission of ten new Member States in 2004 could have been a good opportunity to consider the issue of the retroactive implementation of information provision, in connection with the function it has in fighting tax fraud. Political considerations probably prevented this. Likewise, retroactive implementation was not applied to the Savings Directive. This also seems a political choice, probably dictated by the fear that it would make acceptance of the directive even more difficult.

However, the European Court of Justice in a decision concerning assistance with the collection of custom duties according to Directive 76/308 EU forced Greece to provide assistance to Italy, even though Greece, at the time that the request was made in connection with a case of fraud, was not yet a member of the European Community.[166]

### 4.3.7. Conclusion

From the analysis of the commercial scope of the exchange regulations, it appears that the possibilities for exchanging information have expanded continuously over time.

In Article 26 of the OECD Model convention, an expansion was implemented in 2005 to cover all types of taxes, from central and local authorities, including obligatory social security. The link thus disappeared to the rest of the tax treaty of which the stipulation is part, making it more useful for combating fraud and equally

165. By the way, in the dynamic interpretation method advocated by the Committee on Fiscal Affairs, there is also an element of retroactive effect because newer commentaries are applied on earlier treaties and because this new meaning takes precedence in issues of friction between new national meanings of treaty terms over what was valid at the time of concluding the treaty. Thereby, the newer commentaries and meanings 'act' retroactively, without this being explicitly stated in the treaty. See for the discussion on this, s. 3.6.
166. ECJ, 1 Jul. 2004, Cases C-361/01 and C-362/02. See also V-N 2004/39.24.

applicable to a wide range of issues as the Strasbourg Convention (as far as information exchange is concerned). This promotes the uniformity of international exchange law. The expanded scope applies only to the newest treaties, however. Because this is not a 'clarification' of the treaty text, the new terminology cannot be applied to earlier treaties.

The commercial scope of the multilateral version of the OECD Agreement comes close to the intention of the Strasbourg Convention: exchange of information is mandatory regarding direct taxes on income, profit, capital and wealth, and consumer taxes such as inheritance and gift taxes levied by the central government. Taxes imposed by regional or local authorities, and indirect taxes can be included. The benefit of this broad design is questionable because most committed jurisdictions prefer the bilateral version, which allows the states more freedom in the choice of categories falling under the exchange obligation. Provision of information in the obligatory categories may not be refused.

European Directive 77/799 applies since 2003 only to the direct taxes and the insurance tax, while the exchange of VAT data, including those concerning intra-community transactions, has been placed under Council Regulation 1798/2003. To this belongs the Implementation Regulation 1925/2004, regarding the automatic exchange of a number of VAT data.

With the establishment of Council Regulation 2073/2004, the exchange of data on excise duties, which originally fell partly under Directive 77/799, is also arranged separately.

For a convergence of obligations concerning the exchange of information from bilateral treaties with those from Directive 77/799, we assume that the directive takes precedence based on Article 5 of the EU Treaty and jurisprudence from the European Court of Justice concerning the intrinsic precedence of Community law over national and international law. States that decide in mutual consultation to apply a more restricted exchange stipulation instead of the broader stipulation in Community law would frustrate the 'full implementation of Community law', be it regulations or directives.

A new aspect in the OECD Commentary is the permission to provide information from the period before a tax treaty came into force if the exchange takes place after agreeing on the obligation. Retroactive implementation is considered admissible in international law (Article 28 of the Treaty of Vienna and Article 1 of the First Protocol of the European Convention of Human Rights (ECHR) under the following conditions: its possible implementation must be explicitly established by the states in the agreement, it must derive from the public interest, and it must be bound by legal conditions. Conditions that have been presented in a recent decision from the European Court of Justice, in Dutch legislation and jurisprudence from the Supreme Court of the Netherlands, and in the literature include extensive misuse of the existing law or the risk for the development of substantial notification effects damaging to the treasury.

In the field of the exchange of information, retroactive implementation means that a particular taxable fact that took place before a treaty came into force will be provided to the other state. This does not concern modifying the competence of the treasury to collect fiscal information, nor the taxability of an income category as such. Thus it cannot concern a violation of the taxpayer's expectation about the fiscal effect of his/her actions. Any expectation concerns only the avoidance of actual taxation. Regarding this aspect, the taxpayer should not be protected.

Specifying a (maximum) period for the retroactive effect in the exchange of information provision can provide security for the states and their taxpayers who have to supply the information.

## 4.4. Objectives for the Exchange: Extended and Narrow Exchange

### 4.4.1. OECD Model Convention

The exchange of information provision in the OECD Model convention names two objectives for the exchange obligation; 'the carrying out of this Convention, or of the domestic laws of the Contracting States'.[167]

This wording deviates from that in the 1963 version, where these objectives are linked by the conjunction 'and'.[168] The replacement by the conjunction 'or' took place in the first revision of Article 26 in 1977. As a result, van Raad and Milders questioned in 1963 whether a cumulative requirement was being established. The fact that the 1963 Commentary already mentions exchange to benefit 'the correct implementation of the Convention, *and* also of the internal laws of the Contracting States' suggests to me that the intention from the start was to create two separate objectives.[169]

This double objective is known in the literature as the 'extended exchange', in contrast to the 'narrow exchange'.[170] With extended information exchange the sole essential incentive for the exchange lies in the question of whether the requesting state can impose tax in a particular case. The stage of the taxation activity in the requesting state during which the information is requested is not important; it can even be during fiscal prosecution procedures against tax fraud, according to Vogel.[171] Given the apparent intention of the Commentary to establish as broad an information obligation as possible, the term information should be defined

167. The prevention of tax fraud also falls under the last objective, as explicitly stated in s. 6 of the 1963 Commentary.
168. See also van Raad/Milders (1988), 62.
169. OECD Commentary, 1963, Art. 26, para. 3.
170. These terms were first used in Menck (1971), 57, and since then have become generally accepted.
171. Vogel (2003), Art. 26, Rz. 43. The national states are indeed free to impose rules on the provision of evidence in their judicial procedures. A Dutch judge has in the past set a deadline for the production of evidence through information obtained from abroad (the Antilles). After waiting for eighteen months, no new deadline was permitted. HR 17 Apr. 1991, BNB 1991/161.

broadly.[172] Vogel feels that Article 26 aims to cover general information, for example the standard pricing of goods in a particular branch, and the *interpretation* of certain treaty stipulations in a mutual agreement procedure. I doubt whether that is sensible. It would mean that the interpretation of a term in the mutual agreement procedure must be kept secret, which is not in keeping with the norm of transparent government action.[173]

The inclusion of general, not personal information under Article 26, and thus under the requirement of confidentiality, would make sense only if that information had strategic importance for the states in their fight against tax evasion. In my opinion, that is what is meant by 'sensitive information' (about 'risk analysis techniques or tax evasion schemes') in paragraph 5.1 of the 2005 Commentary. This explicit mention places such information under the requirement of confidentiality, which possibly allows it to be exempted from disclosure earlier in such cases. This seems a sensible use of the addition to me.[174]

### 4.4.2. Narrow Exchange (Model Convention on Double Taxation)

The term 'narrow exchange' means that the states are obliged to exchange only information that is required for the implementation of the stipulations of the treaty. It must be about the application of a treaty stipulation, meaning that the taxpayer's tax arrears under the treaty would differ if it were not implemented.[175] The national law implementation can be affected by the result of this exchange; for example, if it appears that a taxpayer, in contrast to the information he/she supplied, does not have a fixed residence or office in the other state, but for the narrow exchange stipulation, the treaty implementation must be the *aim*. Because of the importance of information exchange for treaty implementation, almost all treaties to prevent double taxation (even those before 1963) include at least this 'narrow' exchange of information.[176]

The Commentary to the 1963 version gives several examples of information that could be exchanged, for example, concerning the receipt or payment of royalties (including the amount of the sums) or inter-company pricing,[177] but does not clearly classify what is considered the treaty implementation and what the implementation of the national laws. The Commentary on these objectives was expanded in 1977 and the examples used to illustrate the 'narrow exchange' stimulated considerable (especially German) written comments.

172. OECD Commentary, 1977-2005, Art. 26, para. 2.
173. Vogel (2003), Art. 26, Rz. 15. See also the decision HR 29 Sep. 1999, BNB 2000/16, referring to the mutual agreement that the Netherlands and Germany had reached about the interpretation of the term 'temporary' in Art. 10 of the German-Dutch treaty. That was not binding according to the Supreme Court of the Netherlands, because it was not properly published.
174. OECD Commentary, 1977-2005, Art. 26, para. 5.1.
175. K. Vogel 2003, Art. 26, Rz. 41 and Wisselink 1996, 51.
176. For the Dutch system of treaties, the ones with Switzerland (1951) and the Soviet Union (1986) are exceptions. They do not contain fiscal exchange obligations.
177. OECD Commentary, 1963, Art. 26, para. 4.

Because in the international system of treaties, including the Dutch one, there are treaties with a 'narrow' exchange stipulation, it is important to briefly consider the discussion about it. These stipulations were agreed, in deviation from the Model convention, so it can be assumed that states judged it expedient to agree on an exchange obligation with less scope.[178] Thus, I think that this cannot be interpreted subsequently as 'dynamic'.[179]

According to Commentary 1977 the *narrow exchange* should be considered an exchange about:

- the implementation of Article 12 of the Model convention (data to ascertain the amount of royalties transferred between the payer in country B and the authorized person in country A);
- or vice versa to ascertain whether the recipient of the royalties in country A is really established there, and whether he is the definitive authorized person;
- information essential for the correction of taxable profit from the permanent organization in the other state, through information from the headquarters' accounts, about allocation of the profit between affiliated companies in the different states (Articles 7, 9, 12, and 23, Model convention).

In addition, the narrow exchange of information obligation covers:

- information about the source tax on income abroad levied in the other state, and also (counter)information about the value or the profit of real estate in a state, information about the duration of cross-border work of employees (for the 183-day exception in Article 15 of the Model convention), about the residency of the taxpayer in the other state.[180]

In the revision of 2005 this last category was added as an example, as was the information required for the implementation of Article 25 of the Model convention (mutual agreement procedure).[181]

There was considerable discussion in the literature about the example cited in paragraph 7 sub a of the OECD Commentary. The *sum* paid as royalties by the inhabitants of one country to the recipient in the other country (Article 12, Model convention) is not important for the treaty implementation, but for the calculation of the recipient's income according to the national law of his/her state.[182]

---

178. One reason for this could have been ignorance of the legal system of the other state or uncertainty about his/her (or one's own) practical possibilities to provide information on a broader scale.
179. Likewise, Daniels (1987), 20.
180. *Ibid.*, 19.
181. OECD Commentary, 1977-2005, Art. 26, para. 7, points d and e.
182. See Vogel (2003), Art. 26, Rz. 42, who considers the Commentary too generous in this respect. Narrow exchange can refer only to the question of whether a taxpayer on the basis of the treaty rules should be involved in the taxation or not. The Commentary interpretation does not do justice to the intentions of the states that agreed to a 'narrow exchange of information obligation'.

According to Debatin this stretched the meaning of the term 'narrow exchange' until it no longer concerned a clarification of the stipulation, but a substantial modification.[183]

Similar criticism was aimed also at the information cited in Note 7 of the Commentary concerning the distribution of inter-company profits over affiliated bodies in both states (Article 9, Model convention). They should not fall under the narrow exchange either, because Article 9 of the Model convention only specifies *how* the states must determine the profits of affiliated companies (namely, at arm's length).

In my opinion, the criticized examples definitely involve treaty implementation as well. Article 9, second paragraph, concerning the profit allocation of affiliated companies determines that if the 'at arm's length requirement' is not fulfilled; the state where the event took place has no claim to 'relief of double taxation' by the other state.

Whether that is the case can often only be ascertained through the exchange of information. In the example involving Article 12, 'the amount of royalties' is definitely important for treaty implementation, to determine whether according to Article 12, fourth paragraph, it concerns an 'excessive part' of a royalty between affiliated parties, which would fall as bonus under Article 10 or as other income under Article 21, OECD Model convention.

My conclusion is that all examples given in the Commentary certainly are included in the 'narrow exchange'.

### 4.4.3. Extended Exchange (Model Convention on Double Taxation)

The Commentary gives in paragraph 8 the following examples of exchange for the implementation of national laws:

- data about the pricing practice on goods traded between two states between independent companies, to implement the national tax law;
- data about the pricing practice on goods traded from state A to state B, through state C, with which neither state A nor B have concluded a treaty. State A (the requesting state) can for the implementation of its national law ask state B about the purchase price of the goods in state B. One example is a Dutch A BV that supplies goods to D AG in Switzerland, which they then transfer to B GmbH established in Germany. As there is no exchange of information clause in the Netherlands-Switzerland treaty, the Netherlands cannot request any information from Switzerland, but it can from Germany,

183. Debatin (1978), 382 and Debatin (1977), 2064, 2068, 2117. He referred to inclusion of the example in the 1977 Commentary as 'a shift in the possible contents of the information that could hardly get bigger'. See also Wisselink (1978), 50. *Id.* Daniels (1987), 19. Also this author is of the opinion that information referring to the *amount* of the royalty income does not fall under the narrow exchange, as it could only be important for the implementation of the taxation laws in the state that may impose the taxes by reason of the treaty.

if it wants to ascertain whether the prices charged by the Dutch BV to Switzerland were set at arm's length. That seems practical to me, if in this example Germany can estimate the facts through its own investigation, and there is no need for a German request to Switzerland. In the latter case there is a risk that the German request would not meet the requirement of interest in assessing tax in the treaty relationship between Germany and Switzerland.[184]

In 2004 the following example was added:

– data about the way in which the costs of services provided in country A by a contractor from country B are accounted for in its bookkeeping, in relation to the verification of a claim the contractor made for refund of the VAT in country A.[185] This is the first report of information regarding the taxation of an indirect tax.

### 4.4.4. Objectives of Exchange in Other Exchange of Information Rules

The other exchange of information rules do not offer the possibility for exemption by 'narrow exchange', the OECD treaties have, because the link to the other obligations of the tax treaties is lacking. Information must be exchanged according to Article 1, first paragraph of Directive 77/799 if it 'is useful for the determination of the tax liabilities( . . . )' without specifying from which tax law the tax liability derive.

Article 1, paragraph 1, Strasbourg Convention, formulated the objective of the convention as 'providing administrative assistance in fiscal matters', which I think covers the implementation of both the tax treaties and the national laws of the states.

Article 1 of Council Regulation 1798/2003 on VAT states as its objective (paraphrased): establishing rules for the collaboration of Member States in ensuring the taxation of VAT, levied in the Member States on the basis of the so-called Sixth Directive. The Directive has legal force only through national laws, so we can conclude strictly speaking that Council Regulation 1798/2003 serves only the implementation of the national laws.

The OECD Agreement is intended 'to provide assistance ( . . . ) that is foreseeably relevant to the administration and enforcement of the domestic laws of the Contacting Parties' (Article 1).

---

184. Cf. Vogel (2003), Art. 26, para. 54, 1999. Art. 26, para. 8 to of Commentary 2005 warns that the exchange of information connected to the transfer-pricing problem can be 'a difficult and delicate matter', in connection with the reasons for exemptions concerning professional secrets in the second paragraph of Art. 26.

185. OECD Commentary, 1977-2004, Art. 26, para. 8.

### 4.4.5. Conclusion

The exchange of information provision in the OECD Model convention has a twofold objective: the implementation of the stipulations of the tax treaty itself and the implementation of the states' national tax laws (the so-called 'extended exchange'). In addition, there are several tax treaties in which, in deviation from the Model convention, the exchange obligation is limited to data that could be applicable just for the application of the treaty itself. In the 1977 version of the Commentary, some examples are given. Several of them were criticized, such as the information about the sum of royalties paid from one country to another, and data about the distribution of the inter-company profits between affiliated companies in both states (Articles 12 and 9, Model convention). They are particularly important for ascertaining the tax liabilities in the recipient state and thus fall under the extended information exchange. In my opinion, this also includes treaty implementation because the data could be important for establishing treaty misuse with regard to these categories. Several treaties incorporate only a 'narrow exchange stipulation'. As they are stated in terms that deviate from the text of the Model convention, they should be interpreted literally. In my opinion, the previously mentioned specified information could be exchanged under these treaties as well.

## 4.5. Methods of Exchange

### 4.5.1. Development and Compulsory Nature of the Exchange Methods (OECD Model Convention)

To be able to give an impression of the taxpayer's legal position in the exchange of information (in Chapter 7), it is important to determine as clearly as possible the scope of the exchange obligation that his/her state has in a particular case. This also includes the response to the question of whether the treaty obligation extends to the use of a particular *method* of exchange in a specific case.

According to the different versions of the OECD Commentary, the exchange obligation in the OECD Model convention shows increasing diversity over time concerning the methods to be used as well. Here the influence of the other international regulations for mutual assistance is felt, although sometimes with a delay.

Departing from the basic requirement that the exchanged information must be *'foreseeably relevant'* for the other state, the exchange of information upon *request* from another state can be seen as the most obvious method. With this method the requested (supplying) state at least has some point of reference for the existence of this relevance, although it does have the right (in terms of international law) to review this marginally.[186]

186. I shall elaborate in Ch. 7 on the extent to which the state also has the *duty* toward its taxpayer to review the interest when assessing tax. In any case, the request must contain points of reference required for this review. See also Vogel (2003), Art. 26, Rz. 18 1988.

In this respect, it is quite understandable that all exchange regulations acknowledge at least this method of exchange. In the OECD Agreement, it even is the sole obligatory method, like it was in the first Commentary on the OECD Model convention in 1963.[187] In the revision of 1977,[188] automatic exchange[189] and spontaneous exchange of information were added, in imitation of Directive 77/799, which appeared in the same year.[190] In 2000, paragraph 9.1 of the OECD Commentary emphasized that these methods could be combined and that states could also use other methods, such as the authorization of civil servants in investigations in the requested state and conducting simultaneous investigations.[191] This reveals the influence of the Strasbourg Convention. In the 2005 version of the OECD Commentary I observe that influence as well, where the Commentary mentions for the first time in its history the fundamental right of protection of privacy for taxpayers and the possibility for the states to protect this in their separate treaties.[192]

The choice of wording in paragraph 9 of the OECD Commentary: 'the rule laid down in paragraph 1 (.) *allows* information to be exchanged' (with the previously mentioned methods) induces questions about the obligatory nature of the listing. The objective of the exchange of information provision does not give us cause to interpret the wording as a noncommittal choice option for the states, but rather as a space that must be granted from necessity to be able to vary the methods of exchange according to the circumstances.

### 4.5.2. Development and Compulsory Nature of Methods in Other Regulations

In the Strasbourg Convention, as in Directive 77/799,[193] along with the exchange upon request, automatic exchange was clearly specified as an obligation from the beginning.[194] Spontaneous exchange is made mandatory in several specified situations.[195] To what extent these regulations actually do make automatic or spontaneous exchange of *certain* data obligatory will be treated later (see sections 4.4.5.6. and 4.4.5.7).

---

187. OECD Commentary, 1963, Art. 26, para. 7 states: 'The rule laid down in paragraph 1 of the Art. presupposes that information shall be exchanged only on application.'
188. OECD Commentary, 1977-2004, Art. 26, para. 9.
189. Massive exchange via the creation of data flows.
190. This is the exchange of information that states come across in their own taxation activities.
191. OECD Commentary, 1977-2004, Art. 26, para. 9.1.
192. *Ibid.*, Art. 26, para. 10 refers in this sense to the Council of Europe Convention for the Protection of Individuals with regard to Automatic Processing of Personal Data of 28 Jan. 1981.
193. Directive 77/799 77/799/EU, Arts 2-4.
194. Article 3 Directive 77/799 states: 'The countries supply each other regularly and without prior request (–) with information about groups of cases they specify (–).' Art. 6, Strasbourg Convention, states: 'Given the type of cases, and in agreement with the procedures they (. . .) specify, two or more parties automatically (. . .) exchange data.'
195. Strasbourg Convention, Ch. III, Part I, Arts 5-7.

Council Regulation 1798/2003 for VAT exchange is somewhat different. Exchange upon request[196] is mandatory, as is automatic exchange in several cases. Member States do not have the *obligation* for spontaneous exchange.[197]

Let us discuss the different methods.

### 4.5.3. Exchange upon Request

The scope of the obligation to exchange upon request is delineated in the different exchange regulations in the requirements that the *requesting state* on the one hand and the supplying state on the other must meet.

The 'requirements' for the *requesting* state are: (a) restriction to individualized requests, and (b) the 'exhaustion rule'. For the *supplying* state they are: (c) the effort that must be made to comply with the treaty partner's request.

(a) Individualized Requests (All Rules)

In all the versions of the OECD Commentary, from 1963 to 2005,[198] in Article 3 of Directive 77/799[199] and in Article 5 of the Strasbourg Convention,[200] the starting point is that requests for information should be restricted to specific, individual cases, and not refer to groups of unspecified individuals (so-called 'fishing expeditions').[201] One reason for this can be the remark made in the 1963 Commentary that 'wide-ranging requests' are associated with too many administrative problems for the requested state and therefore must be covered in separate agreements.[202] Neither the revised OECD Commentaries, nor Directive 77/799, nor the often lengthy Commentary to the Strasbourg Convention expresses a more precise motive for this restriction.[203] I am assuming that further interpretation is unnecessary, on the basis of the commonly accepted treaty law axiom of the equality of the treaty parties, on the basis of which it is unacceptable for one state to have to entirely subordinate its own interests to those of its treaty partner.

In contrast to the previous discussion, Article 5 of Council Regulation 1798/2003 contains the obligation to provide information on request, '*also* when the request concerns a *specific case*'. This creates the impression that individual

196. Vo. 1798/2003 Ch. XXII, Part 1, Arts 5-10.
197. Vo. 1798/2003 Ch. IV, Arts 17-21.
198. OECD Commentary, 1963, Art. 26, para. 7, mentions 'specific tax cases'. OECD Commentary, 1977-2005, Art. 26, para. 9, under a: 'with a special case in mind'.
199. Directive 77/799/EU, Art. 3, states: 'Countries can request information about a *special* case from each other.'
200. Strasbourg Convention, Explanatory Report, Art. 4, para. 51 and Art. 5: 'exchange on request will relate to a particular case'.
201. OECD Commentary, 1977-2005, Art. 26, para. 5.
202. OECD Commentary, 1963, Art. 26, para. 7. This further explanation was not repeated in subsequent versions.
203. See Malherbe (1991), 50 (General Report Barcelona Conference). He reports that some states may also request only individualized information from their own 'third taxpayers', and thus cannot ask banks for information about all their clients.

requests are the exception. I consider the reason for this different wording to be that Council Regulation 1798/2003 derives from Council Regulation EU 218/92[204] regarding the wholesale, digitalized exchange of data on intra-community transactions, which is only exceptionally followed by individual requests for information.[205] The new regulation also emphasizes the wholesale, digitalized exchange of data flows.[206] This does not mean that the Member States have an unlimited freedom to make requests. Article 40, first paragraph under a of Regulation 1798/2003 on VAT forbids making requests that burden the petitioned Member State inordinately.

The OECD Agreement, which turned out to be confined to exchange upon request, contains in Article 5, paragraph 5, several specifically described 'requirements' that the requests must meet regarding the requirement of individuality. This must be viewed from the position of the 'committed jurisdictions', which will have understood that in almost all cases *they* would be the requested states, and would like to have a guarantee of sufficient relevance for taxation.[207] Thus, for example, a foreign request must include the identification details of the taxpayer to be investigated, the nature of the information and the form in which it is to be provided. It should also contain reference to its purpose, the reasons for assuming that the information can be found in the requested state, and in who's possession it would be. Sceptics have already noted that as a result of this requirement, the Agreement is more a means to find what the other state already knows than to discover what it does not yet know.[208]

(b) Exhaustion Norm (OECD Model Convention on Double Taxation)

The equality of parties described above, as a norm for interstate relationships, also underlies the second 'requirement' imposed on a request concerning the apportioning of the effort made between the states: the so-called *exhaustion rule/subsidiarity principle.*[209]

This means that the requesting state, before making a request of its treaty partners, must first use its 'usual' sources and possibilities. The term 'usual' in my view refers to the normal 'information gathering powers' a state has at its disposal, such as examining the files in question, asking questions, or starting a tax examination on the taxpayers' premises.[210] From the first version of the OECD

204. Council Regulation of 27 Jan. 1992, OJEU L 24. See Bomer (1993), 1275.
205. Making individual requests was only envisaged in the 'follow-up' of the exchange, if the data about certain transactions did not match those from other states (so-called third phase). See also Ordinance AFZ 93/2990M, V-N 1993/16, 2672.
206. Like data about intra-community transactions, VAT identification numbers, electronic services.
207. OECD Covenant, Art. 5, Commentary para. 57.
208. McLure (2005), 95.
209. Term from Wisselink (1996), 39. In the German literature the term '*Subsidiaritätsprinzip*' is also used. See e.g., Schaumburg (1998), para. 19.7 1328.
210. See also van Raad (1987), 224.

Commentary,[211] the rule links up with information and cooperation obligations of the taxpayers toward the treasury, found in all legal systems.[212] The question that arises in the context of the main motive of this study is to what extent this exhaustion rule influences not only the relations between the states and their taxpayer but also the mutual relations between the states. The question is explored in more detail in section 7.3.1, but to answer it we must first establish here whether not complying with this exhaustion rule *between states* is unlawful. Vogel interprets this aspect of the OECD Commentary strictly. In his opinion, this means that '*die innerstaatlichen Auskunftsquellen müssen ausgeschöpft werden*'. Otherwise, he believes the request cannot be deemed 'necessary'.[213] I see the situation differently. In my opinion the Commentary does not provide cause to conclude that this is a 'rigid' requirement. Paragraph 7 in the 1963 Commentary, which concerns only the exchange upon request,[214] mentions standard sources of information 'which should be relied upon in the first place' and then notes that 'assistance (. . . ) would therefore *normally* be requested when the information from the regularly available sources is insufficient'.[215] This reading has vanished from the later versions of the Commentary, but in my opinion it still applies. The use of the conditional verb form and of the word 'normally' in the original reading definitely does not refer in my view to a *command* to the requesting state. This allows room to evaluate principles such as proportionality and efficacy, which could oppose the implementation of the rule.[216] Given that viewpoint, I think that the request for information, or its provision without observing the exhaustion rule, is not considered unlawful in terms of international law.[217] Especially in the context of the fight

---

211. OECD Commentary, 1963, Art. 26, para. 7. In the revised OECD Commentary, 1977-2005, Art. 26, para. 9.
212. See also Malherbe (1991; General Report, Barcelona Conference), 46 ff. about the limits of the fiscal cooperation obligation of third taxpayers in the different states.
213. Vogel (2003), Art. 26, Rz. 16, thinks that not complying with the standard of exhaustion is a reason for the requested state to refuse an exchange (the same level as a lack of interest in assessing tax).
214. I believe that has to do with the fact that at that time, it concerned the first version of the Commentary, and exchange on request was the most natural method of exchange.
215. OECD Commentary, 1977-2004, Art. 26, para. 9.
216. I refer to Art. 47 a of the Dutch General Tax Law that, despite the treasury's legal right to ask a company for all information concerning foreign mother and daughter companies, nevertheless prescribes in treaty situations to make a request to the treaty partner first; thus the international exhaustion 'rule' is broken. Also, the European Court of Justice appears to advise a direct appeal to the international exchange of information in cases of doubt of whether a national legal stipulation must be applied in cross-border situations (decision C I/93 Halliburton). See also ECJ, 15 May 1997, C-250/959 (*Futura*), in which Luxembourg was not allowed to *demand* of a non-resident company to support its claim with proof of bookkeeping in Luxembourg. The state Luxemburg should have requested information from the other state, instead of laying the burden of proof solely on the company. Also in that case, the exhaustion rule was not decisive.
217. The OECD report Tax Information Exchange between OECD Member Countries, Paris 1994, para. 4 states about this principle only that the providing state can assume that the requesting state has exhausted its own sources.

against tax fraud, it is conceivable to imagine circumstances in which the exhaustion rule is counterproductive. The greatest risk associated with a strict interpretation of this rule for the states is that an investigation in the requesting state (if part of the standard steps to take) could alarm the taxpayer there. It could give him/her the opportunity to warn his/her counterpart in the other state. Then a request to the other state would be useless, because the evidence there would already be gone. I consider this a greater risk for the efficacy of the information exchange than any delay in providing the raw data. Also, the strict manner in which the rule is formulated creates exaggerated expectations about the verifiability. The rationale of the standard of exhaustion, namely, protecting the requested state from unnecessary exertion, means that the state in principle has the right to verify its compliance by the treaty partner.[218] How extensive this verification must be depends on its national legislation.[219] The territoriality principle, however, forbids a state from conducting investigations on the territory of another state without its permission. The requested state cannot do more than rely on what the treaty partner communicates about this point on request. In addition, the interstate trust in the correct implementation of the treaty, which is the foundation of the international exchange, makes verification a delicate issue. In that connection, I think it is better to modify the OECD Commentary, to clearly create room for the requesting state's own judgment about the question of whether in a particular case the exhaustion rule can be observed.

This would make the Model convention align better with the views in Directive 77/799 and the Strasbourg Convention.

Exhaustion Rule in Other Regulations

Article 2 of Directive 77/799 and Article 40, first paragraph under b of Council Regulation 1798/2003 does justice to the open nature of the exhaustion norm as it was discussed earlier. They determine that the requested state is not obliged to comply with a request when it becomes apparent that the requesting state has not first exhausted all possible ways of obtaining the information that it could have used in this situation 'without endangering the intended result'.

This is similar with Article 19 of the Strasbourg Convention. The latter states that the requested state is not obliged to comply with a request if the requesting state has not applied all available means, 'unless this ( . . . ) would lead to inordinate difficulties' for the requesting state.[220] The Commentary envisages only a limited role for this rule and advises the states to use it prudently. The requesting

218. Specific conditions associated with a request can give the state a reason to doubt the requesting country's diligence, such as experiences from the past. Also, for a request to a new treaty partner, where the legal system is still being developed, more detailed verification is sometimes considered desirable. It is rarely possible, however.

219. Vogel (2003), Art. 26, Rz. 17, 1987.

220. In conformance with the scope of the Strasbourg Convention, requests regarding all areas of assistance provision are meant, thus also those concerning the collection and the serving of documents. Strasbourg Convention, jo. Explanatory Report, Art. 19, para. 179.

state's compliance is restricted by the proportionality argument, according to the Commentary.[221]

In these regulations, the idea is thus clearly incorporated that the exhaustion rule is an instrument for ensuring the balance between the states under continuously changing conditions. The *possibilities* for verification are restricted to asking the competent authorities of the requesting state questions about it, as was apparent above. To prevent delay, the Strasbourg Convention requires the states to report the extent to which they exhausted their own options when submitting their request for information.[222] In general, however, the interstate trust between treaty partners will lead states not to ask for further verification.[223]

The requirements imposed on the request for information, specified in Article 5, fifth paragraph of the OECD Agreement, normally include a declaration by the requesting state that it used all available means in its power to collect the information itself (Article 5, fifth paragraph, point g). However, those methods or means are excluded that would lead to 'disproportional difficulties'. Paragraph 63 of the Commentary clarifies that when a comparison of the efforts required by both states reveals that the information could be obtained more easily in the requested state, the exhaustion principle does not apply.[224]

### (c) Investigation Obligation for the Requested State (OECD Model Convention)

The obligation to comply with requests from the treaty partners is not only circumscribed by the requirements imposed on the request itself (and thus on the requesting state; the exhaustion rule) but also by estimating the efforts the requested state is assumed to have made.

The original OECD Model convention from 1963 did not mention this, nor did Note 7 of the relevant Commentary. The efforts which could be expected of the providing state are only considered in the Commentary in the third paragraph of Article 26, point b.[225] This point creates the possibility for the requested state to refuse to comply with a request if the collection of the requested data would conflict with its own legislation and 'the *normal* course of administration'. The 1963 Commentary[226] defined this term as 'the *normal procedure* of tax determination', which was originally understood expressly to mean *not* doing '*special investigations*' for the other state.

This was changed in the OECD Commentaries since 1977. The requested state can no longer make such an *investigation* dependent on the national interest in assessing tax, but is obliged to collect the requested information in the same

221. Strasbourg Convention, jo. Explanatory Report, Art. 19, para. 180.
222. Strasbourg Convention, Art. 18, para. 1(f), and Explanatory Report, Art. 18, para. 175.
223. In Dutch jurisprudence, this has been examined several times. I shall discuss it in s. 8.4.
224. Oberson (2003).
225. OECD Commentary, 1963, Art. 26, para. 11.
226. OECD Model Convention on double taxation 1963, para. 2(b), jo. OECD Commentary, 1963, Art. 26, para. 11.

manner as it would do for its own purposes. 'Eine Kehrwendung' (a turn-about) according to Vogel.[227]

From that time, it has become clear that all means the requested state possesses to obtain information should be used to comply with the other state's request, even if they are only called on for *that* reason.[228] In the 2005 revision of Article 26 of the Model convention, this obligation to investigate was finally added in the treaty text itself.[229] The '*information-gathering measures*' of the requested state must be employed even in cases in which the state does not need the information for its own taxation. According to the Commentary, inclusion of this paragraph reflects a practice that had been going on for years in the affiliated countries.[230] I wonder whether this was the real reason to formulate this obligation so prominently in the treaty text. The referral in the Commentary to the OECD report 'Improving Access to Bank Information for Tax Purposes' from 2000, which contains the same obligation, suggests that this confirmation of the obligation to investigate serves to deprive states of their argument to resist information exchange about savings accounts.[231] The Committee of Fiscal Affairs did not see this expansion of the exertion obligation for the states as a *substantial* modification of the treaty obligation.[232] This means that a tax treaty modelled after the version of 1963 should be interpreted dynamically in this respect.[233] I agree with this. The states' competences and the taxpayers' obligation to cooperate are not expanded in themselves. For these reasons, I agree with the Committee on Fiscal Affairs that also for treaties concluded before 1977 there is an obligation to use all the investigating powers on behalf of the other state. This differs only in treaties incorporating a deviating stipulation on that point *after* that date.

The latest Commentary still emphasizes that states must provide the information to the best of their ability in the form requested by the requesting state, except if this form is unknown in their own administrative practice.[234]

### Obligation to Investigate in Other Regulations

In Directive 77/799 the obligation to investigate is included in the text of Article 2, second paragraph: '*if necessary* the (...) requested state institutes an investigation', the term '*if necessary*' clearly referring to the necessity for a foreign request.

227. Vogel (2003), Art. 26, Rz. 37. 1991.
228. OECD Commentary, 1977-2003, Art. 26, para. 14.
229. Article 26 OECD Model Convention, para. 4.
230. OECD Commentary, 1977-2005, Art. 26, para. 19.6.
231. See also OECD Commentary, 1977-2004, Art. 26, para. 19.6-19.9. See also s. 6.3.1.1.
232. OECD Commentary, 1977-2005, Art. 26, Preliminary Remarks, para. 4, mentions only the change of the confidentiality clause as 'a point of substance'.
233. Vogel (2003), Art. 26, Rz. 36, 1991 concludes the existence of the obligation to investigate because of the second paragraph of Art. 26, on the basis of which the obligation to take *measures* is restricted in certain cases. This suggests that the measures (instituting an investigation) normally are obligatory.
234. OECD Commentary, 1977-2005, Art. 26, para. 10.2.

In the revision of Directive 77/799 by means of Directive 2004/56, a third paragraph was added, that imposes on the requested Member State the obligation to make the same exertion to obtain the information requested by a fellow Member State as if it had to collect information for its own purpose. Similar wordings are found in Council Regulation 1798/2003.[235]

Article 5, paragraphs 2 and 4 of this regulation take the same tack. The third paragraph adds that the state must make the same exertion as if it was acting for its own taxation or on request from another authority in the same state.

Article 5, second paragraph, of the Strasbourg Convention obliges the requested state to take '*all appropriate* measures' to provide the information that is not available in the files of the requested state.[236] The Explanatory Report defines this as all measures available to the state to obtain the information. The obligation to investigate is restricted by the extent to which the requesting state has complied with the exhaustion rule and by the other grounds for exemptions.[237]

In the *OECD Agreement* the obligation to institute an investigation is found in Article 5, third paragraph. In that article, the requested state is obliged to take all *'relevant information-gathering measures'* to provide the requested data, regardless of whether it needs the information for its own taxation. While this matches the 2005 version of Article 26 of the Model convention, the same cannot be said for Article 5, *paragraph 4* of the Convention. In that paragraph, the requested state is obliged to ensure that its civil servants have the competence to collect the data from its taxpayers. Point b of that paragraph contains a listing of those people to whom this information obligation must apply: banks or other financial institutions, natural persons acting as agent or as fiduciary or as representative of legal counsel. According to the Commentary, this listing was intended to make an appeal to the restrictions of the exchange obligation impossible (conflict with the civil order or involving a commercial or professional secret).[238] The competencies to be created must be sufficiently strong to allow data about legal relationships concerning property of companies, trusts, and foundations to be exchanged. From this extensive point in the Commentary, the important role assigned to bank and property information seems aligned with the (difficult) discussion about it conducted in the years before the new millennium. The result of negotiations achieved in this Agreement concerning bank

---

235. Council Regulation (EU) 1798/2003, Art. 5, para. 2 states: 'With a view to the provision of information meant in paragraph 1, the petitioned authority institutes the requested administrative investigation to obtain this information.'
236. Article 5 is included in Ch. III, Part 1 of the Treaty, dedicated to the exchange of information. The other parts of this chapter, namely Assistance with collection (Deel II) and Serving documents (Part III) are not dealt with in this book.
237. Explanatory Report, Art. 5, para. 61.
238. OECD Covenant, Art. 5, para. 4, Commentary paras 46 and 47. The restrictions on the exchange obligation are several conditions specified in all exchange regulations, in which the providing state can consider itself discharged from its obligation. This includes the argument that provision could act against the civil order or reveal a commercial or professional secret. These arguments can also be misused of course. See Ch. 6 for a more extensive treatment.

information is remarkable because the OECD states individually have not come that far.[239] The European Union has only succeeded with difficulty to unite its own members, and dissident states lying within the European geographic region, under the Savings Directive.

#### 4.5.3.1. *Conclusion for Exchange on Request*

Exchange upon request is incorporated in all regulations as an obligation. It is therefore linked to certain 'requirements' for the requesting and for the providing state. The requesting state must restrict itself to individualized requests (except in Council Regulation 1798/2003), with an assumed interest in assessing tax, and must in principle first exhaust its own options. In most regulations it is (implicitly) acknowledged that an overly rigid view of this 'exhaustion principle' can be counterproductive in cases of fraud. The risk of a strict interpretation of the exhaustion rule, having its effects in the gathering of information stage, may be greater for the effectiveness of the information exchange than any delay in its supplying. This implicit recognition, creating some discretionary freedom for the requesting states, is unfortunately lacking in the Commentary on Article 26 of the Model convention.

Since 1977, the supplying (requested) state was obliged to institute an audit if this was necessary. The Commentary on the Model convention relates this obligation to 'the normal procedure of tax determination' in the state. The starting point was that the investigative efforts on behalf of the requesting state must be just as intensive as the ones the state would have conducted for its own taxation. In the different versions of the OECD Commentary, and later in the text of the Model convention, the obligation becomes increasingly strengthened. It applies also when the particular information is not even important for the requested state itself. This obligation to investigate is incorporated in all other exchange regulations as well. This promotes the effectiveness of the exchange. In the OECD Agreement, the obligation to investigate is even associated with an obligation for the requested state to *create* the essential competencies required for this investigation.

### 4.5.4. Simultaneous Auditing

#### 4.5.4.1. *OECD Model Convention, Directive 77/799, Strasbourg Convention, Council Regulation 1798/2003*

In the following sections, two specifications of the obligation to investigate in cases of a foreign request will be considered. They concern the possibility of foreign civil servants being involved in the investigations instituted for their state by the treaty partner, and simultaneous auditing. These methods were adopted

239. Judging by the report Improving Access to Bank Information for Tax Purposes, 2000, published on <www.oecd.org>. See also the criticism from, e.g., Hay 2003 concerning the milder requirements that the OECD imposed on the commitment of its own members.

from Directive 77/799 and the Strasbourg Convention, respectively, in the 2000 Commentary on the OECD Model convention.

Following the listing in the OECD Commentary of 2000, I shall treat simultaneous auditing first.

Along with the Strasbourg Convention,[240] the Commentary cites as 'sources of inspiration' the Model Agreement for the Undertaking of Simultaneous Tax Examinations of 1992 and the study instituted by the Committee on Fiscal Affairs in 1994 into the methods of fiscal collaboration used in the OECD states.[241]

The method of simultaneous investigations was new in practical terms. It did not require expansion of the competencies of the taxation agencies, assuming that their *national* law already granted them the information gathering powers to fulfil the obligation to investigate, incorporated in all exchange regulations after 1977. The method only adds to this that two or more states institute their investigations into taxpayer(s) (or affiliated group) *simultaneously,* on behalf of shared or related interests, each on their own territory.[242] The aim is to exchange the data obtained, to prevent (affiliated) parties 'modifying' the information to be supplied according to an earlier investigation in another state. Because of the mainly organizational nature of this distinction from normal fiscal investigations, I think that even without incorporating an explicit stipulation in the relevant exchange law, for example, in a non-European state that is not a signatory of the Strasbourg Convention, this method can be used under a tax treaty modelled on the Model convention from before 2000.

In the revision of Directive 77/799 by means of Directive 2004/56,[243] this method was also included for direct taxes, likewise in Council Regulation 1798/2003 for VAT.[244] Thus the coherence of international legislation on this issue was ameliorated.

In all exchange of information rules, the states are autonomous in deciding to participate, but under European exchange law their decision-making must be explicitly motivated. The requesting state has to substantiate its request with enough background information to allow the requested state to judge whether a mutual interest is involved.[245] According to the Commentary to the OECD Agreement, the likelihood of this increases in cases of affiliated companies (able to manipulate their inter-company prices), transactions with tax havens, emerging patterns of fraud and 'non-compliance schemes.[246]

---

240. Strasbourg Convention, Art. 8, paras 1 and 2, jo. Explanatory Report, Art. 8, 78 and 79.
241. See the report Tax Information Exchange between OECD Member Countries: A Survey of Current Practices, OECD, Paris 1994.
242. In the same sense, also Vogel (2003), Art. 26, Rz. 24, 1990.
243. Directive 77/799/EU, Art. 8*ter*. most recently revised by Directive 2004/56/EU, dated 21 Apr. 2004.
244. Council Regulation (EU) 1798/2003, Arts 12 and 13, the latter containing the procedure rules.
245. Strasbourg Convention, Art. 8, para. 1, jo. Explanatory Report, Art. 8, para. 79, Directive 77/799 Art. 8*ter*, para. 2, and Council Regulation 1798/2003 Art. 13, para. 1.
246. OECD Model Agreement for the Undertaking of Simultaneous Tax Examinations, Introduction, point C.

The method does not impose additional burdens on the *taxpayer*. In contrast, for example, for a company with offices in different countries, a coordinated investigation can lead to a reduction of the burden, because the investigations take place over a rather short period, rather than occurring one after another in another state.[247] Despite the fact that in my opinion no specific legal basis is needed for this method, I still consider the stipulations useful, because they protect the balance between the efforts of the requesting and the requested state, establish the decision-making competence of each state, and increase the taxpayers' familiarity with the law.

#### *4.5.4.2. Conclusions for Simultaneous Investigations*

Simultaneous investigations form an important supplement to the instruments available for the mutual information exchange, not because the method creates new competencies, but because of the coordinated nature of the collaboration. For exchanging information about (groups of) internationally operating companies, the method can be effective because of the reduced risk for 'leaking' of essential information. For the taxpayers its coordinated nature can mean a reduction of the administrative burden.

### 4.5.5. Attending Investigations Abroad

#### *4.5.5.1. OECD Model Convention on Double Taxation, Strasbourg Convention, Directive 77/799, Council Regulation 1798/2003 on VAT*

Another specific form of exchange upon request is to combine a request to the other state with a request to allow a civil servant of the requesting state *to attend to* the requested investigation in the other country. From Article 6 of Directive 77/799 this method has found its way to Article 9 of the Strasbourg Convention,[248] to Article 11 of the European VAT Regulation, and in 2000 to paragraph 9 of the OECD Commentary.[249]

To find the background to this method of exchange, it is best to start with the extensive Commentary to the Strasbourg Convention, because the European Directive 77/799 and Council Regulation 1798/2003 do not have their own Commentary. The shorter OECD Commentary on this point, incorporated in the 2005 version of the exchange of information provision, will be examined last.

To begin with, I believe that *this* method of exchange could not be implemented *without* an explicit international law basis. Given the important international principle of exclusive territorial jurisdiction, the presence of civil servants from

247. See also Strasbourg Convention, and Explanatory Report, Art. 8, para. 75.
248. Strasbourg Convention Art. 9, jo. Explanatory Report, Art. 9, paras 85-98.
249. OECD Commentary, 1977-2004, Art. 9, para. 9.1. See also Vogel 2003, Art. 26, para. 24, 1989.

one state at investigations in the other state is not self-evident.[250] It is actually considered a 'transgression of an elementary international law principle' as Pijl puts it, not because foreign civil servants 'are working on the territory of another state' (because that is not the method's intention) but because of the risk of the foreign civil servant influencing the investigation process.[251] There is the risk that the interests of *his* state would predominate, which is in conflict with the principle of equality of the treaty parties in international law relationships, and with the interests of the *taxpayer* being investigated. This will be especially the case when the requesting state is more powerful than the requested state. The bilateral implementation agreement made by civil servants, which is advised for initiating this method in the exchange of information rules, in my view offers insufficient democratic legitimacy, that is, if the method is not expressly brought to the attention of the parliaments of these states, so that it could be deemed to be approved by them. In that respect, it is already a problem that the method is not incorporated in the (Model) treaty itself. The fact that the method requires a specific agreement between the states does not help the situation. Similar agreements made be officials are rarely presented to Parliaments.[252] Apart from this, the states are not *obliged* in any of the regulations to admit civil servants at tax examinations. That does not relieve them however of the obligation to provide the requested information.

#### *4.5.5.2. Attendance at Investigations Abroad: Strasbourg Convention*

The Explanatory Note to the Strasbourg Convention associates the states' freedom of choice with the principle of sovereignty. On these grounds, it recognizes that the presence of the other state's officials in investigations could be considered an 'infringement of the country's sovereignty'.[253] However, rejection of the method by a state does not mean that the request for information can also be refused.[254]

The Explanatory Note assumes that the attendance is limited to the part of interest for the requesting state[255] and that the method is reserved for special cases, like an exceptionally large fiscal interest, a complex matter, or the fact that a certain case can be considered a model for a pattern of tax evasion.[256] The benefits

250. Vogel (2003), Art. 26, Rz. 25, 1990, calls this method: 'the most extensive form of cooperation between tax authorities'.
251. Pijl (1998), 341, correctly criticized the bilateral agreement between the Netherlands and Canada concerning the attendance of civil servants at investigations, because Canada was not a signatory of the Strasbourg Convention, nor a European Member State. In addition, the information clause in the Canadian – Dutch tax treaty did not provide for this method at that time, and neither did the OECD Model Convention. See also s. 4.4.8.
252. In all regulations specifying this method, it is assumed that states wanting to implement it will make bilateral agreements. Mostly neither these agreements are presented to parliaments.
253. See Strasbourg Convention, jo. Explanatory Report, Art. 9, para. 87.
254. Strasbourg Convention, Art. 9, jo. Explanatory Report, Art. 9, para. 94.
255. *Ibid.*, Art. 9, para. 93.
256. *Ibid.*, Art. 9, para. 91. These are also the limiting conditions agreed in Dutch bilateral agreements with other parties to the Strasbourg Convention, or with other Member States of the European Union and the Netherlands Antilles.

of this method include the speed with which the cooperation can take place, its less formal nature, and the production of a more complete and coherent image of the international relationships of certain taxpayers, which is especially important in cases of tax fraud.[257] Given the Preamble to that Convention, and its appeal to the states to protect the interests of their taxpayers, this one-sided emphasis on the benefits of the informal nature of the method is somewhat disappointing. It is this informal nature that can carry risks for taxpayers. The Explanatory Note leaves the states free to agree that the requested investigation will be conducted *by* and under the complete control of the fiscal authorities *of* the requested state,[258] or to give the visiting civil servant his/her own implementing competencies within the legal framework of the requested state.[259] The latter option, in my view, is risky (perhaps too risky), given the balance between the two states' officials and the risk of unequal positions.

#### *4.5.5.3. Attendance at Investigations Abroad: Commentary on OECD Model Convention on Double Taxation*

Since 2000, the OECD Commentary also includes the possibility of conducting 'a tax examination abroad', under the condition that the laws of the states allow this. In the 2005 version of the Commentary, paragraph 9.1 likewise mentions the (more extensive) competence to interview taxpayers or to investigate his accounts.[260] This suggests an active step by the foreign civil servant. The example given by the Commentary in my view is confusing: the case in which a taxpayer may keep his accounts in the requested state.[261] In those cases, I think this does not involve an *exchange* of information, but the implementation of the national tax law of the requesting state, which of course can take place only with the explicit consent of the country. The exchange of information obligation is not affected by this. The same misunderstanding is expressed in the OECD Survey of Current Practices of 1994. Assuming that this report is based on statements from the OECD states, we can conclude that not all states fully comprehend this instrument of the 'participation of foreign tax officials'.[262]

257. Strasbourg Convention, Explanatory Report, para. 85 gives cases of international work loan.
258. Strasbourg Convention, Art. 9, para. 2, elaborated in Explanatory Report, Art. 9, paras 95 and 96.
259. Explanatory Report, Art. 9, para. 88, but then within the legal framework of the requested state.
260. Some states require for the institution of a fiscal investigation at least also a national interest in assessing tax, for example, in Japan and the United Kingdom. (See Observation 21 on the Commentary.)
261. OECD Commentary, 1977-2004, Art. 26, para. 9.1.
262. In 1994, the presence of foreign civil servants at investigations in the requested state was not yet included in the OECD Model convention. Section 88 of the Survey vaguely describes the exchange practice of states of the different international communities.

### *4.5.5.4. Attendance at Investigations Abroad: Community Rules*

Directive 77/799 has incorporated this method since its origin in 1977, like the Council Regulation 1798/2003. In Article 11 of this Regulation it is even taken further. Member States have the option for foreign civil servants to visit the tax offices of the requested state and have access to certain files there.[263] Given the Preamble, the intention for this extension must undoubtedly have been to accelerate the speed and the efficacy of the exchange. This also entails the risk that the visiting foreign civil servant may act too independently, and in doing so may infringe on the fiscal confidentiality in the visited as well as in the recipient state,[264] not to speak of the lack of transparency. The requirement of giving copies of relevant documents directly to the visiting civil servant creates risks against the background of the administrative law concepts about confidentiality of the taxpayer whose assessment is to be established, and freedom of information for the public. The obligation for the states to explicitly assign a competent civil servant for this method of information exchange does not take this risk away.[265] It can at best *limit* the risk of unlawful government actions, under the condition that these specially assigned officials are well trained and consciously supervised. The risks for the taxpayer's position mentioned here will not be entirely eliminated.[266]

### *4.5.5.5. Attendance at Investigations Abroad: OECD Agreement*

Article 6 of the Agreement describes two possible forms of attendance of foreign officials: the first, established in the first paragraph, maintains that a state permits the officials of the other state to interview taxpayers and examine their files, if they have received written consent to do so. The Commentary expressly states that the decision to permit access to a foreign official lies solely with the requested state, and that the visiting official does not have any competence to force opening of the files.[267] For states with few personnel available to deal with requests for information, this could be a good alternative, according to the Commentary.[268] Although

263. If the files contain the requested information, copies must be provided to the visiting civil servant (Art. 11, para. 1, Council Regulation 1798/2003).
264. States have their own fiscal confidentiality legislation, which is contravened by the exchange obligation if in a particular case, the conditions for the exchange of information are met (the proper treaty basis, and information falling within the objective scope of the prevailing obligation). The obligation to confidentiality of the supplying state is then transferred to the receiving state through the so-called confidentiality clause in Art. 26, para. 1 (after 2005: Art. 26, para. 1).
265. See Art. 3, para. 4, Vo. The competent civil servant is appointed as competent authority for the provision of information, under the guidance of the central competent authority. He may make requests independently and provide other states with information.
266. See Ch. 7 for the general position of the taxpayers being investigated.
267. OECD Covenant, Art. 6, Commentary, Art. 6, para. 66. This method somewhat resembles the data collection at tax offices by foreign civil servants in Council Regulation 1798/2003 (Art. 11, para. 1). There is, however, no condition imposed of gaining the taxpayer's consent.
268. OECD Covenant, Art. 6, Commentary, Art. 6, para. 67.

that may be true, the requirement of written consent from the taxpayer, however positive it seems in terms of legal protection, will not promote the actual use of this possibility.[269]

In addition, a requested state *can*, on the basis of Article 6, second paragraph, permit a foreign civil servant to be present at 'the appropriate part' of an investigation on its territory, started on request of a treaty partner. The Commentary instructs that such – thoroughly justified – requests for attendance should be made only for important affairs, and when the attendance provides benefit for the results of the investigation. The interest of the investigation should not be measured only by the quantity of tax yield in each case, but by a possible link with structural patterns occurring in special branches, says the Commentary.[270]

#### *4.5.5.6. Conclusion for Attendance at Foreign Investigations*

Permitting a civil servant from the requesting state to attend an investigation conducted for his/her state represents a breakthrough of the principles of sovereignty and territorial jurisdiction characterizing international law. Therefore, I believe that this method should be based on a relevant treaty stipulation. Separately from this, an agreement made by public servants of the two states has too little democratic legitimacy, and there are international law and public law risks for excessive influence exerted by the civil servant. This could especially occur when the states are unequal in power. Therefore, in my view, the fact that the legal foundation of this method is only in the OECD Commentary, makes it questionable, because it does not involve explicit mentioning in the separate tax treaties themselves. The Explanatory Notes sent to Parliaments in the ratification procedure should make up for this deficiency.

In all regulations, it is assumed that for the implementation of this method between states a bilateral agreement is needed, to establish the conditions under which this can take place.

The Strasbourg Convention emphasizes that this method is meant for important and complicated affairs and that the visiting official may only be present at those parts of the investigation that are relevant for his/her state. The same applies in the OECD Agreement.

Council Regulation 1798/2003 for VAT and the OECD Agreement both acknowledge the possibility of attendance outside a specific investigation, during which the visiting civil servants can examine files. I think that the use of this method requires extensive regulation, because of the risk of infringing the confidentiality rule and of the lack of transparency concerning government actions. The Agreement also recognizes the possibility that the visiting official could conduct interviews. Making this dependent on the written consent of the taxpayers involved removes much of the risky nature of this method, but calls its usefulness into doubt.

---

269. Gyönghi Végh (2002), classifies this under the 'first line of protective measures' of the OECD Agreement, formed by the restrictions on the exchange obligation.
270. OECD Covenant, Art. 6, Commentary, Art. 6, para. 67.

### 4.5.6. Automatic Exchange

#### *4.5.6.1. OECD Model Convention on Double Taxation*

Even if the exchange upon request is considered the oldest and most obvious exchange obligation, the first OECD Commentary confirmed that before 1963 bilateral agreements referred to the 'regular and automatic exchange of information'.[271]

Since 1977, it has been possible according to the Commentary ('the rule laid down in paragraph 1 *allows* . . . ') to implement automatic data exchange. This is a form of exchange in which certain categories of income are systematically provided to the other state. The wording refers to a certain periodicity and quantity of data.[272] This is a manner of exchange in which the taxpayer does not have to be approached directly in each individual case because the exchanged data concern files of already collected information, which were prepared with the help of withholding agents or taxpayers. The method is intended for situations in which treaty partners recognize structural risks of tax evasion resulting from their economic relationships. They can try to avoid a multitude of such requests by instituting a flow of data through arranging a bilateral agreement. Once the agreement exists, exchange based upon it is obligatory. The choice to make such an agreement depends so strongly on practical and organizational circumstances in the states (for example, the massive quantity and periodic availability of certain data) that it cannot be imposed as an obligation within the framework of the Model convention. The good faith governing the legal relationship between the states demands, however, that a state would consider a proposal to initiate a flow of data seriously. The starting points must be that the prevailing standards regarding the benefit and usefulness of data in one state cannot be imposed on other states[273] and that the advantages and disadvantages are evenly shared.[274]

The Committee on Fiscal Affairs considers automatic exchange an important instrument, as is evident from the development since 1981 of standardized forms,[275] a Standard Magnetic Format,[276] a Model Memorandum of Understanding

271. OECD Commentary, 1963, Art. 26, para. 8. It is thus striking that Vogel (2003), Art. 26, Rz. 19 feels that in treaties modelled after the Model, automatic exchange is not acceptable. He also recognizes that this is not considered so by most countries in practice and that Germany also makes agreements for automatic regulations (e.g., with the Netherlands) on the basis of a similar treaty.
272. OECD Commentary, 1977-2004, Art. 26, para. 9.
273. Vogel (2003), Art. 26, Rz. 33, 1990, discusses a decision of the Swiss Federal Court (no. 101, 1b, BGE 160) from 1975, between Switzerland and the USA, in which that is established.
274. See also the OECD report 'Tax Information Exchange between OECD Member Countries' of 1994, para. 79.
275. See the 'Recommendation of the Council Concerning a Standardized Form for Automatic Exchange of Information under international tax agreements', C (81) 39/FINAL (5 May 1981).
276. See the 'Recommendation of the Council Concerning a Standardized Magnetic Format for Automatic Exchange of Tax Information', C(92) 50/FINAL (23 Jul. 1992), revised in 'Recommendation of the Council of the OECD on the Use of the revised Standardized Magnetic Format for Automatic Exchange of Tax Information', C (97) 30 FINAL (10 Jul. 1997).

for the automatic exchange of information, and from the attempts to introduce an international Tax Identification Number,[277]

In the past few years, this method of cooperation has been practiced by the Netherlands increasingly often.[278]

Keen and Ligthart correctly point out that in automatic exchange, 'the real issue' is whether and to what extent the states can actually use this exchanged information for their taxation.[279] This requires technological and organizational adjustments in the separate states.

#### *4.5.6.2. Automatic Exchange in the Strasbourg Convention and Directive 77/799*

In Article 6 of the *Strasbourg Convention* ('parties exchange'), in Article 3 of Directive 77/799 ('the Member States provide each other') and in Article 17 of Council Regulation 1798/2003 ('the Member States switch to'), the automatic exchange of information is formulated as an obligation.[280] The question is how this relates to what I observed in connection with the Model convention about this method's dependence on the practical and organizational possibilities of the states, and the resulting non-obligatory nature of this manner of exchange. In my opinion, the differences in nature of the stipulation in various regulations are justified because Directive 77/799, Council Regulation 1798/2003 and the Strasbourg Convention are multilateral agreements, in which the affiliated states explicitly focus on the common objective: arranging mutual assistance that is as efficient as possible. Their intention thus differs from that of the treaty partners in fiscal treaties, which conclude a tax treaty for various reasons. The common commitment of parties in a multilateral agreement means that all states may be expected to implement the differences in the methods specified in the agreement as faithfully as possible and thus take any essential national measures. In Directive 77/799 the implementation obligation is generated by the supranational nature of the

277. Recommendation of the OECD Council on the Use of Tax Identification Numbers in an International Context, C (97) 29 FINAL (23 Mar. 1997). See also OECD Commentary, 1977-2005, para. 9.
278. So-called Memoranda of Understanding were concluded with France, Belgium, Germany, Canada, Denmark, Australia, Estonia, Lithuania, Sweden, Poland and Spain between 1996 and 2004. This Memorandum concerns the (automatic) exchange of information and sometimes also the attendance of foreign civil servants.
279. Keen/Ligthart (2006), 91.
280. Article 6, Strasbourg Convention states: 'with regard to categories of cases and in alignment with procedures that they agree upon, two or more parties automatically exchange (. . . ) data'. Art. 3 of Directive 77/799 reads: 'the Member States provide each other with (. . . ) information for groups of cases they specify in the framework of the consultation procedure as alluded to in Art. 9'.

    Art. 17 of Council Regulation 1798/2003 states: 'without prejudice to the stipulations in Chs V and VI (intra-community transactions and e-commerce, ASG), the Member States switch over to automatic or structured exchange of the information specified in Art. 1 in the following situations (. . . )'.

European legal order, while the Regulation creates obligations directly. After all, the imperative formulation of the automatic exchange method in Directive 77/799 does not appear to guarantee a flourishing practice of the exchange of data flows, as is apparent in the Preamble to the new Council Regulation 1798/2003. It mentions the limited scope of the automatic (and spontaneous) exchange of information under Directive 77/799 as one of the reasons to subsume assistance in the field of VAT under one regulation.

#### *4.5.6.3. Automatic information exchange: Council Regulation 1798/2003 on VAT*

Council Regulation 1798/2003 collects automatic and spontaneous exchange together under Chapter IV: 'Exchange without prior request'. Article 17 mentions 'automatic or *structured* automatic exchange'. According to the definition (Article 2, point 14, Council Regulation), this latter term means the systematic exchange of specified data, at the moment that they are found. Although with automatic exchange, the data to be provided already are available in data files, and it can be done at a set time, structured automatic exchange is dependent on the moment at which the data are found during examinations for the state's own taxation. This method closely resembles spontaneous exchange, which will be treated in section 4.4.5.7.

I define the term 'structured' based on the entirety of measures that are meant to enable the inspectors to be alert for these data during individual tax examinations and to ensure that they reach the competent exchange authorities. The Member States are obliged to take these 'administrative and organizational measures'.[281]

Automatic or structured exchange is made mandatory in several cases:

- when the taxation in the country of destination depends on information from the country of origin;
- when infringement of the VAT legislation in the other country is suspected;
- and when in the other state there is a risk of tax loss.

This enumeration refers to fixed patterns of fraud risks already recognized by the Member States and resulting from the economic relationships between the Member States of the European Union.[282]

Article 18 of the Council Regulation prescribes specific agreements between states, in which the data categories, the deadlines and other practical aspects are arranged. Participation in the exchange of particular categories of data and the choice of the method of exchange (automatic or structured automatic) are determined by the separate states. This makes it possible that the European Commission orchestrates multilateral agreements, in which a more differentiated participation by the different states can provide efficiency advantages, depending on the extent to which specific risks occur in their system. One example of this is Council

281. Council Regulation 1798/2003, Art. 20.
282. These economic concerns are also often 'tax-driven' as well.

Regulation 1925/2004 (Implementation regulation),[283] which lists several categories of data that should be exchanged automatically or in a structured way. This concerns data on non-resident taxpayers, about statements of intra-community deliveries that do not match the statements from the communal Value Added Information Exchange System (VIES)[284] and data about distance marketing. The exchange of data on intra-community deliveries of new means of transportation (cars, airplanes and vessels, motorbikes), for which a separate agreement was concluded earlier,[285] is included under the regulation. For all categories, the Member States must state which of the methods (automatic or structured) they choose. The exchange takes place as far as possible via the computerized information-exchange systems supplied by the European Commission, and according to the legal rules of Council Regulation 1798/2003.

#### *4.5.6.4. Conclusion*

Automatic exchange (the initiating of data flows) is a suitable method for states to counteract the structural risks for tax fraud as a result of their specific economic relationships. The method is strongly dependent on the technological developments and the level of organization in the states and can therefore not be made mandatory outside the EU. The use of the data received will require technical and organizational measures in the states.

### 4.5.7. Spontaneous Exchange

#### *4.5.7.1. OECD Model Convention*

Spontaneous exchange has been defined since 1977 in the OECD Commentary with the example of a state 'having acquired *through certain investigations*, information that it supposes to be of interest to the other State'. The requirement that the information to be exchanged must be 'necessary' or 'foreseeably relevant' for the taxation of the treaty partner is difficult to fulfil in such situations, especially if must serve implementation of its national law. The Commentary therefore imposes the lighter requirement of *assumed* interest in assessing tax to make supplying the information legal.[286]

---

283. Council Regulation (EU) 1925/2004, of 27 Oct. 2004, PbEU L 331 of 5 Nov. 2004 on implementation of several stipulations in Council Regulation (EU) 1798/2003.
284. The VIES system is a computerized file (**V**alue Added **I**nformation **E**xchange **S**ystem), in which the states provide each other with all intra-Community deliveries supplied by companies in their state. The delivery in the one state must correspond to an acquisition in the other state.
285. Agreement of 7 Nov. 2002, Memo, State Secretary for Finances, dated 29 Nov. 2002, no. DGB2002/6753M, Stcrt. no. 234. See also (V-N 2002/60.15). A list of the choices the states made in the methods of exchange was included in this agreement: automatic or 'intensified spontaneous'. The latter term was replaced in the Implementation Council Regulation by the term 'structured' exchange.
286. OECD Commentary, Art. 26, 1977-2005, para. 9, point c.

Also, with regard to spontaneous exchange, the question arises of the obligatory nature of the method, in connection with the question of whether this also applies to treaties modelled after the older Model convention.

In my opinion, the first question should be answered in the affirmative, from the viewpoint that in 1977 the states wanted to create an information obligation 'to the widest possible extent'.[287] This implies that the exchange of information about individual cases must not only depend on the existence of a request for information. Facts of which a state is unaware simply *cannot* provide an incentive to request information.[288] Moreover, the information is generated as a 'by-product' of the states' national taxation activities, and so there is no disproportionate effort needed in the supplying state, nor can there be a lack in practical options to comply with this obligation.

The second question, regarding the legitimacy of spontaneous exchange on the basis of treaties modelled after the 1963 Model convention has led to a discussion in literature.[289] This was strongly influenced by the authors' views on the role of the Commentary in the interpretation of the OECD Model convention, and by the associated reading of the dynamic treaty interpretation established by the Committee on Fiscal Affairs there (see section 3.6).

Several (Dutch) writers feel that for spontaneous exchange under a treaty modelled after the 1963 OECD Model (which acknowledged only exchange on request) an explicit agreement must be made between the states[290] or that spontaneous supplying of information under an 'old' treaty is only justified if in the relevant exchange of information provision a specific fraud-combating objective is provided.[291] Others feel that the 1963 version of the Commentary is overruled on this point by the revised version.[292] Vogel is of the opinion, on the one hand, that tax treaties should be interpreted according to the version of the Model convention that was valid when they were created (which would mean that for treaties based on the 1963 version, the spontaneous provision of information would not be 'permitted'), but on the other hand, admits that the large majority of OECD countries feel that spontaneous exchange under the treaties is permitted. For both viewpoints, he can cite supporting decisions from German, Belgian, and Dutch jurisprudence.[293]

In my opinion, there is nothing in the wording of the first paragraph of Article 26 that would allow us to suppose that the intention was to *forbid* or to exclude spontaneous exchange. Nor does paragraph 7 of the 1963 Commentary imply a *ban*

287. *Ibid.*, Art. 26, 1977-2005, para. 3.
288. Vogel (2003), Art. 26, Rz. 22 1989, refers to German jurisprudence in which an obligation to provide information spontaneously is only accepted in cases in which due to a failure to provide it, no taxation would be done in either state.
289. The 1963 version of the OECD model Commentary only mentions exchange on request.
290. See Daniels (1987), 35 and Wisselink (1996), 44.
291. van Raad/Milders (1988), 60.
292. van de Ven (1990a), 19.
293. Vogel (2003), Art. 26, Rz. 20, 1988.

of the use of other methods of information exchange.[294] I feel that not listing these methods in the 1963 version was due to the states' lack of experience with the recognition of the cross-border aspects of their subjects' activities. In that light, the expansion of the methods of exchange can be considered the response to the questions states struggled with in practice. I therefore agree with the Committee on Fiscal Affairs that this modification in the Commentary is a *clarification* of the original concept, not a substantial modification. Therefore, in my view, Article 26 of the Model convention should be interpreted dynamically, like is recommended in the Introduction to the Commentary.[295]

The manner in which the information is exchanged within the various methods (in writing, or via secure electronic communication systems) is left to the states to decide.[296]

#### *4.5.7.2. Spontaneous Exchange in Directive 77/799*

In Directive 77/799 spontaneous exchange is incorporated in Article 4, first paragraph, as an obligation:

> The competent authority of the Member State shares, without prior request, the information specified in Article 1, paragraph 1, that it is aware of also with the competent authority of every other interested Member State, in the following situations:
>
> a) the competent authority of the Member State has reason to suspect that in another Member State an abnormal exemption or reduction of tax exists;
> b) a taxpayer obtains an exemption or reduction of tax in one Member State which for him/her should amount to taxation or increase of tax in the other state;
> c) transactions between a taxpayer of one Member State and a taxpayer of another Member State are routed through one or more other countries in such a way that a tax savings is generated in one or both Member States;
> d) the competent authority of a Member State has reason to suspect that tax saving took place in another Member State by means of an artificial transfer of profits within a group of companies.

> With this 'framework', the general requirement of fiscal relevance of the information to be exchanged, which is not always 'foreseeable' for the providing state, is objectified in general terms.

---

294. See *Ibid.*, Rz. 23, 1989. An example of Dutch jurisprudence is the decision by the Council of State of 24 Jul. 1991, V-N 1991/5, 2476 about the existence or not of an obligation for spontaneous exchange based on the treaty with Belgium. The judge decided that the obligation existed, although the tax treaty was concluded under the operation of the 1963 OECD Model convention on double taxation. This decision hardly has a justification.
295. OECD Commentary, 1977-2004, Introduction, para. 33.
296. OECD Commentary, 1977-2005, Art. 26, para. 10.

The enumeration contains the minimum obligation for the spontaneous provision of information.

- On the basis of Article 4, paragraph 2, this obligation *can* still be specified in bilateral negotiations by states. Then they can use a collective analysis of certain patterns emerging in the cross-border contacts of their taxpayers, and try to combat these through spontaneous exchange.[297]
- Article 4, paragraph 3 opens up the possibility for states to provide each other spontaneously with the type of information specified in the first paragraph that they are aware of in other, unanticipated or unforeseeable cases.

The reading of the enumeration in Article 4, paragraph 1 was not clear from the start. This was apparent from the prejudicial questions the Dutch Council of State put to the European Court of Justice in 2000 about the interpretation of Article 4 of Directive 77/799. The questions were (paraphrased):

- does the term 'reduction of tax' mean that this reduction must be contained in an express action by the competent authorities of the other Member State?
- how should the term 'abnormal' be defined in this connection?
- if Article 4, paragraph 1 under a of the Directive is not applicable, can an obligation for the spontaneous provision of information be derived from Article 4, third paragraph?

On 13 April 2000 the European Court of Justice decided that: the reduction of tax does not have to be the result of an explicit action by the other Member State, but there must be a suspicion that this exemption or reduction will actually take place. The term 'abnormal' must be defined as 'unjustified'. After supplying these answers, the Court did not see the necessity for answering the third question about the obligatory nature of the third paragraph of Article 4 of Directive 77/799.[298]

#### *4.5.7.3. Spontaneous Exchange in Council Regulation 1798/2003 on VAT*

Council Regulation 1798/2003 distinguishes between exchange upon request and exchange without prior request, discussed in separate chapters. Chapter IV covers the automatic and the structured automatic, as well as the spontaneous, exchange. According to the definition stipulation this means irregular provision of information

297. One example is (was) the sizeable emigration of pensioners from the Netherlands to countries such as Belgium and France, which led to the suspicion of tax evasion. The Netherlands can at the time of learning about the emigration request the other state to keep it informed, so that tax can be levied.

298. HvJ EU, C-420/98, (W-N). See V-N, 1999/14.8, and V-N 2000/22.7 (decision), and European Taxation, July 2000, 22.

without prior request to another state.[299] According to Article 19 of the Council Regulation, there is no obligation to do so.

#### 4.5.7.4. *Spontaneous Exchange in the Strasbourg Convention*

Just like Directive 77/799, Article 7 of the Strasbourg Convention makes spontaneous exchange mandatory in several cases. The enumeration matches that of Directive 77/799, to which the Commentary refers.[300] In addition, Article 7, second paragraph, obliges the states to take implementation measures to enable spontaneous exchange. After all, the assumptions about eventual risks of tax evasion in the other state (also mentioned in Directive 77/799) can only arise in the inspections conducted for its own taxation. According to the Commentary, it is the individual weighing and assessment by the inspector ('the experienced eye') that generates the benefit of this method compared to automatic exchange.[301] To accomplish this, the tax authorities must be aware of the importance of this method for the exchange of information as a whole, and the information found must reach the competent exchange authorities quickly.

#### 4.5.7.5. *Conclusion*

Spontaneous exchange of information is the supplying of information that is not requested. It is found by states in their own taxation activities, and deemed of importance for the other state. The method is not incorporated in the text of the OECD Model convention, as it is in Directive 77/799 and the Strasbourg Convention. Nevertheless, I think that it is considered obligatory in the OECD law also, because of the intention, laid down in the Commentary to create as broad an information obligation as possible. The spontaneous exchange of information forms an essential supplement in that context. In the Commentary on the Model convention, the assumption of relevance for taxation in the other state is not made concrete by naming specific cases in which the risk existed of an inadequate taxation in the other state, as was done in Directive 77/799 and the Strasbourg Convention. The Regulation 1798/2003 on VAT does indeed mention the spontaneous exchange, but as a possibility, not as an obligation. The OECD Agreement does not include the spontaneous exchange at all.

## 4.6. Subjects of Exchange

Along with the objective restriction of the exchange obligation (in terms of the *information* that can be provided), the obligation is also defined through the *subjects* involved in the exchange. These are the taxpayers to whom the exchanged

299. Council Regulation (EU) 1798/2003, Art. 2, point 14.
300. Strasbourg Convention, Explanatory Report, Art. 7, para. 70.
301. *Ibid.*, paras 72 and 73.

information refers and the exchanging authorities. I believe that the taxpayers from whom the exchanged information is obtained should also be considered subjects in the exchange.

## 4.6.1. Circle of Taxpayers/Subjects

### *4.6.1.1. OECD Model Convention on Double Taxation*

In the 1963 version of Article 26, the *circle* of taxpayers who could be involved in the exchange of information corresponded to the entitlement to treaty protection and thus to residency in one of the treaty states (or both of them).[302] In fact, the unequivocal establishing of the fiscal residence was originally one of the most important reasons for creating the information exchange clause.

Since the revision of the Model convention in 1977, Article 1 of the tax treaty did no longer applied for the implementation of the information clause, 'so that the information may include particulars about non-residents', according to the Commentary.[303] This clearly reveals the unique nature of Article 26, compared with the entirety of the treaty stipulations.[304] This means that the information obligation also applies to a taxpayer who has only a source of income in both countries, without there necessarily being a case of double residency.[305] In contrast to the Committee on Fiscal Affairs, which sees this addition as a clarification of the original text,[306] I think that the revision of the stipulation in 1977 has brought about a substantial expansion of the subjective scope, which cannot influence the interpretation of the 'older' treaties.[307]

The 'non-residents' about whom information can be requested and provided will often not be the ones whose tax liabilities must be established. France, for example, for purposes of levying corporate tax there, can ask the Netherlands for information about payment transactions of a shareholder from a French corporation that is resident neither in France nor in the Netherlands, to determine whether through this shareholder money is being recycled to other shareholders of the corporation.[308] This applies also to those who are indeed resident in one of the

302. OECD Model Convention on double taxation 1977-2005, Art. 1 jo. Art. 4.
303. OECD Commentary, 1977-2005, Art. 26, para. 2.
304. Vogel (2003), Art. 26, Rz. 55, talks about a stipulation that is 'removed from the area of application of the other regulations of the DBA standards'.
305. See also van de Ven (1990b), 13.
306. The Committee on Fiscal Affairs states in the report Tax Information Exchange between OECD Member Countries: A Survey of Current Practices, 1994, para. 22 ff., that the personal scope was never restricted to inhabitants of the treaty states. Incorrectly, I think.
307. In the same sense Vogel (2003), Art. 26, Rz. 78. See also Gangemi (1990), 28, who feels that the addition, if intended as a clarification, is entirely unnecessary. He considers the 'acceptance' or not of the dynamic interpretation primarily a result of a state's (or a judge's) opinion about the status of the Commentary. Docclo (1999), reports that also in the Belgian literature the modification of Art. 26 of the 1977 Model Convention is not considered a clarification of this point. Also, van Raad/Milders (1988), 62.
308. The information must then be collected e.g., by a Dutch bank.

treaty states. To ascertain the profit of a corporation in country A, country B can be asked to collect information from transaction partners of this company.

Despite this subjective expansion, Wisselink's description of Article 26 Model convention as a framework for an 'unlimited and worldwide sphere of action for information exchange' could be criticized.[309] On the basis of its confidentiality clause, the information received from a treaty partner may not be transferred to *third* countries without a separate agreement in the tax treaty, as the European Directive 77/799 allows.[310]

The position of the taxpayers in the involved states (as subject of an information request or as supplier of information), which is the subject of this study, is not explicitly considered in the exchange of information provision. Only the Commentary refers sporadically to it in the interpretation of the grounds for exemptions from the exchange, which I shall discuss in Chapter 6. An implicit reference to the position of the taxpayer is to be found in the confidentiality clause. Its contents will be discussed in detail in the next chapter.

#### *4.6.1.2. Circle of Taxpayer/Subjects in Other Regulations*

The Strasbourg Convention states in Article 1, third paragraph, that assistance must be provided 'regardless of whether the person involved is an inhabitant or a subject of a Party or of another state'. That treaty thus has the same subjective scope as the OECD stipulation since 1977.[311]

Directive 77/799 has no separate stipulation concerning the subjective scope, and also the Preamble makes no allusion to this whatsoever. Starting from the objectives of the Directive given in the Preamble, which are the ensuring of a correct national taxation in the Member States, the protecting of fiscal justice, and the countering of disturbances in competition resulting from international tax fraud, it seems unlikely that a limitation to information about inhabitants is meant.[312] I maintain that between the Member States all information that could be relevant for taxation can be exchanged, even if they concern non-residents of the states. The same is true for the Regulation on VAT.

The OECD Agreement covers the exchange of information with former tax paradises, 'committed jurisdictions', where in fiscal legislation the term

309. Wisselink (1996), 46.
310. OECD Commentary, 1977-2005, Art. 26, para. 12.2 (new) opens up the possibility of transferring the data received to a third state only if the states arranged this explicitly in their mutual tax treaty.
311. This thus also includes the assistance with collection and the serving of official documents, which the Strasbourg Convention also envisages. Strasbourg Convention, jo. Explanatory Report, Art. 1, para. 17 to 22.
312. Gangemi (1990), 43 seems to assume so. This means he has not answered the question of whether two Member States on the basis of the Directive can exchange data about non-residents *outside* both Member States. (It is also striking that he incorrectly considers the Directive as applying only to direct taxes, while at that time Directive EU/79/1070 was already expanded to cover indirect taxes).

'inhabitant' does not have the meaning it has in the OECD Model convention or in Community law. Article 2 of the Agreement determines the subjective scope of the agreement in terms other than residency. Information must be provided if the authorities have it, or it is *in the possession* of or under the power of disposal ('control') of 'persons within its territorial jurisdiction'. Given the nature of the agreement, the information may certainly refer to non-residents of the 'committed jurisdictions'.

### 4.6.2. Competent Authorities/All Rules

In all exchange of information rules the 'competent authorities' are specified as those under whose responsibility the exchange must take place. They are also to be considered 'subjects' of the international information exchange.

Article 3, first paragraph, of the Model convention does not define the term; it only gives the states the task to specify these authorities explicitly in their separate tax treaties. According to the Commentary, this is a result of the wish of most states to entrust the implementation of the tax treaty to an executive body rather than the highest tax authorities.[313] Usually, special central agencies are designated as competent authorities for the data exchange, which are part of either the Ministry of Finance or the tax authorities, more or less directly under the control of those ministries.[314] Their task is not described further in Article 26, but it is evident that it should consist of the implementation of the information exchange (managing it). It includes keeping up the essential contacts with treaty partners and with their own tax authorities and checking the actual exchange against the conditions and principles established in the international agreements. The written communication method, standard procedure between the states, works best given the complexity of the material and the criteria on the quality of evidence imposed in fiscal procedures.[315]

The prescribed process of information exchange via the central agencies is thus connected with exercising due caution that the international 'command' of loyalty to the treaty partners implies. Deviation from this leads, I think to illegality of the exchange under international law.[316] If this happens, states should confront each other about this. In cases of serious and recurring breach of this prescription, they could unilaterally suspend the exchange (at least temporarily).[317] The question of whether this illegality on the part of the treaty partner should lead

313. OECD Commentary, 1963, Art. 3, para. 7. See also the explanation in OECD report Tax Information Exchange between OECD Member Countries, 1994, para. 71. For the Strasbourg Convention, see Explanatory Report, Art. 3, para. 44.
314. This was taken up within the different workgroups of the Committee on Fiscal Affairs, and also the EU has created its own secure network for the exchange of data on VAT.
315. Studies should be done on how modern means of communication like a secure Internet connection between the different competent authorities could increase the efficacy.
316. That would then apply to information obtained in a direct, informal contact between civil servants in different tax offices on either side of a country border.
317. Following on from Art. 60, para. 3 of the Treaty of Vienna.

to rejection of the *received* data in a fiscal procedure will be answered by each state differently. A similar case was presented to the Court of Antwerpen in 1995. The data that the Belgian inspector received directly from a Dutch tax unit was not accepted as evidence in a fiscal procedure.[318] In my opinion, this is correct: the compulsory nature of this international law stipulation means that information obtained otherwise than through the competent authorities was obtained illegally and must not be accepted in fiscal procedures. In some criminal cases against Dutch taxpayers who concealed their Luxembourg savings accounts, judgments had to be made about the admissibility of the data received from Belgium. They were supplied spontaneously by the competent authorities of Belgium. Therefore they were considered acceptable evidence by Dutch Supreme Court, although it was not quite clear how they had come into the possession of the *Belgian* authorities in the first place (given the fact of Luxembourg's bank secrecy).[319]

#### *4.6.2.1. Competent Authorities in the Strasbourg Convention*

The term 'competent authorities' is mentioned, but not defined, in Article 3 of the Strasbourg Convention. The Explanatory Report explains that this is due to the diversity of forms of assistance acknowledged by the Convention, and the different ways in which the parties have organized their taxation.[320] The Appendix indicates which administrative body the various parties to the Treaty designated. Most of the articles in the first part of Chapter 4 mention 'the states' or 'parties' that exchange, except for Article 9, which arranges the attendance of foreign civil servants.

#### *4.6.2.2. Competent Authorities in Council Regulation 1798/2003 on VAT*

According to the Preamble, the objective of this regulation is to intensify the cooperation between the Member States of the European Union, with the aim to stop cross-border tax fraud in the field of VAT. To this end, the exchange of information must be coordinated from Central Liaison Offices established by each Member State, which have several clearly described tasks and responsibilities assigned to them. The most important one is keeping up the contacts between the Member States. In addition, Article 3, third paragraph, of the Council Regulation opens up the possibility of also assigning *regional* liaison services or even *individual* competent civil servants who would act as competent authorities themselves, but under the responsibility of the central office. States are not required to do so, but recital 12 of the Preamble clearly states that the Council expects it to

318. Judgment from the Court of Antwerp of 15 Jan. 1996, Revue Générale de Fiscalité, nos 6-7, July 1996, 206. See also Docclo (1999).
319. See ruling of Dutch High Court 21 Mar. 2008, LJN BA 8179.
320. In Art. 3, para. 1(d), refers only to Appendix B, which lists the competent authorities of all parties.

improve efficiency. Especially for states that are organized as a federation, or very extended states, this decentralization can have that effect. Special efforts will be needed to ensure the legitimacy, transparency, and uniformity of the government acts.

### *4.6.2.3. Conclusion*

The scope of the exchange obligation is partly determined by the (legal) persons whose information can be exchanged. The original version of the Model convention covered only the inhabitants of the treaty-party states. Since 1977, the requirement of residency has been removed from the Model convention, and having an income in a state is sufficient to make a (legal) person the subject of information provision. This broad scope has increased the potential efficacy of the information exchange.

Strasbourg Convention also does not have an explicit 'requirement of residency', nor does the OECD Agreement. The latter regulation is concerned with whether the information on a taxpayer of the requesting state falls under the decision-making power of (legal) persons in the requested state. The community nature of Directive 77/799 and Council Regulation 1798/2003 means that it focuses on data about inhabitants of the European Member States.

Other subjects in the exchange are the 'competent authorities' specified in all regulations as the sole responsible agencies for the application of the exchange of information rules. This delegation clause brings the exchange of information outside the diplomatic field of influence and allows the exchange ultimately to be positioned in (or close to) the tax administrations, which can promote applicability. The centralized nature of this organizational design can improve the legitimacy and correctness of the government acts and will also promote uniformity of the policy. It could, however, also lead to unnecessary bureaucracy. For the European Member States the decentralization of this executive power, as envisaged in Council Regulation 1798/2003, may provide a solution, if professionalism and uniformity of policy can be safeguarded.

## 5. SUMMARY AND CONCLUSIONS

1. The international exchange of tax information (also described as *mutual supplying* of it) should not just be approached from an international law perspective; it should be considered an action of government toward the taxpayers obliged to provide the information that is to be exchanged. The provision of this information takes place within a legal relationship (asymmetrical by definition) of the government with its taxpayers. This relationship is based on tax law, the source of the government's information gathering power and the taxpayer's duty to cooperate. Within this legal relationship, the government, being the strongest party, has the legal duty to treat its information-providing taxpayers as equal partners as far as possible. This requires a careful weighing of their interests.

2. This specific government task derives from an international law relationship of that government with another state, which aims to have the treaty partners promote each others' interests. The convergence of both legal duties and the issue of their mutual relationship arouse curiosity about the extent to which this *international* law framework also provides *room* for considering the interests of the taxpayers *within* those states.

3. A positive aspect here could be the fact that in twentieth-century international law, on both the global and the European levels, ethical norms have been given a place. They have left their mark on charters and treaties on human rights, formulated by international communities such as the United Nations and the European Community. Legal values, for example, freedom and equality, and principles derived from them, such as duty of care by the stronger government toward the weaker citizen, have similarly been emphasized in international law. In fiscal treaty law, discussions were conducted in the 1960s about a fair system of apportioning of taxation rights between country of residence and country of source, which could reduce the wealth gap between the states. The leading principle in this discussion was the moral term equity.

4. However, the recent OECD campaign against the so-called 'harmful tax competition' displayed little of this ideal. The substantial criticism against this campaign in the international literature rightly pointed out the lack of an ethical approach aimed at justice in the international tax law within the OECD, and at the one-sided emphasis on the interests of the rich Western states.

5. Within this campaign the exchange obligation from the Model convention was so widely accepted as an instrument for the states to promote *each others'* interests that it became a standard in itself. States had to comply so as not to be labelled 'harmful'. From this point of view, the question of how to protect the taxpayers' position in this context gains in importance.

6. In the analysis of the exchange obligation, it appeared that its development began in the first versions of Article 26 of the OECD Model convention (from 1963 and 1977). The line of thought within the OECD from which it sprang clearly left its mark in European Directive 77/799 of 1977, which also added its own elements. Joint efforts by the Committee on Fiscal Affairs of the OECD and the then European Community led to the Strasbourg Convention of 1988. Because it also covers measures in the field of tax collection and serving of fiscal documents, this treaty can be considered an integral codification of the mutual assistance law, which influenced in turn the Model convention and the European exchange law. The development of the exchange of information obligation is most evident in the continuing evolution of the OECD Model convention and the associated Commentary.

7. All of the regulations specified here establish an *obligation* to exchange data that is necessary or 'foreseeably relevant' or *could be* 'useful' for the implementation of the states' tax laws (and through Article 26 of the Model convention also for the other treaty stipulations). Until now, in the mass of tax treaties concluded from 1950 on, a less broad exchange of information obligations exists that, for example, apply to only treaty implementation, whether combined or not with applicability to national anti-misuse stipulations.

8. The objective scope of the exchange obligation was heavily revised, especially in the Model convention. Until 2000, it extended only to the direct taxes specified in the tax treaty. In 2000, following on from the Strasbourg Convention, Article 26 declared the exchange obligation to apply to 'taxes of every kind or description', regardless of whether they were levied on the central or regional level. In the Community exchange law, a rearrangement took place in 2003. Since then, European Directive 77/799 covers only direct tax and insurance tax. For exchange of information about VAT, Council Regulation 1798/2003 was established in Europe. Both regulations contain an obligation to serve official documents for the other Member States. With the realization of Council Regulation (EU) 2073/2004, the exchange of data on excise duties was arranged separately.

The subjective scope of the regulations covers inhabitants and non-inhabitants of the states, except in the original version of the OECD Model convention (1963). Implementation is meant to be done by the competent authorities. Its background was formed by the strict rules for confidentiality and use, which made central supervision essential. Regulation 1798/2003 makes room for designating local or individual competent authorities, in addition to the central office.

9. All exchange rules, except the OECD Agreement, recognize three main methods of exchange: upon request, automatic, and spontaneous. In the Model convention itself, they are not even specified. The fact that the last two appeared at first in the 1977 Commentary stimulated a discussion about the question of whether spontaneous exchange was also obligatory on the basis of older treaties. The Committee on Fiscal Affairs felt that the treaties must be interpreted dynamically on this point. This concept has since become widely accepted. It accords with the intention of the OECD states to realize the broadest possible exchange of information.

10. The *requests* for information must meet the following criteria in all exchange regulations:

- they may refer only to individualized cases (except those based on Council Regulation 1798/2003);
- in general, they may be made only after the requesting state has exhausted all of its own options. This exhaustion principle is transgressed in most regulations if the requesting state's investigative activities would be counterproductive. This restriction considerably reduces the chance that in fraud cases a later request for data in the other state would be superfluous because the taxpayer being investigated in the requesting state can warn his/her counterpart in the other state to dispose of the data. I consider this impediment in the *collection* of the data a greater risk to the effectiveness of the exchange than any delay in the process of the supplying. It is therefore regrettable that this exception to the exhaustion rule is not incorporated in the OECD Commentary;
- the states have had an investigation obligation to comply with a foreign request since 1977. This was increasingly emphasized. All regulations determine that a state must conduct an investigation for the other state in the same way as it would for its own purposes. According to Article 26 of

the 2005 Model convention, this also applies even if the requested data are not important for the requested state's own taxation.

11. Several variants (discretionary) to this obligation to investigate *upon request* from the treaty partner have been developed over time:

- Since 1977 Directive 77/799 has contained the possibility for the *attendance of civil servants* from the requesting state at an investigation in the requested state. This method does require a special agreement between the states. The Explanatory Report to the Strasbourg Convention, which also contains this possibility, gives as the added value of this method the realization of a completer picture of the international relationships of the taxpayers, and results being obtained more quickly, especially given the more informal nature of the cooperation. The Explanatory Report, however, does not consider the consequences this informal nature could have on the investigated taxpayers' position.
- In 1994, this variant was also included in the Survey of Current Practices from the Committee on Fiscal Affairs, and in 2000, also, in the Commentary to Article 26 of the OECD Model convention.
- The 'foundation' of this method in the OECD Commentary (instead of in the Model convention itself) is deficient in my view. I believe the risk of influence exerted by the other state that can be the consequence of the use of this method requires a basis in the tax treaty itself. This increases its recognizability for the parliamentary representatives and the taxpayers being investigated, and those for whom the attendance of foreign civil servants could have consequences. This applies even more to the attendance of foreign tax officials on the basis of the OECD Agreement, because of the likely unbalanced relationship between an OECD state and a 'committed jurisdiction'. The possibility that the visiting tax official can interview the taxpayers himself is also risky in this light. The question is what protection the requirement of consent can offer in these situations.
- Council Regulation 1798/2003 on VAT additionally contains the possibility for civil servants of the requesting state to be present in the *tax offices* of the other state and have access to their files. I feel this demands additional exertions from states to safeguard the careful weighing of interests of the states and the taxpayers whose information is sought and supplied.
- The second variant of the obligation to investigate, derived from the Strasbourg Convention, concerns the possibility of conducting *simultaneous investigations* of the same, or affiliated, or otherwise mutually involved taxpayers by two or more states, each one on their own territory. The Explanatory Report to the Strasbourg Convention gives as benefits the possibility of joint preparation and harmonization of the investigative method. This gain in efficiency would also benefit the taxpayers because of the possibility of reduced administrative burden. In 2000, this variant was also incorporated in the Commentary to the OECD Model convention. The method was adopted in the revised Directive 77/799 and in Council

Regulation 1798/2003. In all these regulations, states can refuse to participate in these simultaneous investigations, but they must provide reasons for doing so. Because of its primarily organizational nature, I feel this method is applicable without being explicitly included in an international treaty-obligation.

12. *Automatic exchange* (creating data flows between states) was incorporated in the OECD Commentary in 1977 and in Directive 77/799. The method is intended for situations in which treaty partners recognize structural risks of tax evasion because of their specific economic relationships, which could be overcome by periodically exchanging certain categories of data. It is highly dependent on the level of administrative organization of states, for example, concerning the availability of digitalized data files, and is therefore not mandatory in the OECD Commentary. The Committee on Fiscal Affairs has had digital formats developed, along with a standard agreement for automatic exchange. Experiments have also been done with the implementation of an international fiscal number. More attention will have to be paid to the usefulness of the data in the states' tax systems and the problems they encounter. This also applies to the data flows exchanged at the European level.

In Council Regulation 1798/2003, automatic data exchange is made mandatory with regard to intra-community deliveries and acquisitions and data about electronic services. For this the computerized VIES system is used. In Council Regulation 1925/2004 (Implementation Regulation), several more categories of data are listed that should be exchanged automatically (at fixed times) or by way of 'structured automatic' exchange (no fixed times). This concerns data about non-resident taxpayers, about statements of intra-community deliveries, about distance marketing, and about transactions concerning new transport vehicles. States have to specify which of the methods of supplying they choose.

13. *Spontaneous* exchange concerns information derived from the states' own taxation process that a state suspects could be important for the taxation of the other state. More than an assumed interest in assessing tax is not expected by the 1977 OECD Commentary. That, of course would not be possible.

In Directive 77/799 and the Strasbourg Convention, the assumption of relevance for levying of tax in the other state was made objective by enumerating the cases in which the obligation is considered to exist, for example, the occurrence in the providing state of a tax rebate, reduction, or exemption that should lead to an increase of tax in the other country; the supplying state's knowledge that certain cross-border transactions are being conducted over several countries' or that profit transfers are being done within a group of companies. The states can also add other cases after mutual consultation.

Council Regulation 1798/2003 on VAT recognizes the automatic and the spontaneous, as well as the structured exchange, which concerns categories defined in advance but without fixed time points.

Spontaneous exchange is not mandatory in the Regulation. It stresses automatic and structured exchange.

Chapter 5

# Terms and Conditions Relating to the Exchange: Secrecy and Use

## 1. INTRODUCTION

The main question of this study concerns the existence of a legal obligation for states exchanging data with their treaty partners to protect the interests of the taxpayers or withholding agents from whom they gather the information. We concluded that this legal obligation may be deduced from the legal relationship between the tax authorities and their taxpayers, on which their powers are based. This legal obligation, we saw, has to be fulfilled within the framework of the international legal relationship of this state with its treaty partners, to which it promised assistance.

The second question was whether it was at all possible to take the interests of taxpayers into account within the scope of an international obligation that is first and foremost mainly oriented on the interests of the states. The answer to that question requires an analysis of the international duty to exchange information, and this was done in three chapters.

In the preceding chapter, the contents of the various duties to exchange information were discussed: the various taxes, their purposes and methods, and the efforts both the requesting and the requested state are expected to make.

Until now, this analysis indeed reveals the exclusive orientation of the states toward their interests, recognized by the Organization for Economic Cooperation and Development (OECD) Committee on Fiscal Affairs and many authors,[1]

1. Cf. the OECD Report on Harmful Tax Competition, An Emerging Global Issue, Paris 1998, para. 92. In this Report, the exchange of information is seen as an important means to fight this phenomenon. Cf. also the Model Agreement on the Exchange of Information on Tax Matters, developed for states not wishing to be qualified as tax havens in the previously mentioned Report.

although in some cases this obligation may also serve the interests of taxpayers.[2]

Apart from this, all duties to exchange information 'foreseeably relevant' for taxation contain stringent conditions and warranties with regard to the secrecy and the use of the data. Whatever may have been the darker purpose of these provisions, it is clear that especially this condition of secrecy will *also* affect the position of the taxpayers. Therefore it could provide a basis for the answer to the core question of this study with regard to the relationship between the international exchange of information and the obligations of states toward their information providing taxpayers.

In this chapter, the scope of the secrecy clauses in various exchanges of information rules will be investigated, following the same scheme as before: a thematic discussion of the various elements of the secrecy clauses, based on the elements drawn from the OECD Model convention. In the following chapter, the consequences of the duty of secrecy for the information-providing taxpayers, as well as for the taxpayers in the receiving state, will be discussed.

## 2. SECRECY IN THE OECD MODEL CONVENTION

As a rationale for the *secrecy clause*, the OECD Commentary merely states that mutual assistance between states '*is feasible only*' if the condition of secrecy of the information received if fulfilled, without indicating why this is so.[3] This could be seen as an implicit recognition of the fact that states, in their struggle against tax fraud, need to be able to exchange confidential documents within an 'internal' space. Another reason could be the recognition that tax secrecy is an essential standard for constitutional states in their relation with their taxpayers. This standard would deserve explicit protection in the exchange of information with other states because of the fact that, as the data disappear from its jurisdiction, the supplying state is no longer able to fulfil its constitutional obligation.[4] Exchange of information would therefore not be feasible if the convention would not *transfer* that obligation to the receiving state. Thus states may claim performance from each

McLure (2001), 330 describes the exchange of information as one of the 'benefits' in view of which states are prepared to waiver part of their sovereignty in tax matters. Cf. also Vogel (2003), Art. 26, Rz. 4, where he claims that the provision on the exchange of information serves '*allein den nationalen Interessen* der Vertragsstaaten'. Schaumburg (1998), para. 19.46 points out that the exchange of information is not only of importance to the receiving treaty partner, but based on the principle of mutuality, also to the supplying state itself.

2. This may especially be the case for the taxpayer of the receiving state, if his representation of the facts is confirmed by the foreign data. As the exchange of information improves the enforcement of tax laws, it may provide a level playing field for taxpayers. The advantageous competitive position of fraudulent taxpayers (as their tax burden is lighter) is thus cancelled.
3. OECD Commentary 1977-2005, Art. 26, para. 11.
4. In his 1990, 'General Report of the IFA Conference on the Exchange of information', Gangemi (39) remarks that in nerly all states involved special legal provisions exist which override the duty of secrecy with regard to the exchange of information.

other if they are in breach of this contract, and secrecy in tax matters, in regard to the legal position of taxpayers, is transformed into an *international* obligation.[5] In my view, this 'public law' aspect of legal protection becomes especially clear from the fact that in the secrecy clause, *both* tax authorities *and* judicial authorities are entitled to disclosure of the data.[6]

Therefore the conclusion seems justified that this provision was also intended to create rights citizens may rely on, in spite of the fact that the wording of the clause merely refers to an obligation for *states*. In my view, this implies that the secrecy clause is given direct effect with regard to the information providing taxpayers of the supplying state.[7] Taxpayers are entitled to directly apply to the courts of the receiving state, if the latter falls short of its duty of secrecy. The interest of taxpayers in the *receiving state*, for the calculation of whose tax liability the data are *used*, rather lies in their disclosure than in their secrecy, so that tax assessments may be motivated and taxpayers may defend themselves against them. This (implicit) focus on the position of the information providing taxpayers, apart from the purely international purpose to prevent disclosure of the '*objektive Rechtsgut*' of the information,[8] offers a first glimpse of the typical stratification of the secrecy clause.

The substantial differences between the original version of the clause and the subsequent versions of it in the OECD Model convention are discussed separately in the paragraphs following hereafter. The consequences to the position of taxpayers in the supplying and the receiving state are specified in greater detail in Chapter 7.

## 2.1. Secrecy According to the 1963 OECD Model Convention

### 2.1.1. Absolute Duty of Secrecy

The secrecy clause in the 1963 Model convention reads as follows:

> any information so exchanged shall be treated as secret and shall not be disclosed to any persons or authorities other then those concerned with the assessment or collection of the taxes which are the subject of the Convention.

The 1963 version of the OECD exchange provision requires the information so exchanged to be treated as secret. The duty of secrecy concerns information

5. In the same sense, Vogel (2003), Art. 26, Rz. 60, 1998.
6. Cf. also OECD Report: Tax Information Exchange between OECD Member Countries, A Survey of Current Practice, Paris, 1994, para. 51.
7. Vogel (2003), Art. 26, Rz. 60, describes the direct effect of the secrecy clause amended in 1977. The taxpayer in the supplying state is entitled to legal protection against the disclosure of the data, according to the legal system of the receiving state. Lambooij (1990), 43; Vakstudie Algemeen Deel, Wet internationale bijstandsverlening bij de heffing van belastingen. ad Art. 1, 1–20, also recognizes the direct effect of Art. 26, as well as Docclo (1999), 318.
8. Vogel (2003), Art. 26, Rz. 60, 1998.

already exchanged. It therefore rests with the *receiving state*. It concerns an autonomous obligation under the convention, with no reference to the domestic laws of the receiving or the supplying state.[9] The circle of persons and authorities in the receiving state entitled to have access to the foreign information consists of the persons and authorities (...) concerned with the assessment or collection of the taxes that are the subject of the Convention. According to paragraph 9 of the 1963 OECD Commentary, this obligation also covers the authorities competent to judge disputes on tax matters. Apparently, without being mentioned explicitly in the clause, they form part of the parties entitled to the disclosure of the information in question.[10] In my view, tax courts at any rate form part of the authorities concerned with the assessment or collection of taxes, and thus also of the circle of parties entitled to disclosure as drawn in the first version of the clause.[11]

The 1963 Commentary is very strict and requires that special measures be taken if the law or legal practice do not warrant the secrecy of the data received during court hearings.[12] This will especially be the case if the tax case law decisions in a state are made public. Of course states may mutually agree that the information received is to be used in public hearings, but if they have not done so, domestic law concerning the public nature of court rulings must yield to the obligation under the convention.

### 2.1.2. Circle of Parties Entitled to the Information

Neither the text of the original Model convention nor its Commentary refers in any way to the use of the data for the *preparation* of tax *criminal proceedings*.[13] In my opinion, however, they may be used for that purpose, especially if the treaty partners have specifically incorporated the fight against tax fraud. It is indeed '*sinnwidrig*' – to put it in Vogel's words – to assume that the secrecy clause of the 1963 Model would not permit this use. That would imply that fraudulent taxpayers could escape criminal penalties imposed as a result of the exchange of information, simply because those data could not be used in criminal proceedings.[14] Keeping in mind that in most states, criminal courts are open courts, that use will require advance permission.

9. *Ibid.*, Rz. 59, 1997, refers to an '*eigenständiges internationales Steuergeheimnis*'. Cf. also Gangemi (1990), 39.
10. From para. 54 of the OECD Report Tax Information Exchange between OECD Member Countries, 1994, it appears that this interpretation was intended from the beginning.
11. In the same sense: Vogel (2003), Art. 26, Rz. 80, 2014, who holds the view that the term 'authorities' must be interpreted extensively. In Dutch case law, the view is developed that the tax courts must replace decisions by the tax inspector that they consider incorrect by their own rulings. This is called the 'devolutive effect' of the appeal.
12. OECD Commentary 1963, Art. 26, para. 9.
13. *Ibid.*, Art. 26, para. 6 only refers the *prevention* of tax fraud.
14. Therefore, Vogel (2003), Art. 26, Rz. 70, is of the opinion that the many German tax conventions still modelled after the 1963 Model convention should be interpreted dynamically at this point.

The 'persons or authorities' mentioned in the 1963 version of Article 26, paragraph 1, also cover parties involved in the *collection* of the taxes that are the subject of the convention. The latter has led to a discussion in literature, because the 1963 Commentary explicitly excludes mutual assistance in the collection of taxes.[15] According to some authors, tax collection also was covered by the provision on the exchange of information, as it forms part of the domestic laws concerning the taxes that are subject to the convention, so that Article 26 may be invoked.[16]

In my view, the original Commentary does not contain a 100% ban with regard to tax collection. The term 'administrative assistance' refers to a wider scope than just the *exchange of information* with regard to tax collection. Mutual assistance in the collection of taxes also covers powers and obligations that are only of interest to the collection of taxes, such as the serving of writs of execution or precautionary seizure on behalf of the treaty partner.[17] These measures are excluded in the 1963 Commentary.[18] Use of the *data received* on the basis of Article 26 for the collection of taxes, as the secrecy clause admits, refers to the possibility that foreign data received for the purpose of tax assessment may disclose the existence of a property for which recourse is available. This may thus be used as a motive for a request for mutual assistance in tax collection. In my view, keeping the definition of the purpose of the exchange of information in mind, which only refers to taxation, under Article 26 of the Model convention, tax authorities are not allowed to request this information specifically for that (collection) purpose. It is conspicuous that in the 1963 version of the Commentary, taxpayers in the receiving country are not included in the circle of parties entitled to the disclosure of the information received, although this information may serve as a basis for their tax liability. In Chapter 7, I will elaborate on the consequences of this phenomenon for the position of taxpayers.

## 2.2. Secrecy According to the 1977-2005 Model Convention

In 1977, Article 26 was amended in three ways: (a) A reference to the secrecy legislation in the receiving state was made, (b) the circle of persons and authorities entitled to the disclosure of the information was extended, and (c) the purposes the

15. This mutual assistance must be drafted separately, either by separate agreements or by the introduction of a provision to this end in the tax convention, cf. OECD Commentary 1963, Art. 26, General Observations, para. 2.
16. Vogel (2003), Art. 26, Rz. 80. Cf. also Wisselink (1996), 33, who holds this view, as does Pijl (1998), 349, on the basis of the text of Art. 5 of the Model Convention for Mutual Assistance in the Recovery of Tax Claims of 1981. This article refers to the wider scope of Art. 26 of the 1977 OECD Model convention. Pijl concludes from this that the latter Model includes mutual assistance for both the assessment and the collection of taxes.
17. Cf. also the definition of Art. 1, para. 2 of the Strasbourg convention, Strasbourg, 1988.
18. Since 2003, the OECD Model convention also contains a separate Article for the mutual assistance in the collection of taxes (Art. 27).

information may be used for were extended, especially the possibility to disclose it in court hearings and case law, as well as its use for tax criminal proceedings.

It reads:

> Any information received by a Contracting State shall be treated as secret in the same manner as information obtained under the domestic laws of that State, and shall be disclosed only to persons or authorities (including courts and administrative bodies) concerned with the assessment or collection of, the enforcement or prosecution in respect of, the determination of appeals in relation to the taxes referred to in paragraph 1, or the oversight of the above. Such persons or authorities shall use the information only for such purposes. They may disclose the information in public proceedings or in judicial decisions.

In 2005, this secrecy clause was embedded in a separate paragraph (2) of Article 26 of the Model convention.

### 2.2.1. Relative Duty of Secrecy

Since 1977, the interstate duty to secrecy is not only defined in a substantive sense (by a description of the circle of parties in the receiving state entitled to the disclosure of the information), but also related to the domestic laws on secrecy in the receiving state.[19] This raises the question which should prevail in a specific situation: The definition laid down in the convention, or the domestic laws of the receiving state?

I consider the definition of the circle of parties entitled in the clause as a reflection of the general standard of tax secrecy that, according to the 1990 OECD Report, is valid in all OECD Member States.[20] The data a tax official gathers by virtue of his/her office may be disclosed to only those parties charged with the assessment and collection of taxes, including the courts of appeal and taxpayers themselves. They can be used only for tax purposes.[21] Thus the idea of 'proper confidence', so important in the Commentary, is circumscribed in the revised text of the convention. At the same time, however, secrecy is supposed to be warranted through the *domestic* legislation of the states, because the failure to comply with this obligation deserves to be sanctioned.[22]

---

19. Vogel (2003), Art. 26 Rz. 57, refers to the revised secrecy clause as a relative protection for citizens. Cf. Gangemi (1990), 41 onward, and Malherbe (1991), 64 onward.
20. Cf. the 1990 OECD Report: Taxpayers' Rights and Obligations (A Survey of the Legal Situation in OECD Countries). According to this Report, other basic principles for the protection of taxpayers' rights are: a right of appeal against decisions of tax authorities, and right to privacy in the gathering of tax-related data.
21. Cf. Bentley (1998), 6. He includes the duty of tax secrecy in the 'secondary rights, focusing on the specific operation of the law, concerned with the protection of rights at both a general and a specific level'.
22. OECD Commentary 1977-2005, Art. 26, para. 11.

As a result, however, both the states and the taxpayers are put at risk. The interpretation of the term 'persons and authorities' alone (as parties who are entitled to the data) can be very different.[23] Thus the level of protection for the taxpayer supplying the information in the requested states is uncertain beforehand.

Vogel holds the view that small variations in secrecy will leave the obligation to exchange information '*grundsätzlich unberührt*'. In his view, the 'weakness' of the revised provision is compensated by the strict rules concerning the disclosure of the data to which it refers. Moreover, the linking of the domestic law to the provision of the convention turns compliance with the domestic duty of secrecy by the receiving state into '*eine abkommensrechtliche Pflicht*', the neglecting of which the supplying state may take action against.[24] However, this does not change the fact that the revised provision introduces the risk that the domestic secrecy legislation of the receiving state offers less protection than taxpayers in the supplying state would enjoy under their own legislation, without the latter being able to take action against this.[25] Therefore, according to some, the choice of a state for one or both secrecy clauses can be seen as 'a meaningful test of each State's approach to the issue of confidentiality'.[26]

I am of the opinion that not only the obligation of secrecy under the treaty, but also the legal position of taxpayers should result comprehensively from the provision on the exchange of information. To the taxpayers involved, secrecy is so essential that it simply cannot be left to the unknown domestic legislation of the other state. I will elaborate on this further in Chapter 7.

The general reference to the domestic laws of the other state also implies a risk for the states themselves, because possible exceptions to secrecy in various states, like those in their domestic freedom of information acts, are thus brought within the scope of the treaty relationship.[27]

---

23. Gangemi (1990), 41, with examples of the interpretation of the terms 'persons and authorities' in this connection in countries like the US, Norway and non-OECD Member states such as Brazil and Sri Lanka. Malherbe, too (1991) refers to many variations in the persons and authorities entitled to disclosure of information held by tax authorities in different states.
24. Vogel (2003), Art. 26, Rz. 59. Cf. Daniels (1987), 26. The sanction for breaching the obligation should be that the exchange of information comes to an end.
25. The Dutch Explanatory Memorandum to the tax convention between the Netherlands and The Russian Federation of 27 Aug. 1998, Parliamentary Papers II 1996/1997, 25 347, nr. 268, gives an interesting view of the way in which the secrecy clause is 'motivated' in the negotiations preceding the convention (out of necessity?). After asking questions about domestic laws on secrecy to the partner in the convention, nothing can be done but trust the picture painted by the latter. If in practice it should prove otherwise, measures may be taken through diplomatic channels, the Explanatory Memorandum reads.
26. Gangemi (1990), 41.
27. These domestic exceptions to the duty of secrecy reflect the inconsistency of interests national authorities must represent. Cf. for example Christian (1991) and Vogel (1991), 291 (Confidentiality); the authors indicate that in their states, conflicts regularly occur between the domestic freedom of information legislation on the one hand and secrecy provisions on the other. Schick (2000), refers to the secrecy provisions including their exceptions, making it possible for the American IRS 'to use the disclosure provisions both as a sword and a shield'. Urtz (2000), 46,

An example is the legal battle that arose in the United States when a large publishing concern, based on the Freedom of Information Act, requested the Internal Revenue Service (IRS) to disclose certain international Advance Pricing Agreements (APAs). These had been concluded by the IRS through mutual agreement procedures, and were based on information exchanged between the treaty partners.[28] The question whether the information exchanged within the framework of the aforementioned mutual agreement procedures falls under the exchange of information provision in the tax conventions concerned was answered in the affirmative by the U.S. authorities.[29] On the other hand, it was feared that the U.S. Freedom of Information Act would dictate the internal disclosure of the APAs involved. The fears of the taxpayers and suppliers of information and the partners to the tax conventions involved were heightened by the possibility that the documents that had been exchanged containing background information would have to be disclosed as well. This legal battle caused quite a stir internationally,[30] and was the motive for an amendment of the U.S. secrecy legislation in 1999. The United States was not obligated to disclose the information gathered from other states.[31]

This outcome was corroborated by many authors: the clause in the tax convention must prevail over the domestic law,[32] as the exchange of information between states is drafted as an international obligation with the express purpose to create supremacy of that clause over domestic tax secrecy provisions. As a result of this debate, in the 2005 amendment of the Model convention the disclosure of the information exchanged to others than the parties mentioned in the article is

---

states that the Austrian lECislation on confidentiality in tax matters makes an exception 'if required by law or in the public interest'.

For a description of the various secrecy provisions and their exceptions, cf. a series of articles on 'Confidentiality of Taxpayers Information', *International Transfer Pricing Journal* 7 (2000).

28. *BNA v. IRS*, Nos 96-376, 96-2820, and 98-1473 Daily Tax Report for Executives, Bureau of National Affairs, ISSN 0092-6884, Jan. 1999, and Tax Management Transfer Pricing Report, 4 Jul. 1999, ISSN 1063-2069, and Tax Notes International, 14 Jun. 1999.
29. Article 25 merely created an obligation for states to solve their mutual problems on the applications (and the interpretation) of the convention. It provides no independent power to exchange personal information. That power is embedded in Art. 26. In the same sense Vogel (2003), Art. 26, Rz. 7 1984, and Rz. 51, 1994.
30. With reference to this case *BNA v. IRS* the International Transfer Pricing Journal initiated a series of comparative surveys on the ways in which states shape secrecy in tax matters. Cf. The series of articles in the *International Transfer Pricing Journal* 7 (2000): 10, 17, 22, 28, 101, 97, 101, 142, 152, under 'Comparative Survey on Confidentiality of Taxpayer Information'.
31. Cf. Schick (2000), 34 and Wright (2000), 41.
32. Cf. Vogel (2003), Art. 26, para. 62. Also Burns/Turner (2000), stating that in Canada the provision of the tax convention would prevail and no information would be supplied to other parties except the foreign state, not even if the requests to supply this information stem from 'US Access-to-Information laws'. The Dutch Freedom of information Act (Art. 10) there also contains exceptions as to the interests of the Dutch state in maintaining international relationships. Cf. also para. 10.9.

forbidden, 'regardless of domestic information disclosure laws such as freedom of information legislation'. This is also valid for non-personal information.[33]

To the states, this implies extra protection. The OECD Committee on Fiscal Affairs 'creates' supremacy of the international secrecy obligation over the possible domestic legal obligation authorities have to disclose information on government actions. *Third parties* filing a request for disclosure of internationally exchanged information (as happened in the case of the previously mentioned U.S. publishing company), would have no chance of succeeding.

In some states, however, international law has no supremacy over domestic laws (e.g., the United States, the United Kingdom, and Austria).[34] Thus, these states are able to draft new domestic laws that can refute the provisions of conventions.

Apart from that, there is something to be said for the more stringent view in the Commentary: the feasibility of the obligation to exchange of information is not only related to the protection of the information taxpayers supply. It also presupposes a freedom for the states to be able to communicate confidentially, especially in the fight against tax fraud or tax evasion. In this connection, they must be able to exchange suspicions as well as facts. The financial interest states have must count heavily. This interest is not served by the disclosure of their correspondence. This is also true for the background information which 'accompanies' the request for information. This information too will have to be kept secret by the requested state.[35] The duty of secrecy extends to all tax information exchanged between the states under the tax convention. In some countries, the exception with regard to foreign information in domestic laws on freedom of information was already common practice.[36]

The general interest that *outsiders* may have in the freedom of information concerning government actions in fact forces the supplying states to take into account three kinds of interests. The interest of the state and its treaty partnerly in the best possible secrecy of the data; those of the taxpayers in the supplying or the receiving state may be secrecy as well as disclosure.;[37] There are also those of the critical citizen looking for transparency of government actions. Therefore this

33. OECD Commentary 1977-2005, Art. 26, para. 12.
34. Vogel (2004), concludes that of the forty-two *European* states, at this moment there are still thirteen that do not recognize supremacy of the law of treaties over their domestic laws.
35. Likewise Schaumburg (1998), para. 19.40. For a dissenting opinion, cf. Daniels (1987), 26, where he claims not to be able to find 'good reasons' to deny the taxpayer access to the international requests for information. In my view, he fails to recognize that a request for information in itself usually contains data about the taxpayer in the requesting state, and that the latter of course is entitled to the secrecy of his data.
36. As it appeared from the IFA Conference in 1990, Gangemi (1990), 40.
37. For example, if those taxpayers do not have an independent right of information and wish to check the exchange of 'their' data.

'OECD doctrine' on the supremacy of the international secrecy provision will have to be developed further in international case law.[38]

This amendment of Article 26 is also explicitly valid for non-personal information. From the angle of the states, this has the advantage that this information too can successfully resist a request with regard to disclosure. The disadvantage of bringing this kind of information under the secrecy provision is, however, that it becomes more difficult, not to say impossible, to pass it on to authorities occupied with side issues such as money laundering or the fight against corruption. These are not (officially) meant by the authorities assessing tax liabilities or prosecuting tax fraud. The fact that the OECD Committee on Fiscal Affairs is thoroughly aware of this problem can be gathered from paragraph 12.3 of the Commentary, added in 2005 and creating the possibility for the states to reach a mutual agreement on allowing the use of the supplied information by 'other law enforcement agencies'. Thus the position of the OECD Member States was strengthened. This is indeed advantageous in cases of tax fraud. Moreover, the additional paragraph offers more protection of the correspondence between states against 'outsiders'. However, for constitutional states, a warranty of transparency of government actions is too essential to waiver in individual cases without a proper weighing up of the interests. The awareness that in some situations the more stringent duty of secrecy may turn against taxpayers cannot be detected in the new Commentary. This is the same for the criteria to come to a proper balancing of interests (such as the interest of the states to exercise oversight on the one hand or the interest of citizens in transparency of government actions on the other hand. (Cf. paragraph 7.3.2.).

### 2.2.2. Circle of Parties Entitled to the Data

The second amendment to the 1977 secrecy clause concerns the extension of the enumeration of persons and authorities entitled to the information. Since then, it includes the 'courts and administrative bodies, involved in the assessment or collection of, the enforcement or prosecution in respect of, or the determination of appeals in relation to the taxes' in the *receiving state*. The Commentary also includes taxpayers in that state, as well as their legal counsels and possible witnesses.[39] How this right of access of the taxpayer to these data is implemented in tax proceedings will be established by domestic legislation. (Cf. paragraph 7.4.2) In principle, the information is not envisaged for other authorities than the tax authorities, even though states may mutually agree to incorporate a provision that a

38. In the Dutch practice of the international exchange of information, this balancing of interests has been the topic of discussions several times, and although the taxpayers wanted disclosure, the administrative (and tax) courts ruled in favour of secrecy in most cases. Cf. Amsterdam (tax) Court of Appeal, 13 Nov. 2003, V-N 2004/7.8, Administrative Jurisdiction Division 29 May 2000, V-N 2000/31.2, Administrative Jurisdiction Division 1 Apr. 1986, AB 1987/534, Administrative Jurisdiction Division 16 Dec. 1997, V-N 1998/ 6.6. Also District Court of The Hague, 26 Jul. 1995, Infobulletin 95/786. Dissentive: 's-Hertogenbosch Court of Appeal, 25 Mar. 2003, FUTD, nr. 38, 22. Cf. extensively para. 10.9.
39. OECD Commentary 1977-2005, Art. 26, para. 12.

more ample use is possible, if that use would also be possible in the supplying state and if that state would grant permission for that use.[40]

The 2005 version of Article 26, paragraph 2 of the OECD Model convention is extended with the phrase '*the oversight of the above*'. The OECD Commentary itself considers this a turning point. Which it is, if compared to the standpoint hitherto taken in paragraph 12, that the supervisory bodies first were excluded from the information received. The Commentary interprets the notion 'oversight bodies' as administrative bodies responsible for the decision-making on disclosure to the taxpayer, his legal counsel, or possible witnesses.[41] Why the extension to the *decision-making* supervisory bodies was made is not explicitly explained. In my view, its rationale must be found in the assumption that, at variance with the main rule, in certain situations the taxpayer, his legal counsel, or witness should not have access to the information obtained. This could have a connection with the 'priority rule' introduced by the OECD Committee on Fiscal Affairs for the international secrecy rules above the domestic 'freedom of information' rules on standards of transparency of government actions. Conflicts between these two systems of law could then perhaps be better not put exclusively in the hands of the tax courts. In my opinion, this priority rule should never be construed to deny the taxpayer *himself* access to received *information* determining his tax liability.[42]

The extension to the 'oversight bodies' may also be useful in connection with the extensively widened scope (since 2000) of the duty to supply information to 'taxes of every kind or description'. Because this may include taxes levied by 'political subdivisions and local authorities', the information could in principle also end up with local administrative bodies, and these may be less experienced or familiar with the enforcement of the duty of secrecy in tax matters. The possibility of an 'adjustment' of their actions by a higher tier of government could then offer the necessary warranties. On the basis of Article 26, (new) paragraph 2, the 'oversight bodies', too, are bound by the limitation that the data may be used only for tax purposes.

States may mutually agree with their contracting partners not to incorporate this extension in their specific tax convention (cf. the Commentary). Under the condition mentioned earlier that on the one hand the taxpayer will not be denied the access to the information received, and on the other that the information may also be used by the oversight bodies within the limits of the secrecy provisions, this extension, in my opinion, can be deemed justifiable.

40. *Ibid.*, para. 12.3.
41. *Ibid.*, para. 12.1 defines the oversight bodies as 'bodies including authorities that supervise tax administration and enforcement authorities as part of the general administration of the Government of a Contracting State'. E.g., bodies existing in may states such as the Council of State, The Court of Audit, Parliamentary Petitions Committees, and The National Ombudsman.
42. This does not mean that I wish to comment on his right of access to the correspondence between the states, at least not at this point.

### 2.2.3. Extension of the Use of the Data

As of 1977, it is expressly determined that the information supply may also be disclosed to those in charge of the '*prosecution in respect of (...) the taxes referred to*'. The term 'prosecution' in the text of the convention refers to criminal proceedings, in which the information may be used for the prosecution of *tax* offences. The 1977 Commentary also includes 'witnesses' in the parties entitled to the data. It is also appropriate for criminal proceedings that as of 1977, Article 26 allows disclosure of the data in public hearings and rulings, even if the identity of the taxpayer is revealed by it.[43] Consequently, the substantial nature of this amendment cannot be automatically carried over to the tax conventions based on the 1963 version of the Model convention, which is also the view of the OECD Committee on Fiscal Affairs. Information disclosed by public legal proceedings may from then on be used for other purposes as well (cf. paragraph 13 of the Commentary).[44] However, this does not imply that 'additional information', too, may be disclosed by the tax authorities. My interpretation of this cryptic note is that such disclosed data as such may be used for other purposes,[45] but may not be the 'starting point' of an additional request to the other state for the other purpose, from the receiving or from the requested authorities.[46] If states object to the disclosure of data in public (criminal) proceedings, they should exclude this possibility in their separate tax conventions.[47] In that case the main rule applies: the receiving state is not allowed to use the information for other than tax purposes.[48]

For the *assistance in the collection* of taxes as such, the Commentary referred to the possibilities in the Strasbourg Convention. It did so until 2003, the year in which Article 27 was incorporated in the Model convention. (About the *use* for tax collection purposes of *data* obtained on the basis of mutual assistance for tax assessment purposes, see the preceding paragraph).

43. OECD Commentary 1977-2005, Art. 26, para. 13.
44. The Dutch Instruction on the supply of information determines that data obtained by the Dutch tax authorities and used for tax purposes, may also be used by other authorities mentioned in the Instruction. However, not the information itself must be forwarded, but only the tax liability after correction with the help of the information received.
45. Wisselink (1996), 52 thinks that what is meant here is 'additional information outside the identity of the taxpayer'.
46. An example of (in my view) unlawful 'additional information' is that tax data already disclosed in one country would also indicate fraud with regard to social security contributions. These data may be used as an indication, but should not lead to the situation that this country applies for additional information to solve this problem, and certainly not for the supplying state to furnish the additional data.
47. At any rate, the data that were possibly disclosed in criminal proceedings should be obtained exclusively by administrative means. Mutual assistance in (tax) criminal proceedings, involving criminal penalties, is only possible through separate conventions. (For the Netherlands: European Convention on Mutual Assistance in Criminal Matters, and Benelux Treaty on Extradition and Mutual Assistance in Criminal Matters). For The Netherlands, the domestic procedure with regard to the exchange of information within the context of mutual assistance in criminal matters is embedded in Articles 552h-552s of the Dutch Code of Criminal Procedure.
48. OECD Commentary 1977-2005, Art. 26, para. 12.

In 2005, a more effective exchange was made possible by opening the possibility in the Commentary to forward data to third countries, if states have *explicitly* incorporated this in their tax convention.[49] Apart from that, the strict ban on disclosure and use of the data outside the 'classic' circle of entitled persons and authorities is mitigated in the sense that 'the sharing of tax information (. . .) with other *law enforcement agencies* and judicial authorities on certain high priority matters' becomes possible.[50] What is probably meant is the fight against money laundering or income from criminal behaviour, against corruption and financing terrorism. States having incorporated the transfer of tax data for the previously mentioned purposes in their domestic laws and aspiring at a more extended use of these data should explicitly agree on this use in their tax conventions.

### 2.2.4. Conclusion

The duty of secrecy for data received from abroad serves the interests of the states but those of taxpayers as well. This conclusion may be drawn from that fact that the information received may be disclosed not only to tax authorities and the taxpayer himself, but also to the tax courts.

Within this framework, relating the duty of secrecy to the domestic law of the receiving state (in the 1977 Model convention) must be seen as a mitigation of the absolute duty of secrecy of the first version of the Model convention. This phenomenon is only partly compensated by the exhaustive list of persons and authorities entitled to the information. The protection this clause may offer in a specific situation is in fact unclear.

With regard to the amendment of Article 26 of the OECD Model convention in 2005 the conclusion may be drawn that the OECD Committee on Fiscal Affairs has successfully tried to improve the position of the states. This was mainly realized by creating supremacy of the secrecy obligation over the 'freedom of information' legislation of the states. However, the effect of this effort will eventually be determined by the courts because of the different manners in which domestic and international law relate within the states and because of the necessary balancing of interests in each individual case.

## 3. SECRECY CLAUSES IN EUROPEAN LAW: DIRECTIVE 77/799 AND VALUE ADDED TAX REGULATION

European exchange rules in the field of taxation are to be found in Council Directive 77/799 (including the various Directives in which it was amended and value added tax [VAT] Regulation 1798/2003 (including the corresponding Implementation Regulation 1925/2004).

49. *Ibid.*, Art. 26, para. 12.2.
50. *Ibid.*, Art. 26, para. 12.3.

## 3.1. Secrecy in Council Directive 77/799

### 3.1.1. Relative Secrecy

From the beginning, the secrecy clause of Article 7 of Directive 77/799, as well as the OECD provision, has been related to the domestic laws of the Member States. An essential difference with the OECD Model provision can be read in Article 7, paragraph 2 of the Directive. There the supplying state has the right to decline the exchange of information if the secrecy provisions of its treaty partner offer less protection than its domestic laws and if the receiving state is not willing to take additional measures. This ground for exception serves both the interests the *states* have in the secrecy of the data and the interests of the taxpayers having supplied the information. Thus, Directive 77/799 leaves the Member States more room for the protection of the position of the taxpayers than the OECD Model provision, especially after the last revision of Article 26 of the Model convention. I will further elaborate on this in Chapter 7.

### 3.1.2. Use of the Data: Collection, Prosecution, Forwarding, Use in Criminal Proceedings

Based on Article 7, paragraph 1 of Directive 77/799, the information received may be used only for the assessment of tax liabilities and tax audits, including the imposing of administrative penalties with regard to the taxes listed in Article 1. Therefore the authorities having access to the information include persons directly involved in tax assessment and tax audits and in proceedings in which penalties are imposed. Since the amendment of the Directive in 2003[51] does no longer cover indirect taxes, apart from direct taxes, social security contributions, mentioned in the Directive 76/308 (the Recovery Directive).

The reference to the Recovery Directive is meaningful. It makes clear that slowly but surely, a more integrated vision of mutual assistance between states is developing, in which assessment and recovery are equally important. Like the Recovery Directive since 2001 made possible mutual assistance in the recovery of direct taxes, including social security contributions,[52] the revised Directive 77/799 introduces mutual assistance for the *levying* of taxes on those contributions.

Within this context, it is to be regretted that in spite of the bringing into line of the objective scopes of the two Directives, the *recovery authorities* are not listed in Article 7, paragraph 1. The use of the information obtained for the recovery as a sign for the existence of properties for which recourse is available is therefore not

51. In Council Directive nr. 2003/93 of 7 Oct. 2003, amending Council Directive nr. 77/799 concerning mutual assistance by the competent authorities of the Member States in the field of direct and indirect taxation. This Directive was drafted simultaneously with the new Council regulation on administrative cooperation in the field of value added tax. Cf. V-N 2003/58.4.
52. Recovery Directive nr. 76/308/EEC was last amended in Council Directive nr. 2001/44/EC of 15 Jun. 2001, cf. V-N 2002/5.33.

self-evident, but is subject to *the prior consent* of the supplying state, (Article 7, paragraph 3) and to the condition that this use would also be permitted in the other state. Thus, also after the amendment of 2003, Directive 77/799 is (still) at variance, in a negative sense, with Article 26 of the OECD Model convention, under which article the use of this information for the tax collection was possible as of 1977. In this amendment, the opportunity was missed to improve the effectiveness of the international exchange of information. Moreover, this would also have meant a recognition of the fact that in order to reach the goal of fair taxation, assessment of tax liabilities, imposing tax assessments and the collection of taxes are inextricably linked.

Another difference with the OECD rules can be seen in Directive 77/799 where the use of the data for *prosecution* with regard to the taxes listed in that Directive is concerned.[53] Contrary to what Gangemi seems to argue, I am of the opinion that the use of information obtained for criminal proceedings is not included in the main rule of Article 7, paragraph 1.[54] That Article creates a right of access, apart from the taxpayer and the officials of the tax authorities, for persons and authorities directly involved in the procedures concerning '*the assessment*' of the tax liability, possibly including the imposing of '*administrative penalties*'. Although Article 7, paragraph 1 does allow use of the data in open court, subject to prior authorization of the supplying state, as well as their listing in court rulings, this does not yet create a basis for the use of the data in tax *criminal tax* proceedings, even if in most states the latter are judged in open courts. For use of the data in criminal proceedings, a remedy must be sought in the third paragraph of Article 7. This opens up the possibility of use 'for other purposes', inasmuch as this (e.g., criminal tax proceedings) use is also allowed in the supplying state. The wording is not altogether clear where it concerns the question of whether the latter is subject to prior consent or not. Literally taken, it seems that prior consent of the supplying state is not required, at least if the receiving state already *knows* that criminal use of foreign data is allowed in the other state.

Yet it would be preferable to request the other state's prior consent, to prevent the interference of criminal proceedings in two countries. Moreover, prior consent implies that the supplying state may also obtain relevant information on the importance of the information supplied by it. For efficiency reasons, quicker proceedings to seek this consent made mandatory in Directive nr. 2004/56 concerning the use of the received tax information in *open court* should also apply to this use in *criminal tax* proceedings.[55]

53. From amending Directive nr. 2000/93/EEC of 27 Oct. 2003, to the amendment of Directive nr. 77/799, in which mutual assistance in the field of VAT was brought under Council Regulation 1798/2003, Council Directive nr. 77/799 also concerns taxes listed in the Recovery Directive. Cf. V-N 2003/58.4.
54. Gangemi (1990), 46.
55. Council Directive 2004/56/EC of 21 Apr. 2004 amending Council Directive nr. 77/799/EEC concerning the mutual assistance of the competent authorities of the Member States in the field of direct taxation, certain excise duties, and taxation of insurance premiums OJ EU L 127/70. Article 1 of that Directive determines that states willing to give their permission to use

With the amendment of the Directive 77/799 in 2003 also the transfer of data to a third Member State on the basis of Article 7, paragraph 4, was bound to the prior consent of the supplying state. Although this does not further the efficiency of the exchange, it cannot be denied that the original supplying state may have interests that are incompatible with the forwarding of the information to a third Member State, such as an unequivalent secrecy legislation in that third state, or the absence of reciprocity.[56]

### 3.1.3. Conclusion

The secrecy obligation in Directive 77/799, as well as that of the OECD Model convention, is related to the domestic laws of the receiving state. However, the difference is that the Directive allows the supplying state to decline the exchange of information if that other state is not capable or willing to offer the same protection as in the supplying state. Therefore this clause offers more protection to the state, but basically also to the taxpayer.

This directive differs in a less favourable sense from the Model convention with regard to the use of the data as an indication for recovery, which even after the amendment of Article 7 of 2003 still remained subject to explicit prior authorization.

Also on that occasion, opportunities were missed by not combining the required prior consent of the other state on the point of use of the data in *criminal proceedings* with the newly drafted quicker procedure for prior consent for the use of the information *in open court*, prescribed in Directive 2004/56.

## 3.2. Secrecy in Regulation 1798/2003 on VAT

### 3.2.1. Relative Secrecy

The main rule of the secrecy clause in Regulation 1798/2003 is embedded in Article 41, paragraph 1. The duty of secrecy, in the same manner as in the Model convention and Council Directive 77/799, is related to the domestic laws of the receiving state, but also to the secrecy standards in 'similar provisions valid for the authorities of the Community'. This refers to Directive 95/46/EC (the so-called Privacy Directive). Articles 10 and 11 of that Directive create informational rights for citizens, to whom data are related and also contain grounds for

transmitted data in open court and court rulings must do so at the time of transmission, so that no separate exchange of letters is necessary afterwards. The preamble of this Directive presents this as an improvement of efficiency. Cf. V-N 2004/31.4.

56. The absence of reciprocity is one of the grounds on which a state, in the Model convention as well as in the Directive 77/799 (and the Strasbourg Convention) may decline or refrain from supplying information. Cf. Ch.6, s. 4 hereafter.

exception.[57] From a viewpoint of protection of the taxpayer, this (vague) reference does not outweigh the *absence* in this paragraph of the possibility for the supplying state to require extra measures in situations in which the secrecy of the requesting state offers less protection. It is hard to understand why this extra protection for states and citizens, embedded in Directive 77/799 for direct taxes and taxation of social security contributions, would not have to be valid for the exchange of information for VAT purposes.[58]

To put it shortly, Article 41, paragraph 5 creates an obligation for the states to limit the scope of the rights citizens have on the basis of Articles 10, 11, paragraphs 1, 12, and 21 of the so-called Privacy Directive, inasmuch as this would be necessary to warrant the financial interests of the states, (in Article 13 sub e of that Directive).. This provision will be discussed in more detail in Chapter 8.

### 3.2.2. Use of the Data: Collection, Prosecution, Forwarding, Other Use (Criminal Proceedings)

Apart from the assessment of VAT liabilities,[59] the data received and the administrative control of these data may also be used for the *recovery* of indirect taxes and for the customs and taxes for which Council Directive nr. 76/308 (the Recovery of tax claims Directive) was drafted. As of 2001, apart from the VAT, the latter also covers certain agricultural levies and insurance premiums.[60] The use of the data for the recovery of tax claims does not require the separate consent of the supplying state. This serves the correlation between the assessment of tax liabilities and the recovery of tax claims, at least in the field of VAT. These VAT data may also without further ado be used for the *levying of* direct taxes, and vice versa, via the reference to the Recovery Directive, in which they are incorporated as of 2001.

The reference in Article 7, paragraph 1 of the VAT Regulation to legal proceedings involving the application of *penalties*, as well as the rights 'of *suspects and witnesses*' in '*proceedings involving breach of tax legislation*' implies the possibility of use of the data in criminal proceedings, without the consent of the

57. Council Directive nr. 95/46/EEC of 24 Oct. 1995 on the protection of individuals with regard to processing of personal data and on the free movement of such data, OJ EU L 281, 31. Art. 10 of this Directive creates a right of information for citizens, in case the data were obtained from themselves, Art. 11 refers to data not directly obtained from citizens, and Art. 13, sub-para e of the Directive creates an exception to that right of information if this would jeopardize the economic and financial interests of the state of the European Union.
58. This is all the more so because the extension of the Union has seen the entrance of Member States in which rule of law traditions are not yet deeply rooted.
59. Article 1 of The Council Regulation determines the substantive scope, being 'taxes on the added value of supplies of goods, services, intra-community acquisitions and importation of goods (...)'.
60. Council Directive 76/308/EEC of 15 Mar. 1976, on the mutual assistance for the recovery of claims resulting from certain levies, duties, and taxes, OJ EC L73 (the recovery Directive), most recently changed in Directive 2001/44/EC. The taxes listed are certain agricultural levies, customs excises resulting from the Euratom decision, and as of 2001 also taxes on income and wealth and insurance premiums.

supplying state. The rights enjoyed by the listed parties in the receiving state should be warranted, in accordance with Article 41, paragraph 1. The advantages in the field of efficiency and the disadvantages (the risk of interference of criminal proceedings in both countries, mentioned in the preceding paragraph), also apply here. The latter may be solved by using quick prior consent proceedings such as the one mentioned in the Directive 2004/56 could solve this problem. Based on Article 41, paragraph 4 of the regulation, forwarding the data received to a third Member State does not require prior consent, except if the requested state explicitly wishes to reserve this prior authorization. In connection with the above discussion, it is conspicuous that this forwarding of data is bound by the obligation to *notify* the supplying state, and the use in criminal proceedings does not. However, the knowledge of use of the data in criminal tax proceedings seems no less important than that of forwarding them to another Member State. The mandatory notification of the supplying state of the fact that the information is forwarded to third parties is valuable in itself, because the forwarding of the data supplied becomes clear to the supplying state, which may complete the 'profile' of certain taxpayers. The possibility contained in the provision for states to opt for *prior consent* may be of interest for the original supplying state and its taxpayers in connection with the level of secrecy protection in that *third* state.[61] The reciprocity element may also be of interest to the original supplying state.[62]

However, based on Article 36 of the Council Regulation, requiring prior consent is necessary if information is transmitted to a third state *outside* the European Union, and if the receiving Member State wishes to use the data *for other purposes*, (cf. Article 41, paragraph 3). This prior authorization *must* be granted if the domestic legislation of the supplying state allows for such use in the state itself. In Directive 77/799, granting prior authorization was left to the decision-making power of the supplying state. Here the more imperative nature of the Council Regulation comes to light.

### 3.2.3. Conclusion

The VAT Regulation does not contain a possibility for the supplying state to refuse information if the level of protection in the other state is too much at variance with its domestic legislation; thus it offers less protection than Directive 77/799. Especially as a result of the strong extension of the Union, this may only enhance the risks for states (and their information providing taxpayers).

The effectiveness of the exchange is increased by allowing the use of the data for recovery, without prior consent. For use of the data in criminal proceedings,

---

61. In that situation, prior authorization of the forwarding of data to third countries creates a possibility to make a reservation. This seems justified because of the less direct connection between the original supplying state and the ultimately receiving state.
62. Other interests of states hampering the supply of information would be the sovereignty of domestic legislation or the element of reciprocity no longer lying with the original state once the data supplied are forwarded. Cf. Ch. 6.

prior authorization is not required either. However, in my opinion, the disadvantages this implies (possible interference of criminal proceedings in the Member States and less feedback for the supplying state) outweigh a possible advantage with regard to efficiency.

For the transfer of information between Member States, notification of the supplying state suffices, except if states have mutually agreed on prior authorization. Such a requirement should be preferable, because it can offer protection to the original supplying state against a possibly uncertain warranty of secrecy. For the same reasons, prior authorization of the transfer of data to *third* countries outside the European Union is justified and desirable because it is for possible use of the data for other purposes.

## 4. THE SECRECY CLAUSE IN THE STRASBOURG CONVENTION

### 4.1. Relative Duty of Secrecy

The duty of secrecy in the receiving country is related to the secrecy legislation of that state on the basis of Article 22, paragraph 1 of the Strasbourg Convention, and as in Council Directive nr. 77/799, the supplying state may require that his domestic, more stringent rules are applied. The Explanatory Report presents the secrecy clause explicitly as a means for the protection of the 'legitimate interests of taxpayers'.[63] This does not mean that those taxpayers actually enjoy a better protection under the Convention than under the bilateral conventions, as Gangemi rightly states, nor that the 'sensitive question of the timely notification of the taxpayer' is thus solved.[64]

### 4.2. Use of the Data: Collection, Prosecution, Forwarding, Other Use (Criminal Proceedings)

The purpose of the Strasbourg Convention is worded as follows in Article 4: exchange of information 'foreseeably relevant to the assessment and collection of tax, and for the prosecution before an administrative authority, and for the initiation of prosecution before a judicial body'.

Here, too, the circle of parties entitled to disclosure of the data consists of persons and authorities (including the taxpayer himself or his representatives), involved in the assessment, collection, prosecution, and conduct of proceedings with regard to taxes listed in the specific bilateral convention between two parties. These include the oversight bodies in the states.

---

63. Strasbourg Convention, Explanatory Report, Art. 22, para. 205.
64. Gangemi (1990), 45.

The Strasbourg Convention offers the parties the possibility of making all kinds of reservations within the scope of the Convention; thus states may interpret the obligation to exchange information differently.[65] This harbours two risks:

- In the first place this may lead to a situation in which, if only few reservations are made between parties, the circle of parties entitled to the data will be very large, and also local authorities, or authorities involved in social securities, may be included in it.[66] Possibly, this large potential of users is the reason that supervising bodies of government are granted access to the data,[67] so that the enforcement of this tax duty of secrecy outside the *central* tax authorities may be controlled.[68] Other than tax authorities may also be able to benefit from the results of the exchange of information. If this has led to a correction of the tax liability, this corrected liability may be transferred to other authorities, as long as the data themselves are kept secret, the Explanatory Report reads.[69]
- The second consequence of the potentially varied objective scope of the Strasbourg Convention is its lack of clarity. Therefore Article 22, paragraph 3 explicitly prohibits the use of the data received for taxes or a field for which the supplying state has made a reservation in the process of ratification.

Before 2001, the Netherlands made a reservation as to indirect taxes.[70] If another party to the Convention had not made such a reservation, or if the Netherlands would have received data with regard to direct taxes, which might also be of use for VAT, that state would not be authorized to use that information. The Netherlands would not even be authorized to ignore their own reservation when using the data *received.*[71]

Based on Article 4, paragraph 2 of the Strasbourg Convention, at variance of Article 26 of the Model convention the supplying state must give prior

65. Cf. the Strasbourg Convention, Art. 30, and Explanatory Report, Art. 30, paras 262-269. These reservations may be made with regard to the kind of tax (levied or not by the central tax authorities, direct or indirect taxes), in the field of mutual assistance (assistance in the recovery, or assistance in the notification). However, the exchange of information about centrally levied direct taxes is a minimum requirement for states to enter the Strasbourg convention.
66. Strasbourg Convention, Explanatory Report, Art. 22, para. 208.
67. *Ibid.*, Art. 22, para. 206 speaks of 'Bodies responsible for the supervision of the administration of the tax laws (...) having the power to look into individual tax cases'.
68. As we have seen, in the 2005 version of the OECD Model Convention the 'oversight bodies' are listed as parties entitled to the information, as a result of the extension in 2000 of the objective scope of Art. 26 to all taxes, also those levied by local authorities.
69. Strasbourg Convention, Explanatory Report, Art. 22, para. 209. Cf. also note 50 to Ch. 5 s. 2.2.3 about the Dutch practice.
70. Cf. the Dutch Kingdom Act of 26 Jun. 1996, implementing the approval of the Convention on mutual assistance in tax matters, concluded in Strasbourg on 25 Jun. 1988, Parliamentary Papers 1995/1996, 24 452 (R 15 51), nr. 3 (Explanatory Memorandum), 4-8.
71. The reservation was abolished in a letter of the State Secretary for Finance to the States General, 2000-2001, 27 595 (R16 75). Cf. also V-N 2001/10.8.

authorization for the use of the data received as evidence in *criminal proceedings*, while Article 22, paragraph 2 also requires prior consent for the use in open court.[72] The Explanatory Report recommends the states to grant this prior authorization as much as possible or to use the possibility to omit the requirement of prior consent from their bilateral relationship, in order to not hamper the exchange of data unnecessarily.[73] Inasmuch as 'the prosecution with regard to tax' of the party to the convention is at stake, I consider the requirement of prior consent useful. That is because, as I have mentioned before, interference of criminal proceedings may be avoided if criminal liability exists in both states and because of the useful feedback it may yield to the supplying state about the activities of its taxpayers.

To enhance efficiency, states might use the swift prior consent procedure dictated in the amended Directive 77/799 with regard to the use in open court, as I have proposed earlier.

Article 22, paragraph 4 of the Strasbourg Convention contains (as does Directive 77/799) the possibility to use the data *for other purposes* than those listed in paragraph 2, if such use is legally possible in the supplying state and is authorized by that state.[74] According to the Explanatory Report, the combination of both conditions offers sufficient warranty for the protection of the right of privacy of the taxpayers. However, to me, this is not entirely true. The requirement of prior consent gives the supplying state the opportunity and the *discretion* to take the interests of its information-providing taxpayers into account. The answer to questions such as whether it uses this discretion and whether the taxpayer may force the tax authorities to balance his/her interests cannot be found in this provision. In Chapter 7, the position of this taxpayer will be discussed in further detail. During the '*travaux préparatoires*' of this Convention, the possibility of extended use was seen as an 'innovative element'[75] in comparison to the OECD Model convention. In the 2005 amendment of Article 26 of the OECD Model convention, this difference was abolished.

The possibility to *transfer of* information received to a third party is embedded in Article 22, paragraph 4 of the Strasbourg Convention. As in Directive 77/799 and in the latest OECD Commentary, this is subject to the authorization of the supplying state. The Explanatory Report states as a motive for this consent that this requirement may prevent states receiving data they would not be able to legally obtain otherwise.[76]

This risk may occur if information that is covered by a reservation is transferred by mistake to a third party without mentioning that reservation. If the Netherlands would have supplied information to France under the reservation with regard to indirect taxes already mentioned, France would not be able to

72. This is also true if the taxpayer in the receiving state wishes to use the supplied data in open court (e.g., in divorce proceedings). Strasbourg convention, Explanatory Report, Art. 22, para. 210.
73. Strasbourg Convention, Explanatory Report, Art. 22, para. 211.
74. *Ibid.*, Art. 26, para. 216.
75. Gangemi (1990), 47.
76. Strasbourg Convention, Explanatory Report, Art. 22, para. 217.

use that information for the assessment of indirect taxes. It would have been able only to pass on the information to a third country, under the same restriction. The requirement of prior consent enhances the control of the original supplying state and is therefore also in the interest of the taxpayer having provided the information. This is also true for the possibility thus created for the supplying party to test its secrecy standards against those of the other party (in this case a third country).

#### 4.2.1. Conclusion

In the Strasbourg Convention, too, the secrecy of the data supplied is modelled after the standards in the receiving state, the supplying state having the right to decline a request for information, as in Directive 77/799, if the other state is not willing to adopt the more stringent standards of the supplying state.

The circle of parties entitled to the data encompasses policy making or oversight bodies, perhaps because of the extra supervision considered necessary in connection with the principally very large objective scope, in which also local authorities can become users of the information.

Use for recovery purposes is possible, which enhances the effectiveness of the exchange. For the use of the data in open court prior authorization is required, as is the case for use in criminal proceedings or other use. The requirement of prior consent is especially valuable in the prevention of interferences between proceedings, and in complementing the 'profile' of taxpayers in the supplying state. Efficiency could be increased by requiring prior consent simultaneously with the request for information. Prior consent is also required for the transfer of information to a third party. This offers the supplying state a possibility to control whether any reservations it made were respected and gives it the opportunity to test its secrecy standards against those of the other party.

## 5. SECRECY IN THE OECD MODEL AGREEMENT[77]

### 5.1. Absolute Duty of Secrecy

Article 8 of the OECD Agreement dictates that 'any information received by a Contracting Party shall be treated as confidential'. The fact that no reference is made to secrecy standards in the receiving states constitutes an absolute duty of secrecy.

This reflects the relationships for which the Agreement was designated and which, put euphemistically, are not characterized by a large amount of confidence of the states in each other's legal systems. It is not to be wondered that especially the 'committed jurisdictions' (hereinafter the jurisdictions) intended to create the utmost warranties for secrecy in the receiving OECD Member States. The confidentiality of the data must be respected in order 'to protect the legitimate interests

77. Agreement on the Exchange of Information on Tax Matters, Paris 2002, see Ch. 1.

of taxpayers', as the Commentary puts it.[78] The latter emphasizes that secrecy applies to all information received by both states (the requesting and the receiving state). In this respect, it refers to Article 5, paragraph 5 of the Agreement, in which the information is listed, which the requesting state must 'include' in its request.[79]

### 5.2. Use of the Data

The circle of parties entitled access to the information is largely similar to that drawn in the Model convention. 'The oversight bodies' are not included, and from the Commentary it becomes clear why that is not necessary. If they had been listed in the Model convention in order to introduce the possibility of separate decision-making on disclosure of the information received to the taxpayer or his legal counsels or witnesses, the Global Forum did not envisage their intermediation. Taxpayers *may* have access to the information received, paragraph 96 of the Commentary reads, but it is not an obligation, and it may even be desirable that the taxpayer in the receiving state is not aware of the information received. The latter serves the protection of the party having supplied the information. Whether protection is necessary, the exchanging states will have to decide mutually.[80] This more detailed explanation in the Commentary refers to the atypical population of 'taxpayers' former tax havens may have to deal with.

Use of the data in open court is allowed. Explicit and written prior consent is required from the supplying state for use of the data other than for tax purposes or tax criminal proceedings or transmission to other 'jurisdictions'.

## 6. SUMMARY AND CONCLUSIONS

1. All exchange obligations have *the secrecy of the supplied data* by the receiving state as a *conditio sine qua non*. This reflects the need of states for secrecy in their fight against tax fraud, but also the will to protect taxpayers/suppliers of information. This conclusion may be drawn from the fact that in all rules and regulations not only the tax authorities, but also the judicial authorities are mentioned as parties entitled to the information received.

2. The *1963 version* of the Model convention contains an *autonomous* duty of secrecy, not related to the domestic law of the receiving state. This absolute duty rests on the still existing tax conventions from that period, because the subsequent amendment of the text of the Model convention cannot be interpreted as a clarification of the original text. Thus, there is no room for a dynamic interpretation of the clause.

78. Commentary to the OECD Agreement, Art. 8, para. 94
79. Cf. OECD Agreement Art. 5, para. 5, Commentary Art. 5, para. 95.
80. OECD Agreement Art. 5, para. 5, Commentary Art. 5, para. 96.

Under this version, the data received cannot be automatically disclosed in public court hearings or court rulings. The states must incorporate mutual agreements on this in their conventions. The information is destined for the tax authorities and the judicial authorities and may be used only for the assessment of tax liabilities and for the collection of taxes. In spite of the fact that an explicit reference to the use for criminal proceedings is missing, it is assumed that the latter is possible if the supplying state gives its permission to do so.

3. The amendment of Article 26 of the *OECD Model convention* in 1977 allows for the disclosure of received data in open court hearings and court rulings without further ado, as well as the use for (tax) criminal purposes. In my view, it would be preferable to introduce a requirement of permission, in combination with an expedited procedure to obtain it. This could offer a strong signal for the supplying state and could also prevent any interference of criminal proceedings in the states. Data once disclosed may also be used for other purposes, but cannot lead to further requests for information for those other purposes.

4. The 1977 OECD Model convention establishes a duty of secrecy that must in part be 'filled in' with reference to the secrecy legislation of the receiving state. This creates risks for both the states and the taxpayer whose data are supplied to the other state. Although the latter thus acquires a legal position in the receiving state, the scope of this protection is uncertain. This uncertainty is especially true with regard to the conflicting interests that may exist in the receiving state with regard to secrecy and disclosure of data based on claims of transparency of government actions.

5. In the 2005 version of Article 26 of the OECD Model convention, it is established that the duty of secrecy under the convention must have supremacy over any domestic freedom of information act in the receiving state. Since then, the information also may be passed on to general oversight bodies in the receiving state. This was possibly prompted by the wide scale of taxes, also levied by local bodies, covered by the international exchange of information from 2000 on. This extension of the possibilities for disclosure was not a clarification, but a substantial amendment of the former version. Therefore it cannot have retrospective effect on previously concluded tax convention by dynamic interpretation. As of 2004, other use of the data is possible (e.g., in the fight against money laundering, corruption and terrorism), provided that such use is internally allowed in both states and they explicitly agree to do so. Finally, in 2005, the forwarding of the data to other states was permitted, if states have incorporated this explicitly in their separate tax conventions.

6. In my view, the purpose of all of these amendments is better protection of the interests of the states. Hardly any attention, or none at all, was paid to the position of the taxpayer having provided the information.

The secrecy clause of the Model convention does not create the possibility for states, laid down in Directive 77/799 and the Strasbourg Convention, to require extra measures of secrecy to protect their taxpayer information supplier in case the levels of protection are at variance.

7. In the *European rules on the exchange of information* the secrecy clause also refers to the domestic secrecy legislation of the receiving Member State.

However, under Directive 77/799, the supplying state may require that the data are kept secret according to its own domestic legislation, if the latter offers more protection. Regulation 1798/2003 on VAT does not refer to this possibility.

8. European rules are also at variance with the OECD Model convention with regard to the use of the data. Directive 77/799 contains a requirement of consent for the use of the data in open court hearings. The corresponding procedure was streamlined in the amendment of the Directive as a result of the coming into force of Regulation 1798/2003 on VAT. Permission is also required for the use of the data for the collection of taxes (recovery). This does not further the effectiveness of the exchange.

The use of the data in criminal proceedings is not mentioned in so many words. It may be assumed that it is covered by 'other use', of Article 7, paragraph 3 of Directive 77/799. Although it is not quite clear whether permission is required in each individual case (also if the receiving state already knows that the other use is legally permitted in the supplying state) a requirement of consent would be preferable, for the same reasons as mentioned above.

The received data, which since the 2003 amendment of the Directive 77/799 may only *concern* direct taxes, may also be *used* for indirect taxes.

9. *The Regulation 1798/2003 on VAT* does not mention the use of the data in open court. However, the data can be used for tax criminal proceedings without permission, under the condition that no rights of suspects and witnesses are violated. The VAT information also may be used for the collection and the assessment of other taxes, that is, those mentioned in the Recovery Directive concerning the collection of taxes (including direct taxes). Forwarding of data is possible only to a Member State after notification to the original supplying state.

10. By referring to the Privacy Directive, the VAT Regulation expresses the Council's view on the position of the information-providing taxpayers. It refers to the informational rights the parties involved have on the basis of that Directive with regard to processing of data. They should be limited if (in the opinion of the Member States), they jeopardize the 'important' financial interests of the states involved. These limitations also should be invoked by the Member States for the exchange of information. However, the Privacy Directive regards only natural persons, whereas in a Council Regulation regarding VAT, legal bodies will certainly be involved as well.

11. In the *Strasbourg Convention*, the secrecy clause is explicitly presented as a means to protect the position of citizens. The duty of secrecy is also related to the domestic law of the receiving state, but the supplying state may require that its own domestic laws be applied if the latter offer more protection.

The circle of parties entitled to the information also encompasses, apart from the taxpayer and his representatives and the tax and judicial authorities, those applying tax criminal law. Besides the parties mentioned, oversight bodies are also entitled to the data. Perhaps this is due to the very large scope the exchange may have under this Convention, so that local, less experienced authorities also may be compelled to apply the secrecy rule in tax matters. This could require more supervision.

12. If the requesting state in 'accepting' the Strasbourg Convention has made a reservation for a certain kind of tax or for a field of mutual assistance, it is not allowed to use the received data for those purposes, even if the supplying state would not have made such a reservation.

Disclosure of the data in public proceedings requires permission, although the Explanatory Notes call for either a broad policy in this respect, or the abolishment of the permission requirement by mutual agreement. If data supplied have led to a correction of the tax liability, the corrected amount of taxable income may be passed on to authorities other than tax authorities in the receiving state without the special permission of the supplying state, as long as the information itself is not supplied. Under the Strasbourg Convention, forwarding of the information to third countries requires permission.

13. The Strasbourg Convention offers the possibility to require extra warranties on secrecy from other parties, resulting in a better protection of the information providing taxpayer.

# Chapter 6

# Limitations to the Obligation to Exchange Information

## 1. INTRODUCTION

In previous chapters I argued that, in addition to fulfilling a contractual obligation between states, the international exchange of information is also a form of government action with regard to its taxpayers who have to provide the information. Although the nature of the legal relationship between states is symmetrical, the legal relationship between the state and its citizens, in legal terms, is characterized as being asymmetrical.[1] The state, which is the most powerful party, must *protect* the interests of its citizens by weighing them against national interests. When acting within the framework of the international exchange of information, this weighing of interests must also include the Contracting party's interests.

To unravel the balance between both legal obligations of the states in the previous chapters the different obligations under international law were analyzed with regard to the international exchange of information. The following issues were examined – the objectives, the scope of the obligation to exchange information, the methods, and the necessary efforts of the Contracting states. The analysis shows that this obligation is almost exclusively focused on the protection of the tax interests of the Contracting states. Until now, only a weak trace of the existence of a state's legal obligation toward its information suppliers has been found, in the warranty of secrecy regarding information by the receiving state. This indeed also protects the information provider in the supplying state. Without running

1. The duty of care of the treaty partners under international law means that they will interpret and implement their agreement in good faith, and subject to that agreement they shall weigh the interests of their treaty partners against their own interests. In principle, both parties are expected to show the same efforts.

ahead of the analysis of the interests of these taxpayers that are discussed in the next chapter, we can thus far conclude that the protection of their position in the supplying state leaves much to be desired.

The analysis of the rules and regulations is not complete without focusing on the fact that this obligation to lend assistance between what, by definition, are equal states cannot be absolute or complete. To this end, all the regulations on the exchange of information contain limitative lists of cases in which states can consider the obligation as nonexistent.

## 2. OBLIGATIONS AND LIMITATIONS

The conditional character of the obligation to exchange information arises from the axioms of sovereignty and equality of the parties, which so strongly characterizes international law. Based on this principle, it is impossible for one state to be reduced to be merely instrumental to the aims of the other state. Obligations under international law are bound under the domestic political interests of the Convention parties,[2] whose freedom to be able to maintain their tax legislation and practical implementation is what is most essential in this respect.[3]

The right to exchange information therefore always includes a list of considerations that can limit the obligation to provide information. This creates discretionary room for states within which they can protect their domestic interests.

In Community legislation on the subject of exchange of information this is more complicated. Of course also the Member States are sovereign states, with equal positions, but at the same time their political aims are framed by this very membership. The European Court of Justice repeatedly pointed out that 'while direct taxation falls within their competence, the Member States must none the less exercise that competence consistently with Community law'.[4] This in turn raises questions about the role and function of the principle of the sovereignty of domestic law as it is laid down in Article 8, paragraph 1 of the Directive 77/799 on mutual assistance. I will elaborate on that later.

Now that within the formulation of the exchange information provision, the position of the taxpayer is not or is hardly regulated, this discretionary room could offer the information-supplying state opportunities to fulfil their duty of care under public law by also taking into account the interests of these taxpayers.[5] The

2. Additionally, a state obviously has the right to refuse the enforcement of the provision in view of a violation of the scope of the provision on the exchange of information. In the sentence: Vogel (2003), Art. 26, Rz. 107.
3. Gangemi (1990), 31 refers to the refusal of states to adapt their tax laws and practical implementation of the needs of the other states. In his opinion, this is expressed in the preamble to the London and Mexico Model Conventions of the League of Nations in 1946.
4. See, inter alia, Case C-451/05 *Elisa*, C-319/02 *Manninen* at paragraph 19; and Case C-157/05 *Holböck*, at para. 21.
5. Schaumburg (1998), para. 19.46, speaks of '*ein Konfliktfeld*' for the information-supplying state between its own interests and those of the taxpayers.

framework of international law does bring with it that the taxpayers' interests must also be 'affected' by the limiting provisions. Only if this is the case, can they be involved in the assessment.

To establish to what extent taxpayers' interests are parallel to those of the state, the limitations on the exchange of information obligation need to be examined more closely. In view of the fact that they act as exceptions to the obligation to provide information, they shall hereafter be referred to as the 'grounds for exception'. For the exchange of information on request, the term 'grounds for refusal' also could apply.[6]

It should be considered that a state's own room for judgment, which it is given on the grounds of these provisions, contains certain risks. In the literature these are referred to as the 'Achilles heel of International Assistance'.[7] Even within the European Community (EC), where Member States, although sovereign in matters of tax legislation, are bound to the demand of consistency with European Convention, states can become frustrated in their aims to combat tax evasion. The cause of this is the limitation to the exchange of information obligation regarding the sovereignty of domestic laws laid down in Article 8, paragraph 1 of the Directive 77/799, comparable to OECD tax treaties. In the *Elisa* case of the European Court of Justice, it turns out that even the 'priority' of Community law offers no 'answer' in situations in which the domestic law in the requested Member State does not offer the possibilities to gather the information needed. In these cases, in spite of the EC Treaty freedoms, the Member States may conclude a specific treaty in which they *exclude* a category of taxpayers from an advantageous rule, but they are not allowed to make the existence itself of an exchange of information obligation in the other country to a *general* condition to grant 'foreign' taxpayers an equal treatment. 'Taxpayers themselves should not be excluded a priori from providing relevant documentary evidence enabling the tax authorities of the Member State imposing the tax to ascertain, clearly and precisely, that he/she is not attempting to avoid or evade the payment of taxes', the European Court of Justice ruled in the *Elisa* case.[8]

Even though it is usually in the state's interest to behave cooperatively, it could have reasons for showing an unresponsive attitude. The discretionary provisions, laid down in Article 26, paragraph 3 of the 2005 Model Convention, Article 21, paragraph 2 of the Strasbourg Convention, Article 8 of Directive 77/799, Article 40 of Regulation 1798/2003 on value added tax (VAT), and Article 7 of the OECD Agreement, give it this possibility, even if these limitations are used improperly.[9] This can frustrate the international exchange of information.

---

6. Wisselink (1996), 59 ff.
7. van de Ven (1990b), 35.
8. Case C-451/05 *Elisa*, about the application of the reduction on the French tax on immovable properties at para. 96. Also see Case C-39/04 *Laboratoires Fournier* at para. 25 about the application of anti-abuse laws and the opportunity foreign taxpayers should get to prove their fiscal integrity, and case-law cited there.
9. Gangemi (1990), 32 mentions a 'self restrictive character of the formula'.

Though ideally, the good faith that the treaty partners owe each other and the effect of the principle of reciprocity will create a barrier against too broad a use of the discretionary powers.[10]

Various reports from within and outside the OECD show that, in practice, most states do not interpret the limiting provisions too prohibitively.[11]

## 2.1. Text of the Limiting Provisions

What are the circumstances that could give cause to states' interests being harmed, whereby they consider themselves relieved of their obligation to exchange information? According to the wording of the *Model Convention* in Article 26, paragraph 3 they are as follows:

The states are *not* obliged:

(a) to carry out measures at variance with the laws and[12] the administrative practice of that or of the other Contracting State;

This ground for exception serves the sovereignty of the states by presupposing that their national and (implementing) rules with regard to gathering or obtaining information on tax matters are essentially independent of the treaty partner's wishes. In the rest of this chapter, I shall refer to this as the sovereignty argument. Additionally, an extra restriction is included in the form of the principle of reciprocity. States are not even required to use the powers they do possess, if the other state does not have the same powers:

(b) to supply information[13] which is not obtainable under the laws or in the normal course of the administration of that or of the other Contracting State;

These grounds for refusal, in particular, concern the means by which information is gathered from taxpayers and how it is kept available. This is ultimately determined by what the law, the state's domestic tax audit practice, and the administrative organization permit and enable. Here, reciprocity also forms the starting point;

(c) to supply information which would disclose any trade, business, industrial, commercial or professional secret or trade process, or information, the disclosure of which would be contrary to public policy (ordre public).

---

10. Article 26 of the Vienna Convention mentions: 'Every effective treaty binds the parties and must be implemented by them in good faith'. Art. 31, para. 1 of that convention repeats this command for the interpretation of the treaty.
11. Gangemi (1990), 30 ff. See also the OECD Report Tax information Exchange between OECD Member Countries: Survey of Current Practices, 1994, and OECD Commentary 2005, para. 19.6 (on the willingness to conduct audits).
12. The original version contained the word 'or'.
13. The original version contained the word 'particulars'.

This assumes a certain amount of parallelism between the (economic) interests of the taxpayers whose information is exchanged and those of the state. The state can use the existence of these interests as an argument for refusing to disclose information.

Additionally, the states' other political interests are protected by the argument of the '*ordre public*'.

It is striking that in the 1994 OECD Survey of the practices on the exchange of information, states primarily mention the lack of reciprocity, business or professional secrecy, and the violation of the public order as limiting provisions.[14]

Until now, the wording in the regulations on this subject has remained the same. However, in the thinking of the OECD a development has taken place. It is reflected in the different versions of the Commentary[15] and mainly concerned the terms '*normal course of administration*' and '*trade or professional secret*'. In the 2005 version of the OECD Model Convention, this has led to the adding of two new paragraphs to the text of the convention, in which these terms are further 'elaborated'.

Community Law

Article 8 of Directive 77/779, headed 'Limits to exchange of information' is the example for other Community rules. It provides:

1. This Directive shall impose no obligation to have enquiries carried out or to provide information if the Member State, which should furnish the information, would be prevented by its laws or administrative practices from carrying out these enquiries or from collecting or using this information for its own purposes.
2. The provision of information may be refused where it would lead to the disclosure of a commercial, industrial or professional secret or of a commercial process, or of information whose disclosure would be contrary to public policy.
3. The competent authority of a Member State may refuse to provide information where the State concerned is unable, for practical or legal reasons, to provide similar information.

### 2.1.1. Specific Provisions

The Strasbourg Convention adds two other arguments to these three 'classic' arguments, that also occur and are formulated slightly differently in the Directive

14. Tax Information Exchange between OECD Member Countries, A Survey of Current Practices, OECD, 1994, para. 44.
15. See also Calderon (2000), 462. He points out that since the 1970s a huge increase has been seen in the number of tax treaties with a provision on the exchange of information, the scope of the provision, and the use that is made of them.

77/799 and in Regulation 1798/2003 on VAT. Pursuant to Article 21, paragraph 2 sub-paragraph e, a state is not required:

> to lend assistance if and in as far as it considers the taxation in the requesting state to be in violation of the generally accepted taxation principles or to the provisions of an agreement for the avoidance of double taxation, or with any other agreement which the requested state has entered into with the requesting state

Sub-paragraph f of this article also refers to the lending of assistance outside of the obligation:

> if the application of this Convention would lead to discrimination between a national of the requested state and nationals of the requesting state.

*Regulation 1798/2003* also includes grounds for exception 'a disproportionate administrative burden' of the requested state.

The OECD Agreement, in Article 7, paragraph 3 adds as argument the suspicion or knowledge that the requested information is meant 'to administer or enforce a provision in the tax law of the requesting party (. . . ) which discriminates a national of the requested party'.

The fact that the treaty law allows states a certain amount of freedom here does not mean that they can also use this with respect to their citizens. A characteristic of the rule of law is that government actions in that state are bound by the norms and laws that are formulated in public debate and should therefore be made known to its citizens and be 'enforceable'. That is why states must lay down the way in which they want to handle the discretionary freedom of the provision on the exchange of information in their domestic laws.[16] This is mainly important because the grounds for exception are almost exclusively formulated from the perspective of the supplying states. If they are also to be used on behalf of the taxpayers' interests, they must be included in the national legislation.[17]

The weighing of interests as permitted under paragraph 3, could result a state supplying information, in spite of the applicability of a 'ground for refusal or exception', if this is permitted under its national legislation. A state that does this remains bound under 'the framework (. . . ) of the Convention'.[18]

16. Compare Davis (1969). He asserts that most of the injustices in the legal practice result from discretionary powers that are too broad. The law is much more frequently enacted on an individual level than realized by the legislator. This mainly has disastrous effects for the application of the principle of equality. According to him, this discretion should be restrained by formulating 'standards' for and by the implementing bodies. In 2006, in the Netherlands this is referred to as the 'unity of policy and implementation'.
17. Schaumburg (1998), para. 19.60, mentions grounds on which Germany is not required to supply information, such as not complying with the principle of exhaustion, lack of reciprocity (taken from Article 26 Model Convention), and the principle of proportionality. The Dutch WIB has also adopted the grounds for refusal, but contrary to Germany's practice, the Netherlands has formulated them as an imperative. See hereafter para. 10.8.
18. OECD Commentary 1977-2005, Art. 26, para. 17. Also see Strasbourg Convention, Explanatory Report, Art. 21, para. 195. Also see Vogel (2003), Art. 26, Rz. 110.

The grounds for exception are handled point by point below.

I shall apply the same thematic approach as in the previous chapter, and base this on the OECD Model Convention and the corresponding Commentary. From the first version of this Model convention, this served as an example under which limitations to the obligation to exchange information have almost literally been adopted in the 1977 European Directive 77/799, the Strasbourg Convention, European Regulation 1798/2003 of 2003 and the OECD Agreement.

## 3. SOVEREIGNTY OF THE DOMESTIC LAWS OR ADMINISTRATIVE PRACTICE

In most regulations, the sovereignty argument consists of two components, and these may or may not be worded separately. The first concerns 'not *having to take measures*', (OECD Model Convention Article 26 paragraph 3, sub-paragraph a, Strasbourg Convention, Article 21, paragraph 2, sub-paragraph a, Directive 77/799 Article 8, paragraph 1, and Article 7, paragraph 1 of the OECD Agreement). The second component relates to not having to provide *unobtainable* information (OECD Model Convention Article 26 paragraph 3, sub-paragraph b, Strasbourg Convention Article 21, paragraph 2, sub-paragraph c. Under European law this is called (not being required to) *conduct an inquiry*, or not *being required to provide information* (Directive 77/799 Article 8, paragraph 1, VAT Regulation Article 40, paragraph 2).

In all cases, the criterion is the domestic law or administrative practice with regard to obtaining tax information, based on the general principle of international law that states have the right to pursue their own objectives, without being able to be *forced* to make exceptions solely on behalf of the other state.[19] The supplying state is protected against supplying information if this would mean having to violate its domestic sovereign national legislation and administrative practice.[20] If the information-gathering powers of one state are much weaker than those of the other state, the 'sovereignty argument' can induce this other state to conclude a more limited tax treaty and to create domestic legislation that excludes some of the taxpayers of that state from advantageous tax rules.[21] This is accepted

---

19. Also see the OECD view on this in the debate on tax competition. The right of states to establish tax laws according to their own insights is fundamental and inviolable, even if this affects other states. OECD Report: Harmful Tax Competition, An Emerging Global Issue, Paris 1998, para. 26, 15. On the influence of the administrative procedures of the European Court of Justice on the tax laws of the Member States, van den Hurk (2003), 155. Also see McLure 2001, 328, who focuses on the effect of market forces on the tax politics of the individual states as a result of globalization. This results in restrictions to the tax sovereignty of the states, which are established unilaterally or via negotiations.
20. According to Vogel (2003), Art. 26, Rz. 111, 'administrative measures' should be understood to mean all administrative actions that states must take to comply with a request for information, irrespective of which public body takes them.
21. Case C-451/05 *Elisa* 2005, at para. 55.

even in the case law of the EC, even if this would hamper the 'freedoms' of the EC Treaty.

The sovereignty argument is meant to protect the interests of the state who has to supply the information, but it also serves both states to maintain their integrity in their relationship with their citizens. The Explanatory Report to Article 21 of the Strasbourg Convention explains this with regard to the requesting state: 'This rule is important in safeguarding the rights of the taxpayer, since it prevents the applicant state from making use indirectly (...) of greater powers than it possesses under its domestic law.'[22] I shall discuss this public-law aspect in the next chapter.

## 3.1. Sovereign Domestic Laws

The ground for exemption pertains to the entire tax legislation concerning the obtainability of information on behalf of taxation and its implementation.

Within this context the most relevant components are:

- the national statutory investigative powers of the tax authorities;
- the rights of taxpayers, within the framework of taxation, such as the obligation of secrecy regarding tax matters, taxpayers' rights to information, citizens' rights to not have to incriminate themselves, and the statutory right to not be required to disclose certain confidential communication to the tax authorities (the 'solicitors' privilege').[23]

### 3.1.1. The Tax Authorities' Powers

The obtainability of information is dependent on the 'information-gathering powers' in the sovereign domestic laws of the treaty partners, and their content is therefore diverse. The Commentary to the Model Convention has attempted to objectify this term through further descriptions.[24]

From the 1963 version of that Commentary (with the previous Article 26, paragraph *two*) the term is linked to the term 'normal course of administration', whereby the latter is defined as the 'normal procedure of tax determination' in the requested country. As shown in Chapter 4, this initially did *not* include conducting special audits among taxpayers or third parties.[25] Information that is 'obtained' in this way can contain only information that the tax authorities already have on the grounds of the requirement to submit a tax declaration (the 'readily available

22. Strasbourg Convention, Explanatory Report, Art. 21, para. 189.
23. The state can invoke this right both under the sovereignty argument (OECD Model convention), and under the argument concerning business or professional secrecy (OECD Agreement).
24. In 2005 this tightening of the rules was also incorporated in the text of the Model Convention itself.
25. OECD Commentary 1963, Art. 26, para. 12.

information')[26] or information that is readily obtainable from the taxpayer or third party, depending on which options the state has.[27]

The question arises as to whether a requested state can refuse a request based on such an 'old' tax treaty because the information can be obtained only through inquiries, even if the state's legislation does provide for such inquiries?

Two aspects are important here:

- The first is that such a treaty is on strained terms with the altered insights on the pursued treaty efforts, as laid down in the Commentary. Under the direction of the Committee on Fiscal Affairs (CFA), it is generally accepted that old treaties must be explained within the meaning of the new Commentary, as these may be considered to reflect the new insights of the OECD community. However, the requesting state cannot enforce this so-called dynamic interpretation.[28] This may even be wrongful if the treaty partners *deliberately* used the divergent previous version of the existing Comment.
- The second consideration is that a request to the foreign country also could be possible and useful under the oldest version of the obligation to exchange information. The tax authorities of the requested state can view the foreign request as a signal of a possible *national* taxation interest and may conduct an investigation on behalf of the national taxation. In such a case the often 'draconian powers' of states to gather information on behalf their national taxation of taxpayers can be used to for the other state as well.[29] The reason for the requested state to act like this could be a major tax interest in the other state. In doing so, the state is not violating the exchange of information provision, which asserts only a 'minimum position', and by no means prohibits further efforts on behalf of the other state.[30] Whether or not a state acts wrongfully with regard to the audited taxpayer depends on the question of whether the circumstances fall under the '*détournement de pouvoir*' (abuse of power). Only the requested state itself is able to assess this. For this reason, the requesting state cannot enforce such a position on its treaty partner.

The freedom that states have to appeal to their legislation and administrative practice can also lead to a circular argument, if the states have not expanded their national powers to conduct tax audits beyond the national taxation interest and subsequently appeal to the lack of this power to refuse requests for

---

26. In some tax treaties the exchange is limited to this. For example in the Dutch treaties with Germany (1959), Denmark (1957), and in several recent treaties. Also see para. 9.2.
27. Also Wisselink (1996), 62.
28. Some authors (and possibly also judges) do not agree with this view. See para. 3.6.
29. The term is by Bentley (1998), 157. He has observed this view among the majority of the OECD states. Also see Winkler (2006), 96, 99 ff., who observes a strengthening of the states' powers of the states and as a result the undermining of taxpayers' rights, partly as a result to the international exchange of information on taxes.
30. See the OECD report: Tax Information between OECD Member Countries, A Survey of Current Practices, 1994, para. 48.

information.[31] Literally speaking, they are not in violation of the treaty, which also refers to the national legislation and administrative practice. Therefore, in my opinion, Article 27 of the Vienna Convention does not apply.[32] There is also no general rule of international law that determines that international law always automatically has supremacy over provisions of domestic law. This depends on the interpretations that the individual states have laid down in their constitutions. In some states, there is no supremacy of international law and the rule applies that the 'youngest' legal rule takes precedence over the old rule (the *lex posteriori* rule).[33] Other states, among them the Netherlands, have only a constitutional precedence for directly applicable provisions of international law. With the discretionarily formulated restrictions of the obligation to supply information, however, this cannot be the case.[34]

To slightly limit the risk, in the revision of the OECD Commentary in 1977, the states are asked to show more commitment, also concerning the institution of special audits for the sake of the treaty partner.[35] From this point on, states are no longer free to not apply the administrative instruments at their disposal on behalf of the treaty partner, even if this is exclusively in the treaty partner's interest. The requested information must be gathered *in the same way* as would occur on behalf of the state's own levying of taxes, according to paragraph 14 of the OECD Commentary.

However, the Committee on Fiscal Affairs did not consider this sufficient. The way in which the restriction was formulated in the Commentary meant it included the risk for a misconception that the states would be required to provide only the information that they also gathered on behalf of their own levying of taxes. This can be concluded from Article 26, paragraph 4, added in 2005. The requested states must apply their 'information-gathering measures' to obtain the requested information, 'even though the other State may not need such information for its own tax purposes'.[36]

However, according to the treaty text, this does not mean that the grounds for exception under Article 26, paragraph 3, no longer apply.[37]

The OECD Commentary presents Article 26, paragraph 4 as the explanation of the situation in practice for conducting special audits without a national tax

31. There are states that link the investigative power for the foreign taxation interest to the existence of a national taxation interest. An example is Japan, which has laid down an 'observation' for this purpose in the Commentary.
32. Article 27 of the Vienna Convention alleges that a party may not invoke its national laws to justify not implementing the convention. This does not apply to elements of the convention that acknowledge national law as standard.
33. Sometimes, like in the United States, the supremacy of the new law over the existing treaty is dependent on the question of whether the new law is specifically intended to 'override' the treaty.
34. See Ch. 4, s. 4.3.
35. See Ch. 4, s. 4.6.1.
36. Also see OECD Commentary 1977-2005, Art. 26, para. 19.7.
37. OECD Model Convention, Article 4 alleges: '*the obligation contained in the preceding sentence is subject to the limitations in paragraph 3*'.

interest.[38] This is a slightly odd argument. If the previous Comment 14 of the OECD Commentary were faithfully complied with, then why would another provision be required? This may have been in view of the expected accession of new economically and politically important countries that did not participate in the forming of ideas on this point within the OECD. Whatever the Committee on Fiscal Affairs' motivation for expanding the provision may have been, it does mean that states can no longer use the argument of conflicts with their domestic legislation or administrative practice solely because the information cannot be gathered *because of the lack of a state's domestic taxation interest.*

The OECD Commentary with this article gives states that have doubts on the 'information-gathering powers' of their Contracting states the suggestion to include a separate clause in their tax treaties on behalf of modifying the 'legislation, rule-making or administrative arrangements' in this field.[39] The question remains if the states concerned are willing to accept this language.

Article 26, paragraph 5 of the OECD Model Convention 2005 goes a step further. States cannot simply refuse to supply information for the simple reason that it must be gathered from 'a bank, other financial institution, nominee or person acting in an agency or fiduciary capacity, or because it relates to ownerships interests in a person'. This contains clear indications of the difficult debates on banking secrecy that long kept the OECD in its grasp.[40]

In my opinion, by recognizing the sovereignty of the supplying state's domestic legislation, this also means that states should refrain from *using* information as a result of which their treaty partner would appeal to the sovereignty argument.[41]

### 3.1.2. The Rights of Taxpayers (Model Convention, Other Regulations)

Paragraph 15 of the OECD Commentary with Article 26, paragraph 3, Model convention, sub-paragraph a, also classifies under the 'internal laws' of the states, which could prevent the exchange of information, those laws that concern the rights of the citizens in these states. They are approached differently in the several regulations on the exchange of information.

---

38. OECD Commentary 1977-2005, Article 26, para. 19.6.
39. OECD Commentary 1977-2005, Article 26, para. 19.9.
40. This comment in the OECD Commentary also relates to the hereafter examined grounds for refusal concerning business or professional secrecy.
41. An example of this is the case of the Luxemburg bank details that were obtained by Belgium via a search warrant and that were spontaneously supplied to the Netherlands, in spite of the Luxemburg 'banking secrecy'. In this case, it can be alleged that the information should not have been obtained in Luxemburg within the context of the administrative exchange of information while Luxemburg was unable to use its discretionary power of 26, para. 2 (now 3) to still supply the information. In my opinion, this makes the information obtained by Belgium wrongful. The Dutch (criminal) courts for the most part judged the obtaining of information by the Netherlands as lawful. Also see Vogel (2003), Art. 26, Rz. 106, who was unaware of this specific case.

### 3.1.2.1. Rights in the Tax Audit Process

It is not only the way in which the tax authorities' powers in a state are regulated that can limit the statutory obtainability of information, and so also the exchange of information, but also the duty to lend assistance of the taxpayers, including certain rights taxpayers are able to enforce *in the tax audit process.*[42]

Here I am referring to the rights to oppose the *gathering of information* by the government, for example, via the right to object and appeal in the event of third-party audits.[43]

According to Vogel, the taxpayer can appeal to such rights, even if the information to be gathered is intended for another state; however, this circumstance cannot strengthen the taxpayer's rights, nor can it make an appeal on the grounds for refusal concerning business and professional secrecy (see hereafter). In principle, the exchange of information is obligatory, and '*nach Article 26 Abs. 2, bezieht sich der internationale Auskunftsverkehr auch auf Geschäfts-und Gewerbegeheimnisse, dem ersuchten Staat wird in diesem Bereich lediglich and Auskunftsermessen eingeräumt'*.[44] I understand Vogel's point of view to mean that the grounds for exception cannot result in a direct right of appeal for the taxpayer. This seems correct to me. It is true that until now the grounds for exception have been almost exclusively formulated from the states' perspective.[45] I am of the opinion that these rights can (and should be) the vehicle via which to weigh the taxpayers' interests. However, this is only possible after the information has been gathered by the tax authorities.[46]

### 3.1.2.2. Rights of Information

As of 1977, the Commentary explicitly mentions as example the obligation of some states to notify the information-providing taxpayers in advance of an

---

42. This does not refer to, in the previous paragraph mentioned right to information on the fact of supplying the information as such.
43. In the Netherlands in 1997, as argued by the Working Group for aspect of legal protection under tax law (Geppaart – Flinterman) see V-N 1997, 1716, Schaumburg (1998), para. 19.59, mentions rights existing in Germany to refuse information and to inspect documents and the right to a hearing before an investigation *for parties that are required to lend assistance*, at the time of writing, the legislative proposal Legal Projection for Audits by the Tax Authorities, submitted by members of parliament Dezentjé Hamming and Crone. Submitted, Official documents 2005/2006 30645. Also see Winkler (2006), 113 ff.
44. ('On the basis of Art. 26, para. 2 the international exchange of information, also concerning business secrets, just entitles the requested state to exchange information.') Vogel (2003), Art. 26, Rz. 114, 2022.
45. Only with regard to the hereafter examined grounds for refusal on business secrecy, does the OECD Commentary mention taxpayers' interests that can also be weighed by the state.
46. See the judgment of the Court of Amsterdam, 13 Nov. 2003, V-N 2004/7.8. The judgment makes a clear division between the stage of gathering the information requested by a foreign country (whereby the taxpayer has a duty to lend assistance) and the decision-making stage on the supply of information (whereby the Dutch taxpayer has a right to information).

intended supplying of information. According to the OECD Commentary until 2005, states must mention the existence of this obligation and the possible consequences to the Contracting States.[47] The 1994 OECD Survey refers to the hindering effects which are based on some nationally enshrined 'taxpayers' guarantees', because these can lead to lengthy procedures.[48]

This comment is further elaborated in the last revision of Article 26 Model convention and the Commentary in 2005. Although the added Comment 14.1 is the first mention of acknowledging the value of a right to information to avoid mistakes in the supply of information and to improve the 'compliance' of taxpayers, it mainly refers to the risk that such a right would entail to the interests of the requesting state. In urgent cases, it should be possible to suspend the notification to the taxpayer or in cases in which this would undermine the results of the enquiry in the requesting state.[49] This shall be examined more extensively in the discussion of the position of the taxpayers involved in the exchanged of information.[50]

#### *3.1.2.3. Ban on Self-Incrimination*

OECD Commentary 2005, like the example set in the OECD Agreement, also mentions self-incrimination as a right of taxpayers that could obstruct the gathering of information by the tax authorities and so also the exchange of information. This applies in cases in which there is a risk that information can be used on behalf of criminal-law proceedings concerning tax matters.[51] In these cases, the requested state can refuse to supply information in view of a violation of its own domestic laws, but this ban on self-incrimination can hardly play a significant role in the exchange of information between the states. This is in view of the fact that only the party who risks becoming a suspect is entitled to this, whereas for the exchange of information between the states, most of the information must be obtained from third parties such as banks or contracting parties in transactions between organizations'.[52]

### 3.1.3. National Secrecy Laws, No Grounds for Exception (All Regulations)

According to the OECD Commentary, the domestic laws that the supplying states could appeal to on the grounds of Article 26, paragraph 3 a and b, do not include the

47. OECD Commentary 1977-2005, Art. 26, para. 14. See Vogel 2003, Art. 26, Rz. 110, 2021.
48. Tax Information Exchange between OECD Member Countries, A Survey of Current Practices, OECD 1994, para. 44.
49. OECD Commentary 1977-2005, Art. 26, para. 14.1.
50. See Chs 7 and 8.
51. This right was first mentioned as a limiting factor for the exchange of information in the Report Tax Information Exchange between OECD Member Countries, A Survey of Current Practices, OECD, 1994, para. 69.
52. OECD Commentary 1977-2005, Art. 26, para. 15.2, and OECD Agreement, Commentary Art. 7, para. 74.

national legislation on *secrecy*.[53] This is because the obligation of secrecy with regard to the provided information is passed on to the receiving state. The commentary to the OECD Agreement also alleges that in spite of the existence of a ground for refusal the supplying of information still occurs, 'the person concerned cannot allege an infraction of the rules on secrecy'.[54] This ban appears to have been formulated too strictly, in view of the existence of the grounds for exception in case of a 'professional or business secret'. In my view, the last mentioned refers more to the situation that certain information is also a 'secret' for the supplying state or cannot be obtained in a regular way. I will discuss this more elaborately in paragraph 6.5.1.

The ban on appealing to the rules of tax secrecy is not mentioned in the – otherwise elaborate – Explanatory Report to the Strasbourg Convention, and as previously mentioned, Directive 77/799 and Regulation 1798/2003 do not contain any notes at all. However, I am of the opinion that this prohibition should also apply in the other regulations. After all, the *international* obligation to exchange information was created for the very purpose of overruling the national obligation of secrecy in the states on behalf of the treaty partner's interests.

### 3.1.4. Taxpayers' Rights in Other Regulations

The Strasbourg Convention clearly recognizes the importance of domestic laws for taxpayers. Article 21, paragraph 1 expressly mentions that the treaty may not infringe on people's rights pursuant to the legislation or the administrative practice in the requested state. Until now, no such general 'guarantee' has been included in the Model convention and the Commentary. There, taxpayers' rights are considered an obstruction to the exchange of information, which should not be implemented too far. The more citizen-oriented perspective of the Strasbourg Convention seems to be continued in the separate grounds for refusal that are laid down in Article 21 of the Strasbourg Convention.

Article 21, paragraph 2, sub-paragraph e, of the Convention mentions as extra ground for exception that the exchanging of information would serve taxation in the requesting state that infringes on the generally accepted taxation principles. The Explanatory Report mentions as examples taxation of a confiscatory character and the existence of draconian sanctions in the other state.[55] The limiting of the obligation to exchange information in view of 'the generally accepted taxation principles', especially in the explanation given in the Explanation, refers to a higher abstraction level than the sovereignty argument as such. Here, not only is recognized the inviolability of the existing tax legislation in both treaty states, but also the existence of more general standards of decency with which all tax laws should comply.

53. OECD Commentary 1963, Art. 26, para. 10, and OECD Commentary 1977-2005, Art. 26, para. 14.
54. OECD Agreement, Commentary, Art. 7, para. 71.
55. Strasbourg Convention, Explanatory Report, Art. 21, para. 200.

Article 21, paragraph 2 of the Strasbourg Convention also allows the parties to refuse to supply the information, if in their opinion this violates the provisions of the *tax treaty* that exists between parties. This means no information needs to be exchanged if this were to lead to double taxation, or if the requests are made on the basis of other definitions, or within the framework of other measures than allowed under that treaty.[56] Insofar as this stipulation is similar to Article 26, paragraph 1 of the Model convention, that makes the exchange of information for the applicability of the national legislation only obligatory, 'insofar as the taxation there under is not contrary to the Convention'.

Additionally, a human rights' aspect is mentioned in sub-paragraph f of Article 21, paragraph 2 of the Strasbourg Convention, which also mentions possible discrimination of a national from the requested state in the requesting state as ground for refusal. On further consideration, this provision seems superfluous because the prevention of discrimination pre-eminently fits with generally accepted taxation principles and is therefore already covered in sub-paragraph e (and by paragraph 1 of Article 26 of the OECD tax treaties existing between states). The Explanatory Notes to these parts of Article 21, in my opinion, has rightly been criticized as superfluous and gratuitous by some authors.[57]

European Directive 77/799 in its exception provision (Article 8) makes no specific mention of any taxpayers' rights that could limit the obligation to supply information, although the national legislation, among which are statutory rights of taxpayers, can also limit the obligation to exchange information on the grounds of that Directive.

Regulation 1798/2003 on VAT does mention specific rights of taxpayers, namely, the rights to information that taxpayers in the Member States can have on the grounds of Directive 95/46 EC[58] but judges that not the obligation to exchange information, but that these rights should be curtailed, if this would cause harm to the financial interests of the states.[59] These rights to information are not mentioned in Article 40 (the exception provision), but in Article 41, paragraph 5, as part of the secrecy clause.

The OECD Agreement, Article 7 does not include the 'sovereignty argument'. This may be due to the rudimentary nature of tax legislation and administrative practice in the jurisdictions for which the Agreement is intended, (and which to some taxpayers constitutes the appeal of these jurisdictions).[60]

56. Strasbourg Convention, Explanatory Report, Art. 21, para. 201, mentions as examples taxation on the grounds of other than permitted withholding tax rates or based on a different definition of a permanent establishment.
57. See den Boer (1988). Also see Wisselink (1996), 204, and Helfrich-Laubrock (1987), who as standpoint of the international business sector mention that the draft treaty makes too few requirements on protecting the taxpayer, mainly with regard to infringement of business or commercial secrets.
58. Directive 95/46/EC of 24 Oct. 1995, OJ L 281. (The so-called Privacy Directive).
59. Also see above in Ch. Ch.5, s. 3.2.1.
60. Article 7, para 1 provides a protection for the *requested state* against a lack in the reciprocity. See para. 6.4 hereafter.

Legislation aimed at protecting the interests of their taxpayers does exist in most of these jurisdictions, as evident from Article 7, paragraph 3, the specific protection of the national laws concerning the confidentiality of the counsellor-client relationship.[61] Herein detailed attention is paid to the definition of the terms 'confidential', 'attorney' and 'solicitor'.[62] This detailed description appears to have little to do with respect for the legislation of a sovereign treaty partner, but seems more focused on placing these laws 'between bounds', so that the obligation to exchange information does not still become illusory. The provision is very similar to the so-called business secrecy argument that is examined further on.

### 3.2. Sovereign Administrative Practice

The sovereignty argument does not extend just to the domestic *laws*, but also to the administrative *practice* of the requested (or spontaneously supplying state). The term 'administrative practice' is mentioned in all regulations. In the absence of the sovereignty argument in the OECD Agreement, this term is used only indirectly in connection with the reciprocity argument, and in this case with regard to the *other* state.[63]

#### 3.2.1. Definition: OECD Model Convention, Strasbourg Convention

The term 'administrative practice' is not further defined in either the OECD Commentary, or in the Explanation to the Strasbourg Convention.[64] The context reveals that here the term also refers to the obtaining or gathering of information by the tax authorities (in practice).[65] It is assumed that this means every practical implementation with regard to obtaining information that is based on a law or a binding implementing regulation. This includes rules and agreements, or implementing rules and agreements with information suppliers who are subject to taxation, including so-called 'gentlemen's agreements' with banks.[66]

---

61. OECD Agreement, Commentary Art. 7, paras 85, 87, 89.
62. *Ibid.*, paras 86, 88, 90.
63. The OECD Agreement does not include grounds for refusal concerning the infringement of the national legislation or practice in the requested state, as seen in Ch. 6, s. 2.1.1., but only the argument of the lack of reciprocity (see hereafter Ch. 6, s. 4.1).
64. Neither in the Report Tax Information Exchange between OECD Member Countries, A Survey of Current Practices, OECD, 1994.
65. Also see Vogel (2003), Art. 26, Rz. 111.
66. Like in the previous Dutch Code of Conduct for tax authorities – banks, whereby in principle the banks were indemnified against questions on behalf of a foreign taxation interest. (In 1998 this was replaced by the Regulations on Information from Tax authorities/Banks, of 1 Apr. 1998, no. AFZ98/1228, *Government Gazette* 1998, 70). Another example is the limited informational duties of third parties for tax consultants.

In this respect, I am referring to my commentary in paragraph 6.3.1.1 on the investigative powers of the tax authorities, as manifested in what the OECD Commentary calls the 'normal procedure of tax determination'. This refers to subordinate regulations in which these laws are incorporated.

Also, with regard to the term 'administrative practice', which includes the connotation of 'normal handling', the next versions of the Model Convention and Commentary were increasingly restricted. Vogel considers every general means of handling by the administration to be an administrative practice, even if it is not prescribed as binding.[67] By including the administrative practice in the grounds for exception, the principles of efficiency and proportionality also play a role.[68]

It is noticeable that over the course of time the text of the Model convention and the Commentary concerning the administrative practice has appeared to become more divergent. Article 26, paragraph 3 of the Model convention 2005 formulates the grounds for exception for 'a Contracting State'. Paragraph 15 of the 2005 Commentary, however, speaks of the *requested* state. Article 21 of the Strasbourg Convention and the Explanation refer only to 'the requested state',[69] whereas both commentaries also mention the spontaneous and automatic exchange of information as compulsory methods of exchanging information. This raises the question as to whether this 'sovereignty argument' may not be applicable to the other methods of exchange. In my opinion, this argument applies to all methods of exchanging information. The inviolability of a state's domestic law, in addition to the interests of the supplying state, also serves as legal certainty for the state's citizens. The fact that, here, the perspective of the exchange on request was chosen is possibly because the exchange that underlies the treaty partner's request is the archetype of the exchange of information.[70]

### *3.2.1.1. 'Laws and Administrative Practice'*

Another textual divergence is observed in Article 26, paragraph 2, sub-paragraph a, of the Model convention. Since the revision in 1977, this provision contains the phrase 'measures at variance with laws *and* administrative practice', whereas in the original version of the article, one of the circumstances already appears sufficient for a state to consider itself relieved from the obligation to exchange information ('laws *or the* administrative practice') and the Commentary in paragraph 14 (old) uses the conjunction 'and' and paragraph 15 uses the conjunction 'or'.

The question is whether this results in a double requirement of conflict. In that case, a state could less easily consider itself entitled to refuse to supply

67. Vogel (2003), Art. 26, Rz. 112.
68. See Vogel (2003), Art. 26, Rz. 101 for the German situation, in which a general *Wirtschaftlichheitsprinzip* is formulated in the legislation.
69. Strasbourg Convention Art. 21, para. 1, in conjunction with Explanatory Report, Art. 21, para. 198.
70. The OECD Report Tax Information Exchange between OECD Member Countries, 1994, generally assumes that the obligation to exchange information is greatest on requesting information.

information. This would be disadvantageous to that state, because its discretionary room is restricted, but also to the taxpayer who has provided the information. This is because before supplying the information, they could benefit from the fact that only one of the two elements of the sovereignty argument needs to be weighed against their interests.

In my view, no part of the Model convention or the Commentary gives cause to assume that the use of the word 'and' in the revised text of Article 26 by formulating a cumulative requirement had the objective of reducing the discretionary room of the states compared to the original version. In the corresponding Commentary, no attention is paid to the alteration, and, as previously mentioned, the old terminology is maintained in Comment 15. It is defensible that the use of the conjunction 'and' in the Model Convention only means that both circumstances (infringement of the law, infringement of the administrative practice) could give cause for refusal and not that the refusal is possible only if they both occurred simultaneously.[71] My preference would be to maintain the current terminology, because this is the same as the grounds for refusal as laid down in sub-paragraph a of Article 21, paragraph 2 of the 1988 Strasbourg Convention, and to Article 8 of Directive 77/799. Both provisions mention 'legislation *or* administrative practice'.

Any disputes arising from the varying text could be solved via a mutual agreement procedure pursuant to Article 25 of the Model convention.

### 3.2.2. Sovereign Law and 'Administrative Practice' in Other Regulations

#### *3.3.2.1. Strasbourg Convention*

The above-mentioned incorporation of the term 'normal procedure of tax determination' in the OECD Model Convention (paragraph 3.2.1.1), has created some 'static' between the Strasbourg Convention and the Explanation to Article 21, paragraph 2 sub-paragraph c of the Convention. This simply mentions that a state that has these powers, but 'does not in practice *normally* use' is not *required* to use these on behalf of the treaty partner. The Explanatory Report does not distinguish on the ground of the reason why these are not used.[72] This explanation, which originates from 1988, in my opinion does not correspond with the new paragraph 4 of Article 26 OECD Model Convention.[73] There, states are obligated to supply information that is *not of interest* to their *domestic* taxation (and that they will *normally* not obtain). If states have entered into a tax treaty on the basis of the

71. In the Dutch situation there is a (slight) chance that a court will decide on the text as included on the basis of the Dutch Standard convention in tax treaties. This could occur in treaties whereby both language versions differ on this point, but are equally authentic. A taxpayer could present the English text as basis for the court and could try to enforce the 'or' variant, as a result of which the Netherlands would sooner be able to invoke the grounds for refusal as formulated imperatively under the Dutch rules on the international exchange of information.
72. Strasbourg Convention, Explanatory Report, Art. 21, para. 189 and 195.
73. Also see Vogel (2003), Art. 26, Rz. 113.

OECD Model Convention, but are also party to the Strasbourg Convention,[74] in my opinion, this causes tension between both opinions regarding to what extent the sovereignty argument can apply.

Article 27 states that the Convention does not impose restrictions on the application of other regulations and is not limited by these either. The Explanatory Report explains that 'the most effective instruments *can* be used in any particular situation'. In my opinion, to retain the broadest possible discretionary power, non-European states[75] could base their exchange on the Strasbourg Convention.

It would be wise if the Coordinating Body, which is responsible for developing the Strasbourg Convention[76] and whose members are also members of the OECD, were to modify the Explanation on this point, to put them in line with the OECD Model Convention.

#### *3.3.2.2. Directive 77/799*

In Directive 77/799, the sovereignty argument was laid down in Article 8, paragraph 1. States are not obligated to conduct inquiries or to supply information if their domestic laws or administrative practice does not permit them to conduct an audit for their domestic objectives or to gather or *use* information. It is difficult to place this last word because the grounds for exception would limit the obligation, and are therefore formulated from the perspective of the *supplying* state. This may refer to the situation that the law of the supplying state also prohibits the use of the information that it receives through a request for information, for example, for reasons relating to the privacy of taxpayers. The lack of an explanation or commentary means this cannot be said with certainty.

#### *3.3.2.3. Regulation 1798/2003 on VAT*

Regulation 1798/2003 under Article 40, paragraph 2 includes the same provision as Directive 77/799. Paragraph 1 of that Article names two other grounds that limit the obligations to exchange information: (a) if the nature and the number of requests from the other Member State would impose a disproportionate burden on the requested state and (b) if the requesting state has not exhausted its domestic normal sources (for the so-called standard of exhaustion see paragraph 4.4.6.1).

74. An example of this is the relationship between the Netherlands and the United States.
75. Strasbourg Convention, Art. 27, para. 2, obliges the European Member States in the consolidation of the treaties in their mutual relationships to opt for regulations that fall under European law.
76. Strasbourg Convention, Art. 24, para. 3, in conjunction with Explanatory Report, Art. 24, paras 229-230 and 242-243.

### *3.3.2.4. OECD Agreement*

As previously observed in the OECD Agreement, neither domestic law nor the administrative practice forms a reason for a state to consider itself relieved of the obligation. This may be due to the rudimentary stage of the tax legislation and administrative practice in the states for which the Agreement is specifically intended.

### *3.3.2.5. Conclusion*

An analysis of the sovereignty argument as included in the OECD Model Convention shows that over time this has been increasingly curtailed via the incorporation of the term 'normal procedure of tax determination' and by expanding the expected efforts, even if no domestic taxation interest exists.

The effect of the sovereignty argument is ultimately curtailed in the 2005 version of the Model convention through the recommendation to the states to make the realization itself of the 'information-gathering powers' by the treaty partner an item for the treaty negotiations.

The analysis shows that national rights of information for data suppliers in the Model convention are considered with some suspicion. The possibility to appeal to national bans on self-incrimination (in the Model convention) is restrained through a strict definition. This is partly explainable because of the risk that states will make wrongful use of the sovereignty argument to avoid the obligation to exchange information. This mainly seems to be the background to the lack of this limiting provision in the OECD Agreement of 2002.

The Strasbourg Convention seems to adopt a more positive approach to taxpayers' rights; however, because any further explanation is missing, the statements are of a somewhat noncommittal nature.

## 4. RECIPROCITY

In the exceptions, the obligation to exchange information is not only restricted through impossibilities in the legislation and/or administrative practice of the requested (supplying) state, but also by those in the *other* (requesting) state. This makes the principle of reciprocity explicit in the rules on the international exchange of information. This requirement of reciprocity is seen in the Model convention in Article 26, paragraph 3, sub-paragraphs a and b; in the Strasbourg Convention in Article 21, paragraph 2, sub-paragraphs a and c; in the Directive 77/799 in Article 8, paragraph 3; in Regulation 1798/2003 in Article 40, paragraph 3; and in the OECD Agreement in Article 7, paragraph 1.

These regulations mention two aspects of reciprocity: reciprocity with regard to *actively* using *powers* to obtain information and with regard to the availability of information as such. I shall examine both aspects because they relate to (the different) possibilities of *obtaining* information. I shall also base this on the

OECD Model Convention and Commentary, because these have the longest and most documented history.

### 4.1. Reciprocity in the Model Convention

The Commentary with the Model Convention motivates the requirement of reciprocity since 1963 as follows, 'A Contracting State *cannot* take advantage of the information system of another state, if it is wider than its domestic system',[77] This comment is formulated based on the perspective of the exchange on request, the only form of exchange that was required on the grounds of the original Model convention.[78] This use of words is also maintained in the later versions of the Commentary, although in my view the '*general principle of reciprocity*'[79] also applies to the spontaneous and automatic exchange.

To 'weigh' this argument, the reciprocity standard must be subjected to a closer examination.[80]

The reciprocity standard concretizes the principal equality of parties in a symmetrical legal relationship under international law (as well as in interpersonal relationships) that involve obligations of means. This entails that a party cannot expect more in advance than has been agreed and not more than it is will to provide. However, it may make such requests. Treaty partners are also free to provide more than may be expected under the legal relationship. The reciprocity standard is not really aimed at maintaining the balance between parties per interaction, but rather at enforcing at certain 'bandwidth' within which parties can consider each other as treated equally. This ideally allows room for flexibility, whereby parties can vary their efforts according to the importance of the specific situation. Therefore, in my opinion, it is justified to speak of the *principle* of reciprocity.

For the exchange of information, the reciprocity standard is described as not *being required to supply* information that another state could not or would not be willing to obtain or supply, in accordance with its domestic legislation or practice. However, serious reasons may exist (international fraud prevention for example) as to why in certain cases a state would be willing to supply information, in spite of the lack of reciprocity.[81]

Contrary to normal symmetrical legal relationships, the choice in the mutual assistance relationship does not allow the same amount of freedom to both participants in the relationship. The discretionary character of the provision, and the

77. OECD Commentary 1963, Art. 26, para. 11.
78. *Ibid.*, Art. 26, para. 7.
79. *Ibid.*, Art. 26, para. 11.
80. To correctly understand term reciprocity it is important to realize that here the term 'reciprocity' refers to the 'horizontal' of two legally equivalent contracting parties. This as opposed to a more 'vertical' definition of reciprocity as recognized in the legal relationship under *public law* (e.g., in the Netherlands General Administrative Law Act).
81. See Gangemi (1990), 32 for the flexible or strict ways in which different states deal with the principle of reciprocity.

freedom of implementation, in my opinion, exists only insofar as a state is the *supplying* party. The supplying state that adopts a flexible attitude and, in spite of the lack of reciprocity, still supplies information subject to predetermined conditions still takes its domestic statutory 'information-gathering powers' as guiding principle, as required by the principle of legality.[82] The requesting state that acts outside of the reciprocity is acting beyond it. By making a request to another state that it would not be willing to grant, the state is benefiting from the broader options of its treaty partner, meaning it will obtain information that is not simply provided for under its domestic regulations or administrative practice. This is on strained terms with the principle of legality that prescribes that all government actions are based on laws, in a manner that is knowable and predictable to its citizens. The pre-formulating in the national legislation of the conditions subject to which reciprocity shall be abandoned does provide certainty on the circumstances under which a state would be willing to do this, but not the consequences that could occur in a specific situation. This concerns the many different statutory options in the different states, that – albeit theoretically – give the requesting state an unlimited range of possibilities that are indeterminable to the citizen.

In my view, this is the background of the comment that was included in the Commentary from the first version Model convention: namely that 'a Contracting State *cannot* take advantage of the information system of the other state, if it is wider than its domestic system',[83] whereby the term 'contracting state' should be read to mean *requesting* state. To what extent it is acting illegally for the requests for information[84] does not concern the supplying state and cannot be evaluated by it either.

The OECD Commentary has always considered risks involved in too strict an enforcement of the principle of reciprocity by the supplying states, because this causes the interaction to be limited to the lowest of the two levels of statutory and administrative options in the countries concerned, 'so the Contracting State will exchange very little information, or perhaps none at all'. The 1963 version of the Commentary already suggests that, if necessary, the states should jointly aim to alleviate this effect of the principle of reciprocity by making agreements on this within a 'mutual agreement' procedure.[85] Comment 18 of the 1977 revised Commentary also leaves the mitigation of the possible effects of the reciprocity argument, to the states that 'may find it appropriate to broaden the scope of the exchange (…)'. The 2005 version of the OECD Commentary, in Comment 15.1, takes the first step toward incorporating the reciprocity argument as such, because it is no longer declared applicable to whether or not the same specific *procedures* exist in the other state. I consider this to be correct: in such a case an

82. The state must include the conditions under which this flexible attitude shall be effectuated on the *supplying* of information in the national laws. (Examples include cases of serious international fraud, large international money flows, or a major interest of the other state.)
83. This phrase is also included in Comment 189 of the Notes to the Strasbourg Convention, and in Comment 73 of the Commentary with Art. 7 of the OECD Agreement.
84. Vogel (2003), Art. 26, Rz. 110 and Schaumburg (1998), para. 19.76.
85. OECD Commentary 1963, Art. 26, para. 11 (in the revised version para. 18).

appeal to the reciprocity argument would infringe on the task of Comment 14 of the OECD Commentary to the states to apply all available means on behalf of the Contracting partner. Vogel limits the obligation of means on the supplying state to what it and the other state would *normally* also do.[86]

The 2003 OECD Commentary includes an example of a ruling procedure that does exist in the requested state, but not in the requesting state. According to the Commentary, this last-mentioned fact cannot serve as an argument for the requested state to refuse information on a ruling. On the other hand, the same version of that Commentary expands the validity of the reciprocity argument to the application of the ban on self-incrimination among the different treaty partners.[87]

So the reciprocity argument concerns the fact that information that is obtainable in the state itself, but not in the other state, does not *need* to be supplied.[88] The most striking example obviously concerns the obtainability of bank details, which, in some states, the tax authorities cannot access. On the grounds of the reciprocity argument, this information also falls outside of the obligation to exchange information. It is obviously in the interest of the supplying state to protect a measure of balance in the international legal relationship. This ultimately means that the exchange of information '*nicht zu einer Einbahnstrasse wird*'.[89] The question of whether the guarding of this balance also represents an interest for the taxpayer is handled in the next chapter.

The obtainability of information that must be acquired via tax audits depends on the national regulations in the field of these audits. If these are less far reaching in one state than in another, this indicates a lack of reciprocity. An example of this would be if in one of the states an enquiry would be conducted only subject to the condition that this concerns a national taxation interest.[90] In this way, the sovereignty argument and the reciprocity argument overlap each other.[91]

The phraseology in the OECD provision that links the term obtainability to the term 'normal course of administration', of normal course of tax determination' gives the term reciprocity a practical connotation in additional to a legal one. It is also important to determine to what extent it is possible to make certain information available to the other state via organizational measures, without requiring too much time, and with a certain measure of preciseness and possibly also periodicity. According to Comment 15 of the OECD Commentary, this also means that a lower

86. Vogel (2003), Art. 26, Rz. 113.
87. See OECD Commentary 1977-2005, Art. 26, para. 15.2. The reciprocity argument can be used only in this respect if the requesting state has a stronger form of protection against self-incrimination in a situation that gives more freedom than the requested state, as a result of which the requesting state would less quickly be required to rapidly supply information.
88. OECD Commentary 1977-2005, Art. 26, para. 19.6.
89. Schaumburg (1998), para. 19.74.
90. For example, this is the case in Japan and the United Kingdom, that have laid down an 'observation' for this purpose in Comments 14 and 16 of the revised Commentary.
91. Like the rule that inquiries must be notified in advance, or must be motivated, or cannot occur multiple times within a specific time frame.

level of organization and administrative efficiency in the requesting state can result in a lack of reciprocity. In the OECD Report from 1994 on the practice of the exchange of information between OECD states, this is referred to as 'factual reciprocity', primarily in connection with producing information flows within the context of the automatic exchange of information.[92]

The fear of a possible frustrating effect of the principle of reciprocity on the exchange of information, visible as of the first version of the OECD Commentary in particular, applies to this factual reciprocity.[93] According to the latest OECD Commentary, the principle of reciprocity is not really applicable to 'practices and procedures' which happen to differ between states, but should be reserved for deviations 'in the overall ability to obtain information' from the requesting state.[94]

This constant striving towards a pragmatic application of the principle of reciprocity ultimately results in the OECD Commentary 2005 formulated starting point that in principle states must assumed that information requested by a Contracting state must also be legally obtainable in the e state itself. This would also mean that the *legal reciprocity* no longer forms a problem.[95] For states that have adopted a rigorous application of the principle of reciprocity this could mainly prove a risk in new relations under the convention. From a practical consideration, an agreement could be made whereby the requesting state standard declares that it would also supply the requested information or the conduct an inquiry in accordance with its regulations. This is laid down in Article 5, paragraph, 5 subparagraph f, of the OECD Agreement.[96]

The fact that this fear of a too factual definition of reciprocity is not shared by every author is evident from Schaumburg's comment that the reciprocity argument does not concern '*nicht auf die rechtlichen, sondern auf die tatsächlichen Möglichkeiten des ersuchenden Staates*'. If the '*Verwaltungseffizienz*' of the requested state (read Germany) is greater than that of its Contracting partners, it is no longer a 'de jure' but a 'de facto' imbalance, and therefore, according to the author, the information should not be supplied.[97] This rigid attitude shows little consideration to states that are less developed in terms of their administration.

92. See OECD Report Tax Information Exchange between OECD Member Countries, A Survey of Current Practices, 1994, para. 46.
93. This warning is already included in Comment 11 of the 1963 version of the OECD Commentary. This is included in Comment 18.
94. OECD Commentary 1977-2005, Art. 26, para. 15. At the International Fiscal Association (IFA) 'Stockholm Conference' in 1990 Gangemi reported the view that concerning participants 'item by item reciprocity should not be required, provided that within the overall context of information exchange, there is generally adequate reciprocity'.
95. This would only be excluded if states have made separate agreements in this respect in their treaty, thus according to OECD Commentary 1977-2005, Art. 26, para. 18.1.
96. Such a method of handling was already recommended by the London and Mexico Model Conventions for the Establishment of Reciprocal Administrative Assistance for the Assessment and Collection of Direct Taxes (and Estates and Successions) of 1946, in Article II of the Protocol. Also see Gangemi (1990). To my knowledge, in the Dutch practice of mutual assistance. this has already been customary for some time.
97. Schaumburg (1998), para. 19.78.

Vogel seems to consider the factual possibilities and efforts of the other state irrelevant, if a state already possesses certain information. In this case, in his opinion, there is no room for the reciprocity argument, because the OECD Commentary automatically assumes that the available information will be supplied. According to the author, the rationale behind the grounds for exception is that a state is not required to change sovereign laws or administrative practice and this is not necessary for information that is already available.[98] I view this differently. The provision alleges that a conflict between the supplying information and the legislation of the requested 'or of the other state' forms a reason, subject to which a state can consider itself relieved of the obligation to exchange information. This means only that the lack of reciprocity is a reason for refusing a request for information and that the 'requirement of reciprocity' serves to protect the inviolability of the domestic legislation, but also serves an independent function, namely, to protect the balance of the relationships under the Convention.[99]

## 4.2. Reciprocity in Other Regulations: Strasbourg Convention, Directive 77/799, Regulation 1798/2003 and OECD Agreement

### 4.2.1. Strasbourg Convention

The Strasbourg Convention places the reciprocity, as with the other grounds for exception, in a more constitutional framework. The Notes to Article 21, paragraph 2 of that treaty views the reciprocity as a guarantee for the rights of the taxpayer in the requesting state. After all 'it prevents the applicant state from making use, indirectly ( . . . ) of greater powers than it possesses under its domestic law'.[100] The Notes to the Strasbourg Convention also 'warns' against too wide a use of the reciprocity argument, which could seriously hinder the exchange.[101] It is unclear whether the reciprocity is mainly referred to from a legal perspective or also from a practical perspective. The advice to the states here is not to seek a solution through joint consultation, but that the requesting state still makes a request for information, in the hope that the other state will not use its 'right of refusal'.[102] As mentioned earliest, in the requesting state this could be on strained

98. Vogel (2003), Art. 26, Rz. 117. This view possibly corresponds with the difference made in the German *Abgabenordung* between obtaining information by means of an audit or otherwise. In the first case, the taxpayer has certain rights of objection.
99. Under Dutch law, the automatic provision of available information is no longer automatically assumed. The Netherlands International Assistance Levying of Taxes Act. Act of 24 Apr. 1986 (WIB), Art. 13, para. 1 sub-paragraph e, contains a *prohibition* on supplying information, on the lack of reciprocity, irrespective of the question whether the Dutch tax authorities have this information.
100. Strasbourg Convention, Explanatory Report, Art. 21, para. 189.
101. *Ibid.*, Art. 21, paras 195 and 196.
102. *Ibid.*, Art. 21, para. 196.

terms with the requirement of legality that makes a state a constitutional state. In my opinion, this recommendation affects the infringement taxpayers' rights, which, according to the introductory provision of Article 21 of the Strasbourg Convention, it aims to protect.

### 4.2.2. Council Directive 77/799

Article 8 of the European Directive 77/799 mentions the right only to *refuse* to supply information, if the receiving state 'is unable to supply such information on legal or factual grounds'. In Article 9 of the Savings Tax Directive, Article 8 of Directive 77/799 has been declared not applicable.[103] A lack of reciprocity can no longer be under discussion, now that the paying agencies in all states pursuant to Article 8 of that directive supply the same information to their tax authorities (or must levy a withholding tax).

Regulation 1798/2003 under Article 40, paragraph 3 mentions the supplying state's right to refuse to give information 'if the (receiving) member state concerned is unable to supply such information on *statutory* grounds'. The lack of an explanation makes it unclear whether this is really intended to fully exclude a lack in factual reciprocity. This could relate to the imperative and supranational character of the regulation, in anticipation of bringing into line the methods and procedures in the different Member States.

The OECD Agreement refers to the reciprocity argument in Article 7, paragraph 1. The Commentary mentions as an example the ban on self-incrimination. If this is the case, and the scope of the statutory ban would be more limited in the requesting state than in the requested state, the requested state would not be obligated to supply the requested information.[104] States are not permitted to expand their powers via the 'detour' of the international exchange of information.

To remove any doubt as to the existence of reciprocity, pursuant to Article 5, paragraph 5 of the Agreement, the requesting state must include a statement to this end in its request, as previously observed. According to the Commentary under Article 7 of the Agreement, the requested state can still refuse if it has grounds to doubt the truthfulness of that statement, but if it supplies the requested information, it does remain within the limits of the Agreement.[105]

### 4.2.3. Conclusion

States are able to protect the balance of their legal relationships via the principle of reciprocity, if this is considered necessary.

The requirement of reciprocity concerns the statutory and administrative powers of states to gather tax information (legal reciprocity) and the availability

---

103. Directive 2003/48/EC of the Council of 3 Jun. 2003, concerning taxation on income from savings in the form of interest payments.
104. OECD Agreement, Commentary Art. 7, paras 73 and 74.
105. *Ibid.*, para. 77.

of the information, as created in the states as a result of organizational measures (factual reciprocity).

Regulation 1798/2003 and the OECD Agreement limit the argument to the lack of *legal* reciprocity. For the regulation, this concerns its direct effect and its supremacy over the domestic laws of the Member States, as a result of which it can have a far-reaching influence and harmonization on the practical implementation in the Member States. For the OECD Agreement, the lack of factual reciprocity between the former tax havens, with their rudimentary organization of gathering tax information, and the OECD states is still so unlikely that the argument would be obstructive.

In my opinion, the view expressed by the Committee on Fiscal Affairs that reciprocity is mainly a legal term, offers the best opportunities for active and smooth cooperation between the states. The one-sided focus on the differences in procedures and number of cases in which information is exchanged has an unnecessarily hindering effect, except if there are indications of a lack of willingness by the other state to meet its obligations.

The commentaries mainly emphasize the position of the requesting state. States should not be allowed to expand their information-gathering powers via requests to other states. The principle of reciprocity forms an argument. The Strasbourg Convention also considers the principle as a form of protecting '*legitimate* rights' of the taxpayers (in italics author). In my opinion, this mainly concerns taxpayers in the requesting state. In the 'hands of' the supplying state, the principle of reciprocity is considered a risk in view of the immobilizing effect that a strict enforcement could have on the exchange. The question as to whether the principle also affects the legal position of the taxpayer in the supplying state that needs supply the information is not answered by the Strasbourg Convention or the other regulations on the exchange of information. This is further elaborated on in Chapter 7.

## 5. BUSINESS OR PROFESSIONAL SECRET; '*ORDRE PUBLIC*'

In addition to the conflict with domestic laws or national administrative practice with regard to gathering information that is relevant on behalf taxation, or with the principle of reciprocity, the risk that a business, trade, industrial, or professional secret shall be revealed can also be a reason why a state will not disclose information. OECD Model Convention, Article 26, paragraph 3, sub-paragraph c, also names 'commercial secret and trade process'. For the sake of brevity and because the OECD Commentary makes no distinction between the different 'secrets', I shall refer to this as 'business secrecy' in the rest of this chapter. The same ground for exception is included in the Strasbourg Convention in Article 21, paragraph 2, in sub-paragraph d; in the Directive 77/799 in Article 8, paragraph 2; in Regulation 1798/2003 in Article 40, paragraph 4; and in the OECD Agreement in Article 7, paragraph 2.

The text of this grounds for exception has not been altered since it first occurred in the 1963 version of the Model convention. The development of ideas that have since occurred within the OECD on this subject, is reflected in the Commentary, mainly in the 2005 version.

## 5.1. Definition of Business Secrecy

### 5.1.1. OECD Model Convention

The text of the OECD Model Convention and the Commentary lack a definition for the terms 'business, professional, or industrial secret',[106] and it should therefore be assumed that the used terms can relate to the multitude of economic activities by a taxpayer in a state.

Until the 2005 version of the OECD Commentary, the explanation of the terms proved problematic. A '*lex fori* interpretation' on the grounds of Article 3, paragraph 2 of the Model convention fails on the fact that the terms do not occur in all national tax legal systems. Therefore, according to Vogel, the level of secrecy between the states would differ too much.[107] He derived a workable definition from German law: it must pertain to knowledge that only a limited group of individuals has and that can be exploited in the market, because they benefit the owner over other persons.[108] The term 'business secrecy' in the new Comment 19.2 of the Commentary is described in almost the same way. This is in regard to information that represents a *considerable* economic interest for the (taxpayer or) the supplying state, and of which the unauthorized exploitation could cause *serious* harm to the taxpayer. In other cases, this information is already sufficiently protected under the secrecy clause. The fact that a *tax liability* arises as a result of the 'disclosure' is not considered harmful. This modification to the OECD Commentary is expected to greatly reduce the problems of interpretation underlying the enforcement of the provision on the exchange of information and possibly also its implementation, mainly because, in my opinion, this modification has the character of a clarification of a previously undefined term and is therefore also applicable to previous versions of the OECD provision on the exchange of information.

In the OECD states, it is generally assumed that business secrets as referred to in this article cannot exist between a permanent establishment and the head office.[109] Opinions differ with regard to its existence between affiliated organizations. Vogel disputes the opinion that competition is not possible between different

106. Schaumburg (1998), para. 19.79 and Vogel (2003), Art. 26, para. 120, 2025. Multiple terms may have been included to include as many different references of 'business secrecy' as possible in the domestic laws of the states.
107. Vogel (2003), Art. 26, para. 119, 2024.
108. *Ibid.*, para. 121, 2025. Also see Schaumburg (1998), para. 19.80, 1333.
109. Also see OECD Report Tax Information Exchange Between OECD Member Countries, 1994.

divisions of a company in different countries, and that therefore in these cases they cannot appeal the argument of business or professional secrecy. In his opinion, the background to the ground for exception lies in protecting the economic interests of the supplying *state*.[110] However, it cannot be denied that taxpayers' interests are under discussion (as acknowledged in Comment 19 of the OECD Commentary), in my view, it seems essential how taxpayers themselves define their interest in certain situations. Daniels uses the explanation of the Convention text and the Commentary, and German jurisprudence to come to a number of 'business secrets', such as a company's plans or quotations, but mainly also the (technical) knowledge that is of such economic importance, and which, according to the company's actions (also for affiliated companies), it wants to keep secret. This can also include a company's pricing policy with regard to the different countries. In my opinion, retaining secrecy on these matters could also be of importance between different divisions.[111]

Under Belgian legislation, a Belgian company that paid fees to Italian commercial agents was also included under business secrecy.[112]

## 5.2. Developments with Regard to Business Secrets

The role that the grounds for refusal concerning business secrecy played in the context of the Model convention has altered in the course of time. The 1963 version of the OECD Commentary mentioned it still neutrally, as an extra (international) protection for states that possess special national rules regarding secrecy for specific information.[113] The 1977 version already indicates a fear of the possible effects. The grounds for refusal could also serve on behalf of refusing certain taxpayers' rights, according to Comment 19 (and this is the only place where the Commentary mentions the taxpayers' interests), but this determination must concern serious interests. A too-broad interpretation of the term 'business secret' would render the exchange of information ineffective. It should be emphasized that states have the freedom *not* to appeal to the limitation and that taxpayers cannot defend themselves by appealing to national secrecy laws. After all, the obligation under the Convention imposes the obligation of secrecy on the receiving state.

In Comment 19.1 of the 2005 Commentary, the scope of applicability of the grounds for refusal is limited in a general sense. It is emphasized that the exchangeable information is already protected by the general secrecy clause of Article 26 and that states should not use their discretionary room here if they do not have a

110. Vogel (2003), Art. 26, Rz. 122 and Schaumburg (1998), para. 19.79, which mentions the risk of economic espionage. Also see Reuter (1975-1976), 419, which refers to the threat of 'leaking' information in countries that have powerful state enterprises.
111. Daniels (1987), 32. Also see Wisselink (1996), 70 and Oliver (1995), 116.
112. Brussels Court, 5 Sep. 1980, European Taxation 1987, 87.
113. OECD Commentary 1963, Art. 26, para. 13.

reasonable suspicion that the taxpayer concerned will experience consequences that are 'incompatible with information exchange', whatever that means.

### 5.3. Business and Banking Secrecy

From the very beginning, the so-called 'banking secrecy' has been given a special place in the development of ideas involving these grounds for refusal, although it is already protected under the grounds for exception of Article 26, (old) paragraph 2, sub-paragraph a (the domestic laws and/or administrative practice), and Article 26, paragraph 2 sub-paragraph b (the obtainability of the information). In the original version of the Commentary, banking secrecy was already freely mentioned as an example of secrecy regarding special kinds of information existing in many states. This was the reason for adopting it in the (former) paragraph 2 of Article 26.

After the revision of the Commentary in 1977, until 2003, Comment 19 contains a reference to the freedom of states 'to add further dispensations from the obligation to supply information', such as information that is subject to 'special protection on banker's discretion'. In a report on the Stockholm Conference on the international exchange of information in 1990, Gangemi reported that according to the contributions of the different states, the term 'business secrecy' is mainly used with regard to bank details.[114]

In 2005, the many years of debating within the OECD in the 1990s left its mark on the added paragraph 5 of Article 26.[115] This explicitly ends the long 'accepted' practice in the Commentary of some countries to refuse to supply information (whether or not by invoking business secrecy) solely because of the fact that it originates from banks or financial institutes.[116] In Comment 19 of the Commentary, the reference to the *banking* secrecy has been removed, this is in line with the conclusion that most OECD countries already exchange bank details,[117] and referring to the international developments in the forming of ideas on (the abolition of) banking secrecy, as laid down in the Model Agreement[118] and in the OECD Report, Improving Access to Bank Information for Tax Purposes of 2000.[119] Information held by agents or trusted representatives or information concerning ownership ratios can also no longer simply be protected under professional secrecy, not

114. Gangemi (1990). For the opposing view that according to general views business secret does refer to banking secrecy, see Malherbe (1991).
115. Prokisch (2004) mentions the OECD Report Taxation and the Abuse of Bank-Secrecy that was already published 'as far back as the early 1980s'.
116. Also see OECD Commentary 1977-2005, Art. 26, para. 19.2.
117. OECD Commentary 1977-2005, Art. 26, para. 19.10
118. See Barnard (2002), 1042.
119. OECD Commentary 1977-2005, Art. 26, para. 19.12. Regarding both reports it is worth remarking that they have been completely conceived from the perspective of the tax administrations, which somewhat explains the difficult nature of the debate on banking secrecy. Also see Prokisch (2004), 11.

even if this is deemed so under the state's laws, according to the OECD Commentary.[120]

The question that arises here is to what extent the Committee on Fiscal Affairs infringes on the sovereignty of the states, by encroaching on national legislation. In my opinion, the Commentary here is trying to influence the national laws, not by prescribing how they should read, but by excluding a certain means of interpretation as part of the mutual assistance between states. Winkler argues that this influence has also had (some) results in Switzerland and Austria,[121] where certain laws have been formed or misused to escape the obligation to exchange information. These cases do not meet the good faith that the Contracting states owe each other in the implementation of their agreement. The difficult nature of the 'banking-secrecy debate' within the OECD (and within the European Union [EU]) gives cause to assume that fear of the Committee on Fiscal Affairs is not completely unfounded, and at the same time shows that a change in the attitude of the states can be achieved only through endless persuasion. Based on the fact that the banking secrecy does not just harm the treasuries of the states, but can also serve to cover up activities that are objectionable from a social point of view, the preparatory committees deserve praise for the persistence that they showed in the debate.

### 5.4. 'Solicitor's Privilege'

A different category of 'further dispensations from the obligation to supply information', which states were able to add to the 'secrets' in sub-paragraph c of the grounds for exception, according to the OECD Commentary the information that originates from certain professionals. The 'attorney-client privilege' of lawyers, counsellors, or legal representatives of taxpayers is discussed in the new Comment 19.3 of that Commentary. Actually, just like banking secrecy, this concerns exceptions of national law to the obligation to provide information by taxpayers on the tax authorities.[122] This privilege should therefore be classified under the sovereignty argument. The fact that this privilege is treated as a business secret in the new Commentary could be due to a practice of improper user. Comment 19.3 acknowledges the existence of this privilege in the states, but on behalf of the obligation to supply information, it defines the number of cases subject to which the right can be appealed to in relation to other states. This is possible only if it concerns information communicated between counsellors and their clients as part of the confidential advisory relationship, not if obtained by these persons in their capacity as shareholder, trust holder, and/or director.

Correspondence with the counsellor that is aimed at withholding certain documents concerning the identity of a shareholder, director, or the person entitled from the tax authorities, cannot be included in the privilege. According to the

120. OECD Commentary 1977-2005, Art. 26, para. 19.13.
121. S.A.Winkler, 2006, p. 21 and 142 et seq. (Switzerland) and 162 et seq. (Austria).
122. Malherbe (1991), 53.

Commentary, the designating of information as falling under the privilege is possible only by the court in the state in which the right is appealed to and must be in accordance with the legislation of that state. Within this context, this is the state that must supply the information. An appeal to this privilege and the 'adjudication' by the 'the courts of the requested state', to which the Comment refers, in any case implies that the holder of that right in that state should at least be aware of the proposed notification. This corresponds to the view as already expressed in the literature regarding business secrecy in general, that its application as ground for exception '*nur im Benehmen mit dem Betroffenen geprüft werden kann*'.[123] This seems to be an appropriate conclusion: if the interests of the taxpayer concerned also can be considered, as alleged by the Commentary, and if a state wants to invoke these grounds for exception against its treaty partner, then it would seem obvious that the taxpayer has a right to information in these cases. (For a more elaborate explanation see Chapter 7).

Paragraph 19.4 OECD Commentary contains a text proposal for states that want to separately arrange the application of the privilege in their own tax treaty.

## 5.5. Business and Professional Secrecy in Other Regulations: Strasbourg Convention, Directive 77/799, Regulation 1798/2003, OECD Agreement

### 5.5.1. Strasbourg Convention

In the Strasbourg Convention, business secrecy is included as grounds for exception in Article 21, paragraph 2, sub-paragraph d. The text of the provision in the Strasbourg Convention literally corresponds with that of the Model Convention, as it applied until 2004. This also lacks a definition for the term 'business secrecy'. Because of the fact that the rules on the international exchange of information are so interwoven, as a result of the fact that parties of the Strasbourg Convention also participate as members of the OECD in the development of ideas within that forum, it is safe to assume that the previous comments on the demarcation of the term 'business secrecy' will also apply to the Strasbourg Convention.

The Notes to the Treaty differ from those of the OECD Commentary. Business secrecy is firstly mentioned in Comment 197, which discusses whether states can impose specific requirements and conditions on the receiving state upon supplying certain information. That 'would indeed be preferable', according to the Comment, because the information would then be supplied. The special requirements for this 'earmarked information' can pertain to secrecy or special conditions such as

123. Vogel (2003), Art. 26, Rz. 121. In the same sentence: Oliver (1995), in which he discusses the OECD Report Tax Information Exchange between OECD Member Countries of 1994. Business secrecy is 'closely connected to the right of the taxpayer to be informed about any proposed exchange', because the state is often unable to establish if a fact or circumstance will result in a secret.

'notification of the taxpayer'. This would mainly be applicable in cases relating to business secrecy, according to the Notes.[124] In view of the question that the Comment aims to handle and that is aimed at the handling of information in the *receiving* state, the comment concerning the '*notification to the taxpayer*' is difficult to understand. It seems evident that the extra warranty for secrecy must be realized in the receiving state,[125] whereas the 'notification to the taxpayer' concerns the *requested* (supplying) state, and therefore cannot be imposed as a condition on the receiving state. Or the comment would have to mean that the requested state 'notifies' the requesting state that it will provide only a special piece of information after consulting the information-supplying taxpayer.[126] This explanation would match the reference in the Notes to the careful weighing of the taxpayer's interests that are required for an appeal to business secrecy, if only to limit appeals to this argument.

### 5.5.2. European Directive 77/799

Directive 77/799 also lacks a definition of the term 'business secrecy' and an official explanation; here, the same applies as aforementioned regarding the interweaving of the rules on the international exchange of information of the different communities. The states that were members of the EC at the time of the formation of Directive 77/799 in 1977, were also members of the OECD. It is therefore only logical to assume that the notion regarding business secrecy in the OECD 'working party' also forms the background to the provision in question in Directive 77/799. Because of the lack of official commentary, it is not possible to ascertain whether the grounds for refusal concerning business secrecy in the perspective of European law also serve the weighing of the taxpayers' interests. The text of Article 8, paragraph 2 of Directive 77/799, which in this respect explicitly mentions the possibility of *refusing*, contains no indication of this, and neither do the similar provisions of the OECD Model Convention. Here, the reference to the interests of taxpayers is discussed only in the commentary. In my opinion, the same applies to Directive 77/799 that these grounds for exception *by their nature* also refer to the (financial) interests of taxpayers and so in principle can be used as an instrument by the states to weigh the taxpayer's interests.

124. Strasbourg Convention, Explanatory Report, Art. 21, para. 197.
125. See Vogel (2003), Art. 26, Rz. 60, which the taxpayer 'seinen eigenen, im nationalen Recht des Empfängerstaates begründeten Anspruch auf Geheimhaltung' toedicht, 'durchsetzbar gemäß nationalen Recht' and irrespective of obligation under international law. This comment was used in connection with the OECD Model Convention, but in my opinion, it is also applicable to the secrecy clause of the Strasbourg Convention, which also uses the national secrecy laws of the receiving state as basis.
126. Unfortunately the comment is not further elaborated in the often verbose Notes. Strasbourg Convention, Explanatory Report, Art. 21, para. 198 just like the OECD Commentary warns that business secrecy 'not must be taken in too wide a sense'.

### 5.5.3. Regulation 1798/2003 on VAT

Article 40, paragraph 4 of the regulation is identical to the one contained in Directive 77/799. The regulation also lacks an explanation. In view of the origin of the Regulation, it is safe to assume that for these grounds for exception, the same applies as observed with Directive 77/799.

### 5.5.4. OECD Agreement

The Commentary at Article 7, paragraph 2 of this Agreement, just like the OECD Commentary (in my opinion rightly so), observes that business secrets will play only a limited role in the exchange of information pursuant to that agreement, because the exchanged information usually contains passive income, which does not involve commercial, industrial, or business activities. The Commentary does not include a definition of the term 'business secrecy', except that this includes patents and so forth held by holders in the requested state and therefore may occur in financial records.[127] Information held by banks, financial institutes, or with persons acting as agents, representatives, or holders, cannot be considered a business secret merely on the grounds of *this* reason. National legislation that, contrary to Article 5, paragraph 4 of the Agreement, does *not* provide for an obligation to exchange information for the persons and institutes toward the tax authorities, is overruled by the Agreement, according to the commentary.[128]

The 'solicitor's privilege', (handled under business secrecy in the Model Convention), is elaborated separately in Article 7, paragraph 3 of the OECD Agreement. In principle, it is an acknowledged form of professional secrecy. Unlike in the OECD Model Commentary the Commentary to the Agreement does not warn to interpret the privilege in a limited way. This could be explained by the fact that a certain privilege (that creates a barrier to information gathering by the government) in the 'committed jurisdictions' plays a much more essential role than in the OECD states, where a more balanced system of obligations and rights has been created for the taxpayer. The precise delineation of the 'communication' between client and counsellor that falls under the client-attorney privilege and the term 'confidential information' is striking. It is essential that the communication takes place within the framework of legal advice, whether or not in preparation of a legal procedure. Correspondence that is aimed at hiding information, or a person's identity (for example the person entitled) from the authorities cannot be included under the privilege, which is neither the case under the Model Convention. The reciprocity argument is also applicable to this privilege. In as far as this is 'more flexible' in the requesting state than in the requested state; the state's duty to supply information ceases to exist.

---

127. OECD Agreement, Commentary Art. 7, para. 79-81. The Commentary only really sees an application for the argument by a third party that must guard the intellectual property regarding certain processes on behalf of another party.
128. OECD Agreement, Commentary Art. 7, para. 82.

### 5.5.5. Conclusion

In the same way as with other grounds for exception, the argument of business secrecy is subject to 'wear' mainly in the OECD regulations. Primarily in the latest OECD Model Convention and Commentary, the role of the argument is increasingly limited through further specifications. The privilege of banking secrecy (as specimen of business secrecy) is no longer automatically accepted as a ground for exception to the obligation to supply information. This is the result of many years of debating within the OECD regarding banking secrecy and 'harmful tax competition'. In my opinion this is correct. In the past, business secrecy has often served as a cover for practices which were on strained terms with the tax laws of the national states.

## 5.6. Public Order (All Regulations)

The term 'public order' is in the OECD Commentary,[129] and the Explanatory Report to the Strasbourg Convention[130] and the Commentary to the OECD Agreement is vaguely defined as the 'vital interests of the State itself'. This can be understood to mean economic and political interests of the supplying state. In the literature the term is also explained as the interest which the state has in maintaining the key values of its domestic legal system. These are only at stake under extreme circumstances, for example if it is plausible that the receiving state would use the information in a manner that, according to the judgment of the supplying state, goes against the fundamental principles of the rule of law.[131] The Commentary with the 2005 version of the OECD Model Convention and the OECD Agreement include the following examples: requests by states made within the context of political, religious, or racial oppression. And therefore the argument of the '*ordre public*' not only pertains to matters of security or the supplying state's political survival, but also the constitutional content of the tax laws in the other state, apparently considered important enough to be mutually assessed by the states. Against this background, it is hard to understand why states have been given discretionary freedom with regard to this point. This is also at odds with the provision under Article 26, paragraph 1 of the Model convention, that the obligation to exchange information applies only to the extent that the levying of taxes under domestic law '*is not contrary to the convention*'. This provision also refers to a constitutional element such as the prohibition on discrimination, which is standard included in the tax treaties.[132]

In paragraph 6.2.1.1, I already mentioned the argument of Article 21, paragraph 2, sub-paragraph e, of the Strasbourg Convention, which alleges that

129. OECD Commentary Art. 26, 1977-2005, para. 19.5.
130. Strasbourg Convention, Explanatory Report, Art. 21, para. 201.
131. Vogel (2003), Art. 26, Rz. 123.
132. See Ch. 4, s. 4.3.2.

a state is not obligated 'to lend assistance if and in as far as it considers the taxation of the requesting state to infringe on the generally accepted taxation principles or with the provisions of an agreement to avoid double taxation'. The examples given in the Explanatory Notes (a confiscatory character of the legislation in the other state, or a disproportional sentencing) unmistakingly refer to criteria for assessing the constitutional content of legal systems.[133] Here, the grounds for exception is also formulated discretionarily, as well as in sub-paragraph f of Article 21, paragraph 2, concerning the prohibition of discrimination.[134] This is even more striking because the Strasbourg Convention, in the introduction of Article 21, considers the taxpayers' right to be so important.

### 5.6.1. Conclusion

The argument of the public order not only provides protection for 'the vital interests of the state itself' but also legitimizes an inter-State assessment of the states on crucial elements that determine a legal system's constitutional content. Therefore, it should not have a discretionary character, and neither should sub-paragraphs e and f of paragraph 2 of Article 21 Strasbourg Convention. Rather, it should be formulated as a condition. To this end, it could be combined with the 'ban' of Article 26, paragraph 1 of the OECD Model Convention to exchange information if this is in violation of the tax treaty.

## 6. OTHER LIMITATIONS

At this point it is wise to once again mention that, in addition to the previously mentioned grounds for refusal, the description of the obligation to exchange information itself can also result in the refusal to exchange information. A state has the right to refuse the exchange of information if the requested information *cannot* be relevant on behalf of the levy of taxes and/or (under a tax treaty according to the Model prior to the year 2000) does not concern taxes mentioned under the Convention, if information is requested under a 'minor' provision on behalf of the national legislation of the requesting state, if subject to an 'important' provision on the exchange of information the national tax laws on behalf of which they are requested are not in accordance with the Convention, if the secrecy or rightful use cannot sufficiently be guaranteed, and if a request is actually a 'fishing expedition'.

133. Strasbourg Convention, Explanatory Report, Art. 21, paras 200 and 2001.
134. Strasbourg Convention, Art. 21, para. 2 subpara. f, gives grounds for refusal if the exchange of information 'can result in the discrimination between a national of the requested state and nationals of the requesting state'.

## 7. SUMMARY AND CONCLUSIONS

1. The legal relationship between states is characterized by the principles of sovereignty and equality of the partners: one party can never simply be a means to serve the objectives of the other party. That is why the obligation to exchange information can never be absolute. That is also why, as of the 1963 version of the OECD Model Convention, the rules on the international exchange of information mention several circumstances whereby states can consider themselves relieved from the obligation to exchange information and where they have room to weigh their domestic interests against those of the treaty partner.

2. Next to a legal relationship under international law, the exchange of information also presumes a legal relationship under public law between the state and the taxpayer who must provide the information. In this asymmetrical legal relationship, states also have a duty of care with regard to the taxpayer's interests.

3. An analysis of the formulations of the *obligation* to exchange information showed that the existing regulations contain no references to weighing the taxpayer's interests.

Therefore, it is important to examine whether the limiting provisions offer reference points for the states to fulfil their duty of care toward their information-providing taxpayers.

The weighing of interest of and by treaty partners turned out to be possible in the following cases:

- If a state's obligation to exchange information would force it to act in violation of its domestic legislation or 'administrative practice' with regard to obtaining tax information, or if the information is not obtainable within the framework of the normal procedure of tax assessments, audits, and levies. I referred to this as the sovereignty argument.
- If these circumstances do not occur in their own state, but in the other state, then I referred to this as the reciprocity argument.
- If a risk of revealing a business secret existed, or if there was a threat to the public order.

4. The above-mentioned grounds for exception occur in all existing regulations on the exchange of information. Additionally, the Strasbourg Convention in Article 21, paragraph 2, still acknowledges the right of the supplying state to consider itself relieved of the obligation to supply information:

- if, in its opinion, the taxation in the other state which serves would infringe on the generally accepted principles (of the rule of law), for example, if, in that state, this would result in draconic measures against the taxpayer there;
- if there is a fear of discriminating taxpayers in the receiving state.

5. Of relevance with regard to the sovereignty argument is that not all national tax laws can serve as grounds for exception. The supplying state cannot appeal to its domestic laws regarding tax secrecy, because the characteristic feature of the mutual assistance is that the national obligation of secrecy is set aside on behalf

of the other state's needs. The obligation of secrecy for the received information is also transferred to that state.

Whatever rights to information that taxpayers might have with regard to the exchange of information, laid down in their national laws, they cannot serve as grounds for *exception*, according to the commentary to the OECD Model Convention, the Strasbourg Convention and the OECD Agreement.

The Model convention has also restrained the right of states to appeal to national prohibitions on self-incrimination through a strict definition of the applicability. This is explainable because of the general risk that the sovereignty argument will be wrongfully used. This could explain the fact that these grounds for exception are not included in the OECD Agreement of 2002. The rights of taxpayers with regard to the process of information gathering by their state do fall under the sovereignty argument.

The Strasbourg Convention seems to approach taxpayers' rights in a more positive way, however; because any further elaboration is missing and the statements are of a somewhat noncommittal nature.

The sovereignty argument primarily concerns the manner in which statutory or administrative powers to obtain certain information are regulated in a country. In the next versions of the OECD Model Convention, the discretionary freedom under which states can appeal to that argument is increasingly restricted via a more precise description of exactly what falls under the 'normal procedure of tax determination': which statutory powers or powers under the 'administrative practice' must states use (all investigative powers) and in what cases (also without a tax interest). The validity of the sovereignty argument is curtailed in the 2005 version of the Model convention via the recommendation to states to discuss the formation of the 'information gathering powers' described in the Model convention in the negotiations.

6. The *reciprocity argument* concerns the fact that actions undertaken by the supplying state for gathering information, in the *other* (requesting) state would infringe on the laws or administrative practice in that state. In this case, all regulations regarding the obligation to supply information will cease to exist. The term 'reciprocity' is a means to guard the balance in the (horizontal) legal relationship between states. This mainly provides for the *legal* obtainability of the information concerned. In practice, this is also determined by how a state manages its tax information or by the setting of priorities regarding tax matters.

According to the OECD Commentary and the Explanatory Notes to the Strasbourg Convention, this factual reciprocity may not be misused as an argument to frustrate the exchange of information. I share this view, because such misuse infringes on the good faith that the Contracting States owe each other.

In my opinion, the supplying state can set aside the argument, if this discretionary power is laid down in its legal system. This creates room to weigh the importance of balance of the treaty relationship with the other state; these are mainly the relevant international interests at that time. On making *requests* that infringe on the reciprocity, the state will expand the possibilities to gather information outside of its legal system and will thereby come to be on strained terms with the principle of legality. After all, even if this possibility regarding the requests for information was laid down in the law, in my opinion, this would still not meet the requirements that the law should be made known and be transparent. This is because there are many states with which information can be exchanged, so that it is unclear to citizens to what extent the deviation of the domestic law on their behalf could go in practice.

7. The *business secrecy argument* concerns the risk that the exchange of information will reveal certain commercial secrets. This argument allows states to protect themselves against economic espionage, for example. However, the Commentary to the Model convention and Strasbourg Convention view this argument as a means to weigh the economic interests of their *taxpayers* against those of the other state. This creates the risk for wrongful use of the grounds for refusal. That is why the later versions of the OECD Commentary contain warning on a too-broad use.

The 2005 version of the OECD Commentary is the first to contain a definition of the term 'business secret'. It understands it to mean a fact or circumstance that concerns a major economic interest, which, if this were revealed to the other state, could cause serious harm to the state or the taxpayer. Compared to previous versions, the scope of the argument is limited: information of banks and financial institutes, including that of ownership ratios, is excluded. Moreover, an appeal is justified only if a state has a *reasonable* suspicion that the taxpayer in question could suffer harm from the exchange. This implies that a state, before invoking business secrecy, should consult with the taxpayer. This also applies if a state, in order to avoid the obligation to supply information, wants to appeal to a 'solicitor's privilege' as laid down in its legislation. This right is acknowledged both in the OECD Commentary and in the OECD Agreement, but in the OECD Agreement it is restricted through a precise description of the conditions under which this applies. Neither of the conventions establishes a *right* for the taxpayer to be heard. This restriction of the privilege in the OECD Agreement and in the Model convention is certainly understandable, mainly when considered against the background of many years of debates on banking secrecy and 'harmful tax competition'.

8. The argument of conflict with (risks to) the *public order* pertains to the interests that concern the continued existence of the state ('vital interests of the state itself'). In the 2005 version of the OECD Commentary and the Commentary to the OECD Agreement, the description also contains cases in which the information should be used for a discriminatory taxation. In my opinion, the term 'public order' also has a connotation that can be used with the grounds for exception of 'infringing on the generally accepted taxation principles', which, according to the Notes to the Strasbourg Convention, is understood to mean taxation with a confiscatory character or a disproportional sentencing. Both arguments can serve as a verification instrument for the constitutional content of another state's legal system. This is why, in my opinion, these should not be formulated discretionarily, but rather should have the characteristic of a condition to the obligation to exchange information.

In anticipation of the next chapter, it can be concluded that some of the grounds for exception of the different regulations concerning mutual assistance give states the room to, in addition to their domestic interests, also weigh the interests of their taxpayers against the interest of the treaty partners. What these interests are, and how these can be protected by the states, shall be examined in that chapter.

Chapter 7

# Interests of the Taxpayer

## 1. INTRODUCTION

The preceding analysis of the rules on the international exchange of information calls for a recollection of the questions raised with regard to the subject of this study. The first question, on the existence of a legal duty for the states to take into account the position of taxpayers in the international exchange of information[1] was answered positively in the first chapter of this study. The relational legal notion that was taken as a starting point in regard to both citizens and governments as participants in a legal relationship on the basis of administrative law. In concrete terms, this means that the powers to collect tax-related information, as well as the duty to supply it, are deemed to be embedded in the legal relationship that exists between the tax authorities and the taxpayer or withholding agent who has to supply the information.[2] Applied to the exchange of information such a legal relationship is becoming manifest by the decision of the state that in a specific situation, a duty to exchange information exists and that it is prepared and willing to comply. Such a decision can be 'triggered' by a request for information from another state; by the fact that in collecting information for the national levying of taxes. information is found that is possibly of importance to supply spontaneously to a partner in a convention; or by the intention of states to establish a mutual regular data flow.

The principle of legality within this legal relationship prescribes that duties of citizens (and therefore also of taxpayers) can be imposed only by means of legislation. An extension of the scope of those duties to the levying of taxes in foreign

1. In fact, not only the taxpayers but also withholding agents may be involved as suppliers of information in the cross-border exchange of information. For the sake of brevity in this Ch. 1 will continue to use the term 'taxpayer'.
2. Gribnau (1998), 264, points out that actions not aimed at legal consequences, such as providing factual information, can under certain circumstances lead to a new legal consequence.

countries must therefore be embedded in legislation. The latter must also provide a sufficient basis for monitoring of and defence against these government acts. However, in accordance with the modern, relational notion of law, the legal position of citizens is not only protected by the principle of legality. In the more social notion of law that arose in the last century, the direction is mainly determined by the legal value of equality. This was a reaction to the strong emphasis on the freedom and autonomy of individuals in the preceding period. Combined with the relational notion of law, this socialization meant that all legal relationships (whether between individuals, between legal persons, or between citizens and governments) must be governed by the rule that, whenever possible, the other party must be treated as an equivalent participant.[3] This implies that a legally unequal (asymmetrical) legal relationship like that in administrative law, the government as the most powerful party has the responsibility to monitor the balance between parties, by taking into account the interests of individuals and legal persons in the exercise of its powers.[4] The same is true for legal relationships between citizens and the tax authorities.

Moreover, in the preceding chapters, we found that the rules on the international exchange of information, although almost exclusively focused on the interests of the partners to the convention, also create scope for the states to weigh their own interests. This discretionary scope is delineated in the so-called grounds for exemption.

All of this being said, we must now answer the question as to how the duty of care of the state toward its taxpayers can be fulfilled within the framework of the international legal duty to exchange information, as was analyzed in the preceding chapters. This question breaks up into two sub-questions:

- Which interests of taxpayers deserve protection with these specific government acts, in view of the international duty these acts are based on? and
- How should this protection be realized?

Answering these questions requires a description of the specific position of taxpayers in the application of the convention provision. For in doing so, their interests become clear. To that end the convention provision analyzed in the preceding chapters will in this chapter be reviewed from the position of the taxpayer. Here too, the best basis is the Organization for Economic and Cooperative Development (OECD) Model provision, because of its influence on the rules on the international exchange of information as a whole, due to its long and well-documented development process.

This new analysis will be focused less on the differences between the details of the various regulations and more on their points of similarity. From this analysis, it will become clear at which points the protection of the interests of the taxpayers

3. Happé (1996) calls this the political-philosofical principle of equality, from which the right to equal treatment is deduced. Also see Ch. 2.
4. This is also the leading idea behind the drafting of the Dutch General administrative law Act. Cf. Parliamentary Papers II 1988/89 nr. 21 221, nr. 1 and 3 (Explanatory Memorandum), 11-12.

could be combined with the duty to weigh the interests of the partners to the convention as laid down in international law. In other words, it must become clear to what extent the interests of states in supplying or not supplying information can be more closely aligned with those of taxpayers.

## 2. (GENERAL) POSITION OF TAXPAYERS IN THE EXCHANGE OF INFORMATION

To taxpayers, the most essential legal consequence of the existence of a duty of information for the states they live in is that information provided by them and therefore at least related to them is supplied to third parties (i.e., foreign tax authorities). Thus, this duty relates potentially to one of the most important elements in the position of the individual in its relationship with others. The availability of certain data on the one hand and the need to obtain these data on the other are among the most important factors determining the mutual interdependence of individuals, but also that between individuals and the government. Information is essential for the possibilities of an individual to achieve its freedom. Having more information at one's disposal than someone else creates a superior position. The latter is especially true for personal information.[5] From the perspective of the relational notion of law, this kind of informational supremacy is seen as a threat to the balance that, in ideal situations, governs the legal relationships between individuals among themselves and between individuals and their government.[6]

This general fact gained a stronger overtone as a result of the quick increase of the practical importance of information as from the seventies of the last century: the 'new industrial revolution'.[7] This also caused the risks for the individuals concerned to increase. In its turn, this gave rise to a discussion in the Western world about the way in which their risks involved in collecting, exchanging, and using information by market parties or governments could be reduced. The outcome of that discussion was the drafting of principles of sound data processing. The most concrete international result of that discussion can be found in the 1995 European Privacy Directive, which creates a right to information with regard to all forms of processing personal data.[8]

---

5. Cf. the Dutch Personal data protection Act. Parliamentary Papers II 1997/1998, 25 892, nr. 3 (Explanatory Memorandum), 3.
6. Of course, this does not change the fact that the right of citizens to information is not an absolute one, but is related to the context of the legal and factual situation.
7. Cf. the Dutch Personal data protection Act, Parliamentary Papers II 1997/1998, 25 892, nr. 3 (Explanatory Memorandum), 7.
8. The Council Directive 95/46/EC of 24 Oct. 1995, concerning the protection of natural persons with regard to personal data processing and the freedom of movement of these data, OJEC L 281 (hereafter the Privacy Directive), defines *personal data* as: 'any information relating to an identified or identifiable natural person' and *processing* as: 'any operation or set of operations which is performed upon personal data (. . . ) such as collection, recording, organisation, storage (. . . ) disclosure by transmission (. . . )'. The international exchange of information is covered by both definitions, albeit that it does not refer only to natural persons, but also to legal persons.

This informational point of view, related to the rather legal-philosophical approach shown earlier of states and taxpayers as participants in an asymmetrical legal relationship in which the burden of the taxpayer must be kept at an acceptable level through the duty of care of the state, makes it clear what kind of legal protection is needed in this field.

This conclusion is underlined by the fact that the legal obligations of taxpayers in other states were extended continuously during the last decades, as is shown in previous chapters.[9] For the Model convention, I mention the 1977 extension of the scope of the obligation to non-residents and of the obligation of means of states to carry out special examinations, as well as the extension of the scope of mutual assistance to spontaneous and automatic exchange. The two last mentioned are identical to those incorporated in the 1977 Directive 77/799.[10] In 2000, the object of exchange in the Model convention was extended to 'taxes of every kind or description'. The methods of exchange were amplified by the presence of foreign officials in tax examinations as well as simultaneous audits, both after the method described in the Convention on Mutual Administrative Assistance in Tax Matters.

This development has caused an increase of the number of cases in which taxpayers can be required to provide information. For them, this means an increase of their burden, without a direct connection between taxation and consideration, in the individual sense as well as in the form of 'public goods'.[11]

Following this line of thought, it becomes clear that a dialogue will be necessary between the government and the taxpayer as a provider of information,

---

9. Cf. Chs 4-6 which contain an analysis of the rules on the international exchange of information as embodied in the OECD Model convention, 1977-2005, the Council Directive of 19 Dec. 1977 EC, concerning the mutual administrative assistance of the competent authorities of the Member States in the field of direct and indirect taxation (77/799/EC), the Convention on the Mutual Administrative Assistance in Tax Matters of the Council of Europe and the OECD concerning mutual administrative assistance in tax matters (1988), which came into effect in 1995. The Netherlands is a party to this Convention since 17 Jul. 1996 (Approval Act of 26 Jun. 1996, Stb. (*Bulletin of Acts and Decrees*) 382). In addition, rules on the international exchange of information are to be found in the Council VAT regulation 1798/2003 (EC) 1798/2003, of 7 Oct. 2003 concerning mutual assistance in the field of VAT between the EU Member States, which until that date was laid down in the Council Regulation (EEC) 218/92 and the OECD Agreement on Exchange of Information on Tax Matters, <www.oecd.org>.
10. This duty to cooperate may also enter the equation under the 'force' of the 1963 Model Convention, albeit that the states are not obligated to perform special tax audits under that convention (Cf. above, para. 5). According to the Explanatory notes, the taxpayer will (have to) be engaged in it in the same way as is usual 'in the normal procedure of tax determination' in his country. An example is the taxpayer answering questions arising from the foreign request.
11. Kimman (1999) mentions the direct benefit principle, in which taxes are seen as the citizens' consideration for the services of the state. Other authors stress the fact that for taxation to be legitimate in the eyes of the taxpayer, the taxpayer must be able to detect a connection with quid pro quo by the government. If this connection is no longer visible, tax ethics will deteriorate, these authors claim. Although the phenomenon of 'inadequate acceptation of standards' in his volume refers to Dutch tax ethics only, there is no reason to assume that this would be different elsewhere.

in which the interests of the latter are focused on and may be weighed by the state. Bearing in mind that in modern rule of law states the standard of good governance and that of transparency are inextricably connected the necessity of a right of information for the taxpayer involved appears inevitable.[12] Later in this book, this right of information will be focused on in the context of the practical implication of legal protection in the international exchange of information.

### 2.1. Conclusion

Gathering all together, it becomes clear that the convention provisions that are the framework of the international exchange of tax information by states should not only allow for a weighing of the mutual interests of the states, but should also guarantee a weighing of the interests of the state against those of its taxpayers who are obliged to provide the information. A publication of the government decision concerning the exchange of information to the taxpayer concerned is essential for the monitoring of this weighing.

## 3. POSITION OF THE TAXPAYER IN THE PRESENT RULES ON THE INTERNATIONAL EXCHANGE OF INFORMATION

The primary sources of the rules on the international exchange of information were mentioned in the previous chapters. In chronological order, these concern the OECD Model convention, the Directive 77/799, the Convention on the Mutual Administrative Assistance in Tax Matters (Strasbourg Convention), the OECD Agreement for Exchange of Information on Tax Matter (OECD Agreement), and the Council regulation EC 1798/2003 on cooperation in the field of value added tax (VAT).

Substantively, the provisions relative to this study appeared not to differ greatly from each other, especially because in 2000 the text of the Model convention was linked to the provisions of the Strasbourg Convention. The OECD Agreement established in 2002 differs from the other instruments inasmuch as its provisions exclusively concern the exchange upon request. Because of this substantive compatibility, in this chapter the position of the taxpayers is viewed on the basis of the OECD Model provision, because it applies to the largest group of states and is the best documented.

---

12. At a European level, this transparency standard is reflected in the Regulation (EC) 1049/2001 of the European Parliament and of the Council regarding public access to European Parliament, Council and Commission documents, 30 May 2001, OJEU L 145. Cf. Curtin (2000), 7-41.

### 3.1. OECD Model Convention

When reading OECD law, it is striking that the position of the taxpayer is hardly ever dwelled on in either the text of the Convention or the Commentaries: 'not even slightly' to say it in Calderon's words.[13] Since the last decade of the previous century, other authors regularly criticized this as well.[14] Their criticism was mainly aimed at the fact that according to the authors, compared to the protection of the taxpayer, in Article 26 of the Explanatory notes, too much emphasis was laid on the improvement of efficiency in the exchange of information.[15] This is the more striking because in the period mentioned, the international attention for human and civil rights certainly increased. In its 1994 report Tax Information Exchange between OECD Member Countries, the OECD Committee on Fiscal Affairs itself[16] mentions as an example its own 1990 survey regarding Taxpayers' Rights and Obligations[17] and the International Fiscal Association (IFA) Conferences on international information exchange and tax secrecy.[18] Other examples are case law of the European Court of Human Rights (ECHR), in which the application of certain fundamental rights was enforced in tax matters,[19] the entry into force of the European Privacy Directive mentioned previously and the codification of the right of informational self-determination in some countries.[20]

In spite of the fact that many authors have criticized the weak position of the taxpayer in Article 26 of the OECD Model convention, and in spite of the plea for the creation of a right of information for taxpayers,[21] the references in the previously mentioned 1994 OECD report did not lead to the insertion in the Model convention of any right of the taxpayer to information about the exchange of information he/she provided.[22] It can be seen from the subsequent versions of the Commentary to the Model convention that the informational protection of these taxpayers is unfortunately still seen as a matter that concerns only the

13. Calderon (2000), 462 onward. He is not entirely right, as we saw. The OECD Explanatory notes mention the taxpayer in the Explanatory notes to the grounds for refusal with regard to commercial, industrial or professional secrets.
14. Distaso (2000), 47 onward.
15. Calderon (2000), 465.
16. OECD Report Tax Information Exchange between OECD Member Countries, A Survey of Current Practices, 1994.
17. OECD Report Taxpayers' Rights and Obligations, A Survey on the Legal Situation in OECD Member Countries, Paris 1990.
18. Cahiers de Droit Fiscal International LXXV b., 1990, Report on the Stockholm Conference (Exchange of Information) and Cahiers de Droit Fiscal International LXXVI b., 1991, Report on the Barcelona Conference (Protection of Confidential Information in Tax Matters).
19. Like the *Oztürk* case, 21 Feb.1994, NJ 1988, 937 regarding the applicability of Art. 6 ECHR (the right to a fair trial) when imposing tax fines.
20. Like in Germany, Spain, Switzerland. See Calderon (2000), 465, and Oberson (2003).
21. See Gangemi (1990) and Malherbe (1991).
22. Oliver (1995), 116, who in his review of the OECD Report on Tax Information Exchange between OECD Member Countries, A Survey of Current Practices (1994) concludes that the information provision applies the rules with regard to the rights of taxpayers all too flexibly, especially with regard to the detection of a trade secret.

individual states and, moreover, increasingly causes uneasiness with regard to the efficiency of the exchange of information.

This is shown by the fact that the 1995 version of the Model Commentary contained a neutral statement of the fact that some states created a notification right concerning the exchange of information abroad in their legislation,[23] whereas the latest version of the Explanatory notes (2005) has been altered. From then it was worded as a warning that 'notification procedures' are not allowed to obstruct the efforts of the requesting state or to unduly delay the exchange of information.[24] Against this background, the possible advantages of a notification procedure that are also mentioned (such as the prevention of errors and the furtherance of the compliance of taxpayers) pale into insignificance.

## 3.2. OECD Agreement

The notion mentioned earlier on 'rights to prior notification' in the Commentary of the 2005 Model convention was copied from the OECD Agreement.[25] As shown in the commentary to Article 1, in creating possibilities to exchange information, the Agreement purports to find a balance between the 'rights and safeguards secured to persons, by the law or the administrative practice of the requested Party' and the need for the exchange of information. That balance consists in the fact that rights have to be respected as long as they do not 'unduly prevent or delay effective exchange of information'.

The commentary makes it clear that the provision was also inserted to draw the requested Party's attention to its responsibility for a proper use of these rights. Improper use occurs when the invocation of a right is intended to frustrate the exchange of information or has that effect or is delayed to such an extent that the information becomes useless. To avoid this, according to the commentary a notification procedure before the exchange would in any case have to contain an exception for fraud cases or in cases in which the examination in the requesting state would be undermined. The weighing of the interests of taxpayers is referred to only in the context of the exchange of business secrets, but there too, the tone is mainly defensive.[26]

23. Such a right of information then had to be communicated to the partners to the treaty. OECD Explanatory notes 1977-2005, Art. 26, para. 14.
24. OECD Explanatory notes 1977-2004, Art. 26, para. 14.1.
25. Cf. Oberson's critical review of 2003, 14 onward. Cf. also Barnard (2002), 1041. It must be kept in mind that this Model Convention is designed for the exchange of information with former tax havens, and is aimed at a different kind of taxpayers, namely those who commit tax fraud.
26. Cf. Ch. 6, s. 5.5.

### 3.3. Strasbourg Convention

In the preamble of this Convention, the first condition mentioned for mutual administrative assistance is the adequate protection of the rights of taxpayers. These include a right to the protection of their privacy.[27] This point of departure can also be found in Article 21, first paragraph of the Convention, which, by way of 'principal statement' states that 'nothing in this Convention shall affect the rights and safeguards secured to persons by the laws or administrative practice of the requested state'. Although this rule of law notion seems a step in the right direction, compared to the Model provision (and also to European legislation on this subject), it was never developed concretely, as we have seen.[28]

### 3.4. European Rules on the International Exchange of Information

The low amount of attention paid to the taxpayer's interests in the OECD exchange rules is – although to a lesser extent – also a shortcoming in the European Council Directive 77/799. In its preamble, the 'fundamental rights of citizens and enterprises' are only mentioned with regard to the secrecy of the information to be exchanged. As we saw in Chapter 5, in this respect, the text goes further than the text of the OECD Model convention. A Member State is entitled to *refuse* the exchange of information, if the secrecy provisions in the requesting state should offer less protection than its own. At the point of the weighing of interests, the Council Directive is less clear than the Model convention: even the existence of a notification procedure in some Member States is never mentioned in the preamble, no more than the interests of taxpayers regarding commercial, industrial, or professional secrets. This is striking, because during the preparation of the Directive the European Parliament did in fact elaborate on this topic. The result was the Resolution containing the advice on the draft Directive presented to the Council of Europe on April 5, 1976.[29] The proposed legal protection consisted of a right of appeal for taxpayers against the judgment of the Member States on the confidential nature of tax data and their disclosure. According to the European Parliament, the taxpayer providing the information could thus defend himself against possibly unlawful use of the information.[30] The advice was of no avail. The recent changes in Directive 77/799 as a result of the coming into effect of the VAT Council regulation 1798/2003 also contain no reference to the weighing of

27. Strasbourg Convention, Preamble, third and fourth consideration.
28. Cf. Ch. 5, s. 4.1 above and the critical notes mentioned there.
29. Resolution implementing advice of the European Parliament concerning the directive proposal mentioned in n. 5, OJEU, 13 Dec. 1976, C-293/34-35. Cf. Wisselink (1996), 154, for the background of the Directive.
30. Advice of the European Parliament, OJEC of 13 Dec. 1976, nr. C-293/35.

interests of taxpayers or to their informational position.[31] That is striking too, because the regulation itself does contain a statement on that subject,[32] with reference to the Directive 95/46 EC (the so-called Privacy Directive).[33] This legal framework, and the significance it has for the legal protection of taxpayers with regard to the exchange of information, will be discussed in paragraph 7.3.3.3, and more closely examined in Chapter 8.

## 3.5. Conclusion

It becomes clear from the previous section that in the present OECD rules on the international exchange of information as well as in the Community legislation in that field, the protection of the interests of taxpayers needs improvement.

Especially in the legal instruments of the OECD,[34] it is striking that none of these instruments contains a fundamental statement on the necessity of informational legal protection of taxpayers, from the rule of law notion that a state must be transparent in its actions and must weigh the interests of its citizens in a reasonable way. This is remarkable in itself, as we have seen in the previous chapter that especially a correct application of the provisions concerning commercial, industrial, or professional secrets depends on the contacts between tax authorities and their taxpayers.[35]

On this basis, a common set of standards for the OECD countries, a 'level playing field' for the protection of the rights of taxpayers will not come to light. In my opinion, this neglect of the necessary reciprocity in the legal relationship between the state and its citizens is a shortcoming in the rule of law quality of the OECD rules on the international exchange of information, and in the end it will

31. Changes made in Directive 2003/93/EC, in which the substantive scope of the EU Mutual Assistance Directive was adapted, and Directive 2004/56/EC containing more specific procedural regulations.
32. Cf. Art. 41, para. 5 of that Regulation. However, the latter does not contain the possibility Member States have to refuse the supply of information based on the fact that secrecy legislation offers less protection in the other state. Cf. also Ch. 5, s. 3.2.
33. Directive 95/46/EC of the European Parliament and the Council of 24 Oct. 1995 concerning the protection of natural persons with regard to the processing of personal data and the free movement of those data. OJEU L 281 (Privacy Directive).
34. One of those instruments in my view is the Strasbourg Convention, although the Council of Europe was also involved in its drafting. However, for the purpose of monitoring the practical implementation and its development, the Strasbourg Convention was transferred to the Coordinating Body, which itself comes under one of the Working Parties of the OECD Committee on Fiscal Affairs.
35. Article 26, para. 3, s. c of the OECD Model convention, Art. 7, para. 2 of the OECD Agreement, and Art. 21, para. 2(d) of the Strasbourg Convention determine that a state is not obligated to supply information if there is a risk that a trade, professional, commercial or industrial secret could be disclosed (Cf. Ch. 6, s. 5). The commentaries to the Articles all refer explicitly to the interests of taxpayers.

frustrate its efficiency.[36] The OECD Committee on Fiscal Affairs should take its responsibility in this matter. It should formulate in the provision on the exchange of information a minimum obligation for the Member States to add a (form of) notification procedure in their legislation, so that taxpayers in all states involved are able to defend themselves against the unlawful (negligent) supplying of information by their public authorities.

The Community rules on the international exchange of information show a more differentiated picture. In its provision on secrecy, the Directive 77/799 offers more possibilities to Member States to protect their taxpayers against the disclosure or abuse of information by another Member State, but does not in any way refer to the necessity of a notification procedure for these information-providing taxpayers or a weighing of their interests. Community thinking around the protection of the informational position of natural persons in the processing of their personal data, resulting in the Privacy Directive, has in no way been of influence on the wording of the Directive 77/799. The VAT Council regulation 1798/2003, however, does seek a conjunction to it. There too, however, no reference is made to the duty under rule of law to weigh the interests of taxpayers.

In view of the necessity to improve the position of taxpayers, and the requirement of transparency in the actions of public authorities in that field, the necessity of a notification procedure becomes obvious. Through this procedure, the taxpayer will in any case be informed of the fact that his personal data are being exchanged. If this notification procedure is combined with a course of justice, it is also a means to enforce a careful weighing of interests by the public authorities. Within the context of international law, this leads us to the question (already put up in the Introduction of this Chapter) of which interests of taxpayers are to be considered in this process. In the following paragraphs, these will be discussed, and in the subsequent Chapter this envisaged legal protection will be closer examined.

## 4. INTERESTS OF THE TAXPAYER (IN THE REQUESTED STATE)

From the analysis of the various obligations to exchange information duties, it has become clear that the obligation to exchange information is mainly aimed at safeguarding the interests of the parties at the Treaty. Of origin, these are of a political-economic nature: taxation is essential to the existence of the state and its functioning. Moreover, taxation also serves the 'tax justice', as it is put in the preamble of the Directive 77/799, because it helps to combat fraud and disparities in competition. These effects definitely also serve the interests of the taxpayers. Besides that, at an individual level, taxpayers in most cases also run informational

36. Calderon (2001), already points out that the absence of rights for taxpayers will not stimulate their willingness to cooperate in the exchange of information by their state. Cf. also Gribnau/Meussen (2002), 252.

and economic risks,[37] as I mentioned briefly in paragraph 7.2. The public authorities must exercise due care in this respect and must find a balance between the interests of their partners, their own interests, and those of their citizens, wherever necessary and possible. To this end, international rules drafted for the states must be 'reformulated' from a public law point of view as much as possible. In the formulation of the obligation to exchange information in itself, in Chapter 4 two elements were found in the various regulations that affect the interests of the states: the exhaustion principle and the secrecy clause. We have also seen that the international obligation is not an absolute one, and that the states are free to weigh their own interests against those of a treaty partner in some limited situations. The following elements were mentioned:

- the sovereignty of national legislation;
- the principle of reciprocity;
- the interest of maintaining the '*ordre public*';
- safeguarding the generally accepted principles of taxation;
- the risk for the disclosure of a commercial, industrial, or professional secret.

All of these elements will have to be examined to determine to what extent they also represent interests of taxpayers that should be protected or weighed by the state.

## 4.1. The Exhaustion Rule (The Principle of Subsidiarity)

The so-called exhaustion rule concerns the general starting point that a state, before requesting information from a party to the convention, normally first exhausts its own possibilities. It protects the interests of the requested state against its engagement into unnecessary efforts. However, in paragraph 4.4.6.3, we have seen that the exhaustion rule cannot be considered a *conditio sine qua non* for the exchange of information on request. It is a form of politeness that will govern the mutual protection of interests between states and that follows from the principle of proportionality: the party having a major interest in reaching the goal of the legal relationship is expected to make a major investment. However, this principle would have to yield to that of effectiveness, if circumstances arise in which the exhaustive use of domestic means by the requesting state has counterproductive effects (e.g., in cases of fraud). A focused attention of the requesting state to a certain taxpayer can result in the latter warning his business partner in the requested state (who is to provide the information), which could result in information being manipulated or deleted even before a request is put to the other state. This could seriously frustrate the gathering of information in the requested state. I find this risk more threatening to the effectiveness of the information exchange than that of an announced *supply* of information (by prior notification). Then the

37. Albeit that the result of the exchange of information can also be 'exculpatory' to a taxpayer, because the foreign information exonerates him from a tax liability.

business partner of the in the *requesting* state may of course be alarmed, but manipulation of information by the taxpayer there then seems more difficult because the requesting state already has his eye on him.

The Convention of Strasbourg and the European exchange of information rules (unfortunately not the OECD Commentary) do justice to this risk inasmuch as they create a possibility for the requesting state to deviate from the exhaustion rule, if compliance with the latter should jeopardize the intended purpose of the audit.[38] The provisions are worded as an exception to the requested state's duty to exchange information,[39] although they should in fact be fulfilled entirely by the requesting state and are hardly verifiable by the requested state, or not at all (see paragraph 4.4.5.3).

In the first place, this is so because the requested state is not able to independently check what means were pursued by the requesting state because in the context of international law, first and foremost loyalty to and trust in the party to the convention are presupposed.[40] Besides that, if the requested state were to carry out such a check, the latter should include a search into the whole of statutory instruments in the field of information gathering powers of the requesting state to be able to interpret the terms 'usual sources of information' and 'information gathering powers', as well as all related policy rules. Finally, such a check would not be appropriate inasmuch as the discretionary opinion on the counter-productivity of the '*usual* sources' is left to the requesting state. A check by the requested state, if any, can therefore be only marginal. It may be focused only on the question of whether, under the given circumstances, the requesting state could reasonably have reached that conclusion (on the counter-productivity of the usual sources), and even then the requested state can do nothing but rely on the statements of the requesting state.[41]

*A fortiori*, this is also true for the *taxpayer* providing information in the requested state, although the latter is not bound to principles of interstate trust and loyalty in a treaty context. Moreover, with regard to the exhaustion rule, its

38. Cf. Art. 2 of the Mutual Assistance Directive, and Art. 19 of the Convention on the Mutual Administrative Assistance in Tax Matters.
39. Article 2, para. 1 of the Mutual Assistance Directive reads: 'the requested state *need not comply with the request* if it appears that the requesting state has not exhausted its own usual sources of information, it could have utilized without running the risk of endangering the attainment of the sought after result' (italicization ASG) Art. 19 of the Convention on the Mutual Administrative Assistance in Tax Matters reads: 'The requested state shall not be obliged to accede to a request if the applicant state has not pursued all means available in its own territory, except where recourse to such means would give rise to disproportionate difficulty' [italicization author].
40. That is also the opinion of the highest Dutch administrative Court (Council of State) in these matters, as is shown from its ruling of 22 Jun. 1993, RO1.92.0053, Judicial Division of the Council of State, FUtD, 29-7-1993/nr. 143, in a case concerning a request made to Australia, in which The Netherlands, according to the party involved, should have carefully tested Australia's compliance to this principle. The Dutch Council of State ruled that the competent authority was entitled to rely on the statement of the requesting party.
41. This trust can be deemed to be unjustified only when the requested state has reasons to suspect the other state of not observing the rules in this point.

interest can lie only in the possibility of the request being superfluous and as a consequence in the 'unnecessary' reliance on his duty to cooperate in tax matters. However, the 'superfluous' nature of the request by the other state can hardly be made plausible either. For that matter, an audit by the other state can also yield new points of view. The conclusion must be that the exhaustion rule cannot be deemed to serve an interest of taxpayers worth protecting. It is to be considered a standard of instruction to the states, to be deviated from under circumstances such as provisions in the Community rules on the international exchange of information with regard to time limits. Therefore, in Chapter 4, I advocated a more clear expression of it in the international provisions and Commentaries, especially in the OECD Commentary. An open standard, to be interpreted by the states as they see fit, will offer more room for manoeuvre in the fight against tax fraud. Besides that, a possible solution would be for the states to inform each other at every request about what means they have used.

### 4.1.1. Conclusion

The exhaustion rule is a regulating mechanism to efficiently apportion the efforts of the states in the exchange of information, in which variations are possible and desirable according to the circumstances of a specific case, such as those defined in the Directive 1977/799 and the Strasbourg Convention. Thus, the risk for the taxpayer (the intended provider of the information) in the requested state being alarmed is mitigated and therefore, the 'disappearance' of data in the requested state even before the request is received. Moreover, this rule should not be treated as an excuse for the requested state to refuse the supply of information. The facts about compliance to the rule by the requesting state cannot actually be judged by the requested state, and, besides that, determining the import of the term 'usual' sources or means in the other state is extremely cumbersome. The interpretation of the exhaustion rule must be left to the requesting state, and states must rely on each other with regard to their compliance to the agreement.

The rule is not intended to protect an interest of a taxpayer in the requested state with regard to the collection of tax information. In this context, his duty to cooperate in a tax audit does not depend on the answer to the question of whether a certain audit is necessary or not.

Based on this requirement of due care, the requested state does of course have a duty toward its taxpayer to make sure whether *a priori* there are no obstacles resulting in the audit to be cancelled.[42]

42. E.g., because the request does not originate from the competent authority, or because it does not fall under the scope of the treaty-obligation, or has another defect that the requested state can *a priori* detect itself.

### 4.2. The Importance of Secrecy

Beside the scope of the duty to exchange information, in all provisions on information exchange embedded in the various regulations, we find the rule of law perspective as well. The receiving information requires the protection of its confidentiality. The circle of persons and instances that, on the basis of that clause, are entitled to those data also includes appeal courts. From this, the conclusion may be drawn that this clause is not only, and even not in the first place, designed to serve the interests of states, but those of the taxpayers in the supplying and the receiving state (cf. paragraph. 5.2).

#### 4.2.1. Absolute Duty of Secrecy

As we have seen, the original version of the Model convention contained an absolute wording of the requirement of secrecy.

We concluded (in paragraph 5.2.1) that the nature of this provision, which is also aimed at the protection of citizens' rights, implies that it is directly enforceable for the taxpayer involved in supplying of information, that is, before the Court of its own state.[43] However, this does not help the taxpayer in country A if he wishes to enforce the repair of a breach of confidentiality with regard to information his state provided to state B. The duty of secrecy is vested in state B, and if his data are unlawfully disclosed or used by the tax authorities, the providing taxpayer in state A is empty-handed. Only a state, or an organization possessing Legal personality, can hold state B accountable for the non-fulfilment of his duties under the treaty.[44]

As became clear in paragraph 4.3, the question of mutual liability of states in the field of tax treaties has only recently received the attention of international bodies, especially within the framework of the fight against so-called harmful tax competition. Although in the OECD report on that subject, the exchange of information is turned into a standard, the latter is merely of an international law nature and has nothing to do with the attitude of states toward their taxpayers.[45]

If the requested state wishes to protect its taxpayer (and in my view, it should do so) under the current system, actually only a form of 'diplomatic protection' could produce a result.[46] Heavier remedies are charging the other state with breach of international treaty, and eventually suspending or ending the treaty, although the latter will probably not be used immediately.

43. The Court may then (dependent on the constitutional ranking order between domestic and international law in the state concerned), in the event of conflict between domestic and international law, exclude domestic law.
44. Cf. Kooijmans (2000), 104. E.g., acts of the ambassador or consul of one state on a political level, addressed at the authorities of the state in which they are accredited. Cf. van der Bruggen (2001), 134.
45. OECD Report on Harmful Tax Competition, An Emerging Global Issue, OECD 1998, paras 53, 64 and 92. Cf. also Van der Bruggen (2001), 116. He points at the fact that the OECD did not draft standards of liability in this report either.
46. Cf. Kooijmans (2000), 104-107.

However, the so-called 'diplomatic protection' sees to the general duty of states to treat subjects of other states being in their territory with decency.[47] For an appeal on this principle, it should first be extended to the specific phenomenon of the fiscal exchange of information and the confidentiality duty that is a part of it. It is not so sure states will agree on that extension. The greatest uncertainty for the taxpayer who supplied information is, however, that in respect of these actions, seen from an international law perspective, he is without rights. He depends entirely on the willingness of his state to address its treaty partner, apart from the question of whether the other state will recognize its liability, and is prepared to render him legal rehabilitation.[48] The fact that in the rules on the international exchange of information taxpayers remain 'invisible' thoroughly weakens their position.[49]

The culprit is the fact that the obligation to enter into a mutual agreement procedure on the taxpayer's request, as worded in Article 25, paragraph 1 of the Model convention, does not apply to (this clause of) the information provision. This stipulation concerns an action that results in *taxation* not in accordance with the provisions of the Convention.[50] This could be taxation in the requesting (receiving) state, which leads to double taxation, or discrimination as a result of the exchange of information. The affected taxpayer (in the receiving state) is then entitled to request a mutual agreement procedure. However, this rule does not apply to the *supplier* of information in the requested state, who is not receiving an assessment and who wishes to appeal against a defect in the confidentiality or use of the information. Article 25, paragraph 3 OECD Model convention could possibly offer a solution here, as the latter creates an obligation of means for the states to mutually discuss problems in the application of the convention. This would mean that the Commentary should clearly indicate that problems concerning a breach of international secrecy as well as the corresponding liability of states should be covered by that provision[51] and that states be obliged to find a solution.

It is to be regretted that in the amendment of Article 26 of the Model convention, when information exchanged under the mutual agreement procedure was

47. The assumption that it concerns subjects of another state being *in their territory*, makes it doubtful whether this instrument may serve its purpose here, as the taxpayer supplying information lives or stays exactly in the requested state.
48. By way of compensation, or public rectifications if necessary and desirable.
49. Cf. also Brodersen (1987), 471 onward, who in this respect speaks of 'a serious flaw' in the international exchange of information. Cf. also Casley/Henshall 2000, 28, who describe the exchange of information as a 'somewhat opaque process' for the taxpayer.
50. Based on that paragraph, states are under the obligation to process a request for a mutual agreement procedure if a taxpayer of one of the states feels that he is unjustly taxed as a result of the incorrect or unreasonable application of the rules of apportionment of the tax treaty.
51. OECD Commentary, Art. 25, para. 32 in connection with para. 3 reads: 'difficulties of a general nature which concern a category of taxpayers, even if they have arisen in connection with an individual case normally coming under the procedure of paras 1 and 2 of this article'.

explicitly brought under the secrecy clause, this aspect of the connection between Article 25 and Article 26 was not taken into account.[52]

### 4.2.2. Relative Duty of Secrecy

Since 1977, in most regulations the interpretation of the duty of secrecy is left to the legislature of the receiving state,[53] (including the exceptions states have entered in their legislation, for example, because of developments in the field of freedom of information). In paragraph 5.2.2.1, I elaborated on the fact that this dependency creates certain risks for the supplying states. This is, of course, also true for the taxpayers in the requested state.

Vogel deems the position of the information-providing taxpayer not that awkward:[54] in his view, the validity of the domestic rules on confidentiality of the receiving state, enforced by the provision in the Convention, implies that legal protection created in that state with regard to a breach of confidentiality is open to the taxpayer in the supplying country. This would give the taxpayer supplying the information '*einen eigenen anspruch auf Geheimhaltung*' to claim the confidentiality of that information.[55] In its turn, this implies that the taxpayer in the other state should be regarded as an interested party.

This may in itself be true, but that does not offer the taxpayer in the requested state any substantial warranty. It is far from certain that the legislation of the receiving state will offer him the same protection as his own state, let alone that to conduct legal proceedings in another state may be a cumbersome and costly matter. In this respect, Vogel never mentions the necessity of awareness of the taxpayer with regard to the fact that information concerning him is being supplied. Yet this knowledge must be considered essential for conducting legal proceedings.

However, in the end, even Vogel admits that, as a result of the differences that may occur between states in the field of secrecy legislation, expectations of taxpayers, if any, with regard to the protection of their interests will sometimes prove to be rather '*unrealistisch*'.[56]

The single phrase 'persons and authorities concerned with assessment or collection, the enforcement and the prosecution of taxes (. . . )' to whom, according to the OECD Model convention, access is granted to the information received, may

52. Since the amendment, Art. 25, para. 4 reads that all information exchanged in a mutual agreement must be kept secret on the basis of Art. 26, para. 2 of the Model Convention.
53. Of the modern conventions, only the OECD Agreement contains an absolute duty of secrecy.
54. Vogel, and the other authors, mostly comment on the de OECD Model provision, but in my view, their remarks at this point are also relevant for Community law.
55. Vogel (2003), Art. 26, Rz. 60, 1998. Cf. Calderon (2000), 467, who concurs. Cf. also Verbruggen (2001), who, with regard to the possibility to hold states liable in a general sense, also quotes dissenting opinions.
56. Vogel (2003), Art. 26, Rz. 115, and Calderon (2000), 466. Of equal tenor Urtz (2000), 43 who draws the reader's attention to the very weak position of taxpayers. This would be the cause of the fact that case law is sparse. Although breach of secrecy does occur, and is liable to punishment, the taxpayer is not entitled to be a party in proceedings concerning the admissibility of the exchange.

harbour a large diversity of administrative bodies. In his survey of the Stockholm Congress, Gangemi gives some striking examples of this phenomenon.[57] From subsequent, although less systematically comparative literature, a broad scale of authorities emerges, all of which could have access to the information supplied.[58]

Against this background, to conclusively prove (or to make a reasonable case for) government actions to be wrongful would require cumbersome legal research by the aggrieved party. Besides that, to establish the liability of the government, the aggrieved party will have to engage in factual research to present causal evidence. His own state is under no obligation to assist him in this, because in international law, this is only common practice in case of subjects who live or stay in the other state as foreigners.

This is clearly a *lacuna* in the legal protection with regard to the exchange of information, and it should be filled. In my view, here lies a task for the OECD Committee on Fiscal Affairs, because both the Model convention and the Strasbourg Convention fall under its jurisdiction, as well as for the European Commission, which prepares the legislation of the European Union. A focal point in this discussion should not only be the efficiency of the information exchange, but also the necessity and assumptions for the protection of the taxpayer's legal position in the exchange of information by their governments.

### 4.2.3. Solutions by Changes in the International Conventions

In my view, the above mentioned discussion should contain the following elements;

- Rethinking the relative character of the warranty of secrecy. Much is to be gained if the secrecy clause in the exchange of information provisions could be worded autonomously, so that the entire scope of this rule of law obligation, so essential to taxpayers, would show comprehensively from the provision in the treaties.[59] This would increase certainty for both taxpayers and states.
- Developing a train of thought on how the liability of the receiving state for defects in the application of the secrecy clause can be practically shaped. One could envisage that, in case the secrecy clause was not met, the receiving state may be held accountable by the requested state to restore the taxpayer's rights. This could be done by exclusion of evidence in the tax

57. E.g., Gangemi (1990), 41, mentions the Stock Exchange Commission and the Central Bank for Brazil, as well as the Central Statistic Office for Norway.
58. Cf. the series Confidentiality of Taxpayer Information in the *International Transfer Pricing Journal* (2000), mentioned several times before.
59. The amendment of the text of the OECD Model convention and the Commentary in 2005 is a step in that direction. It established that in case 'freedom of information' is invoked, legislation with regard to the information supplied the international secrecy provision prevails. This is of special importance when interstate correspondence is involved. To both the states and the taxpayers/providers of information this mitigates the risk that information would be disclosed. OECD Commentary 1977-2005, Art. 26, para. 12.

procedure as a result of negligence of the administrative organ, by awarding compensation or by offering apologies to the taxpayer. The inclusion of such an international provision will prevent discord between the states on the existence of liability as such and the duty to repair.

- The liability claim could be established through a round of negotiations between the two states, and this round may be instituted by taxpayers by means of an application under the conditions mentioned in the convention or established by the individual states.[60] For the OECD countries, Article 25 of the Model convention would be suitable for that purpose after amendment.
- A minimum option is that, in imitation of the Strasbourg Convention and the Directive 77'799, the secrecy provision of Article 26 of the OECD Model convention would be extended with a possibility for the requested (supplying) state to create additional conditions with regard to secrecy in the receiving state, if the supplying state suspects that the legislation of the receiving state, or its policies in this field, would offer the taxpayer/information supplier insufficient protection.
- And finally the duty of information providing, apart from the *conditio sine qua non* of secrecy, should also contain the condition that the taxpayer in the requested state should be granted a right of information, so that he is able to verify the legitimacy of the actions of his government, and to check the correctness of the information supplied by his state.[61] After all, his government crosses its duty of tax confidentiality (albeit on proper grounds) and transfers this duty to another state, in which it has no jurisdiction at all. Thus, it exposes its taxpayers to the risk for unlawful disclosure or processing, without being able to repair a defective policy of confidentiality. Therefore it is of interest that taxpayers are at least informed of the fact that information he supplied is passed on. Then they can check their own status or to hold the other state liable if necessary.

Such a layout of the secrecy clause would greatly improve the position of the taxpayer, as well as the quality of the rules on the international exchange of information, also because of the effect that it would have on the negotiations about individual double taxation conventions. At that stage, states may want to ensure their own position and practice, as well as those of their treaty partner in tax secrecy matters, more thoroughly than has been the case up to now.[62] Thus, at this point, a level playing field can be created for all states and citizens pertaining to the international communities mentioned.

---

60. Cf. for the shortcomings of Art. 25 as an instrument for legal protection, see paras 4.2 and 7.3.2.
61. Some authors truly consider this a gap in the Model convention: Urtz (2000), 46; Distaso (2000), 52; and Casley/Henshall (2000). Furthermore, Bentley (1998), 46; Calderon (2001), 464 onward; and Schaumburg/Schlossmacher (2000), 522.
62. From the contributions to the IFA Conference on the exchange of information, Gangemi (1990), concludes that most states do not specifically look into the secrecy legislation of their intended party to the convention. They rely on the latter's good faith.

### 4.2.4. Solutions for the States

The discussed proposals alone will not be suitable to improve the position of the taxpayers in the exchange of information. As is true for the international exchange of information as a whole, they will have to be supported by and embedded in domestic legislation and executive measures. Of course, the latter can be changed in the direction indicated above and amended without interference of the bodies mentioned previously.[63] The duty to exchange information does not contain a ban on informing the taxpayer about a decision to supply information or to balance the interests of taxpayers. The Commentaries to the ground for exemption with regard to commercial, industrial, or professional secrets in the OECD Model convention and the OECD Agreement even refer to this fact. Moreover, in Chapter 6, it became clear that all regulations provide for a (well-defined) discretionary margin in which states may balance their own interests against those of their party to the convention, and that within this margin, there will basically also be room for the parallel interests of taxpayers.

To implement this, states may individually take the following measures:

- With regard to the warranty of secrecy, they can, in their domestic legislation, insert the possibility for taxpayers/providers of information to address their domestic tax authorities if a breach of secrecy occurs in the other state. In turn, they can discuss the matter with their treaty party and, if necessary, request a restoration of rights.[64] The domestic legal system should also explicitly provide for the admissibility of the taxpayer in the receiving state in those cases in which the state itself (as the receiving state) fails to maintain the secrecy of the information received.
- Apart from that, the previously mentioned legislation should in any case also contain the right of information for the taxpayer/provider of information, as described above. Thus, the taxpayer may check whether the supply of information by his government was lawful and whether the information supplied is correct. Such a right may also be a first step toward checking the processing of information by the other state.[65] To this right of information arguments may be linked that represent those interests of taxpayers. Thus, a careful balancing of interests could be enforced. One of those arguments could be that the secrecy of the other state does not meet the standards applying in the taxpayer's own state. This taxpayer would then have to

63. The disadvantage of a purely individual approach by the states is, that a level playing field will not come into effect.
64. Brodersen (1987) calls this takeover of a claim for compensation based on wrongful government actions by the other state as a solution for cases in which a tax assessment is made with the help of foreign information which was obtained unlawfully there.
65. In many cases, obtaining knowledge of the actions of the receiving state will be hardest to realize. In a general sense, relying on the good faith of the other state will surely be justified. On the other hand, administrative practice can be obstinate in any state, regardless of the quality of its legislation, and in some states this is more true than in others. In those cases it helps if a taxpayer at least knows that his information was supplied to that country.

be able to require that his own state would request a more extended warranty of secrecy from the party to the convention, or that the supply of information be omitted.[66]

Such a right of information can of course have different shapes, dependent on the measure in which the taxpayer must cooperate in the supply of information or dependent on the reason why it is supplied or of other circumstances. This will be addressed in the next chapter.

### 4.2.5. Conclusion

In the exchange of information, the requested state transfers the duty of confidentiality, so crucial to the taxpayer, to the receiving state, although it is not possible for the requested state to verify or influence the observance of this duty by the receiving state. The obscurity arising for the taxpayer's position, as he is the supplier of the information, is darkened further by the fact that, based on the rules on the international exchange of information, secrecy must partly be observed according to the legislation of the other state. The fact that legal proceedings may be started in the receiving state can hardly remedy this. To hold the other state liable is a cumbersome affair, leaving aside the fact that it is unclear what level of protection the legal system of the other state may offer. This weak position of taxpayers creates the necessity to review the relative nature of the duty of confidentiality, as well as the liability for breach of confidentiality. Also, a right of information should be created for the taxpayer involved. As a result of these changes, together with the position of the taxpayer, the constitutional content of the rules on the international exchange of information, and maybe the national practice on confidentiality of tax-related information must in some states be improved. The states could also create this right of information individually, together with a sound court procedure, so that the taxpayer having supplied the information may check the balancing of interests by his state. In case the states as *receivers* of the information should fail to observe the confidentiality of information, the domestic law should offer an opportunity for the taxpayer/supplier of information in the other state to bring proceedings in case he has suffered damages as a consequence of it.

## 4.3. Other Interests of Taxpayers

Apart from the interest of secrecy of information and the correctness of the information itself, it must be examined here which other interests of taxpayers are affected by the exchange of information.

66. Cf. also Schaumburg (1998), para. 19.74. He points out that in Germany, such an argument may be used by the taxpayer during the hearing. If insufficient observance of secrecy is suspected in the other state, the supply of information must be refused.

Every information provision formulates by means of the grounds for exception various situations in which states deem themselves to be discharged of the obligation to exchange information. To the requested state, each of those situations represents a possible interest. It can weigh its own interest against the interest of its treaty partner. If this process has a negative result for the other state, this interest becomes an argument against that state to refuse or omit the supplying of information.

In Chapter 6, interests such as the sovereignty argument; the reciprocity argument; the argument of commercial, industrial, or professional secrets; and the public order argument were discussed. Inasmuch as these interests affect the position of taxpayers, they may, as was the conclusion, be involved by the requested state in the balancing of interests mentioned previously. Therefore, Gangemi speaks of the 'first line of protection for the taxpayer'.[67] Because the reliance on the grounds for exception is worded optionally, the way in which the states prepared to balance those interests is not the object of the rules on the international exchange of information.[68] However, for the sake of legal certainty, at this point the states must embody the choices they make in their domestic laws.

Hereafter I shall try to analyze what those choices should look like, in other words, which interests of *taxpayers* are worthy to be balanced by their state through the grounds for exception. Within the framework of the protection against arbitrariness, and in accordance with the requirement of transparency and verifiability of government actions, these interests should in my view be handed over to the taxpayers as arguments. This could take place through the creation of statutory rights to lodge an appeal.

### 4.3.1. Sovereignty of Domestic Legislation and Administrative Practice

These grounds for exemption, which appear in all regulations on the exchange of information except the OECD Agreement, protects the sovereignty of the states and their inalienable right to pursue their own purposes through their domestic tax legislation, without being forced to include exceptions purely for their treaty party.[69] These grounds for exemption make it possible for the state to meet the rule of law requirements of legal certainty and predictability of government

67. Gangemi (1990), 34.
68. Although recent developments in the rules on the international exchange of information (especially those of the OECD) do show a curtailment of the discretionary freedom (Cf. Ch. 6 for this topic).
69. Cf. also the OECD viewpoint on this in the discussion about harmful tax competition. The right states have to draft tax bills as they see fit is essential and inviolable, even though this would affect other states. OECD: Harmful Tax Competition, An Emerging Global Issue, Paris 1998, para. 26, 15. Cf. also Daniels 2000, on the influence of the case law of the European Court of Justice on the sovereignty of domestic tax legislation.

actions.[70] According to Vogel, a rule of law state '*ist nicht befugt zu Handlungen die nach seinem innerstaatlichen Recht gesetzwidrig sind*'.[71] It does not further the legal certainty of taxpayers when laws can incidentally be put aside *a posteriori* on the request of another state. Thus, these grounds for refusal also serve an interest of the information-providing taxpayers, and they must be able to invoke it. In this respect, it is remarkable that the OECD Agreement does not contain these grounds for refusal.[72] The Commentary to that agreement does not provide a motive for this decision. In Chapter 6, I indicated that this *lacuna* might be linked to the fact that the Agreement is established by the OECD for the exchange of information with former tax havens, which because of their nature attract an atypical population of taxpayers. A contributing factor would be that the tax legislation in this kind of state, if anything, certainly will offer protection against the international exchange of information, by deliberately limiting the tax authorities' scope of information gathering powers and will be anxious to strengthen the position of their taxpayers by strong secrecy legislation, as we shall see hereafter.

#### *4.3.1.1. Conclusion*

The sovereignty argument confirms the essential inviolability of the legislation of each individual state. The latter can be overridden only by the state itself, if in its opinion the interest of the party to the convention, or the common interest, would justify this. The fact that the parties to a convention cannot force each other to do so, provides certainty to the taxpayer in the requested state about the scope of his duties. The OECD Agreement does not know this argument, possibly because to the former tax havens, the limited scope of the taxpayers' duty to supply information was their unique selling point.

### 4.3.2. Reciprocity

The idea of reciprocity was already defined in Chapter 2 as an essential standard for asymmetrical tax legal relationships between the state and its citizens/bodies, a standard that (also) forms a basis for the government's duty to carefully balance the interests of the taxpayers in its actions. In this paragraph as well, balancing the interests by the tax authorities (hence reciprocity) is the subject. Apart from that, the legal relationship between the exchanging states is government by the reciprocity principle, too. If we indicate the first-mentioned form as 'vertical' reciprocity, and the second as 'horizontal', perhaps it becomes more clear what should be looked into here, namely, to what extent, seen from the taxpayer's perspective, an objectivized standard of horizontal reciprocity between states should also be balanced within the vertical reciprocity of his relationship with his/her state.

70. Schaumburg (1998), para. 19.61 considers this one of the 'Absolute *Auskunftsverbote*' (absolute prohibitions for exchange).
71. Vogel (2003), Art. 26, Rz. 111, 2021.
72. Cf. Barnard (2002), 1041.

In paragraph 6.4.1, I concluded that a conflict with reciprocity in all regulations on the exchange of information forms a ground for exemption, but that the supply of information at variance with that reciprocity is not unlawful under *international* law.[73]

As we saw there, in the rules on the international exchange of information, reciprocity is drafted from the viewpoint of the requested state. This implies that the latter is free to either abstain from supplying information on the basis of the legal or factual unobtainability of the requested information in the requesting state or to supply more information than its treaty partner would be able to supply. In this interpretation, reciprocity is conceived as a standard that must be realized in the long run and in a flexible way, according to the interests of states, and is subject to continuous adaptation to specific situations. Thus, the idea in fact obtains the features of a principle.

The choice of a state for a flexible concept of the standard of reciprocity in supplying information may be justified by:

- the general interest of the state as a party to the convention, so that more flexibility from other states may be expected;
- the general interest that by adopting a flexible attitude the fight against tax fraud may be made easier;
- the interest that by adopting this flexible attitude, the state may in the future obtain more benefits from the tax convention for its taxpayers;
- or the interest a state has to ward off criticism from other states with regard to its harmful tax laws by a generous information exchange policy.

A choice for a strict concept of reciprocity could result from:

- a budgetary or financial interest of a state in making the supplying efforts of the other state as light as possible, for example, based on organizational circumstances;
- uncertainty about what may be expected from the other party to the convention with regard to his willing to make efforts;
- strong variations in legal systems concerning information gathering powers in both countries, so that also in the long term a balance will be hard to reach.

Both interpretations are possible and justified under international law. The Commentaries to the various exchange regulations make it abundantly clear that a flexible interpretation is the most appropriate approach keeping the interests of the states in mind.[74] Especially the factual aspects of reciprocity (e.g., data files and audit techniques not being available yet) are seen as improper reasons to decide

73. Cf. Art. 26, para. 2(a) and (b) of the OECD Model convention, Art. 21, para. 2 of the Convention on the Mutual Administrative Assistance in Tax Matters, and Art. 7, para. 1 of the OECD Agreement.
74. Cf. also s. 6.4.

not to supply information. However, for the taxpayer, the strictest concept of the reciprocity standard is the most advantageous.

Does a state therefore have a duty toward its taxpayers to adopt the strict concept of the standard of reciprocity? To answer this question, it must be established what interest taxpayers may have in the strict application of reciprocity, and the relationship between this interest and the interests of the states mentioned previously. The interest of information-providing taxpayers may exist in the fact that as a consequence of the reciprocity principle, the chance of a distortion of competition will arise if their state supplies information and the other state does not. For example, especially the imminent distortion of competition as a result of defective reciprocity has complicated the discussion about the drafting of the Saving Tax Directive. The choice of a state for either a flexible or a strict application of the reciprocity principle will have to be embedded in the legislation of the states. The principle of legal certainty requires that government actions concerning citizens are transparent and predictable, meaning that the underlying principles are known to all.[75]

#### *4.3.2.1. Conclusion*

In my view, although an all too strict application of the standard of reciprocity may indeed hamper international cooperation, states in applying this standard have a legal duty to take into consideration the interests of the information suppliers. This requirement will especially play a role when entrepreneurs supply information, because of the consequences a lack of reciprocity may have for their competitive position. Therefore, I do not share Schaumburg's view that the principle of reciprocity merely protects the balance of legal relationships between states, and not 'den *Individualinteresse des durch die Auskunft Betroffenen*' as well.[76]

### 4.3.3. Commercial, Industrial, or Professional Secrets/Rights of Information

The ground for exemption with regard to a commercial, industrial, or professional secret offsets the duty to exchange information if complying with this rule would disclose business, commercial, or professional secrets. This 'secret' is to be considered as a specification of the general secrecy provision of the first paragraph of Article 26. It protects supplying states from the risk for industrial espionage, especially of importance if state-owned companies are involved, but it also creates the opportunity to protect their economic interests (i.e., the interests of vital branches of industry) from the exchange of information and thus to create a more favourable position for them. In the analysis of the grounds for exception in Chapter 6, it became clear that in the course of time the OECD Committee on

75. See also Gribnau/Meussen (2002).
76. (The individual interests of those involved in the exchange of Information) Schaumburg (1998), para. 19.83, 1334.

Fiscal Affairs watched commercial, industrial, or professional secrets with ever-increasing scepticism.[77] This may be gathered from the various draftings of the decision-making powers of states at this point. In the Commentary to the Model convention, the liberty initially granted the states in paragraph 17 of the OECD Commentary to rely on the grounds for exception, has been reduced to 'a certain discretion' when this interest is taken into account.[78] The exchange of information must not be restricted too much. Since 1994 especially, the *banking* secrecy has been the subject of an ever-increasing criticism by the OECD Committee on Fiscal Affairs.[79] It became clear that this criticism eventually resulted in a ban on the refusal to supply information of banks or financial institutions under this provision of exception, in 2002 in the OECD Agreement and in 2005 in the OECD Model convention.[80] However, apart from that, under the influence of the discussion with the committed jurisdictions in the latest OECD Commentary, (and in the OECD Agreement) the notion of commercial, industrial, or professional secrets was expanded with a new privilege, being the solicitors' privilege.[81]

A rather conspicuous example of commercial, industrial, or professional secrets being balanced against international duties can be found in Belgian case law.[82] (The case concerned spontaneous exchange of information by the Belgian tax authorities. The subject was information about commissions paid by a Belgian enterprise to Italian agents). The enterprise commenced litigation on the basis of commercial losses as a result of this exchange of information and won his case. The Court considered the exchange to be unlawful because the tax authorities had not given priority to the protection of the industrial secret of their taxpayer. The Court ruled that taxation of the commissions could have been secured by not allowing a deduction of the payments to the Italian agents from the profits of the Belgian enterprise.

In my opinion, what were actually protected here were the interests of the other parties of the information supplier, that is, the Italian agents. In this case, the secrecy requirement apparently lies in the efforts of the receivers to maintain these payments beyond the reach of their tax authorities, and therefore not in the relation of the Belgian information supplier with another party in the market who could benefit from the knowledge of certain facts. If the commercial interest of the information-providing taxpayer may be served only by keeping the income of

77. See paras 6.5.2 and 3 of this book.
78. OECD Commentary 1977-2005, Art. 26, para. 19.
79. In 1994, appeared the OECD Report Tax Information Exchange, A Survey of Current Practices, 1994, which tried to explain Art. 26 for taxpayers. It was then rather neutral about the risk that the commercial, industrial, or professional secret argument would be misused by states. See para. 64.
80. Also the sovereignty of domestic legislation was no more usable for cases of banking secrets (Art. 26 para. 5), like in the OECD Agreement, which does not contain this ground for exemption at all.
81. OECD Commentary 1977-2005, Art. 26, para. 19.3.
82. Wisselink (1993), 352, in his review of the ruling of the Brussels Tribunal, 5 Sep. 1980 (*European Taxation*, 1987, 87-88).

his overseas agent a secret, he does not have an interest that merits legal protection. If, according to the OECD Commentary 2005, becoming liable to tax in itself cannot be classified under any major loss for taxpayers, the latter being the condition for these grounds for exemption to apply,[83] this is even more true for the elimination of the opportunity to avoid taxation.[84] (Cf. also paragraph 9.4.3).

#### *4.3.3.1. Informational Rights*

However, apart from the interests of the states, the exemption with regard to commercial, industrial, or professional secrets also protects the commercial interests of their taxpayers.[85] The conclusion in paragraph 7.2.1 that the position of the taxpayer in the rules on the international exchange of information (except in the Convention on the Mutual Administrative Assistance in Tax Matters) barely received any attention, must be slightly restated here: the commercial interests of the taxpayers are (implicitly) recognized in all regulations inspired by the Model convention. In fact, this argument is the only place in the OECD Commentaries directly referring to the taxpayer. The various commentaries explicitly stress that this balancing of interests must be done very carefully, meaning in this case that states should not be too generous and should concern only "the true interests" of that taxpayer.[86]

In the 1994 OECD report 'Tax Information Exchange, A Survey of Current Practices' it is suggested that for these true interests to be taken into account, a closer contact with the taxpayer is essential, and in this case, the Explanation to the Strasbourg Convention in so many words refers to prior notification of the taxpayer.[87] In his survey of the this OECD report, Oliver, too, claims that commercial, industrial, or professional secrets are closely connected to the right of the taxpayer to be informed about any proposed exchange, because the state itself often cannot determine independently whether in a certain situation, a commercial, industrial, or professional secret is at hand.[88] For the application of the solicitors' privilege, the same conclusion may be drawn from the latest version

83. OECD Explanatory Notes 1977-2005, Art. 26, para. 19.2.
84. The Dutch Council of State has decided differently in a similar case, concerning commissions paid by a Duch BV to a French agent, via a bank account in Switzerland. The corporation invoked the 'commercial secret' grounds of exception, stating that the exchange had caused damage to its commercial interests. The Council decided that these interests were solely depending from the maintaining of the fraud pattern, which was harmful for the French treasury, and that these interests were not worthy of legal protection. ARRvS. 11 Aug. 1993, V-N 30 Dec. 1993, 41-52.
85. Schaumburg (1998), para. 19.79, 1332.
86. Cf. OECD Commentary 1977-2005, Art. 26, para. 19, and the Strasbourg Convention, Art. 21, Explanatory Report, para. 198.
87. The Strasbourg Convention, Art. 21, and the Explanatory Report, para. 198, refer to the possibility that states are more reticent in the supply of certain data (e.g., because commercial, industrial, or professional secrets are involved) and can therefore adopt special measures, such as prior notification of taxpayers. Cf. Ch. 6, s. 5.5.
88. Cf. also Vogel (2003), Art. 26, Rz. 121, 205.

of the OECD Commentary and from Article 7, paragraph 3 of the OECD Agreement. The detailed regulations characterizing these grounds for exemption also presuppose that the taxpayer or his agent in the 'committed jurisdiction' is at least aware of the cross-border exchange of information.[89] However, in this respect the Model convention does not link the idea of prior notification to commercial, industrial, or professional secrets. It is true that the existence (in some countries), of such a right is mentioned in the Commentary in connection to the sovereignty argument, but the recommendation in paragraph 4 initially merely refers to the states communicating the existence of such a right to their treaty partner. In the 1994 OECD report, this neutral position is converted into a warning against the delaying effect of such taxpayer guarantees.[90] On the other hand, it also admits that the right to prior notification can increase the compliance of the taxpayers who have to communicate, and the possibility of correction will increase the risk for exchanging erroneous information. The 2005 OECD Commentary states that the application of this information right should not harm the results for the requesting state. To avoid the risk for postponement, such a right may yield for the interests of the requesting (receiving) state, which means that tax authorities should be able to suppress it in case of an emergency.[91] This passage largely matches the commentary to Article 1 of the OECD Agreement, in which the right of information, including a possible right of appeal linked to it, is referred to as one of the procedural rights taxpayers may have. Article 1 of the Agreement allows for the application of it, at least inasmuch as that application not unduly prevents or delays the exchange of information. Only the fundamental rights (. . . ) 'may take precedence over the Agreement,' according to the Explanatory notes.[92] It becomes clear from all of this that in the OECD-inspired exchange of information rules, the *necessity* of prior notification is not recognized for a correct application of the commercial, industrial, or professional secret argument. A similar conclusion may be drawn from the Community law with regard to commercial or professional secrets. In the absence of explanatory notes in both the Directive 77/799 and Regulation 1798/2003 on VAT, the provisions concerned are the only source. Neither Article 8, paragraph 2 of this Directive, nor Article 40, paragraph 4 of the regulation make reference to the interests of taxpayers anywhere, and in Chapter 6 it became clear that the Directive totally ignores the existence of informational rights in some states. Regulation 1798/2003 on VAT *does*, however, refer

89. If (in the requesting state or) in a certain situation of doubt arises as to whether a right of nondisclosure is properly invoked, the case must be judged by the Court in the state where this right is invoked (the requested state), OECD Commentary 1977-2005, Art. 26, para. 19.3. Of course this presupposes awareness of the taxpayer in that country of the intended supply of information.
90. OECD Report Tax Information Exchange between OECD Member Countries, A Survey of Current Practices, 1994, para. 44.
91. OECD Commentary 1977-2005, Art. 26, para. 14.1.
92. OECD Agreement, Art. 1, para. 5 refers to rights resulting from 'relevant international agreements on human rights'.

to these rights (albeit not in connection with commercial or professional secrets, but by referring to the Privacy Directive).[93]

In my view, this is a defect in the rules on the international exchange of information. As we have seen, states have a legal duty to take into account the interests of their citizens while performing their actions, which also applies for the international exchange of information. Moreover, a correct and transparent balancing of the true interests of taxpayers is certainly also in the interest of the states. The latter not only applies to commercial or professional secrets, but, as we have seen, also to the secrecy of the information supplied. The Communities should give up their faint-hearted attitude with regard to this right of information and must examine how possible disadvantages could be mitigated in practice. What should prevail is the advantage of better relationships between the states and their taxpayers supplying the information, as well as the improvement of the quality of the information.

#### *4.3.3.2. Conclusion*

Apart from the secrecy clause, in the present rules on the international exchange of information the grounds for exemption with regard to commercial or professional secrets is the only element referring (implicitly) to the interests of taxpayers. As we have already seen when examining the secrecy interest, a structural right for taxpayers to be informed about the (intended) cross-border exchange of their data is indispensable for the protection of that interest. Apart from that, also the correct application by the state of the commercial or professional secret argument creates the necessity to establish such a right. If the state wishes to take into account any risks in connection with commercial or professional secrets of its information suppliers (and in my view, it should use this possibility offered by the international rules), communication with the taxpayer is essential. By establishing a right to be informed for all cross-border exchanges of information, arbitrariness and a lack of clarity will be avoided and the transparency of government actions is furthered.

### 4.3.4. The Public Order/*Ordre Public*

In paragraph 6.6 it became clear that the public order argument in the first place affects the interests of the states, whose task it is to guard that public order (the vital interests of the state, such as state security). According to Schaumburg, the grounds for exemption may, however, also be used to decline the exchange of information if this would be not in accordance with the essential basic values of the legal system of the requested state. Examples are that it would lead to discrimination or political persecution in the receiving state.[94] In this way, this argument introduces a rule of law test to the exchange of information for the actions of governments, and the requested state may decline the exchange of information based on that test, to avoid

93. Regulation (EC) 1798/2003 of 7 Oct. 2003, OJEU L 264, Art. 41, para. 5.
94. Schaumburg (1998), para. 19.80. Cf. also Vogel (2003), Art. 26, Rz. 123.

their participation in practices they consider despicable. It is also conceivable that the other state will adapt its practices, especially if the decision to decline the exchange of information is repeated by more than one party. I have already pointed out that the rule of law character of this argument actually dictates that at this point, states should not have discretionary freedom.[95] A better solution would have been to incorporate this rule of law element more explicitly than has been the case up to now, as a condition to the duty to exchange information itself, especially in the OECD Model convention.[96] A first attempt to do so can be detected in the wording of Article 26, paragraph 1 of the OECD Model convention. As became clear,[97] the wording that the duty to exchange information with regard to the information mentioned only exists 'insofar as the taxation there under is not contrary to the Convention', may be interpreted as a reference to something like general principles of taxation. Similar terminology is to be found in the grounds for refusal of Article 21 of the Convention on the Mutual Administrative Assistance in Tax Matters. In both cases, we concluded that this element of rule of law testing should have been profiled more prominently.[98] The general interest 'affected' by this argument suggests that it also should be at the disposal of the taxpayer in the requested state. It is an instrument to enforce the testing of that argument by his government, for example, if a request from a totalitarian state is received to supply information about a certain money transaction, of which the taxpayer legal body in the requested state is aware that it is meant as a donation to a democratic resistance movement in that country. The taxpayer supplier of information should be able to communicate this fact to his government, so that the latter may take this public order argument into consideration when making its decision. Of course this argument will have to be reserved for extreme situations. Whether this appeal is possible depends on the domestic legislation of his state.[99]

#### *4.3.4.1. Conclusion*

The conclusion may be drawn that the grounds for exception in the various rules with regard to the exchange of information, although they are drafted to put the balancing of interests into place, partly also represent the interests of taxpayers. Now that the international rules on cross-border exchange of information create possibilities for the states to weigh their own interests, and as even in their 'imperative' elements, domestic legal systems are respected, the rule of law requires that the domestic laws of the states use the discretion given for the benefit

95. Cf. Ch. 6, s. 5.6.
96. I assume that the legal order of the European Union contains more instruments to influence the rule of law of the domestic legislation, in the wide-ranging field covered by that legal order. Especially the direct effect of the regulations and the implementation duty of the Member States with regard to the Directives can 'model' domestic law to a great extent.
97. In Ch. 4, s. 4.3.2.
98. In Ch. 6, s. 6.1.
99. Based on Dutch case law, only legal persons having incorporated this in their articles of association may defend the general interest.

of those taxpayers. A right of information with regard to the supply of information, in combination with a right of appeal, gives the information-providing taxpayers the chance to enforce balancing of the interests of the state against their own.

## 5. POSITION OF TAXPAYERS IN THE REQUESTING (RECEIVING) STATE

The legal duty of the government to carefully balance the interests of its taxpayers must cover all government actions and therefore also the tax legal relationship as a whole. With regard to the exchange of information, this implies that the duty to protect taxpayers in the other country also covers those persons about whom information is requested abroad.[100] The question is, to what extent parts of the international rules on cross-border exchange of information influence the position of those taxpayers, too, and which specific interests must be taken into account within this framework. For the answer to this question it must be kept in mind that requesting information from a foreign country is complementary to the powers the tax authorities of a state already have to gather information for the assessment of tax liability. Whether it is lawful is determined by the requirements of lawfulness set in the international information provisions and also by domestic rules about the admissibility of proof. In my view, a state having laid down in law that information will be provided only in case of the existence of an international duty to exchange information, will not be able to reserve the right to request a foreign country to supply information outside the scope of the convention provision. The principle of legal certainty requires that government actions are predictable, and therefore consistent and coherent.

What elements of the information provision affect the specific interests of taxpayers about whom the requesting state may require information?

### 5.1. Exhaustion Rule in the Requesting State

In paragraph 4.4.6.3, we concluded that the exhaustion rule in the various regulations serves the interests of the requested state, which must be protected against unnecessary claims from its party to the convention. It requires no specific duties for taxpayers in the requesting country,[101] but on the contrary is entirely based on the existing domestic legal system with regard to the gathering of tax information by the tax authorities. In that system, the taxpayer in most cases remains the party designated in the first instance to supply information for tax purposes, although we

100. There are states, for example, Germany, that have also incorporated requests for information in their mutual assistance legislation, whereas other states, such as the Netherlands, have only provided for the supply of information.
101. For the position of the taxpayer providing the information, cf. Ch. 7, s. 4.1.

have seen before that exceptions to that rule may be conceivable and desirable.[102] The conclusion drawn there, that the exhaustion rule does not constitute a criterion of lawfulness between states, but only a 'standard of instruction', leads to the situation that it cannot represent an interest of taxpayers in the requesting state either. This may also be concluded from the fact that in certain situations, the application of the principle may be counter-productive to the requesting state. Only if the legal system in the requesting state would contain the rule that, for the assessment of tax liabilities, taxpayers themselves should be addressed first, taxpayers would have an interest in the non-compliance of the exhaustion rule by their state.[103]

## 5.2. Secrecy Concerning the Received Information in the Requesting State

### 5.2.1. OECD Model Convention, Convention on the Mutual Administrative Assistance in Tax Matters, OECD Agreement

The secrecy requirement of Article 26, paragraph 1 of the Model convention concerns the information received, and first protects the interests of the taxpayer/supplier in the requested state. However, also the taxpayer about whom information is requested runs the risk that in another state information (background information supplied in complying with the request) is disclosed about him. In his interest these data (e.g., background information) must be kept secret as well, in the same way this is done on the basis of domestic laws for 'domestic' information. At the amendment of the OECD Commentary in 2005 this was put in so many words.[104] The domestic duty of secrecy in the requesting state is not drafted to protect its taxpayers in the exchange of information, just like the requested state cannot protect its own taxpayers. Therefore, the requested state should warrant the secrecy of that background information. If the request is based on the Strasbourg Convention or on the Directive 77/799, and the level of protection in the other state is presumably lower than that in his domestic legislation, the

102. In Dutch legislation in certain situations, there exists a duty for subsidiaries and sister entities to supply information about their foreign parents and sisters to the tax authorities, except when an adequate international exchange provision applies. In that case, the tax authorities will request that information directly from their party to the convention. Cf. also the *Futura* case of the European Court of Justice (C-250/95) in which the Court in case of doubt about the applicability of domestic laws does not refer to the exhaustion rule, but to the exchange of information. Cf. also CJEC C-9/2, dated 11 Mar. 2004 (Lasteyrie du Saillant). Cf. also Ch. 4, s. 4.6.3, must be Ch. 4, s. 4.5.3

103. Cf. Douvier (2000) for a similar argument with regard to audits relating to transfer-pricing in France, where the taxpayer himself was not addressed first. Thus the dialogue between taxpayer and tax authorities, necessary for a tax audit, would have been ignored.

104. OECD Explanatory Notes 1977-2005, Art. 26, para. 11.

requesting state may (and in my opinion should) require extra protection for the information contained in the request.

To the taxpayer in the requesting state (whose taxation is the purpose of the request) it is also of importance that the lawfulness of the request may be checked, as well as the correctness of the information received. In order to be able to do so, he must rely on the remedies and procedures available in domestic tax law. However, as we have seen, these are determined, among other factors, by the description of the circle of parties entitled to have access to this information, like those in the secrecy provision of the underlying duty to exchange information.[105] If that provision is drafted on the basis of the 1963 version of the OECD Model convention, the position of the taxpayer in the requesting state is not very clear. The 1963 Commentary does not explicitly mention the taxpayer in the receiving state (about whom the information is received) as a party having access to the information received, although this information may lead to tax liability.[106] The result would be that taxpayers would not be able to defend themselves against any factual incorrectness or the unlawful requesting of the information received. This is contrary to the generally accepted rule of law standard that government decisions (like tax assessments) should be properly motivated and that parties involved must be able to defend themselves against them before an independent court of law.[107] The solution for this lack of clarity seems to lie in the interpretation of the phrase 'jurisdiction of disputes as to tax liabilities', for which, according to the 1963 Commentary, the information may be used, that is, in closed hearings. Such a dispute presupposes not only the involvement of the authorities, but also that of taxpayers.[108]

The Commentary to the Model convention, amended in 1977, as well as the Explanatory Report to the Strasbourg Convention and the Commentary to the OECD Agreement, include the taxpayer in the circle of parties having access to the received information, as well as his legal counsels and witnesses if any.[109] Thus, the assessment, calculated with the help of cross-border information, may be motivated. The exchange of information provision, however, does not contain in itself a right that is directly enforceable. The way in which this right of the taxpayer is implemented is determined by the domestic laws on tax secrecy of that state

105. Cf. Ch. 5, s. 2.1.2.
106. This is different only in states in which disputes as to tax liabilities are public domain. Of course, the taxpayers themselves have access to the information. In those cases, their state will have to ask the permission of the other party to the convention to disclose the information. Cf. Explanatory notes OECD 1963, Art. 26, para. 9.
107. Cf. van Wijk/Konijnenbelt/van Male (2002), 490 onward. Cf. also Bentley (1998), 24 and 47 and also the 1987 comparative study by de Moor and van Vugt, in which the administrative law of the Netherlands, Belgium, France, Germany, and the European Union are compared and the conclusion is drawn that these legal systems all use general standards of proper administration with regard to government actions. Cf. also Art. 6 ECHR. More recently also Jans (1993).
108. OECD Explanatory notes 1963, Art. 26, para. 9, and the Convention on the Mutual Administrative Assistance in Tax Matters, Explanatory Report, Art. 22. Also OECD Agreement, Explanatory notes Art. 8, para. 96.
109. OECD Explanatory Notes 1977-2005, Art. 26, para. 12.

(including its exceptions based on the legislation with regard to freedom of information), as became clear in the American case described in paragraph 5.2.2.1.

In my view, based on what is referred to as the motivation principle, taxpayers must be able to successfully require that foreign information with the help of which their tax liability is calculated is disclosed to them.[110] However, the fact that this information will be incorporated in the documents exchanged between the states involved cannot bring this motivation principle in conflict with the interest states have in the confidentiality of their communications.[111]

Perhaps the 2005 amendment of the OECD Commentary can be explained as the result of this friction. This amendment introduced the 'ban' on allowing applications from *outsiders* for freedom of information, and this ban may be extended to the taxpayer, his attorney or a witness by the 'governmental and judicial bodies charged with deciding whether such information should be released to the taxpayer (. . .)'.[112] In my view, the darker purpose of this ban may be found in the fact that states fear a breach of their interest to be able to keep their communications about financial and audit strategy matters confidential. It does deteriorate the position of the taxpayer in the receiving state though. Therefore, to do justice to both the motivation principle and the interest of confidentiality in the exchange of information between states, a distinction must be made in the latter between the supplied personal data as such (of course inasmuch as they refer to the taxpayer himself/) and the rest of the information exchanged between states within the scope of a certain case. Placing this on the agenda and further developing this idea would be a task for the OECD Committee on Fiscal Affairs. The confidential cross-border exchange of documents could then be made available by the state either to the tax court in the appeal proceedings with regard to the rule itself or the tax liability in question, or to the administrative court in proceedings with regard to freedom of information. The respective Courts may then judge the lawfulness of the exchange in question.[113]

### 5.2.2. European Community Rules

As a main rule, the secrecy provision in the Directive 77/799 (Article 7, first paragraph) draws the circle of persons entitled to have access to the received information around the person(s) directly involved in the process of audits and tax assessments and around persons involved in proceedings with regard to tax

110. Cf. de Moor/van Vugt (1987) and also Bentley (1998), 55. The latter speaks of an essential right for taxpayers to know on what grounds the decision of the tax authorities is based.
111. In the cross-border exchange of documents, apart from facts, states may also lay down visions, connections, or suspicions that may be of interest for the interpretation of a certain body of facts in the other state.
112. Cf. Ch. 4, s. 4.5.3.
113. In Dutch case law with regard to the exchange of information the relationship between the duty of confidentiality of the information received based on the law of treaties on the one hand and the standard of freedom of information on the other, the court ruled in favour of the administrative body.

liabilities, including those proceedings involving administrative fines. These proceedings may also be public, if the requested state allows this. Article 7, paragraph 3 of the Directive 77/799 opens the possibility of disclosure for other purposes, including criminal proceedings (subject to consent as well). In these disputes and proceedings, the taxpayer is also involved, so it may be assumed that he will have access to the information received. The assessment of his tax liability or the determination of a fine can therefore always be motivated. The Directive 77/799 nor VAT Regulation 1798/2003 take a clear view on the question of whether inter state correspondence may be submitted. I see no reason to reach a different conclusion for Community law or OECD law. Here, too, lies a (clarifying) task for the European Commission.

### 5.2.3. Conclusion

A rule of law state not only has to protect the interests of its taxpayers if they provide information to be exchanged with the other state, but also if he becomes the subject of a request for information made to the other state. Apart from the requirements of lawfulness with regard to the international duty his state relied on, which also determine the admissibility of foreign proof, there are two elements of the international right of information that seem to affect the interests of the subject in the request for information: the exhaustion rule and the international secrecy clause on information received. It may be said of the exhaustion principle that the position of the taxpayer whose tax liability is being examined is not jeopardized by it. In principle, the taxpayer remains the party designated in the first instance to provide the tax authorities with foreseeably relevant information. In some cases, when suspicion arises of a conspiracy to commit tax fraud, exceptions to that exhaustion rule will be conceivable and desirable.[114] This must be at the discretion of the requesting state. The exhaustion rule cannot be expected to protect an interest of the taxpayer in the requesting state. The duty of secrecy is of interest to the taxpayer, however. It covers all data exchanged, also those included in the request as 'background information'. As a taxpayer in the requesting state he will thus be protected in the other state as well. However, based on international secrecy clause, the foreign information with the help of which the assessment is calculated, may be disclosed to the taxpayer himself, so that he may exercise his right of appeal. Based on the most recent OECD Commentary this rule does not apply to outsiders who require freedom of information on the basis of transparency

---

114. Cf. the Dutch Art. 47 a, para. 3 of the Dutch 1963 State Taxes Act, in which in certain cases an exception to the duty of subsidiaries and sister entities to supply information about their foreign parents and sister entities is the applicability of an adequate international exchange provision. Cf. also the *Futura* case of the European Court of Justice (C-250/95) in which the Court in case of doubt about the applicability of domestic laws did not refer to the exhaustion rule, but to the exchange of information. Cf. also Ch. 4, s. 4.5.3 Cf. also ECOJ EC C-9/2 dated 11 Mar. 2004 (Lasteyrie du Saillant).

legislation, nor to the taxpayer when it comes to *documents* exchanged between the states.

## 5.3. Principles of Sovereignty and Reciprocity in the Requesting State

The texts of conventions limit the obligation to supply information to the boundaries of the domestic laws of the requested state. States need not go any further, as we have seen, and cannot cross those boundaries without breaching the principle of legality. A state 'cannot take advantage of the information system of the other state, if it is wider than its own system', the OECD Commentaries claim. To the taxpayer who is the subject of an international request for information, it is important that his state cannot circumvent these legal options. Of course, this does not alter the fact that *this legislation could* make a difference between the information gathering powers in domestic and cross-border situations. For its role as a requested (disclosing) state, situations may be described in which the state, in spite of a defective reciprocity, may still be able to supply information.

However, requesting states are not able to ignore defects in the reciprocity requirement. If a state deems it necessary to be able to have access to certain information to reach a correct and just assessment of tax liabilities, (such as data gathered from third-party audits of third private persons), this must be included in the tax legislation.

The sovereignty and the reciprocity argument may therefore be deemed to represent an interest of the *taxpayer who is the subject of a request for cross-border information.* His government is not allowed to expand its powers by addressing foreign tax authorities. He must be able to submit this argument to the national tax courts in the appeal proceedings with regard to his tax liability.

### 5.3.1. Conclusion

It can be said that a request for information is an extension of the activities of a state to obtain tax-related information. The scope of the duties of the taxpayer about whom information is requested is not extended by the request for information. The protection of the interests of the taxpayer involved in the request should take place within the legal system of the requesting state governing the assessment of the tax liability. Those interests are to be found in the lawfulness of government actions, seen against the background of international law. This implies that the request should fit in with both the scope of the convention provision and the options with regard to the gathering of information embedded in domestic laws. The duty of care of the requesting state implies that extra requirements are to be set with regard to the secrecy of the information involved in the request, that the tax-related information received about the taxpayer are communicated to him, and that the taxpayer must be entitled put up a defence against these actions. In my view, contrary to the sovereignty and reciprocity argument, the exhaustion rule cannot be deemed to represent interests of taxpayers in the requesting state, worthy of protection.

## 6. LEGAL DUTY TOWARD THE TAXPAYER IN THE OTHER STATE

Some years ago, a discussion arose in Dutch literature on whether the obligation to take the interests of taxpayers in the requested state into account in supplying information should or should not be extended to taxpayers in the other state, being the subject of the exchange of information. In my view, however, no written or unwritten legal obligation toward those taxpayers may be assumed, neither on the basis of the text of the Model convention, nor on that of the Explanatory notes, except for the secrecy of information related to them resulting from the requests for information.[115] The requested state does not have a tax legal relationship with taxpayers in the other state. On the contrary, it supplies the information especially to assist the other state in the implementation of its tax legal relationship with taxpayers. I am of the opinion that, as a maximum, an indirect and general obligation to balance interests of taxpayers in the other state is present in those cases in which there are reasons to assume that the information to be supplied could be used for taxation not covered by the convention. This implies that such use is not in accordance with the requirements set to taxation by a rule of law. In the presence of such a risk, the grounds for exemption of breach of public order can be invoked, so that the information does not have to be supplied. This would fit with the tendency in international law I detected so hopefully at the beginning of Chapter 4, to increasingly withdraw the acceptance of the principles of the democratic rule of law from sovereign arbitrariness and to convert international law from 'a marshalling of the intercourse of sovereign states' into a 'global, justice-oriented legal order'.[116] It is my view that it is the (still) unwritten duty of the states to comply circumspectively or not at all with agreements about the exchange of tax information with states where lack of integrity of civil servants, or the absence of sound appeal proceeding can be assumed.[117] Such reasons could also be (the likeliness of) arbitrariness and disproportionality in the sanctions resulting from the supply of the requested information.[118]

115. Schenk-Geers (1996), 1644.
116. Hirsch Ballin (2000), refers to principles of 'good governance'.
117. I assume that the requested state did not already detect these defects during the negotiations preceding the convention. In that case it might have been better if the convention were not drafted (in that form).
118. Meant are rights included in the European Convention on Human Rights, in the United Nations' 1948 Universal Declaration of Human Rights and the International Covenant on Civil and Political Rights. See Kooijmans (2000).

## 7. SUMMARY AND CONCLUSIONS

1. Compliance with the international duties of states to supply information to their treaty partners can take place only through the legal duty of the (third party) taxpayers to cooperate. That duty to cooperate follows from the tax legal relationship between these information providers and the requested state and that relationship should be extended for the benefit of the other state. Set against that duty of the information-providing taxpayer stands the right to a proper and enforceable balancing of the taxpayer's interests. This right stems from the principle of equality that should govern all legal relationships and requires that participants treat each other as equals as much as possible and take each other's interests into account in the best possible way. In asymmetrical legal relationships, this duty of care lies primarily with the most powerful party. In administrative legal relationships that would be the government.

2. The ratio for this duty of care of the exchanging state lies in the risk incurred by the information-providing taxpayer as a result of cross-border exchange of information, without the requested state being able to control or influence possible defects in the maintenance of confidentiality or the use of the information in the other state.

3. During the last decades of the last century, as a result of the rise of the information society, the risks attached to the possession or the right of disposal other parties have with regard to information about an individual became the key area of attention. This resulted in the drafting of informational rights for those involved in the processing of personal data.

4. The international exchange of information legislation should at least warrant the right of the persons involved (in this case the information-providing taxpayers) to be informed of the fact that these data are supplied to another state. Such a right not only serves the purpose of legal certainty, but also that of transparency and verifiability of government actions.

5. However, both OECD rules and Community legislation are defective at this point. In both legal systems, the duty to exchange information is seen from an international angle. This is also true for the secrecy clause, which also regards the position of taxpayers. Both legal systems should, by amending the clause, improve the way in which this interest of the taxpayer is warranted.

6. That secrecy clause should be worded more autonomously, so that the dependency on domestic secrecy legislation is mitigated and an increase of legal certainty is created for information suppliers. It should also warrant a right of information for taxpayers.

7. As a minimum, the OECD Model convention should contain a provision enabling Member States to require extra secrecy warranties or to decline the exchange, if they observe or assume too much of a discrepancy between two levels of protection in their states. This provision already exists in the Directive 77/799 and the Strasbourg Convention.

8. Apart from that, the exchange provisions should contain rules with regard to the liability claim brought on the receiving state in case of non-compliance with the

duty of secrecy and should warrant a fair treatment of complaints a taxpayer may have. OECD Member States should be able to make use of the mutual agreement procedure to this end.

9. Apart from the call for measures coming from the OECD or the European Union to create a level playing field with regard to informational legal protection, the states themselves must incorporate warranties of secrecy for their taxpayers, especially including a right of information for taxpayers providing the information to be supplied. Thus, the latter is able to check whether the actions of his government are lawful, whether the information is correct, and whether his interests were properly taken into account.

10. Within the international duty to exchange information, a reasonable balancing of interests of taxpayers, forming an integral part of the duty of care of governments, is definitely possible, through the discretionary powers supplying states are given on the basis of all international exchange of information rules.

11. Of course, the most conspicuous interests of all taxpayers involved in the exchange (in both the supplying and the requesting state) lie in the lawfulness of the exchange and the correctness of the data. Also of importance to the taxpayers in the supplying state is the secrecy in the other state of the information supplied, the inviolability of domestic legislation, the maintenance of certain reciprocity in the actual exchange, and the extra protection resulting from invoking the commercial, industrial, or professional secret argument. In my view, the exhaustion rule for requests for information cannot be considered an interest of the information-providing taxpayers in the requested state. Rule of law principles such as political freedom and equality of all before the law, which may be incorporated in the public order argument, and the generally accepted principles of taxation should not be laid down as discretionary. Because they are not suitable to be balanced against other interests, they should be conditional for the lawfulness of the information exchange as a whole.

12. Subject to the position of the taxpayer in the *requesting* state about whom the information is received, is that their (tax) interests in the process of tax assessment are already protected. This is implemented through domestic means of redress with regard to the tax assessment (calculated with the help of cross-border information). In the rule of law, this implies that the information received about the taxpayer that is relevant for assessment are made known to the taxpayer, so that he may be able to check the correctness of the data, the lawfulness of the request as such, as well as the processing of his information. The international secrecy provision does in no way impede this.

13. However, friction may occur between the right to secrecy of the taxpayer supplier of information in the requested state and the freedom of information of taxpayers or third parties in the requesting state. In my view, the rule of priority of international secrecy over domestic freedom of information legislation, as laid down in the 2005 Model convention, is justified. The states have as much a right to confidentiality as taxpayers do.

14. A solution must be found for the friction between the right of taxpayers to a substantiated (and therefore verifiable) tax assessment and the interest of confidential cross-border correspondence.

15. Of course, the taxpayer in the requesting state has an interest in his government respecting the inviolability of its domestic tax laws when making a request (the sovereignty argument). Requesting information in violation of the reciprocity principle, indirectly leading to an extension of national ways to gather information, is at odds with the principle of legality.

16. The interests of the taxpayer of the requesting state are tax-related and must be protected by the state having made the request and using the information for assessing the tax liability. The interests of the information-providing taxpayers in the requested state have an informational nature and must be protected by the requested state.

Chapter 8

# Outlines for a System of Legal Protection

## 1 INTRODUCTION

In the previous chapters we have come increasingly closer to formulating an answer to the questions that have concerned us from the start and that pertain to the relationship between states' obligations in the area of international law and public law in respect of the exchange of information in tax matters.

The first question, regarding the *existence* of a legal duty under public law for the government regarding compliance with the obligation to exchange information with other states, could be answered in a general legal-philosophical framework. We concluded that the government must consider the interests of its citizens in all of its actions, on the ground that it is participating, with these citizens, in a relationship of mutual dependence, which should be governed by law. We conceived this law not only as a system of rules and laws, but also as a complex of legal principles referring to legal values and of freedom and equality that, because of the constantly changing circumstances, must be reconsidered again and again. In addition, it appeared that these legal values are subject to development and that in the last century the emphasis particularly shifted to the legal value of equality. This means that every individual is entitled to, in Dworkin's terms, 'equal concern and respect'.[1] This is why, we have seen, participants must consider each other's interests in all legal relationships. It also means that in the relationship under tax law between government and citizen, the government, as the most powerful party, has the duty of care to scrupulously weigh the interests of the taxpayers.[2]

1. Dworkin (1977).
2. Gribnau (1998), 123.

The second question concerned the *possibility* to fit this duty of care within the obligation of exchange of information, as defined in international law, which in its nature is characterized by sovereignty and equality of the treaty parties and by an exclusive mutual focus on their interests. This question could be answered only through an analysis of the obligation to exchange information, its principal elements being the material objectives of scope, obligations of means, and stipulations regarding confidentiality and use, to which the exchange of information between states is bound. Also discussed were the exceptions available to the states to refrain from exchange, to weigh their own interests against those of the treaty partner.

To provide an answer to the third question, regarding the exact *content* of this obligatory consideration of interests, this discretionary freedom had to be analyzed. It appeared that this freedom in principle gave the states the opportunity to consider not only their own interests, but also those of their taxpayers.

This analysis, worked out in Chapters 4-7, showed that in the various schemes, this obligation made hardly any reference to the position of the taxpayer who is to deliver the information to be exchanged, and consequently also very little reference to a legal obligation for the states to protect this position. This deficiency proved to exist, especially in the confidentiality clauses, which leave the protection of the data providers to the national laws of the states and contain no rules to determine their liability.

Also, the obligation of consultation, laid down in Article 25(1) of the OECD Model convention in its current form, proved unable to offer comfort against this deficiency. It seems that with regard to the exchange of information, the states on the one hand conceive their relationship with citizens as a horizontal, reciprocal legal relationship as a result of the development in public law, while on the other hand, as treaty partners, they seem to view the same relationship from the vertical perspective of the classic state under rule of law. The same perspective appears to exist in most states that participated in the 1994 OECD Survey Report, reporting that they had not created any special legal protection for the people involved in the exchange of information. 'The rule therefore, is non existence', says Calderon.[3] This vertical perspective also crops up in the so-called Draft Articles regarding interstate liability, developed by the International Law Committee of the United Nations.[4]

The 'absence' of the taxpayer in rules on the international exchange of information, which met with a lot of criticism in international literature, is not so much the result of an *intrinsic* incompatibility of these rules with the government's legal obligation under public law in this respect, but is more due to this vertical perspective, which renders the taxable supplier of information and his interests invisible.

3. See Calderon (2000). For that matter, this appears to be still so in 2006, from the OECD Report Tax Co-operation: Towards a Level Playing Field, 26 May 2006, regarding national and international transparency in 82 states studied. It showed that warranties for the taxpayers involved in the form of notification with respect to the exchange hardly existed. See Hay (2006), 3.
4. Kooijmans (2000), 115 and T.M.C. Asser-Instituut (2001). Also Van der Bruggen (2001).

After all, Chapter 6 showed that the discretionary grounds for exception existing in all international exchange rules indeed offer starting points for the protection of the taxpayers. They give the states the opportunity to consider not only their own interests and those of their treaty partners, but also those of their taxpayers, at least if those interests may be deemed to be protected pursuant to the ground for exception. In Chapter 7, we concluded that such interests of taxpayers can certainly be identified.

Now that the necessity of protecting the taxpayer, which had been established already from a legal-philosophical perspective, has been outlined more precisely in the substantive-law analysis, we arrive at the last question of this study: *how* might this legal protection take place and take shape in practice?

To answer this question, we must return to what was presented in the last chapter as the most essential legal consequence of the international exchange of information for taxpayers, that is, the violation of his informational position. It must be investigated to what extent standards that were developed for the general protection of this position, may be suitable, or can be made suitable, for the protection of the taxpayer involved in the exchange of information in tax matters. The eventual goal is to 'design' a data processing law that can offer adequate protection for this specific situation. The conclusions of that study should serve as a basis for further development in the domestic legislation of the states on the international exchange of information. Combined with the recommendations presented earlier this study, for amendments in the international treaty law on exchange of information of the Organization for Economic and Cooperative Development (OECD) and the European Union (EU), a general framework of standards can be created for the growing number of states exchanging information and a level playing field for the taxpayers involved in this. It should improve the constitutional quality of the rules on the international exchange of information. As long as the international communities have not generally accepted the standards developed, the design should offer a guideline for states that want to follow their own path in this respect.

## 2 INFORMATIONAL INTERESTS OF CITIZENS

In paragraph 7.2, it was concluded that the interest of the taxpayer involved in the exchange of information lies in the risk that data originating from him, and therefore also pertaining to him, are not 'properly' kept confidential, are used unlawfully by another tax authority, or are not adopted or represented correctly.

This interpretation of the taxpayer's position in terms of information found support in the discussion that took place in the 1970s with regard to the extensive consequences and risks that the developing information society posed to the citizens, especially in the area of personal data. This resulted in the formulation of principles for sound data management in the United States and France,[5] the establishment of OECD Guidelines on the Protection of Privacy and Transborder Flows

5. Blok (2002).

of Personal Data (hereinafter referred to as: the OECD Guidelines)[6] and the Convention for the Protection of Individuals with Regard to Automatic Processing of Personal Data, by the Council of Europe (hereinafter: the European Data Convention).[7] In the same period in Germany, the courts formulated a right of '*informationelle Selbstbestimmung*' (informational self-determination), thus acknowledging the citizen's right to control what information with regard to them may circulate.[8] The Spanish constitution also included such a right.[9] In international terms, the concept was worked out most concretely in the European Privacy Directive of 1995 (hereinafter also called: the Directive), which creates a right to be informed with regard to any *processing of personal information*, such as collection, recording, organization, and disclosure by transmission.[10]

The foundation for these legal instruments had been established before, in Article 12 of the Universal Declaration of Human Rights,[11] Article 8 of the ECHR[12] and Article 17 of the ICCPR.[13] Particularly Article 8 of the ECHR is of great importance, in light of the fact that both private and legal persons, after exhausting national remedies, may invoke this article before the independent European Court of Human Rights (ECHR).

Now the cited sources of law must be examined in more detail, to determine whether the right embodied in them is of any use to the taxpayer who is involved in the international exchange of information by his government.

## 2.1 Characteristics of Informational Law

The development of a set of standards with regard to the collection, possession, and processing of personal data started out with the notion that the possession of information about an individual is a form of power, and *for this reason* poses a risk for the subject of this information. It was acknowledged that accordingly, individuals also may have an interest in the *actual possession of* information that pertains to them, in particular if this information is in the custody of the

6. Paris: OECD. 1981.
7. Treaty of 28 Jan. 1981, Strasbourg, Treaty Series 1988, 7.
8. Vogel (2003), Art. 26, Rz. 74; also Schaumburg (1998), para. 19.32, 1307, which both cite a lot of German literature. Also Schaumburg/Schlossmacher (2000). See also the Explanatory Memorandum to the Dutch Personal Data Protection Act. Parliamentary Papers II 1997/98, 25 892, no. 3 (Explanatory Memorandum), 9.
9. Calderon (2000), 467 and Wisselink (1996). At that time in the Netherlands, it was decided to not include such a right in the constitution. See Advice of the Cals/Donner Committee regarding amendment of the Constitution.
10. Directive 95/46/EG of 24 Oct. 1995 on the protection of individuals with regard to the processing of personal data and the free movement of such data, Official Journal L 281, 23 Nov. 1995 (hereinafter the Privacy Directive) defines personal data as 'any information relating to an identified of identifiable natural person'.
11. Universal Declaration of Human Rights, General Assembly of the United Nations 1948.
12. ECHR, Rome, 1950 (Treaty Series 1951, 154).
13. International Covenant on Civil and Political Rights, New York 1966, Treaty Series, 1969, 100.

government.[14] The idea was that they must have the opportunity to block other people's access to 'their' information. If processing (collection, passing on, use) of this information is deemed to be desirable for society, the data subjects must at least be able to test this processing for compliance with the requirements of lawfulness and due care. This implies that they at least must have knowledge of the various processing steps involved.

A comparison between the previously mentioned OECD Guidelines, the 1981 European Data Convention, and the 1995 European Privacy Directive roughly presents the following unchanging picture. The principle of the regulations is to unite two diverging interests: on the one hand the economic interest that society as a whole has in the freest possible movement of personal information and on the other hand the interest of individuals to be able to shield certain personal data from others.[15]

In this connection, Articles 7 through 11 of the OECD Guidelines contain basic principles of what may be termed sound data management, comprising the collection, storage, transmission, and use of information. These acts, by the parties responsible for these activities, in the various stages must meet the conditions of:

- being bound to a purpose specified in advance, or to a legal provision; and
- legitimacy.

The latter exists when the data subject consents to, has agreed with respect to, or has a vital interest in the processing. In addition, the presence of a legitimate interest of the person responsible or the receiver of the data may cause the processing to be legitimate.

In the latter case, that is, when no consent of the data subject may be assumed to exist, the 'Individual Participation Principle' and the 'Openness Principle' warrant that the subject is notified of the data processing and that he can object to any unlawfulness in this respect.[16]

The same basic principles can be found in Article 5(b) and (c) of the Convention of the Council of Europe of 28 January 1981, in Preamble 28 of the European Privacy Directive of 1995, and in Articles 6, 10, 11, 12 of this Directive, with the proviso that there the term 'processing' is used for the various stages of

14. See Blok (2002a), 116.
15. The OECD Guidelines, Preface, para. 3 state 'the need of balancing competing interests of privacy on the one hand, and freedom of information on the other, in order to allow a full exploitation of the potentialities of modern data processing technologies, in so far as this is desirable'. Also see the Privacy Directive, Preamble 2. Of course there are differences between the rules. For that matter, the European Convention received quite some criticism, in particular on the issue of the ample opportunities for states to raise obstacles for the trans-border data flows and the possibility to set conditions. See in this respect Cuijpers (2004), 17.
16. We also find this 'participation principle' in the OECD Guidelines, Part Two, Basic Principles of National Application, but also in the Arts 7 through 13 and in the European Data Convention, Strasbourg 1981, Arts 8 and 9. In the Privacy Directive, this principle is listed in Preamble 38 and the Arts 10 and 11 (rights to information) and Preamble 45, Art. 14 (the right to object) and Preamble 55, Art. 22 (access to the court).

handling the data and that the rights and obligations of the processor and the data subject are worked out in much more detail.

These principles partly originate from general human rights, such as the requirement that citizens must be able to bring any violation of their informational legal position by others before an independent tribunal (Article 6 of the ECHR) or the right of any individual to receive information from public sources (Article 10 of this Convention). Of course, these basic principles may also be connected with the principles of (good governance?) sound administration, (in particular the principle of fair play), which are part of written and unwritten law in all OECD states.[17]

## 2.2 Basic Principles of Data Processing and the Exchange of Information between States

Of course, to determine how useful the described informational legal standards are in the international exchange of information in tax matters, it must first be examined to what extent the essential elements of data processing law also feature in the legislation on exchange of information in tax matters. In this connection, I select the objective scope, the purpose specification requirement, the requirement of legitimacy, and that of honesty.

The material analysis of the law on exchanging information, presented earlier, in my opinion, justifies the conclusion that the interstate exchange of information can certainly be considered to come under the broader denominator of informational law. This is supported by the 1994 Report 'Tax Information Exchange between OECD Member Countries, A Survey of Current practices', as well as by Preamble 58 of the European Privacy Directive. Tax information that is exchanged to other states, to the extent this concerns natural persons, may be considered as personal data.[18] This type of exchange includes the distinct stages of transmission and use, as covered by the previously mentioned informational law, whereas the government of the disclosing state may be seen as the party responsible for the transmission.

Despite the above observations, it remains a fact that the *collection* of information is not covered by international rules on the exchange of information

---

17. For the Netherlands, see Final Report of the Cals/Donner Committee of 1971, regarding the amendment of the Constitution, 238, where privacy protection is linked with the requirement of 'fair play'. Important for other states is the OECD Report Taxpayers' Rights and Obligations, A Survey of the Legal Situation in OECD Countries, Paris 1990, Introduction, no. 1.4 and General Considerations, no. 2.1, which mentions the fact that in most OECD states the government is observed to adopt a more scrupulous stance toward the citizen from the 1980s onward. Also see Bentley (1998), 7, who also mentions unwritten rights of taxpayers, such as 'expectations to a polite service and courteous treatment by the Tax Executive', which comes close to the criteria of due process of Dutch administrative law. Bentley also asserts (22), that in many countries the protection of taxpayers is more often regulated in a system of administrative rules and principles, rather than in statute. For the role of the general principles of sound administration in European states, see Barents/Brinkhorst (1996), 72-76 and De Moor-van Vugt (1998), 69 ff.
18. Still, such incorporation may lead to problems, as we shall see later on.

between states. After all, collection of information is not necessarily a trans-border activity. Only the *disclosure* of information to a third party (the treaty partner) and the *use* thereof in the other state are covered by the rules on international exchange of information, as we saw earlier. For this reason, collection of information by the controlling states hereinafter will not be treated as a separate subject.

### 2.2.1 Purpose Specification and Legitimacy Requirements

From the previous chapters we could conclude that the rules on the international exchange of information themselves provide for the following basic requirements: the *disclosure* of the tax information and its permitted *use* are bound in the information stipulations to a specific purpose, which has been specified in advance and has been laid down in statutory provisions, namely that of the imposition of (certain) taxations. In addition, this exchange of information must be deemed to be 'legitimate' in terms of informational law, because it 'is necessary for the purpose of the legitimate interest pursued by the controller or by a third party to whom the data are disclosed' (the interests of both exchanging states) that may outweigh the fundamental rights and liberties of the data subjects.[19] Moreover, it may be asserted that the processing of data as part of the international exchange in principle 'is necessary for the performance of a task carried out in the public interest' assigned to the controller or a third party to whom the data are disclosed (the correct and legitimate imposition of taxes).[20]

These purposes and rules of use of the international exchange of information legislation were discussed in the previous chapters. Those rules of law intended to 'contractually' lay down the positions of the *treaty partners* are also the framework within which legal government activities should take place. This 'legality' as such is protecting the individual.

### 2.2.2 'Fair Processing' Requirement

Presently we are most interested in the second basic principle of informational law: that 'if the processing is to be fair, the data subject must be in the position to learn of the existence of a processing operation'.[21] Already mentioned was the 'Individual Participation Principle', stated in Article 13 of the OECD Guidelines and, in a slightly different wording, in Article 8 of the European Data Convention. In these arrangements, the citizen's right of information can be divided into a right of *access* to verify the accuracy and lawfulness of the processing[22] and in a right

---

19. In Chs 6 and 7 we saw that the rules on the international exchange of information indeed offer the possibility of weighing both the interests of the controller and those of the state to which the data are disclosed. The substance of the term 'data subject' will be discussed in the following paragraph.
20. See Art. 7 of the Privacy Directive.
21. See Privacy Directive, Preamble 38 and the Arts 10 and 11, 12, 14, 22 through 24.
22. European Convention Art. 8, part c and Privacy Directive Preamble 41 and Art. 12.

to *object* so that the data subject 'can challenge data relating to him, and have them erased, rectified, completed or amended', according to the Guidelines.[23]

These deliberations with regard to the 'fairness' of the data processing and the individual's 'participation', proved to be laid down in different varieties in the 1994 OECD Report Information Exchange between OECD Member Countries.[24]

The following varieties were distinguished:

- notification rights: rights that warrant that the taxpayer is notified of the disclosure of data to a certain country;
- consultation rights: rights that warrant that a dialogue is established between the taxpayer and his state in respect of the intention to disclose information, offering the opportunity to weigh the different interests;
- intervention rights: rights that warrant that a taxpayer may object against the exchange of data. This right implies that the taxpayer, whose information is being processed, knows what information this concerns, and that he can have an independent court review the legality of this decision. These rights concern in their nature the position of the person interested in the disclosing state that was requested to exchange the information.

The above OECD > Report also showed, as we already concluded, that the majority of the states that were involved in the survey did not proceed to creating such rights for the data subjects in international exchange of information, possibly as a result of the 'silence' of international exchange rules in this respect.[25] This is regrettable. After all, closer analysis in paragraph 7.3.2 shows that the legal position in the *receiving* state most authors see in the confidentiality clause for the taxpayer supplying information proved to exist mostly in theory.[26] Moreover, it comes into being only in cases that the confidentiality of the exchanged data was not properly observed, or if the exchanged data were *used* unlawfully in the state receiving the information. Only in those cases, can the taxable supplier of the information bring an action against the receiving state. In other words, his protection is effective in retrospect.[27] He can challenge only the *disclosure* of information as such in his/her own state, which decided to pass it on to the other state.

Earlier chapters showed that the states that wish to protect the interests of their information-supplying taxpayers had to derive the standards for this from

23. In the legislative history of the Dutch Personal Data Protection Act this combination of requirements is described as the 'transparency principle'. Parliamentary Papers II 1997/1998, 25 892, no. 3 (Explanatory Memorandum), 149.
24. The repeatedly mentioned OECD Report Tax Information Exchange between OECD Member Countries, published in Paris, 1994, is a report of a survey of the exchange practice in the OECD countries.
25. Except for the occasional reference in the OECD commentaries to the *existence* of such information rights in some countries. See Ch. 6, s. 3.1.2 and Ch. 7, s. 4.3.
26. In that case, he might appeal, in the process of the tax assessment and tax imposition, to rights created for this purpose in this state. See also Calderon (2000) and Vogel (2003), Art. 26, Rz. 60 1998.
27. See Ch. 8, s 5.3.4. for the problems this entails for the taxpayer of the disclosing state.

informational law or from other systems, because these standards do not exist in the rules on international exchange of information. The question of which sources of law are most suitable for this will be worked out in further detail in the following section.

## 3 INFORMATIONAL LEGAL PROTECTION IN THE COLLECTION OF THE INFORMATION

The fact that not all states as yet grant their taxpayers the previously mentioned 'participation rights' does not mean that they are completely without protection. After all, paragraph 6.3.1 showed that the gathering of tax information is based on the legislation and administrative practice of the supplying state and that under rule of law these would always be balanced, in some manner, by the rights of taxpayers. Could these rights offer protection in this case?

Of course, it cannot be denied that the rights that taxpayers may bring to bear in the tax examination process in particular also can be important for the *exchange* of data. An example of this is the right taxpayers may have in some countries to be notified in advance of the purpose and the scope of a proposed audit. Such a right might give the taxpayer an opportunity to address the legality of the audit and as such also – indirectly – the legality of or the care observed in the intended supplying of information. However, such a right does not exist in all countries.[28] In cases that it does not exist or apply, for instance, when found information is to be supplied spontaneously or when an investigation is not necessary, any contact between the supplying state and the taxpayer providing the information is no longer self-evident. If specific legal safeguards in respect to supplying information to other states are lacking, the taxpayer might remain completely ignorant of the (intended) supplying of the information, originating from him/ and consequently (also) relating to him, to another tax administration.

Therefore, the conclusion must be that the supplying state can safeguard the taxpayer's informational position only if it adopts specific regulations for the *transmission* of information.

When examining how these regulations should be structured, it is logical to consult standards and instruments for informational protection, developed on the basis of the previously mentioned premises in international law. As such a set of standards, the European Privacy Directive is most eligible, because this is where the envisaged premises and basic principles were worked out most recently. Moreover, pursuant to the obligation to implement the Convention in all European Member States, the Directive may be assumed to have become current law in at least twenty-five countries. This is why it is important to work out if this law system offers sufficient protection for the specific situation that is under examination, or alternatively, what adjustments are required to make it suitable for the

28. In the Dutch situation there is no such *enforceable* right. At the time of writing (2009) the Dutch Parliament is discussing to amend the law on this point.

protection of a taxpayer in the situation that his state discloses 'his data to other states. This examination will focus exclusively on the protective provisions in the European Privacy Directive, rather than on its material descriptions.

## 4 INFORMATIONAL PROTECTION IN THE PRIVACY DIRECTIVE

The evaluation of what protection the directive may offer to the taxpayer involved in the exchange of data will follow in the paragraphs below, based on two questions:

- What protection is being offered?
- Who is being protected?

Some prior explanatory remarks may elucidate this analysis.

Preamble 2 of the Privacy Directive (hereinafter to be called the Directive) states as its aim to respect the fundamental rights and freedoms of natural persons '*notably the right to privacy*'.[29]

This protection must be offered by the party responsible for the processing of the data, referred to in the Directive as 'the controller'. The person who needs to be protected is 'the data subject'. Personal data are 'any information relating to an identified or identifiable natural person'.

In view of this specific intention, it is remarkable that neither the Preamble nor the Directive itself contains a material definition of the term 'privacy'. Preamble 58 explicitly mentions international exchange of information. This makes it clear that tax-related information of or about natural persons should be classified under the concept of 'personal data', even if this would not be so obvious on first consideration.

The protection of natural persons with respect to the processing of personal data must take place through the national laws of the Member States, which must have a certain degree of discretionary freedom in this respect (Preamble 9). The states may adopt a general act or incorporate protection provisions in laws for specific sectors (Preamble 23), and they must provide the proper supervision to ensure the correct application of the law (Preamble 18 and 19).

The basic rule for processing personal data is, as appeared from paragraph 8.2.2, that it must take place *fairly and lawfully* in respect of the data subject. As conditions for this, Preamble 28 and 30 mention that this processing must be in accordance with the legitimate purposes explicitly determined at that time. In the Directive, this is worked out in further detail in Article 6. From paragraph 1, part b, of this article, it may be inferred that when the processing consists of various steps, to wit the collection and further processing, every single step must be compatible with these purposes and therefore must be verified individually for compliance.

29. Thus stated (paraphrased) in Preamble 2 of the Privacy Directive.

The processing steps in the international exchange of information are the acquisition/collection of the data, the passing on to the other state (supplying), and the use thereof. The first two processing steps are performed by the administrative body in the supplying state, and the third step is performed by the administrative body in the receiving state.

But the processing must also be 'legitimate'. The criteria for this were mentioned in paragraph 8.2.2. There we also concluded that the supplying of information in tax matters among Member States, which is obligatory pursuant to a contract concluded between the states, in principle may be considered as permitted. A condition for this is that the interests of the controller and receiver have been weighed properly against the interests and fundamental freedoms of the data subject. As the information exchange takes place in the public interest, the principal requirement of the data subject's consent does not apply in this case.[30]

The question of whether European privacy law should be implemented under private law or under public law will be addressed later.

## 4.1 What Protection?

Any processing of data must be '*lawful and fair*' to the individuals concerned, the Preamble states. This means that this individual has the right to 'accurate and full information' (Preamble 38), that he has a right of access and to verify the accuracy of the information (Preamble 41), and that he, in case of data processing in the public interest, is entitled to object to the processing (Preamble 45). That these rights are not absolute and may be weighed on the grounds of any individual or public interest appears from Preamble 42 and 43 and from Article 13 of the Directive.[31] I will return to this in paragraph 8.4.1.3.

The Privacy Directive assumes that this balance between, on the one hand, the interests of the processing persons and bodies, and, on the other hand, the rights of those whose data are being processed, must be warranted in the national laws of the Member States. These states are allowed a certain degree of discretion in the interpretation of the conditions for restricting these rights.[32] The basic principle of Preamble 38, that individuals concerned must be given *'accurate and full'* information with regard to the processing, is worked out in Articles 10 and 11 of the Directive, which lay down the controller's obligation to provide information. The content of this obligation is partly determined by the question whether or not the data are collected directly from the data subject.

30. See Art. 7 of the Privacy Directive.
31. The grounds for restricting these rights are another individual's right to privacy (Preamble 42) and public interests such as national security, public order, criminal investigations and prosecutions, and important financial interests of Member States or the European Union.
32. See Preambles 9, 25, and 22 in conjunction Arts 5-8 of the Directive.

### 4.1.1 Direct Collection of Data

Article 10 of the Directive pertains to data collected directly from the data subject and 'relating to himself, (so the roles of 'data subject' and 'data provider' coincide). In that case, the controller has the duty to notify the data subject. This obligation to provide information comprises, according to Article 10 *at least* (a) the identity of the controller and (b) the purposes of the processing. For that matter, this obligation exists only to the extent that the data subject is not yet informed or may be deemed to be informed (e.g., if there is a legal provision for the collection of the information that may be assumed to be known).

Article 10, part c, also contains the obligation to provide the data subject with 'further information', such as the recipients of the information, whether the data subject is obliged to cooperate, and the existence of a right of access and a right to rectify. This is only necessary 'in so far as such information, having regard to the specific circumstances in which the data are collected, serves to guarantee fair processing in respect of the data subject', in the wording of Article 10. What is meant by 'further information' in this connection remains vague. I assume that if the information is collected directly from the data subject, the controller must inform the data subject about the recipient of the data and the right to rectify, if this 'further' information is needed to ensure that the data subject gets 'accurate and full' information. The identity of the controller and the purpose of the processing, however, must always be communicated.[33]

The Privacy Directive does not explicitly state the moment that the data subject must be informed. However, especially the fact that any *'further'* information, which the controller, on the grounds of Article 10, part c, is obliged to provide, also concerns the possible existence of an obligation to cooperate, shows that in cases the data are collected directly from the data subject, his information right is linked to the moment of collection.

This leads to the following conclusion.

Article 10 only mentions the *collection* of information, not the disclosure thereof to others. The protection that Article 10 may offer to the data subject in the exchange of information consists of the fact that he at least must be informed of the purpose of the collection, except if he already knows this. This cannot, however, be assumed automatically. After all, a taxpayer will not always be able to determine from his own knowledge, whether a question put forward to him by the tax authorities, concerns any international exchange of information. This means that the taxpayer should be informed that the data are collected for another state.

The question arising with regard to direct collection is, whether *'the specific circumstances in which the data are collected'*, constitute a reason to provide the data subject also with *'further information'*, including the identity of the

33. For that matter, this is also the opinion of the Dutch legislator with regard to the Directive's implementation, as the Explanatory Memorandum with the Dutch Personal Data Protection Act indicates, Parliamentary Papers II 1997/1998, 25 892, no. 3.

recipient.[34] Apart from the fact whether this qualifies as transmission to a 'third party', one cannot be certain there is any 'recipient' at the time of *collection* of the information. After all, even if the data are collected because of a foreign request, the tax authorities will decide whether to disclose the information, after it has tested the data against the grounds for exception of the underlying international exchange of information obligation.[35]

This can be summarized as follows: in case the data to be supplied are collected from the data subject directly, the tax authorities, by virtue of the Directive, must inform the data subject of the fact that the information is being collected in view of a request by a treaty partner. This, however, does not give the data subject any information on the question whether or not the data really will be supplied.

In addition, there is the situation in which data are exchanged spontaneously. Then the data are collected from a taxpayer for the purpose of a national tax debt, and only at a later stage the tax authorities consider these data to be relevant for spontaneous exchange to another state. The taxpayer may be assumed to know the purpose of the data collection (the national tax levy), as well as the identity of the controller, so that in this situation Article 10 of the Privacy Directive would not call for a separate notification.[36] Still, the data subject should be notified of this spontaneous disclosure, by virtue of Article 6, paragraph 1, sub-paragraph b of this Directive. After all, any 'further processing' of the personal data must be compatible with the original purpose of the collection, and of course, be 'fair' and lawful to the data subject. So the data subject must be given 'accurate and full' information on the spontaneous disclosure of data that follows on the collection thereof.[37] Of course, this also applies to the case that the data are collected on foreign request. The data subject must not only be informed of the purpose of the *data collection,* but also of the further processing, that is, the actual supplying, of them. Only then the data subject will be able to test the lawfulness and permissibility of this processing for compliance with the requirements of Articles 6 and 7 of the Privacy Directive or a regulation grafted onto it. Then questions may be raised about the legitimacy of the supplying and the care observed by the administrative body in weighing the subject's interest and that of the receiving state against his rights and freedoms.

---

34. Privacy Directive Art. 10, part c.
35. See the judgment of the Dutch Supreme Court HR 13 May 2005. It clearly delineates the stage of the tax investigation for the purpose of collecting information, which a taxpayer must cooperate with, and which serves to decide if the data will be disclosed. At that time, disclosure is by no means certain yet. The decision in this regard follows afterward. See V-N 2005/35.6, in which the editors argue that the tax authorities may not start such an investigation without proper care.
36. All states under rule of law have tax laws that provide safeguards against any unlawful collection of tax data. These will always include rules regarding a proper identification by the tax authorities and a statutory provision stipulating that the powers of the tax authorities should be restricted to the collection of those data that serve the purpose of determining the tax debt.
37. See Preamble 38 of the Privacy Directive.

### 4.1.2 Collection of Data from Third Parties

The Privacy Directive also distinguishes the case in which certain personal data are *not* directly collected from a data subject, in other words, when the roles of data subject and supplier of the information do not coincide. Article 11 requires that in that case, too, the controller must inform the data subject of his identity and for what purpose, or on the basis of what regulation, the data are being collected (e.g., if the data subject does not yet know this). If necessary, the controller must also give 'further information', such as the relevant data categories, the identity of the recipient of the data, and the existence of a right of access. The time when the data subject must be notified is the moment of data registration, or, if *disclosure* of the data *to third parties* is being considered, no later than the moment of the initial disclosure.

This last situation seems to apply almost perfectly to cases in which personal data are collected from the taxpayer to disclose them to another state, whether on the request of another Member State or otherwise.

The system of Article 11 appears to be as follows: if the tax authorities of the requested state collect such data *about* a person from an employer or a bank, the tax authorities should at least inform the 'data subject'[38] at the moment the data are disclosed.

The data subject in question should also have the right to be informed about the recipient of the data and about the type of data, at least if the specific circumstances in which the further information is being collected should make this necessary, in the controller's opinion. It is my belief that this situation would also give cause for this.[39]

Article 11, second paragraph, of the Privacy Directive eases the controller's obligation to provide information, if this is impossible or involves a disproportionate effort, or if the registration or disclosure is prescribed by law. Apparently, in that case, the data subject must be considered to be aware of the fact that his data are being disclosed.

Again, it is a question of whether the existence of national legislation regarding the exchange of information in a certain country, of which the taxpayer may be considered to be aware, would make this specific right to information redundant.

I do not think so, at least not with regard to individual cases. First of all, in these indirect cases the immediate cause of the data processing is often a request from another state, which the data subject *cannot* be considered to know about from his own knowledge. Moreover, in the exchange of information, the tax authorities may also revert to the possibilities for weighing the different interests under international rules on the exchange of information between states. In other words, even if the data subject was aware of the existence of a foreign request for

38. Who this 'data subject' would be in the framework of the exchange of information is discussed in the next paragraph.
39. The argumentation for this is related with the interpretation with the term 'data subject'. See the following section.

information,[40] he still would not be certain *if,* and if so, *what* data were disclosed. In my opinion, the only case that an individual's right to be informed is not necessary is in case of a structural exchange of data categories, agreed on in advance and having been made known properly (the so-called automatic exchange of information).[41]

Accordingly, the tax authorities should inform the taxpayer in question of the fact that his data are disclosed, on the ground of Article 11.

### 4.1.3 Restrictions on the Rights to Information

The informational rights in the Privacy Directive are not absolute. On the grounds of Article 13 of the Privacy Directive, the requirements of *lawfulness* and fairness, as laid down in Article 6 of the Directive, the right to be informed and the right of access of Articles 10 through 12, and the right of having the operations made public, as stipulated in Article 21, must be weighed against the following interests:

- public interests of the states, such as national security and defence, investigation and prosecution of crimes or *important* economic and financial interests, including budgetary and *taxation* matters and other inspection functions of the states;
- individual interests of the data subject, or rights and freedoms of others.

Of course, only the Member States themselves are able to determine whether in a specific situation one or more of these (public) interests are at stake. This makes this provision discretionary. This becomes particularly clear in the '*important*' economic and financial interests of the states, as cited in Article 13, first paragraph, sub-paragraph e, which are also of eminent importance for our subject, because these are exactly the interests that might lead to a restriction of rights to information in an international exchange of data. This also appears from the Regulation 1798/2003 on VAT, as we have seen.[42] Article 41, fifth paragraph of this Regulation, obliges the Member States to restrict the right to information of the Privacy Directive's Articles 10 and 11, first paragraph, the right of access to data (Article 12) and the right of having the operations publicized (Article 21), if this would harm the protection of the '*important*' financial interests of states as mentioned in Article 13. What would qualify as 'important financial interests' is not specified any further? As a result, different Member States can easily give different interpretations to this provision and the level of legal protection for data subjects can vary significantly among the Member States.

Still, we must keep in mind that the consideration of the these interests may *restrict* the rights of information access and having operations made public, but it does not *eliminate* them. What the term 'restrict' should be understood to mean is

40. For instance, because he has been notified or 'warned' by the data subject from the other state, to which the data pertain and with whom the investigation in the other state originated.
41. The automatic exchange of information was discussed in Ch. 4, s. 4.6.
42. See Ch. 5, s. 3.2.

not made clear in the provision itself, but I think it is plausible that restriction of rights to information particularly concerns any 'further information', which the controllers must inform the data subject of, on the grounds of Article 11 of the Privacy Directive, and which depends on the circumstances of the case. That the 'rights to information' cannot be abolished altogether also becomes evident from the fact that Article 13 does not allow for any restriction of the right to object (Article 14 of the Directive). This right cannot be effectuated if the data subject at least has the knowledge that data pertaining to him are being processed.

### 4.1.4 Right to Object

The right to object is laid down in Article 14 of the Privacy Directive (grounds for appeal) and Article 22 (the authorities in question). It exists *at least* in the cases in which the data subject has no right of consent, if:

- Processing is *necessary* for the performance of a task carried out in the public interest, assigned to the controller (part e of Article 7),
- Processing is necessary for the purposes of the legitimate interests pursued by the controller and its fundamental rights and freedoms (Article 7, part f).

In those cases, the data subject can object to the processing by invoking the national provisions before the authority assigned for this purpose.[43]

However, even the right to object is not absolute: the data subject must have *compelling* and *legitimate* grounds, relating to his particular situation, and this objection may not be prohibited by other national statutory provisions.[44]

In this case, too, the controller (in our case the state) has a substantial margin of discretion to decide when the reasons of a data subject are 'compelling' and 'legitimate', when processing is 'necessary' for the said state's interests, for the controller's own interest, or for the recipient's interest. He also decides whether or not this interest must give way to the fundamental rights and freedoms of the data subject. This discretionary freedom will have to be given an interpretation in national legislation. Preamble 23 explicitly empowers the Member States to do so. They may choose to protect the rights of data subjects by means of a general law, or by laws (either already existing or not) applying to specific sectors.

For our study, Article 14 of the Privacy Directive contains an important point, namely that citizens, with regard to data processing, may indeed have compelling and specific interests (privacy-related and others), with regard to inter-nation data processing, that apparently need to be weighed against the state's public interests. This creates, besides the general rule of law for states to carefully consider their

43. See Art. 22 of the Privacy Directive. If the data subject believes that the controller has violated the provisions of the Directive, he may request administrative relief before the supervisory authority of his country. Any loss incurred as a result of unlawful processing will be borne by the controller, except if the latter can prove that the loss cannot be attributed to him.
44. The second grounds for objection, the anticipated processing for the purpose of direct marketing, I do not consider on the grounds of irrelevance.

citizens' interests, which I discussed in previous chapters, also a more specific standard with respect to the government's disclosure of tax data to another state. We also find such a specification of a general standard in Article 22, which stipulates the data subject's right of access to the supervisory authority and an independent court, as a 'translation' of the right to a fair trial in Article 6 of the ECHR.

These specifications partly do not meet their intended purpose because of the open standards they contain. Particularly, the open formulation of the exceptional provision of Article 13(1) cannot be approved, because it also extends to the basic requirements of Article 6 of the Directive. As a result, not only requirements of adequacy, but also the 'fairness' and the *lawfulness* of the data processing (i.e., also that of the exchange of information), are made a subject of this weighing of interests, as well as the basic requirement that processing must be bound to a legitimate purpose. This to a great extent moderates the legality requirement, which, after all, should be the guiding principle of all government actions under rule of law.

Moreover, restricting the right to object to cases where 'compelling interests' of the data subject are at stake (Article 14) and restricting the information rights in case of *'important'* financial loss for the states (Article 13, first paragraph, sub-paragraph e) will not provide *more* handles for interpretation and the formation of an opinion in a concrete situation than the fundamental rights as such. The necessary national interpretation of these open standards will not benefit the unity of European law.

The term 'important' economic and financial interests of the states (Article 13, first paragraph, sub-paragraph e) should be defined further as the investigation and prosecution of individual fraud or patterns of fraud, whether or not combined with suspicions of flows of funds that could point toward other offences. That would result in a more uniform application of the grounds for exception in the international exchange of information.

For the purpose of applying the right to object of Article 14 of the Directive to the international exchange of information, the interests of information suppliers, as deduced from rules on the international exchange of information in Chapter 7 of this study, should be considered 'compelling interests' within the meaning of Article 14. In this way, the suppliers of data in all states will have an equal opportunity to object.

### 4.1.5 Transfer to Third Countries

The ambition of the authors of the Privacy Directive to protect the citizens of Europe is not limited to European territory. On the ground of Article 25 of the Privacy Directive, any personal data may be transferred to a third country only if that country ensures 'an adequate level of protection'. Whether that is the case must be assessed by the controller in the transferring state, with due observance of the following factors: the nature of the data, the purpose of the processing, the general or local rules of law, and professional rules and security measures applying in the country concerned.[45] If after investigation a negative assessment is made on these points, the European Commission (EC) and the Member States must be notified thereof. If the Commission maintains the assessment, transfer of data in principle cannot take place, except after the data subject's explicit consent, according to Article 25.[46]

On closer consideration, Article 25 seems to contain a certain degree of rhetoric, as further analysis of the stipulations of Article 26 show. Here it is stipulated that the prohibition of Article 25 does not apply in cases that the transfer is necessary in view of interests of the data subject, because of contractual obligations between him and the controller and in case the controller has entered into contracts that protect citizens.[47] In this respect, the level of protection in the other state is either 'guaranteed' by the controller, or the data subject has already considered it at the time of entering into the contract. More risky, however, is Article 26, first paragraph, sub-paragraph d, which allows transfer of data if this is necessary or legally required on 'important public interest grounds'. In that case, it seems the interest of the European data subjects must yield.[48] In view of the pretentions of the Directive to protect a *fundamental* right, these public interest grounds certainly should have been specified more precisely than the present adjective 'important'. An autonomous definition of this term could elucidate the relationship between the 'fundamental' interests of data subjects of all Member States, on the one hand and the necessary transfer of data required on 'important' public interest grounds, on the other hand.

Still, the Preamble attempts to create some clarity, but in relation to our subject, it has the opposite effect. Preamble 58 considers that the prohibition to transfer data without the data subject's consent to countries that do not ensure an 'adequate level of protection' should not be applied, if, inter alia, 'protection of an important public interest so requires, *for example in cases of international transfers of data between tax or customs administrations ( . . . )*'.

It looks like the Preamble wants to propose that the entire exchange of information as such ('the case of international exchange') must be viewed as such an 'important interest', so that any exchange of data in case of an 'inadequate level of protection' would be automatically legitimate. (italics TSG)

Something can be said against this. Rules on the exchange of information between states, even non-Community law, put the importance of the interest of the exchange of information in some situations into perspective, by creating

45. Privacy Directive, Art. 25(2).
46. It would be desirable that so much attention and supervision would also be required in respect of the quality of the confidentiality legislation for the exchange of tax information.
47. The contractual or the pre-contractual obligation, between a data subject and controller (Art. 26(1)(b) or between the controller and a third party (Art. 26(1)(c) must also focus on the interest of the data subject. Transfer of data is also allowed without an adequate level of protection for the defence of a legal claim (Art. 26(1)(d)).
48. The other exceptions mentioned previously, which would allow for the transfer of personal data to countries that do not 'ensure an adequate level of protection' actually do not contain any weighing of interests. These concern the situations in which the data subject also has interests.

exceptions whereby the *disclosing* state can weigh this interest against other interests. As we already saw, this can include the business secret of taxpayers. In this consideration, it is possible in principle that the protection of the data subject prevails over the interests of the other state.[49]

Furthermore, even though the rules on the international exchange of information do not *focus* on the interests of citizens specifically, they do establish a standard protecting their interests by means of the confidentiality clause. After all, the receiving state may use the exchanged data only for specific purposes stated in the convention and may only disclose the data to a limited circle of authorities, including the courts and the data subject to whom the data relate. Chapter 5 showed that these strict rules are also intended to protect the data subject in the supplying state.

With this clause of confidentiality and use, rules on the exchange of information between states have created their own 'level of protection', which *cannot* be put aside because of other interests of states, no matter how 'important' these might be. To the contrary, in view of any differences in protection as these may occur in practice among the states, the European Directive 77/799 created in Article 7, paragraph 2 an extra instrument for the supplying state, to exact even a higher level of protection from another Member State, if necessary, provided the supplying state also applies such a level a protection.[50]

### 4.1.6 Conclusion

For the time being, the question what the content would be of the legal protection that European privacy law could offer with regard to exchange of information seems to be answered. The conclusion must be that especially the data subject's right to information, as stipulated in the Privacy Directive, as such might offer a proper instrument for the protection of taxpayers or withholding agents who are involved in international exchange of information. The broad definition of the term 'personal data' as yet does not seem to stand in the way. In addition, the data subject's right to object also offers opportunities, albeit that the condition that this only applies to 'compelling grounds relating to his particular situation' requires more detailed specification. This should be along the lines of the taxpayer's interests we selected in Chapter 7 on the basis of rules on the exchange of information between states.

Besides this, a point of criticism is the fact that the weighing of interests pursuant to Article 13 may also concern the lawfulness and fairness of processing (and therefore the exchange of information), especially because it concerns

49. I consciously use the term 'level of confidentiality', because of the term 'level of protection' in the Privacy Directive refers to the objective of protecting the individual. In the rules on the international exchange of information, this is effectuated by means of the clause regarding confidentiality and use.

50. The confidentiality clause also protects the data subject in the receiving state. He has the right to be informed of the collected data and in principle may rectify these in the tax proceedings that he may start against a tax assessment that is imposed on him with the aid of these data.

'important' financial and economic interests of EU Member States (Article 13) paragraph 1, (e). In my opinion, this terminology is too vague to be weighed against such essential values of Article 6 as 'fairness and lawfulness of the processing' and specification of a legitimate purpose.

For the international exchange of information, these 'important financial and economic interests of the states', which might restrict the information rights, should be specified as serious suspicions of fraud or tax evasion.

The entanglement of the two legal systems could take place either by including in the Privacy Directive, under the grounds of exception of Article 13 and in Article 14, separate stipulations for the international exchange of data, or by integrating the standards and instruments of the Privacy Directive in European Directive 77/799 and Regulation 1798/2003.

By more clearly delineating standards that are still vague at present, taking into consideration the specific situation of international exchange of tax information, important steps could be taken in the realization of the ambition that resulted in the coming about of the Privacy Directive, that is, to guarantee the lawfulness of the processing of data in general throughout Europe and creating a 'level playing field' for the protection of data subjects, also with regard to data processing between the states. For the protection of data subjects in the exchange of information with other states, data subjects could be protected by including the recommendation for the controlling Member States to demand, if necessary, extra guarantees for their data subjects, like the Directive 1977/79 makes possible. Because the data exchange obligations with non-European states mostly will be modelled on the OECD exchange provision, which has no such option, the European Commission could put this forward in its contacts with the Committee on Fiscal Affairs of the OECD. 'The Working Party' consisting of national supervisory authorities, and set up pursuant to Article 29 of the Privacy Directive, will also have to consult with the Committee on Fiscal Affairs of the OECD, under guidance of the EC.[51]

### 4.2 Who Is Being Protected?

The second question regarding the usefulness of the European Privacy Directive in the exchange of information regarded *the party protected* by this right.

#### 4.2.1 Data Subject in the Privacy Directive

The Privacy Directive has the aim to protect the privacy of the data subject. The definition of this term, in Article 2(a), is as follows: 'any information *relating to* an identified or identifiable natural person (''data subject'')'.

51. See the Arts 28 and 29 of the Privacy Directive and in particular Art. 30(3), which explicitly stipulates, that the 'Working Party' was assigned not only an advisory role, but also the competence to act on its own initiative.

Important for the exchange of information is whether the term 'data subject' means only the person who is the subject of the information or also includes the person from whom the information *originates*. The above formulation fails to make this clear. An analysis of Articles 10 and 11, which pertain to the information rights, without which the protection of the individual cannot be realized, produces the following picture.

Article 10 focuses on the *direct* collection of the information from the data subject. This is the situation in which the roles of supplier of the personal data and the subject converge. 'Member States shall provide that the controller (. . .) provides a data subject *from whom data relating to himself are collected*' (with certain information, ASG).[52] In this instance, there is no gap in the protection.

Article 11, on the other hand, stipulates the situation in which the data, for the purpose of registration or disclosure to a third party, 'have not been obtained from the data subject'. From the formulation of Article 11, it cannot be concluded that the *supplier* of the information can also be the data subject, in the sense that the information is 'relating to himself'. In Article 11, paragraph 1, the Directive implicitly distinguishes two stages: the *collection* of the data and the subsequent *disclosure.* In both stages, there is (the same) 'supplier' of the data, and a controller. In addition, there is also the one to whom the data relates, but only the latter is being protected. That means that the supplier, by definition, is 'not the data subject'. In the wording of the Dutch Personal Data Protection Act he is 'any other than the data subject'.[53] This supplier, who is obliged to supply information, implicitly appears to be considered as no more than the 'holder' of others' personal data, and whose privacy apparently does not seem to be affected by the disclosure of these data. *In the context of privacy law*, the interests of this supplier could not be harmed.

### 4.2.2 Data Subject in the Exchange of Information

For the exchange of information, this exclusion of the supplier as a data subject is problematic. The data also relate to him and the disclosure thereof to a foreign country affects his interests, as we have seen. In addition, in terms of the Directive, the *data subject*, that is, the person who is the subject of the information, in the field of the interstate exchange of information is often residing in the other country. It is the natural person (the taxpayer) in regard to whom another state has requested information, or to whom certain data found in accounts in the disclosing country pertains. The state (the controller) that is responsible for or controls the 'legitimacy' and the 'fairness and lawfulness' of the *collection* and the *disclosure* of the data, must leave the protection of the data subject, when it comes to the *use* of these data, to the other state, who controls their use.

52. Article 10, opening.
53. Parliamentary Papers II 1997/1998, 25 892, no. 3 (Explanatory Memorandum), 152.

Example

An example may illustrate this. Let us assume the following. Member state Germany requests data from the Netherlands, for the purpose of determining the tax debt of house painter X, who has revenues in Germany, but resides (also) in the Netherlands. The request is made to verify whether the painter actually carries out his work from his state of residence, the Netherlands, and actually pays the tax owed in that country, like he states. However, in the Netherlands, X proves to be not officially registered as such an entrepreneur, but is 'working on the side', from whom the Dutch authorities, after some investigation, can collect the requested data. On the basis of Article 10 of the Privacy Directive, X is the data subject, because the information relates to him. As a tax subject of the Netherlands, he accordingly comes under the protection of the Dutch controller who collected and disclosed the information. On the basis of Article 10 of the Privacy Directive this protection (the obligation to notify, or the right to be informed), concerns the *collection* of data, but not the *disclosure to third parties*. With respect to the latter action, X may be considered to be the supplier of the information. Article 10 of the Privacy Directive, however, does not protect X against the risks that this role involves (e.g., the risk for unlawful disclosure or inaccuracy of the data). However, earlier in this chapter I argued that on the basis of Article 6, first paragraph, sub-paragraph b, of the Directive he/ should also be protected with respect to the disclosure. After all, the disclosure to third parties may be considered as a next step in the processing, which should not be incompatible with its original purpose and which of course must also be 'fair and lawful' to the data subject. The data subject, to whom the data relate and from whom they are collected, must be able to test the processing to see if it is incompatible with the original purpose. Because the data relate to him, the painter, in my opinion, has a right to be informed, a right of access and a right to rectify, and a right to object in respect of both the *collection* and the *disclosure* of the data. In the exchange of information the steps of collecting the data and disclosing the data to another country both come under the responsibility (i.e., both are controlled by) the same administrative authority: the competent authority of the supplying state.

The data about house painter X could not be collected directly from him, but from a third party (e.g., an employer or a wholesaler). They are under the obligation to keep records and to cooperate with the tax authorities also for the taxation of third persons. X then would be protected as data subject, by virtue of Article 11 of the Privacy Directive, under the Dutch statutory provision implementing Article 11, with regard to the collection and the disclosure, because the requested data relate to him. However, the *supplier* of the data, (the employer or the wholesaler) to whom the data *also* relate and who may *also* have an interest in their possible disclosure is not protected by Article 11. After all, he is somebody 'other than the data subject'. To protect him also, the phrase 'the one to whom the data relates' should be interpreted in a broad sense, so that the interests of the party obliged to provide the information (the supplier of the data) would also be subsumed under it.

In the above example, the controlling administrative authority in the Netherlands still is obliged to notify at least one of the two persons involved (in this case painter X, to whom the data relate). However, in most cases characteristic of international data exchange, the obligation to provide information would not be relevant at all. In this connection, I refer to the many cases that a person obliged to provide information supplies personal data that 'relate to' another taxpayer who resides in another state.

In this variant, it would concern house painter A, who resides in *Germany,* and who may be suspected, owing to his lifestyle, to earn 'money on the side' in the Netherlands. The Netherlands can acquire the information requested by Germany only from third parties, for instance the wholesaler Y who on the basis of Dutch Tax Law must supply information for the purpose of taxation of third parties. Let us imagine that the wholesaler's records prove not only to supply substantial shipments of paint to A (which is the evidence of A's work in the black economy), but also to other painters in Germany, with the wholesaler giving A an extra discount because of his family relations with A.

In the terminology of the Privacy Directive, painter A in any case is the data subject, because the disclosed data *relate to him.* However, in respect of the *transfer* of the information to Germany, one might also say that the wholesaler from whom the data originated has an interest, if only in view of the risk that it becomes known in Germany that he gives some of his clients preferential treatment, or that data are inaccurate, or that in this specific case the disclosure of these data by the Netherlands is unlawful. But as the supplier of the data, the wholesaler is somebody 'other than the data subject' and therefore presently not protected by the Directive. In interstate exchange of information, the person to whom the exchanged data *relate* (the data subject) has to be protected by the one *in the other state*, who controls 'further processing', in this case, the *use* of the information for the purpose of tax collection in that state. This can be done in the course of tax proceedings, by objecting to the assessment that was imposed with the aid of the foreign data, according to the level of legal protection of that state. In this example, we already know that this use is lawful and legitimate by referring to the underlying legal basis of the confidentiality and use stipulation in international rules on the exchange of information between states. However, the fact that the *collection* of data in the one country (in this example the Netherlands) is 'lawful' within the meaning of the Privacy Directive, and its use in the other state is 'legitimate', does not tell us anything about the question whether the supplying of these data is also 'fair' to the *supplier* of the data. If this were to be so, he should, in the Directive's terminology, be given 'accurate and full information' of at least the fact of disclosure and the data this involved. In other words, the supplier should also be considered as 'data subject', and on these grounds he should at least be informed by the 'controlling' administrative authority of the fact that data originating from him are being disclosed to another country.

### 4.2.3 Extension of the Term Data Subject?

This gap in the concept of 'data subject' in the Privacy Directive results, in my opinion, from the fact that this directive derives its normative direction from the 'fundamental right of protection of privacy'. This connotation of a personal, inviolable sphere for the individual, in which he can organize the most personal aspects of his life without any interference,[54] assumes in respect of the term 'personal data' a strong relationship between the data and the person as such.[55] But this view has the problem that the 'personal data' feature in the international exchange of information do not always demonstrate this strong relationship. To be sure, any tax data may concern a person and, in view of his/her, income also certainly represent a 'personal' interest, both in its relation with the tax authorities and in relation to other individuals and legal entities in society. Furthermore, the 'personal' intimate sphere of one's home, family, religious beliefs, sexual preferences, choice of partner, and the like *may* be affected incidentally.[56] For this reason, tax data in all states under rule of law are protected by confidentiality laws. However, as a result of bringing tax data within the meaning of the concept of Privacy, the 'data subject' in principle can be only a natural person,[57] who as such is the subject of the data. For this reason, the *supplier* of the data is denied the right to information, the right of access, and the rights to rectify and object.

If the concept of 'data subject' from the Privacy Directive is to function in the protection of the position of the taxable natural person who pursuant to the international exchange of information must supply tax data, the term must be interpreted in a broad sense.

However, already in 1977 it was determined that Member States may not add further stipulations to a directive in their implementation laws, because this would derogate the harmonizing effect of the directive.[58] In view of this precept to remain faithful to the directive in the interpretation of the national laws of the Member States, a national court cannot provide such a broad interpretation independently. However, Article 30 of the Privacy Directive provides for a 'Working Party' in the EC that is to evaluate the effects of the directive on the basis of the cases that the citizens have brought before the national supervisory authorities of their states. Any taxpayer involved in the disclosure of data as a *supplier* might bring his case before this Working Party (provided he had found out about the disclosure from his own sources). This is because 'every person' has access to the supervisory authority, not only the ones who on the basis of the directive may be considered as 'data

54. See Westin (1967), who was the first to write about 'informational privacy' and who defined this concept as 'the claim of individuals, groups, or institutions to determine for themselves when, how, and to what extent information about them is to be communicated to others'.
55. Cf. Blok's dissertation (2002).
56. For an example in which privacy is invaded, the description of an action by the Dutch Tax and Customs Administration, see Van Houte (2005), 1078 ff.
57. Accordingly, Preamble 24 and Arts 1 and 2 of the Directive explicitly exclude the applicability of the protection rules to legal persons. Nevertheless, there are authors who believe that legal persons also should have a right of privacy. See Van Strien 1996, who defends that legal persons can also have a right of privacy, because this might protect them against unlimited scrutiny by the government or third parties. In my opinion, this function could be realized at least as well, or even better, without reference to a concept that is only confusing in this context, such as 'privacy'.
58. Court of Justice EC, 5 Oct. 1977, Jur. 1555 (*Tedeschi/Denkavit*).

subject'. In that case, he could argue that he is also a 'data subject' who should enjoy the right to information, the right of access, and the rights to rectify and object, since he, as a supplier, has an interest in the lawfulness of the disclosure and in the accuracy of the data themselves. Perhaps an amendment of the Privacy Directive could be sought by these means.

Whether the supplier can still bring his case before a judicial court after a rejection by the supervisory authority is not entirely clear. Even though Article 22 of the Directive allows 'every person' to seek a remedy before the court, it appears they can only do so in case of 'any breach of the rights guaranteed to him by the national law applicable to the processing in question'. This seems only to refer to the data subject from the Privacy Directive. However, in view of the generally formulated option in Article 28 of the Privacy Directive that 'decisions by the supervisory authority that give rise to complaints may be appealed against through the courts', I take it that Article 22 of the Directive contains a unintended restriction and that the supplier of the data can still go to the administrative or civil court after the supervisory authority rejected the appeal. The court may then, through a request for a preliminary ruling, try to obtain a judgment from the European Court of Justice.

However, even if the definition of 'the data subject' is changed in such a way that it would include the *supplier* of the data to be exchanged, this would still leave the problem of legal persons. In international data exchanges, these very often function as both the subject of the information and the supplier thereof, but they are explicitly excluded from the protection on the ground of Preamble 24 and Articles 1 and 2 of the Privacy Directive. This arrangement is in accordance with the wording of Article 8 of the ECHR, where the terms 'private and family life' pre-eminently refer to natural persons. But this description gave cause for ECHR case law on the question, whether entering business premises may be considered an invasion of privacy. This case law incited some authors and commentators to come up with creative interpretations of the concept of 'privacy', explaining the term in such a way that it may also apply to legal persons. The background for this may be the function of shield against overwhelming government interference, for which privacy law is generally held to be intended. In this view, legal persons should also benefit from this protection.[59] Finaly denied the applicability of the notion of privacy to legal persons, on the basis of a grammatical interpretation of Article 8 of the ECHR, and despite the cases *Chappell* and *Niemietz* before the ECHRs.[60] But since that time, the Court took another step

59. See for example Zwenne (1998), 65 (listed) who grants banks under a duty of disclosure a 'derivative privacy interest'. But the issue is whether this interest is also protected by current privacy law, and on this point he remains silent. Also see van Strien (1996), who wants to confer a right to privacy to legal persons, because this right would protect them against unlimited scrutiny and because it would advance the economic and social development (economic competition). Also see the schedule of Finaly (1998).

60. Finaly (1998), 563. He reached this conclusion after analyzing ECHR of 30 Mar.1989 (*Chappell*), *Dutch Law Reports* 1991, 522 and ECHR of 16 Dec. 1992, *Dutch Law Reports* 1993, 400 (*Niemitz*), with regard to the protection that Art. 8 ECHR would offer against government agencies entering business premises. Both cases were instituted by natural persons. Therefore,

with the *Colas* case and also granted the protection under Article 8 ECHR to legal persons.[61] For that matter, it remains to be seen what the exact meaning of these rulings would be for the applicability of the Privacy Directive to legal persons, because it explicitly *excludes* the applicability to legal persons. Whatever the case may be,[62] I share Blok's opinion that 'the inflation of the notion of privacy'[63] is an obstacle for informational protection in a wider sense and that we need to seek a different basis for protecting both individuals and legal persons against abuse of a dominant position through the processing of information.

### 4.2.4 Conclusion

It must be concluded that the Privacy Directive is not unequivocally suitable for the protection of the *supplier* of the data that are *to be supplied to other states*. After all:

- Article 10 of this Directive as such does not establish a right to be informed (nor the right of access and the right to rectify) for the taxable suppliers with regard to the *disclosure* of information as such. When the information is acquired directly (from 'the person to whom the data relate') the right to be informed applies only to the *collection* of the data and not to the *disclosure* thereof. Still, an obligation for the tax authorities to provide protection may be deduced from Article 6, first paragraph, sub-paragraph b of the Privacy Directive for all subsequent steps of processing, including the disclosure of data to another country. Moreover, the administrative authority's obligation to inform the taxpayer of the purpose of the *collection* (in this case, taxation in another state) could prompt the taxpayer to ask permission to inspect the documents drafted by the administrative authority at a later stage, on the grounds of public access to government information. This could show that the data were disclosed to another country.

Even if this interpretation is accepted, it would offer solace to only a small part of the taxpayers who supply data for disclosure to other states.

In the trans-border context of international information exchange, the data are usually collected from a supplier in the one Member State, while they 'relate to' a (legal) person in another Member State. On the basis of Article 11 of the Privacy Directive, the state controlling the *disclosure* has no obligation to offer protection, neither to the supplier of the data, who is not 'the one to whom the data relate' and whose interest is not acknowledged, nor to the person to whom the data in effect relate. After all, the latter is the 'data subject' with regard to the *use* of the data, which is controlled by the administrative authority of the other state. In the

---

in Finaly's opinion, they did not concern legal persons. Also see the Conclusion of A.G. Geelhoed to CJEC C 301/04 P (*Carbon*), 19 Jan. 2006, point 64, which refers to the ECHR ruling on privacy of legal persons.

61. ECHR 16 Apr. 2002 (*Colas*), no. 3797/97, *Dutch Law Reports* 2003, 452.
62. An analysis of this problem is, despite its great interest, outside the scope of this study.
63. The term is derived from Blok (2002), 17 ff.

terminology of Article 11 of the Directive, the taxpayer supplying the information to be disclosed is not the 'data subject' with regard to the collection. As a result, the reasoning of 'further processing', which must be 'fair' to the *data subject*, cannot confer the right to be informed to the supplier insofar as it regards the intention to *disclose* the information originating from him to a foreign country, nor any right of access or right to rectify or object.

Based on the legal obligation for states to give their citizens with legal rights careful treatment, *also* in the international exchange of information, the Member States of the EU cannot suffice with simply implementing the European Privacy Directive, even with respect to natural persons.

The protection of the data provider in international exchange of information will have to be laid down in a regulation, which recognizes legal persons as being persons with legal 'data processing' rights, and that extends the concept of 'data subject' to the one who has to *supply* the information to the tax authorities and *in this way* has an interest in their passing on. For this purpose, the Privacy Directive should be altered on the previously mentioned points. In my opinion, this would require a change of orientation for the Directive. To protect the specific interests of information suppliers who are involved in interstate data exchange, and to resolve the discussion regarding the informational protection of legal persons, the concept of informational protection should be dissociated from the concept of 'privacy'. A link should be sought with other fundamental rights and standards that may offer protection against data processing. What those might be, we will examine in the next paragraph.

## 5 TOWARD DATA PROCESSING LAW WITH A STRONGER FOCUS ON PROPERTY

The search for an alternative foundation for the right of informational protection than by means of the right of protection of privacy leads us back into history. After all, the concept of 'personal privacy' did not always have such a distinct informational character. It had its own, firm basis in the notion of the classical state under rule of law, which was developed in the early nineteenth century and in which freedom for the citizen was interpreted as absence of state interference.[64] This notion created some distance between the individual and the state and granted the individual a personal sphere, which the state did not have the right to penetrate, except if this was necessary in the public interest.[65] The state had to guarantee its citizens this freedom, even in respect of other individuals. The codification of the classical liberal rights such as freedom of religion, the right of the inviolability of the home, and privacy of correspondence was the consequence of this conception

64. This notion of freedom is also referred to as 'negative' freedom, in contrast to the notion that later gained popularity, in which freedom is understood more as: room for the individual to emancipate toward full participation in society. See Gribnau (1998).
65. Also see Ch. 2.

of the law. Despite the later development toward a more relational and emancipatory concept of freedom under democratic rule of law (positive freedom), the conception of individual freedom as a 'sphere free of the state' has always remained clearly visible in the concept of privacy and in the legal rules pertaining to this, in the past and at present.

### 5.1 Informational Self-Determination

The arrival of information technology in the 1970s gave a new impetus to thinking about privacy. It was acknowledged that these developments increased the risk for the breach of privacy. However, this risk then was not the initial focus of society. In the early years of the information society, the attention was focused much more on the risk for manipulating and influencing the individual's existence, related to *possession* of information about this individual, particularly when, in a relationship of dependence, this information can be collected and passed on.[66]

This fear of an imbalance in social relationships led to the question how this dominance could be checked (put under control?) to protect the weaker parties. In the sphere of private law, one can think of the position of a consumer in relation to businesses, a patient in his relation to the medical profession,[67] and in the sphere of public law, for example, the informational disadvantage of parliament compared to the administration and that of the citizen compared to the state. Some of the standards that were considered to provide a 'solution' for this asymmetrical situation we encountered earlier, such as the individual's right of consent with regard to processing of data that relate to him,[68] the right to be informed, and the right of accessing and rectifying data in case they are processed on grounds of public interest. In some states, these standards were developed further to create a right for the citizen to scrutinize the entire flow of information that relates to him, in all stages of processing.

Schaumburg and Schlossmacher consider this right to informational self-determination a derivative of the individual's right of freedom and its proprietary right, and as such 'an essential feature of a democratic system' that would ensue from the general legal principles that also prevail in international law.

This means in respect to data processing for the purpose of exchanging information, that, to outweigh the freedom and proprietary rights of the interested party, it must meet the requirement of a legitimate general interest, which can be served only in this way. Authors say that the necessity to breach this freedom by means of the international exchange of information is tested in the rules on the exchange of information against the requirement of purpose specification and the proportionality between the means and the end ('necessity'). The necessary weighing of

66. Blok (2002), 117. Schaumburg/Schlossmacher (2000), also mention 'the far reaching knowledge of the actions of an individual' that makes it possible 'to control his actions'.
67. See Cuijpers (2004), on the suitability of private law in particular for the protection of privacy.
68. See Westin (1967), 7 and Sentrop (1973), 208.

interests would be possible thanks to the grounds for exception, which this law contains. On these grounds, the authors believe, the right of informational self-determination can be expressed in the best way. But they have to admit that this right is neither internationally recognized as a fundamental right, for the moment at least, nor is it an absolute right. In certain cases, this right will have to give way to the public interest.[69]

## 5.2 Information as Property

Still, even without necessarily leading to such an all-encompassing right of informational self-determination, the principle on which it is based – information as proprietary object – creates a useful perspective.[70] The basic right to a 'peaceful enjoyment of ( . . . ) possessions' is protected by Article 1 of the First Protocol to the ECHR, in effect applying to 'every natural or *legal* person'. From the case law of the European Court of Human Rights it may be concluded that the concept of property in the ECHR not only pertains to physical goods, but also to rights, licenses, or authorizations, goodwill, and information, that have economic value or significance.[71] The potential economic value of information was acknowledged by the European Court of Justice in proceedings on the presence of business secrets in a certain document for which a right of inspection was claimed. Because of the potential risk that disclosure of the information might cause, the European Commission had to establish the presence of any business secrets by official order, against which the legal person could then appeal.[72]

Such an orientation on the real right of ownership would also warrant the harmonization of data processing law with international rules on the exchange of information between states, and its concept of the business secret. After all, the business secret is, as we have seen, an item of property valuable in money, owned by the information supplying taxpayer in the disclosing state. The supplier's economic interest with regard to the disclosure of information about that 'secret' is, as we have seen, the only interest acknowledged, albeit reluctantly, in the OECD data exchange law, and just there.

The establishment of such a data protection right would also eliminate the necessity of using such a strained concept as a legal person's 'privacy', as a

69. Cf. Schaumburg/Schlossmacher (2000). Also see Calderon (2000) and Vogel (2003), Art. 26, Rz. 74, 2012. Informational self-determination has been included in acts, for example, in Germany and Spain. In the Netherlands it was decided against it, at the time. See Eindrapport van de Staatscommissie bescherming persoonsgegevens's Gravenhage 1976, 22 (Commissie Koopmans).
70. Also see Blok (2002a), 117 ff. and Blok (2002b).
71. Hartlief (1995), 129 ff., thinks that the background of the broad concept of property in the ECHR, which may also include immaterial 'matters', is the 'political-philosophical' intention to guarantee the development of the human personality.
72. CJEC, 24 Jun. 1986, Jur. 1986, 1992.

foundation of the right for a legal person to defend its own informational interests.[73]

In this approach of the concept of data processing, the standards of 'legitimacy' or 'fairness' from the Privacy Directive may remain unimpaired as such. The illegitimate processing of information (without the data subject's consent, or without a legitimate public interest), and the 'unfair' processing thereof (without careful weighing of interests or without notification of the data subject) may then be defined as deterioration of an item of property. Accordingly, the owner or holder of the information starts to play a role as a party having rights.[74] A definition based on the fundamental right of the peaceful enjoyment of possessions would reveal the problem of dominance in the relationships of citizens relative to each other and to the government. As a result, it could establish a harmonization with the legal principles that aim to safeguard the equality of participants in all legal relationships, whether these are 'vertical' or 'horizontal' in nature.[75] For the 'vertical' legal relationship between state and citizen, which is relevant for our subject, we arrive via the First Protocol to the ECHR at standards of administrative law, including the standard of public access to government information.[76] In situations in which this could not be applied, for example, because in a certain state, international exchange of information is not considered an action under public law, it is important to examine whether civil law might offer some form of protection against data processing by the government, and what role the European courts might play in such a case.

## 5.3 Protection through Other Sets of Standards

### 5.3.1 General Standards of Administrative Law

Insofar as standards have been developed in respect of the protection of persons with legal rights in data processing, many countries in Europe implemented these

73. Cf. Zwenne (1998 (listed) who confers to banks a 'right to privacy' that is derived from the privacy right of their clients. Also see van Dijck (1999), judgment of the Dutch Council of State of 12 Jan. 1999, V-N 1999/20.4. (*Technolease*) regarding sections of a file of the Ministry of Finance, which did not need to be disclosed because these concerned 'internal consultation documents'. He concludes that 'the executive also has its protected private sphere'. Alternatively, Finaly (1998).
74. Such an approach of the concept of information is reported in Spanish literature by Calderon (2000). The citizen would be the owner of the information and the tax authorities could only hold this information as the trustee of the taxpayers, which means that it cannot process it without notifying the data subjects thereof. Eventually, the discussion resulted in the formulation of a constitutional right of informational self-determination in Spain in 1998.
75. Also see Blok (2002), 120. The terms horizontal and vertical are by Cuijpers (2004), 3.
76. For the general principles of proper administration in the jurisdiction of the European Court of Justice, see van der Burg (1998), 8. Also see de Moor-van Vugt (1998), 69 ff. and Barents/Brinkhorst (1996), 72 ff.

mostly in administrative laws.[77] This may relate to citizens perceiving the government as a power block, with the risks of processing information by the government being feared the most. The best protection for citizens against this would be an extensive set of administrative standards, designed specifically for such vertical legal relationships.[78] For our subject, too, an administrative protection of the informational position would be most obvious, because of the fact that the international exchange of tax data is a government action. Schaumburg and Schlossmacher base the duty for the state to protect its citizens also in the informational area on the legal values of 'justice and fairness'.[79] These principles also could be identified in the recommendations in the Guidelines with respect to the protection of privacy by the OECD, in the European Data Convention of 1981, and eventually also in the European Privacy Directive. There these values feature in the requirement that any data processing must be 'fair' to the data subject, as well as accurate, accessible, and rectifiable.[80]

Basically, all standards that together make up administrative law aim to bring about that the inequality in the legal relationship between citizen and government is compensated as much as possible. In Chapter 2 we encountered this principle as the undertaking for the state to treat its citizens 'as equals'.

Administrative law has many standards, both written and unwritten, which cannot be discussed within the scope of this study. The principal one, which I mention here, is the generally accepted requirement of *lawfulness* of government action, in relation with the prohibition of misuse of power. A state's international exchange of information should be tested for compliance with international rules on the exchange of information between states. Because this law provides the objective and the direction for government action, it legitimizes these actions relative to the citizen as having a previously described purpose specification that is legitimate and in the public interest, which justifies the imposition of duties on the citizen.

The concept of a state under rule of law requires that the government must act with due care; and with respect to data processing, this requirement is translated in the requirement that if data is processed on the grounds of public interest, for which the citizen's consent is asked, his rights and freedoms must be duly considered.

77. Cuijpers (2004), 4.
78. Cuijpers (2004) points out that these standards also govern the relationship of citizens among themselves, which in her opinion leads to unnecessary bureaucratic rules. With the aid of private law, citizens would be very well able to establish equality in their legal relationships by contractual means.
79. Schaumberg/Schlossmacher (2000), 523.
80. In the Netherlands, informational protection of citizens was first considered to ensue from the principle of fair play, in particular if this principle manifested itself in the requirements regarding the disclosure and inspection of documents in the various 'types' of procedural law. The transparency standard also resounded in these requirements. Parliamentary Papers II 1970/1971, 11 051, no. 1 en 2, 238, and the Report of the Cals/Donner Committee, which advised the Dutch government on the constitutional revision at that time.

I would like to emphasize two of these manifestations of the requirement of due care: the requirement for proper preparation and the requirement for a reasonable weighing of interests.

The requirement for proper preparation comprises much of what I argued for in this study: the notification and, if necessary, hearing of the taxpayer involved, before the decision to supply information to the other state has been implemented.[81] This principle of the dialogue with the taxpayer is applied in many states, and even the data exchange law of the OECD implies it in the grounds for exception concerning the 'business secret'. Earlier, I referred to this obligation for the administrative authority to properly prepare is decisions from the information supplying taxpayer's perspective as a 'right to be informed'. This right, and the subsequent dialogue with the interested party, offers the administrative authority the opportunity to substantiate its decision on better grounds (e.g., by correcting inaccurate information before disclosing it to another country).[82] Conversely, it gives the taxpayer the opportunity to put forward and defend his interests, so that the state may duly consider them.

In Chapter 6 we concluded that international rules on the exchange of information between states, even if they do not create informational rights for taxpayers, do not prohibit, nor do they exclude, this weighing of interests.

In addition, a taxpayer may of course appeal to other principles of sound administration accepted in his state.

When the principles and instruments of administrative law are embedded in a data processing law that is more oriented on real rights, more informational risks may be covered than would be possible by embedding these in the concept of privacy. The interest of the good name and reputation may also be protected in this way, not only of the person to whom the data relate, but also of the natural or legal person from whom the data originate and who for *this* reason has an interest.

Such a reconsideration of the risks of data processing should also comprise the gathering of tax information on behalf of another state and could bring new life to the discussion on the protection of taxpayers against the 'sometimes draconian powers' of tax authorities in gathering this information.[83]

If there are remedies against the actions of the tax authorities in the audit stage, these might, in the absence of an explicit right to be informed with respect to the *disclosure of data*, offer opportunities to the taxpayer who is involved in the

---

81. See van Wijk/Konijnenbelt/Van Male (2002), 284-300. In the legislative history with the Dutch General Administrative Law Act, the citizen's right to being heard is founded on the requirement of proper preparation.
82. The standards of due process, including the obligation to hear a person, are also part of procedural taxation law in most states. In the Commentary to the OECD Model Convention and the Model Agreement regarding the business secret, a dialogue with the taxpayer is implicitly assumed to determine if any data might contain a business secret. (See also Ch. 6, s. 5.) See in this respect also Oliver (1995).
83. For the term 'draconian powers', see Bentley (1998), 157. For the Netherlands, also see van Houte (2005). The Dutch Supreme Court also referred to the powers of the tax authorities as 'very drastic coercive measures'. See HR 10 Feb. 1988, BNB 1988/160.

exchange of information. For example, an obliged notification regarding the purpose and the object of a tax audit could be a signal for the taxpayer that *perhaps*, after weighing the different interests, data might be disclosed. I believe that if the administrative authority notifies the information supplier in respect of the disclosure *after* the investigation, but *before* the actual disclosure, this would be the most scrupulous method to balance the interests of the states in an 'unhampered' collection of data for their treaty partners with the interests of the taxpayer.

### 5.3.2 Protection via the Standard of Public Access to Government Information

A more restricted foundation for the informational legal protection of the taxpayer involved in the exchange of information could be sought in the specific standard of public access to government information. This view was also popular, for a while at least, in the Netherlands in the 1970s.[84] On the basis of this standard, the taxpayer may ask the administrative authority to inspect the documents that it made up or collected about the taxpayer in its files.

This standard is, however, more focused on weighing the public interest of transparency and verifiability of government actions against other public and individual interests that should be protected by the government, such as the informational position or the privacy of natural persons. Besides, in most states, there is an uneasy relationship between the requirement of access to government information and confidentiality of tax information, in particular when it comes to data from tax files.[85] As we Concluded in Chapter 5, the issue in connection with the international exchange of information is complicated even further by the international duty of confidentiality, so important in rules on the international exchange of information and that may be used to prevent tax authorities from spontaneously disclosing interstate correspondence or to prevent taxpayers from requesting this correspondence.[86] In this connection, the legislation on public access to government information applying in the various states will have to contain grounds for exception for cases in which international obligations of other states are at stake, as may be the case in the exchange of information between states.[87]

---

84. See Policy document regarding the constitutional revision policy of 1974, Parliamentary Papers II, 1973/1974, 12 944, no. 2. 38.
85. Calderon (2000), 468. Also Malherbe (1991).
86. See Ch.5, s. 2.2.1 about the recent change in the OECD Commentary (2005) with regard to the relationship between national laws on access to government information and the rules on the international exchange of information, stating that the latter should prevail. The IFA Report Protection of Confidentiality of Taxpayer Information, Cahiers de Droit Fiscal International LXXV1b, 1991, shows that some countries in their access to government information laws make an exception for tax files.
87. See the grounds for exception in the Dutch Government Information Act, Art. 10, para. 2, under (a) risk for relationships with other states, (b) risk for the economic and financial interests of the state and (c) risk for the inspection, auditing, and supervision by administrative authorities. For

### 5.3.3 Protection via the Doctrine of the Unlawful Government Act

In the previous sections, the attention focused mainly on legal standards that determine the lawfulness of the supplying of information to another state and on the possibility of invoking these before the (administrative) courts, but these standards are only an initial means to protect the interests of the taxpayer. After determining the unlawfulness of the government's actions, the question arises whether, and to what extent, the state is indeed liable. Answers to this question may be found in the law of obligations with regard to non-contractual liability. An in-depth examination of the doctrine of the unlawful government act does not fit within the scope of this study, but even without such an examination, legally trained readers may be assumed to be familiar with the conditions for the existence of this liability: the unlawfulness of the action, the attributability or guilt, and the damage and the direct causal link between the unlawful act and the damage.[88] We also find these elements in European case law on liability, which bases itself in this respect on the 'general principles common to the laws of the Member States', which have origins in administrative law as well as private law.[89] Similarly, in the Draft Articles on State Responsibility of the International Law Committee of the United Nations, the concepts of unlawfulness, attributability and the causal link between the unlawful act and the damage prove to be essential for determining (international) liability. Again one may assume that these elements reflect the general basic principles of the laws of the Member States.[90] Some legal systems feature, for the determination of liability, the principle of relativity, which demands that there is a relation between the affected interest and the standard that the injured party claims to be violated.[91] National *administrative* courts may themselves be able to determine the liability for unlawful government action, but in doing so, the court will always be indebted to the (civil) law of obligations, which is the origin of the above doctrine. For this reason, the question of liability is here discussed in relation with the civil judicial process.

---

regulations of other countries, please refer to the series 'Comparative Survey on Confidentiality of Taxpayer Information', *International Transfer Pricing Journal* (2000): 1-7. Also see Ch. 5, s. 2.2.1.

88. See Asser's *Handleiding tot de beoefening van het Nederlands burgerlijk recht*, 12th: (?) Verbintenissenrecht.
89. Article 215(2) EC, defines the liability of the European communities and its institutions. For the influence of international private law on European liability law, see Edward/Robinson (1996340 ff. (Edward/Robinson listed).
90. See Arts 3 and 44 of these Draft Articles on State Responsibility, International Law Committee of the United Nations, 1996 (ILC) revised in 1998 and T.M.C. Asser Institute (2001).
91. This is also known as the 'relativity standard' or 'Schutznorm' theory. A party is allowed the action arising from an unlawful act only if he is also affected in the interest that is protected by the violated standard. Recent case law of the European Court of Justice shows that this requirement is not made there. CJEC 13 Jan. 2005, case C-174/2 (Regional District of Noord Brabant), about an appeal to a support measure against unfair competition, whereas the regional district was not affected at all by unfair competition.

In most legal systems, this judicial process will be considered when the question of liability could not be resolved by means of administrative law, for example because in a country the interstate exchange of information is not considered to be a government decision intended to have legal effect, or because the administrative judicial process offers insufficient protection.[92] In that case, the taxpayer supplying information must be able to take his/her complaints and grievances to another court. He/she has this right on the ground of Article 14 of the International Covenant on Civil and Political Rights (ICCPR) Convention,[93] and Article 6 of the ECHR.

If there is *no* access to an administrative court, the civil court must also determine the lawfulness of the government action. Legal principles, by their nature, are not restricted to individual jurisdictions, as we saw in Chapter 2. Therefore the civil court will also test the government's action for compliance with the statutory provision, with the purpose for which the administrative authority was given its power, with the requirement of the proper weighing of interests and with the standards of sound administration that were developed in the particular state's legal system.[94] In light of the universal character of these principles, this seems plausible for all states under rule of law.[95]

If the disclosure of information *does* subsume under administrative law, the unlawfulness of the data disclosure will have to be determined by the administrative court, whereas the civil court will only rule on the liability.

Apart for perhaps minor differences between the two legal systems (e.g., in the procedural details), the civil judicial process has one essential disadvantage, in my opinion. It does not provide for an obliged *publication* of the government action, although the knowledge that this action took place is a first requirement for instituting a legal action.

In *administrative law* this knowledge is guaranteed in principle, as a result of the administrative authority publicizing the anticipated decision. This enables the dialogue with the taxpayer to come into being, which is so essential for this right, and which may prevent damage. The aggrieved person seeking justice in civil law

92. I assume that administrative jurisdiction is established in a state based on the need for courts with specialist knowledge of and experience in the area of public administration. I therefore expect that in all states under rule of law, the civil court will be sought only after the administrative court proved to be incompetent.
93. Article 14 of the ICCPR explicitly stipulates that this right of access to an independent court and to a fair trial does not only relate to criminal proceedings, but as much to procedures 'to determine his rights and obligations in a suit at law'.
94. In the Netherlands, the civil court can test a government's action for compliance with all standards of sound administration. However, the civil court should exercise restraint with regard to the manner in which the administrative authority has used its power of disposition. Cf. H. Asser's *Handleiding tot de beoefening van het Nederlands verbintenissenrecht*, Ch. X, De onrechtmatige overheidsdaad.
95. See for the application of these administrative standards for other states the previously mentioned reference to the ruling of the European Court of Justice and to the elements for state liability in the Draft Articles of the International Law Committee of the UN (ILC).

must learn from his own sources about the fact that the unlawful act took place or learn this at the moment he experiences its harmful effects.

If the taxpayer supplying information is not given any signal in the information collection stage about the anticipated disclosure, or if civil interlocutory proceedings are not possible, he can only institute a subsequent action for damages. To this end, not only the unlawfulness and damage must be proved, but also the *direct link* between the act and the damage. However, for the taxpayer supplying the information to fulfil this order to produce evidence will prove an almost impossible task. In addition, there is the problem of access to the court in the other state. I first will try to chart the problems existing in three possible situations in which the exchange of data did not take place between Member States of the EU.

#### *5.3.3.1 Liability Due to Unlawful Disclosure*

The 'easiest' part of the issue of proof is – in terms of procedure – to demonstrate the unlawfulness of the *disclosure* as such.[96] The civil-law court of the disclosing state can substantiate this on the basis of international and national regulations and the circumstances of the case. Sometimes this was done already in a prior administrative procedure.[97]

Furthermore, there will only be an obligation for the (disclosing) state to pay damages, if a direct *causal* connection between the state's unlawful action and the occurrence of the damage can be proved or made plausible. This burden of proof is no sinecure.

After all, the damage for the supplier of the exchanged data, for example, consisting of a decrease in trade contracts, reduced competitiveness or harm to his good name or reputation, is mostly inflicted in the other country. Apart from the fact that unlawful actions may have taken place in the receiving state as well (which will be discussed below), reduced turnovers or loss to one's reputation will often occur only when the *government* of the other state has decided to increase the tax assessment of the taxpayer who was subject of the disclosure. In addition, the identity of the taxpayer might be published in the other state's jurisprudence in accordance with national legislation. The question is then if, for example, a reduced turnover in trade is caused by the *disclosure* of the information as such or by the subsequent action of the *other state*.

The facts that must decide this question are difficult to establish in cases such as these, despite the legal access that the taxpayer from the disclosing state has on the grounds of the international confidentiality provision in the receiving state.[98]

96. This does not imply that this would be easy in a *legal* sense.
97. However, we already found that this testing could be only marginal in some points.
98. See Ch.5, ss 2.2 and 3. On the basis of this legal position, I believe the injured party can also appeal to the laws regarding public access to government information in that state, if this would offer possibilities for establishing the facts. Still, it would be a difficult procedure.

### 5.3.3.2 *Shared Liability of States*

The investigation into the course of events in the receiving state regarding the causality between the unlawfulness and loss by and large can have two outcomes: the loss results from the disclosure of the *identity* of the *supplier* of the data to the taxpayer involved or to third parties in the other state, or it results from the disclosure of his *data* to his competitors in this state (which may include state enterprises).

The first outcome may occur through a public tax procedure with regard to the assessment process, which – as was shown in Chapter 5 – is often accepted as a 'calculated risk' in the confidentiality provision between states.[99] In that case, the receiving state might not have acted unlawfully. If the *data* became known outside the permitted institutions stipulated in the confidentiality provision, such as the competitors of the supplier of the information, this gives rise to a 'breach of international obligation', that is attributed to the state on the grounds of international law.[100] In that case, the receiving state would have breached the international confidentiality obligation (in this case, the business secret). If the disclosure of the data had already been determined to be unlawful, there is the possibility of a shared liability of the disclosing state and the receiving state.

This does not make things easier for the injured party. He has very little or no influence on the effort and speed of the necessary investigation in the other state.

### 5.3.3.3 *Liability by Unlawful Use*

The same is true in the event that the disclosure of the data as such was lawful, and the unlawfulness must lie entirely in the receiving state. To be sure, the supplier of information has a means of starting proceedings in the receiving state, as we have seen already, which he may derive from the confidentiality clause in the taxation treaty (or the European regulations), and which grant him, in Vogel's words '*einen eigenen Anspruch auf Geheimhaltung*', before the courts of the *receiving state*.[101] But this taxpayer, who resides abroad, will face the difficult task to prove or make plausible the unlawfulness, the loss, and the causality as such vis-à-vis the receiving state. Another complicating factor is that the receiving state may partly define the obligation of confidentiality itself, so that an 'alien' legal system in perhaps another language must be considered.

But the greatest problem is that the liability of the receiving state comes under international law. The states in question must acknowledge and implement these laws themselves, either in mutual consultations, or by one of the methods of

99. The confidentiality clause of the OECD Model convention provides for the possibility that the identity of the taxpayer is disclosed in a public procedure. Also, in Community law the exchanged data can be used in public proceedings (criminal cases), after consent of the *disclosing* state.
100. Article 3 in conjunction with Art. 10 of the Draft Articles on State Responsibility, 1996 (1998) of the UN International Law Committee.
101. Vogel (2003), Art. 26, Rz. 60.

international settlement of disputes.[102] Paragraph 7.3.2. of this book already showed that the injured taxpayer as yet cannot be a party in this, and that he even lacks the right to force his state to enter such consultations or provisionally bear the costs of the entire loss.

For all of these reasons, I argued in Chapter 7 that, in respect to the international exchange of information, the OECD in particular must develop clear rules for liability of the receiving states regarding compliance with the obligation of confidentiality.[103] As a step in the right direction, I suggested opening the 'mutual agreement' procedure of Article 25 of the OECD Model convention. This provision should not only serve taxpayers who are subject to (double) taxation in violation with the Convention, but also persons who incurred loss as a result of the unlawful disclosure and use of exchanged data that originate from them and who want to establish liability for this. In particular Article 25, paragraph 3, which calls on the authorities to make an effort to solve problems in the interpretation and the *application* of the Convention in mutual consultations, provides starting points for this. Only then, Article 25 could really fulfil the claim of, in the words of the Commentary, 'resolving difficulties arising out of the application of the Convention in the broadest sense of the term'.[104]

In view of these problems regarding the liability and compensation of any loss, I prefer the administrative judicial process for this subject, because the interstate exchange of tax data is performed by the government and because the administrative judicial process is especially designed for settling disputes between citizens and the government. Under administrative law, the administrative authority is obliged to properly publish any decision and to hear the interested party. As a result, the decision may be revised. In this way, risks may be prevented as much as possible. The dialogue with the taxpayer supplying information also reduces the chance of disclosing inaccurate data, which also increases the efficiency of the interstate exchange of data.

### 5.3.4 Protection via European Law

In view of the fact that European law also includes information exchange obligations, the question arises whether the interests of the supplier of data may be protected by the rulings of the European Court of Justice. Of course, this involves the problem that the supplier of information must have knowledge of the fact of disclosure to the other country. If he/she is aware of that, the European law offers two possibilities. The first is to redefine the concept of 'data subject' in the Privacy Directive, by answering so-called preliminary questions, which might solve – in

102. As methods, the International Law Committee of the UN states in Arts 54-60 of the Draft Articles on state liability: intervention by another state (Arts 54-60 mediation, arbitration).
103. I only mention the OECD here because the European legal system does have a higher court that can determine the liability for regulations or actions in violation with European regulations.
104. OECD Commentary 1977-2005, Art. 25, Preliminary Remarks, para. 1. States should also include this in their national law.

part at least – the gap in the legal protection in the interstate exchange of tax data. The second possibility is that of determining and regulating the liability of the states involved in the data exchange.

To realize the first option, the taxpayer supplying the data (a natural person) could argue before the national court that the disclosure was not 'fair' and lawful to him, because he was not informed thereof, as the Privacy Directive stipulates. Furthermore, he can argue that as the supplier of the disclosed information he can also be considered a 'data subject'. Thus his state would not have implemented the Privacy Directive correctly in regard to the exchange of information. The national court can ask the European Court of Justice to answer preliminary questions with regard to the interpretation of the concept of 'data subject'. In this respect, the taxpayer may also derive hope from the fact that the Privacy Directive, in its Preamble, considers the international exchange of information also as a sort of data processing that it regulates (at least if it concerns natural persons). Perhaps a link can be sought with past judgments of the Court, which specify, in the wider scope of the general principles of sound administration, the citizen's right to be heard.[105] Especially the appeal to the right to be heard, which does not only accrue to natural persons, may be suitable to obtain a 'broader' ruling from the Court, which also comprises legal persons. On the grounds of these arguments, a reformulation of the concept of 'data subject', in the sense that it would also encompass the *supplier* of data in the context of the interstate exchange of data, would be plausible in my opinion. As a result, the taxpayer would be able to discuss the lawfulness of the anticipated disclosure of data in a dialogue with the administrative authority, thus possibly *preventing* any unnecessary loss.[106]

Until this amendment is realized, if this even happens, a remedy for the damage is possible only afterwards. (according to my dictionary this is correct) Of course, the question of compensation may also be brought up afterwards, even if in the administrative judicial process in the disclosing state a dialogue did take place, but resulted in a disclosure of data, which entailed the occurrence of loss in the other state as a result of shortcoming confidentiality in the other state. In that case, the supplier of the information is dependent on the ability of instituting an action against the other state on the ground of incorrect application of EU law.[107] The liability case law of the European Court of Justice offers hope in this respect. It has developed since the 1980s in respect of unlawful *legislation* by Member States, consisting of the failure to establish implementation legislation regarding a 'rule

105. See Barents/Brinkhorst (1996), 75 and de Moor-van Vugt (1998), 72. Also cf. ECJ 27 Jun. 1991, C-49/88 Jur. 1-3187 (SAMAD), about the fundamental rights of Art. 6 EVHR, including the right of defence, which are part of the Community's legal principles, ECJ 23 Oct. 1974, 17/74 (*Transocean Marine Paint*).

106. Jans (1999), 151 presents an overview of the basic rights and the general principles of sound administration in the jurisprudence of the European Court of Justice. Also see Barents/Brinkhorst (1996), Ch. 2, para. 6.

107. After all, European Member States are prohibited from holding other Member States liable. See Art. 219 EC.

for the protection of the individual', which breaches an interest of the individual.[108] The liability of the European communities and their institutions is defined in Article 215 paragraph 2, which seeks harmonization with 'the general principles common to the laws of the Member States', with the elements, derived from private law, of unlawfulness (in violation with EC law), loss, and causal connection between loss and lawfulness play a role.[109] The judgment in the *Francovich* case,[110] among others, showed that the conditions for such liability for the Member State are: the relevant provision has to be meant to grant a right to private persons, it must be possible to determine the scope and nature of this right on the basis of the directive, and there must be causal relationship between the state's negligence and the occurred loss. Especially the element of unlawfulness is an important object of investigation for the Court.[111]

Liability is also assumed for unlawful acts by Member States in the *application* of this legislation, that is to say, for the 'acts by which the administration applies general rules in individual cases or otherwise exercises its executive power in an individual manner'.[112] The European Court bases this liability on the principle of loyalty to the community, which requires that Member States do everything in their power to achieve the full effect of the European regulation.

If the receiving state breaches the confidentiality clause of European rules on the international exchange of information, the *legislation* might be failing if the national confidentiality law is not, or insufficiently, adjusted to the mandatory part of the European legal rule, that is, the description of the circle of authorities that are entitled to the information received. In addition, an error might have been made in the application of legislation that is sound in itself and even aims to protect a right of citizens. In that case, the requirement that the purpose of the breached provision is the protection of a right of citizens is also met. But in this case, too, the requirement of causality between the breach of the legal duty and the damage may lead to problems of evidence.[113]

#### *5.3.4.1 Conclusion*

If, because of their strong tie with the concept of privacy, the existing standards for data processing, as found in the Privacy Directive, can be applied only partly to the

108. For liability on the ground of unlawful non-implementation of European directives, see the cases *Frankovich* (C-6/90), *Brasserie du Pécheur*, 1996 (C-46/93), and *British Telecom*, 1996 (C-5/94).
109. For the influence of international private law on European liability law, see Edward/Robinson (1996340. (Edward/Robinson will be listed).
110. CJEC 1991, the cases *Frankovich* and *Bonifaci* C-6/90 and C-7/90, NvJ 1991, 1724. Also see Wattel (1992).
111. Waelbroeck (1996), 329.
112. Cf. van der Woude (1996).
113. de Moor-van Vugt (1998), 100 ff. An extensive discussion of this jurisprudence falls outside the scope of this book. Also see Fines (1996), 29. She point out the economic character of European liability law. In her opinion, the Court too often lets the interests of the European authorities prevail over the individuals.

protection of the supplier of data that is to be exchanged with other countries, then a different data protection right should be designed for this purpose, one that could offer more protection of informational interests to more persons having legal rights than the current right to privacy. The persons protected should include natural and legal persons involved as supplier in the interstate exchange of information. This legal system should not only focus on protection of personal privacy, but have its basis in the fundamental right of the individual to a peaceful use of his possessions. If this data processing right in the legal relationship between government and the supplier of data would be applied via a range of instruments of administrative law, the general principles of sound administration, as developed in most states under rule of law, would also apply to this right,[114] besides the requirement of lawfulness of the government action. The requirement of prior publicizing of decisions under administrative law, combined with the requirement of a proper weighing of interests, would significantly improve the position of the data provider in the international exchange of information. The specific instruments of informational legal protection as developed in the Privacy Directive, such as the rights to be informed, and the rights to rectify and object, could be embedded in this legal system.

In the absence of an adequate means of commencing an action regarding the exchange of information under administrative law, the lawfulness of the government action will have to be tested by the civil court, also on the basis of public-law standards. But liability for any damage, even if it is to be judged by the administrative court, will be determined along the lines of private law.

If the data provider incurs damage in the other state, he faces a heavy burden of proof with regard to establishing any unlawfulness and causal relationship. This also applies to the claim for liability, also because outside the European Union, the concept of interstate liability has been realized to a very limited extent in a practical sense in international treaties.

This could be a task for the Committee on Fiscal Affairs of the OECD. A solution might be to open up the 'mutual agreement' procedure of Article 25 OECD for the actions of states in violation with the information provision in the taxation convention, which caused damage. In addition, it should be included in the national laws that the disclosing state, and not the data provider, will address the treaty partner in cases giving cause for this.

Under intra-Community law, a citizen in principle is able to hold the receiving Member State liable for acting unlawfully. After all, the confidentiality and use clause of the Community rules on the exchange of information aims to protect the individual also, which may be concluded from this provision with adequate clarity. But again, the requirement of causality may be a problem. This makes it more necessary for states to create a form of legal protection for their data providers under administrative law, so that unnecessary damage may be prevented via the

---

114. These could be referred to as 'general standards of proper data management'.

requirement under administrative law of prior notification of the government decision, the citizen's right to be heard, and the possibilities to object and appeal.

## 6 PROPOSALS FOR NATIONAL RULES ON THE INTERNATIONAL EXCHANGE OF INFORMATION BETWEEN STATES

In previous chapters, I presented proposals to improve the position of the taxpayer involved in the interstate exchange of information, through the adjustment of international rules on the exchange of information between states. Such adjustments, enshrined and supplemented in the national laws of states, could establish in the area of legal protection a level playing field in the application of law in a great part of the world. However, this does not dismiss the individual states from the duty to improve the legal position of the previously mentioned persons by means of legislation, even without the supervision of the Committee for Fiscal Affairs or the EC.

Having said this, the question remains what the administrative 'data processing right', as advocated earlier, should contain to be able to protect the person involved in the interstate exchange of information in practice. In answer to this, the characteristics of general administrative law, as described above, must be passed in review once more. In this way, it can become clear where administrative law is in need of adjustment or further specification, with a view to the context of international law of this government action and the specific interests that need protection. The conclusion reached above, that such a right preferably should not be *founded* on the right to personal privacy, of course does not mean that it could not be *consistent* with the protecting instruments from privacy law. After all, this shortcoming of this right for the protection required for international data exchange is not caused by those standards as such, but by the definition of the party they are protecting.

### 6.1 Notification of the Taxpayer

Several times previously I argued that adequate legal protection in the area of transborder data processing by government first of all depends on whether the person involved has a right to be informed. The choice for a system rooted in administrative law was inspired in particular by the requirement of publicizing government decisions.

#### 6.1.1 Proper Publicizing

This requirement ensues from the principles of 'justice and fairness', but is also indispensible for the administrative authority to prepare its decisions properly. The publication (notification) of the decision to disclose information to another state should comprise at least the fact of the disclosure and its purpose. This is also the general rule in the Privacy Directive – albeit with regard to a different party – and in the legal sources preceding this.[115]

Also in accordance with this, the time of notification in principle should be *before* the disclosure of information actually has taken place.

Calderon assumes that in most states a right to be informed already exists with regard to the *collection* of the information, more in particular at the start of a tax investigation, on the grounds of the *standard*, generally accepted in his view, that the administrative authority should communicate purpose of the investigation. This right would then also apply to investigation for the benefit of the other state.[116] Whatever one may think of that, such a link with the *collection* of data, which also features in Article 10 of the Privacy Directive, poses the disadvantage that at the moment of collection it is not yet certain whether or not any data will be disclosed, and if so, what data exactly. This is because the state cannot yet weigh all the interests. Moreover, the choice for this moment of notification is not suitable for cases that an investigation is not required, or that information is disclosed spontaneously.

For this reason, the publication should be linked with the decision to disclose, and it should take place before the actual disclosure, except in special circumstances.

### 6.1.2 Content of the Notification

Besides this, I believe that the 'fair processing' principle from the Privacy Directive means that also the *categories of data* to be disclosed and the *receiver* should be stated. The taxpayer who supplied the information to be disclosed cannot be expected to learn these facts from his own knowledge, whereas it is in his interest to be able to assess if the (anticipated) disclosure falls within the scope of the relevant treaty provision. Not providing 'further information' in the notification (apart from the controller's identity and the purpose), as is possible under the Privacy Directive, would in my view make the legal protection in the context of the international exchange of information rather illusory.

### 6.1.3 Interested Party

Equally crucial as the right to be informed is the definition of the party possessing this right, in other words, the interested party. This is, as argued earlier, in my opinion, not the person *to whom* the disclosed information *relates*, but the person who 'possesses' the information and must *supply* to serve the interest of the other

115. OECD Guidelines on the Protection of Privacy and Transborder Flow of Personal Data and the Convention for the Protection of Individuals with Regard to Automatic Processing of Personal Data, by the Council of Europe, 1981. Also see Ch. 8 s. 2.
116. Calderon (2000). For that matter, Dutch procedural taxation law does not impose such a legal duty on the tax authorities.

state. After all, the supplier runs the risk that his financial position is affected, for example, because his data become known to others and he will be less able to compete; can suffer harm to his good name and reputation, which might worsen his trade relations; or incidentally, intimate matters relating to him/ might be disclosed.

In the exchange of information, the natural or legal person to whom the information 'relates' mostly resides or is registered in the other state and is the one for whose taxation the data may be *used by the receiving state.* This makes the latter, in the terminology of data processing law, the party responsible for the *use* of the data. Under rule of law, the 'fairness and lawfulness' of the *use* of the data is already guaranteed by the procedural tax law of that state, which in relation to the assessment will include the requirement of proper motivation for the administration, the possibility of objection and appeal, and the rules for a fair trial. This legal protection also applies when no foreign data are involved in the assessment, so that it does not involve international law.[117] The view of, for example, Calderon,[118] but also some Dutch authors in the 1990s, and that of the Dutch Ombudsman,[119] that the informational legal protection should apply to persons *to whom the data relate* cannot be upheld in view of the previous arguments.

Similarly, the more theoretical model of thinking which provided an anchor in the previous chapters produces the same outcome, in my opinion. Based on what we indicated above as the function of the law in the relationships between natural and legal persons, that is, to achieve the best possible balance and as much equality as possible, we concluded that the stronger party has the duty to protect the weaker party, by carefully considering the latter's interests. However, this duty ensues from the legal relationship. With respect to the *taxpayer in the receiving state*, the disclosing state only has the legal duty to keep the data that might have been included in a request pertaining to him confidential. This means that the disclosing state cannot protect other – tax-related – interests of this taxpayer. This is the task of the party responsible for the *use* of the data: the receiving state.

Moreover, in the relationship under international law, between the disclosing state and its treaty partner, the disclosing state has promised to protect the tax interests of its treaty partner. For this reason alone, the disclosing state *may not* interfere in any possible conflict of interest between the state requesting the information and the taxpayer of that state.[120]

It may occur that a taxpayer to whom a foreign request relates is also taxable for part of his income or profit in the supplying state. In this case, the data to be disclosed that are collected from this taxpayer also *relate to that taxpayer.* The responsibility of the requested (disclosing) state for the 'fair and lawful' collection, as well as for the disclosure of the data, in my opinion, means that even in this case,

117. Still, the state receiving information does have one obligation arising from international law toward the supplier, to keep his data confidential.
118. Calderon (2000).
119. Report of the Netherlands' Nationale Ombudsman, no. 92/906, V-N 1993, 326.
120. Also Schenk-Geers (1996).

a right to be informed must be granted. The fact that in this case, the data also relate to the taxpayer, and that the taxpayer will enjoy protection under tax law in the other state is not relevant for *this* protection.

### 6.1.4 Time of Notification

As a result of it being firmly rooted in the right to a peaceful enjoyment of possessions and in the legal principles of 'justice and fairness', the right of publication is a strong right. No legitimate interest of the administrative authority can be identified on which grounds the right may be withheld from the taxpayer.[121] Even the government's duty to observe that other basic right, the right of protection of personal privacy, does not stand in the way of the general application of its duty to publicize. After all, the administrative authority can leave out information that is sensitive in terms of privacy of third parties from the publication.

However, I believe that certain government interests mentioned in Article 13 of the Privacy Directive do provide grounds for changing the *time* the notification must take place. Interests such as national security or combating tax fraud[122] are so important, in my opinion, that they may justify a postponement of notification until *after* the disclosure of data, and even the erosion of the legal protection that results from it. Of course the taxpayer should still be given the opportunity to address the administrative authority's weighing of interests, and to have any errors in the data rectified.

Other government interests, comparable to the 'important' financial interest of the state (receiving information) from Article 13, first paragraph, sub-paragraph c, of the Privacy Directive, can only influence the time of notification in relation to the previously mentioned combating of fraud.[123] If this financial interest 'only' involves the ability to impose the tax assessment in due time, it may be stipulated that the state disclosing the data sends the notification to the taxpayer *simultaneously* with the information. In this way, the state receiving information does not need to forfeit its term of imposition, while on the other hand any inaccuracies in the disclosed data can still be reported and communicated in time. For that matter, the state requesting the information is obliged to make its request as soon as possible, to prevent any problems for its treaty partner.

121. Also Art. 13 of the Privacy Directive only refers to measures 'to restrict the scope' of the rights of individuals mentioned in the Directive.
122. In Art. 13, para. 1, of the Privacy Directive the first category is divided in: national security, defence, public security (subparas a-c) and a second category consisting of: the prevention, etc. of criminal offences, and the monitoring and inspection that are related to this (subparas d and f).
123. Article 13, first paragraph, under e of the Privacy Directive mentions besides 'important' financial interests also economic interests. It is not clear what is meant by this addition. In the context of the inter-state exchange of data they seem to coincide, in my opinion.

## 6.2 Objection and Appeal: Assessment Criteria

Together with the right of notification, the rights of objection and appeal included in all administrative law systems (specified in the Privacy Directive as the right of access, and the rights to rectify and appeal) must be made available to the taxpayer involved in the disclosure of information to another country.[124] After all, only the courts have the power to enforce the lawfulness and due care of government actions, if this is necessary. For this reason, I consider of the three types of rights that, according to the OECD Committee for Fiscal Affairs in its 1994 report, existed in the countries (notification rights, consultation rights and intervention rights) only the latter sufficient to protect the supplier of information.[125] According to the definition of the OECD report, it grants the taxpayer the right to have the lawfulness of the exchange assessed, before the exchange of data has actually taken place. This intervention right also fits best within the generally accepted principles that citizens have the right to be heard and they have the right to challenge decisions made by the government.[126]

I mentioned the views of Calderon, who sees the protection of the supplier of information as the possibility to rely for his/her intervention rights on the 'system of appeals' in the state *receiving the information*, and in this way protest against the exchange of information by the *disclosing* state. However, this is only possible if the exchanged data relate to himself/ (his possible tax debt in the other state), and he would be both the data provider (in state A) and the taxpayer (in state B). In that case, he could indeed initiate an action under tax law against the assessment to obtain a judgment on the disclosure. I believe this, according to Calderon, 'indirect' legal protection to be rather too indirect and also too late. As supplier of the data, the taxpayer should be able to protest on the basis of a notification against *his own state disclosing the information*, ideally before the decision to disclose has been made. If he is also the taxpayer in the receiving state, in that quality he could 'restart' the discussion about the lawfulness of the information from the angle of its admissibility as proof. But again, such a case of 'double protection' is rare.

The citizen's right to object and appeal implies the existence of criteria that the government action can be tested against. The general standard for the assessment of the government action is that it always should be grounded in law (the legality

---

124. The OECD Report Taxpayers' Rights and Obligations, A Survey of the Legal Situation in OECD Countries, OECD 1990, 10 and 12, mentions the right 'to appeal against decisions of the administration' under the fundamental rights of citizens in democratic countries.

125. See the report Tax Information Exchange between OECD Member Countries, A Survey of Current Practices, 1994, 66.

126. In addition, the 'intervention right' implies a dialogue between the taxpayer and the administrative authority and therefore serves the principle that the administrative authority must properly prepare its decisions.

For the right to be heard and to defend oneself, see de Moor-van Vugt (1998), 69 ff (*Hoffmann/La Roche* C-85/76). See also Barents/Brinkhorst (1996), 75. Furthermore, see the OECD Report Taxpayers' Rights and Obligations, A Survey of the Legal Situation in OECD Countries, OECD (1990) and Bentley (1998).

principle). However, because the executive has increasing means to create rights, the law has lost its monopoly and lower regulations can also set standards for government actions, next to the codified standards of due process (due care) developed in jurisprudence.[127]

Below I will discuss the legal standards of lawfulness and careful weighing of interests as criteria against which taxpayers involved in inter-state disclosure of data and the court may test the lawfulness of the data disclosure. A discussion of the many other, written and unwritten, principles of sound administration, no matter how important they are, lie outside the scope of this study.[128]

### 6.2.1 Objection and Appeal: Lawfulness

The duty of the government, to be guided in its actions by the law, in our case refers to international regulations, and therefore it is important to determine to what extent such an international obligation is binding for the state *in respect of its citizens*. This is not self-evident, nor equal in all states. Not in all states, an international rule of law applies directly as national law. But even in countries where this is the case, the direct effect will be hampered by the fact that the international provisions for the exchange of data do not exclusively govern all the state's actions in this area. After all, there is nothing in international rules on the exchange of information that prevents states to do more than the information provisions prescribe, or, as in the case of Germany, to disclose information to another state outside such a provision. Only when data are disclosed on the grounds of Regulation 1798/2003, is the obliging character also a fact in a public-law sense. Besides this, the rules on the exchange of information between states also contain discretionary provisions, as we already have seen, in respect of which the legality principle requires that these are laid down by law for the citizens of the state.

The national rules on the exchange of information must therefore explicitly express the legal basis for the exchange of information with other states. Is this exchange only lawful if an international obligation has been entered into, or may the government also disclose information to another state on request or spontaneously? In the latter case, legal certainty demands that the national law formulates autonomous safeguards regarding the confidentiality and the use of the data to be disclosed in the other state and that it be specified what efforts the state will make to assist the other state.

In most cases, however, the disclosure of information to other states is tied to the existence of an obligation under international law. After all, this is the best way to legitimize the breach of the national obligation of confidentiality with regard to tax matters and the use of the national 'information gathering powers' for foreign taxation. In such a case, the international obligations to exchange information will

127. See Gribnau (1998), 161-162. Also see van Wijk/Konijnenbelt/van Male (2002), 267 ff.
128. Also see Calderon (2000), who names as grounds for objection the lack of 'actual legality of the information exchange', on the basis of which the exchange was not obligatory in a certain case or did not take place on the basis of proper weighing of interest.

have to be incorporated or enshrined in national law. The regulations regarding the exchange of information to other states was described from the perspective of international law in Chapters 4, 5, and 6. In the next section, their elements will come under discussion once more as lawfulness criteria for the taxable supplier of information.

###### 6.2.1.1 *Guarantee of Confidentiality of the State Receiving Information*

An essential criterion for lawfulness of the data exchange is the confidentiality guarantee given by the state receiving information. Chapter 5 showed that the data provider has his own legal position in that state on the grounds of this guarantee. But this guarantee starts playing a role only after the data have been disclosed and a possible unlawfulness has already occurred; for that matter, it is mostly exists in theory. Even apart from any unlawful action by the treaty partner, taxpayers in the supplying state run the risk that the confidentiality laws or the legal procedures in the other state offer less protection than those in his own state. This interest should be protected before the disclosure, provided the data provider can obtain the state's attention for this on a special grounds for appeal. Still, he will have to offer thorough substantiation of this suspicion of inadequate protection. The supplying state could then limit these risks in consultation with the state that is to receive the information. In the relationship between the European Member States, there is already a legal basis for this in the confidentiality provision of Directive 77/799, which enables the supplying state to demand extra confidentiality measures from the other Member State, which correspond closer to its own law in this area.[129] In the OECD tax conventions the confidentiality clause should be supplemented in the same manner.[130] This should be coupled to an obligation to start consultation, if an information supplying taxpayer supplier claims to have suffered damage in the other state as a result of the exchange of data. As a ground for appeal, these extra confidentiality measures should be *prohibitive* in nature, so that disclosure of information is not possible as long as these consultations with the other state have not been concluded satisfactorily.

###### 6.2.1.2 *Objective and Subjective Scope of the Rules on the International Exchange of Information*

Also, on the ground of the requirement of lawfulness, the states are not allowed to disclose information that fall outside the objective or subjective scope of the relevant treaty provision, or if there is no obligation to collect this information (and perhaps no national authorization), or if the request is not made by the competent

129. Article 7 of the Directive 77/799.

130. The application seems more complicated than it really is. Such a demand for extra protection of the exchanged data in accordance with the law of the party disclosing the data can be put forward during the negotiations, or afterwards.

authority of the other state. This only different when their domestic law explicitly mentions the discretionary ('ex gratia') information exchange.[131]

### 6.2.2 Objection and Appeal: Reasonable Weighing of Interests

The national rules on the exchange of information between states must also provide for specific arguments for assessing the weighing of interests on which the decision to disclose data was founded. After all, these rules must also affect the taxpayers' interests to be weighed. Apart from the requirements of lawfulness mentioned above, which do not qualify for weighing, the grounds for exception that were formulated in international exchange of information law to protect the interests of the supplying states also can be deemed to regard the interests of the information-supplying taxpayers, as we have seen. These interests must be included in the national rules on the exchange of information between states, as arguments for these taxpayers in their dialogue with the government. In Chapter 7, we defined on the basis of those discretionary grounds for exception for the states arguments that should serve the taxpayers as grounds for appeal. I will let them pass in review below once more.

#### *6.2.2.1 Standard of Exhaustion/Principle of Subsidiarity*

In Chapters 4 and 7, we were acquainted with the exhaustion rule as a means to establish an equal division of burdens between the states. The state requesting information, who benefits from a solution of its taxation problems, should in principle first exhaust its own customary options to obtain the data, before making a request to a treaty partner. The exhaustion rule concerns the interests of the state requested to disclose information, to minimize any unnecessary efforts. Earlier we saw that this principle reaches its limits if there is a suspicion of fraud in the requesting state. In that case, an extensive investigation could prove to be counter-productive. In Chapter 7, we concluded that the data providers also may have an interest in a rejection of the request, on the grounds of a breach of the exhaustion rule. However, I find that this cannot outweigh the interest of states to be able to request relevant data from their treaty partners, even without an investigation in their own state. The degree of discretion of the state requesting the data, and the principle of the exclusive jurisdiction of the state, makes it impossible for the requested state to test compliance with the rule by its treaty partner independently. For this reason, I believe the exhaustion rule cannot serve as an argument or a ground for appeal for taxable suppliers of information in the state disclosing the data.

---

131. German law on information exchange includes this possibility. See Ch. 4, s. 4.1.

#### 6.2.2.2 *The Argument of Sovereignty of Domestic Law*

This argument, which states can use to consider themselves relieved from the obligation to exchange information, concerns the situation that defending the interests of the treaty partner would mean that the supplying state would violate its own laws and/or its own administrative practice. It gives the state disclosing the data the opportunity to meet the requirements of legal certainty and predictability of government actions, as we have seen above, and therefore should be an argument, which the information supplying taxpayer can put forward against its own state. After all, a citizen must be able to trust that his government respects the laws and that the coherence of the legal system is maintained and cannot be broken by all sorts of exceptions, only because of the interests of a variety of different treaty partners.

In view of the importance of legal certainty, I think that this grounds for appeal should be mandatory.

#### 6.2.2.3 *The Argument of Reciprocity*

This argument concerns the situation that the state wanting to disclose data (on request or spontaneously) would be confronted with the situation, that the other state could itself not provide the same information on the grounds of its own legislation or administrative practice. This circumstance relieves the state from the obligation to supply information, by virtue of the grounds of exception in the international rules on the exchange of information.[132] With this argument, we have seen, states can maintain the balance in their legal relationship, but it can also permit a state to put its own economic interests above the common interest of the treaty partners. For the taxpayer who has to supply the data, a strict interpretation of this principle would be more advantageous because it may protect him against any harm to his competitive position relative to the taxable entrepreneurs in the other state. A state's choice for a strict or flexible application of the reciprocity principle is a political one, and it will have to be embodied in legislation in view of the rule of law. The taxpayer supplying information must be able to test for compliance with this choice, for the same reasons as apply to the argument of sovereignty: the taxpayer must be able to predict the actions of his government.

#### 6.2.2.4 *The Business Secret or Professional Privilege*

The grounds of exception regarding the business secret features in all schemes regarding the international exchange of information, and in the OECD rules it is the only provision that in the Commentary refers to the interests of the taxpayer supplying the data, which the states must consider carefully. For that matter, we saw in

132. OECD Model convention Art. 26(3)(a) and (b); Strasbourg Convention in Art. 21(2)(a) and (c); Directive 77/799 Art. 8(3); value added tax (VAT) Assistance Regulation Art. 40(3); and OECD Agreement Art. 7(1). See for the content of this concept para. 6.4.

paragraph 6.5.1 (reference correct) that the due care that the Commentary invokes in particular means that states have to correctly select those interests, so that only the 'real interests' of taxpayers are protected. It must concern information that is known within a small circle only, that can be exploited in economic transactions, and the possession of which by others may cause damage. The concept of business secret comprises technical specifications, plans, and business plans, but also the pricing policy of internationally operating businesses in various countries. It may also include the right to refrain from giving evidence of certain professions. The weighing of interests that is inherent to the application of this argument can be applied only in a dialogue with the taxpayer and is therefore a strong argument for the establishment of a right for this taxpayer to be informed. (Also see paragraphs 6.5.1. and 7.3.3.3.) Furthermore, in the international rules on the exchange of information between states, the risk for impairment of the business secret does *not* result in a *prohibition* to disclose information. Relative to this individual interest, there may be public interests that in the opinion of the states should be given more weight, and accordingly I believe that this ground for appeal should also be given a discretionary formulation. In this way, the states may reserve a degree of discretion to let the public interest prevail.

#### *6.2.2.5 The Argument of Public Order*

In paragraph 6.6, the argument of public order was defined as the political and security interests of the states, or 'the vital interests of the state itself'. The literature considers as part of these interests, which concern the continuation of the state, also those interests that in the general opinion concern the continued existence of states as a legal community. These include the generally accepted fundamental values of democracy and freedom and the dignity of the individual, and the principles of rule of law that are derived from these. If these would be impaired as a result of the exchange of information, a state may refuse the exchange of information. As an example, the OECD Commentary refers to a request for information made in connection with oppression on political, religious, or racial grounds. The possibility of refusal to provide data because of a violation of the 'generally accepted principles of tax law', which only features in the Strasbourg Convention, can be seen in this light.

For these reasons, the argument of public order should be included as ground for appeal in the national rules on the exchange of information between states.[133] Because of its relationship with standards that are essential for the rule of law, I think it should be formulated as a prohibition in the national legislation.

133. Not all states (including the Netherlands) allow *individuals* to use the argument of public order, because it concerns a public interest. In those countries, only interest groups an invoke the argument.

#### 6.2.2.6 *Conclusion*

A set of data processing rules for the international exchange of information should contain the following elements:

- A 'prior notification' of the decision to disclose the data, intended for the data provider, and containing the purpose of disclosure, the name of the state receiving the data, the data categories, and the information itself. In case of compelling interests of states, such as the combating of fraud, it may occur after or at the time of disclosure.
- A clear definition of the interested party. Assuming that the taxpayer to whom the information applies in the receiving state will enjoy protection in that state against unlawful or inaccurate tax assessments on the basis of the received information, the concept of 'interested party' to be protected in the area of *exchange of information* must be limited here to the taxpayer/data provider in the state disclosing the information.
- Specific grounds for appeal. These must be derived from the discretionary provisions in the international exchange of information law, offering the possibilities for the supplying state to refuse or omit the exchange, as the result of the weighing of its interests against those of the treaty partner. The interests of the taxpayers supplying the information can be deemed to run parallel to these.

Included in these are the possibility of asking extra guarantees for confidentiality from the state receiving the data, if this seems to be necessary, application of the argument of sovereignty, the argument of public order, the reciprocity argument, and the business secret argument.

The arguments regarding the confidentiality guarantee, the inviolability of the state's own laws, and the public order should be prohibitory in character because they concern the constitutional degree of the government action as such.

The reciprocity argument should be applied prohibitory to the *making of requests*, in my opinion, because the legality principle demands this. With regard to the *disclosure* of data, which we discussed in this study, I believe that the state supplying the data should be able to weigh the absence of reciprocity, especially if significant interests of the treaty partner are at stake. A prohibition to disclose data if reciprocity is lacking in some circumstances could prove to be too restrictive for properly defending the interests of the state receiving the data, which after all is the objective of the exchange of information. For this reason, this grounds for appeal aims as such on a weighing of interests and should have a *discretionary* formulation together with the business secret argument.

### 6.3 Protection and the Methods of Exchange

Finally, it must be examined to what form of disclosure of data the notification should apply. For this purpose, we must seek a link with the circumstance that makes this necessary, which is that the information-supplying taxpayer involved (a) does not independently know, nor can he be deemed to know, the fact that data originating from him are being exchanged; (b) is obliged to cooperate with this, whereas (c) this could affect his interests.

This situation arises in the case of disclosure of information after an individual *request* by another state and in case of *individual spontaneous disclosure* of data found at a taxpayer.

In addition, there are situations in which the data intended for the other state can be obtained from data files that have been filled by tax declarations of taxpayers and withholding agents. These data can be obtained and disclosed in large quantities, < and (ideally) fill the databases of the tax authorities in a prescribed manner and at a prescribed time.

With this form of exchange, the suppliers mostly are not the individual taxpayers. Of course, they too have an interest in the lawfulness of the data disclosure, as well as the confidentiality and accuracy of the data received. To guarantee the lawfulness of the disclosure of these massive data flows, disclosure should take place only after explicit and proper agreements with the treaty partner, which may and should address the guarantee of confidentiality by the other state, the argument of sovereignty, the argument of reciprocity, and the argument of public order.[134] To warrant the accuracy of the data, the states should, in my opinion, design and monitor an adequate feedback system. Furthermore, the agreement between the states should be published officially.

The massiveness of the disclosure, the extensive bilateral negotiations, and the possibility for those to whom the data relate to start an action in the other state justify in my opinion the omission of an individual notification to the supplier of information.

## 7 SUMMARY AND CONCLUSIONS

1. For an answer to the question *how* the legal protection with regard to international exchange of data should be set up, it is useful to view this exchange as a way of dealing with data, which relate to individuals. As a result, a link may be sought with standards relating to data processing that have been developed since the 1970s in response to the 'information society'. In view of its supranational character and its extensive territorial scope, the European Privacy Directive is the most suitable object of research. Furthermore, its authors believe that it explicitly applies to the international exchange of information.

2. The Directive continues along the line that runs from constitutionally embodied rights to informational self-determination in some states, to international legal sources of the OECD and the EC. On the one hand, the Directive aims to

134. It will hardly ever happen that business secrets are revealed in the automatic exchange of information. As we have seen, such sensitive information often can be established only through individual and rather thorough contact with a taxpayer.

guarantee the economically necessary flow of personal data, and on the other it aims to protect the informational *legal* position of the individual in the information society. All legal sources formulate as basic requirements for the lawful processing of personal information:

- the requirement that the data processing is bound to a purpose specified in advance, or to the law,
- the requirement of legitimacy of the processing, which is made dependent on the consent of the data subject, or a public interest, and
- the requirement of the data subject's participation, consisting of the right to be informed, the right of access and the right to object.

The first two basic requirements were laid down in the international rules for the exchange of information between states as such, and were also discussed in this study. Regrettably, however, the 'principle of participation' was lacking. For this reason, the examination of the Privacy Directive focused on that.

3. Article 10 of the Privacy Directive guarantees the data subject the right to be at least informed about the purpose and the controller of the data processing. In certain cases, also the type of data and the receiver of them are to be communicated. If the data are obtained from somebody other then the data subject (Article 11 of the Directive), the fact of the transfer to a third party must also be communicated before the first transfer or disclosure. The only situation in which notification is not obligatory is if the processing of the data may be assumed to be known already, because of a statutory obligation.

4. In my opinion, the latter is not the case in the international exchange of information. After all, collection of data from taxpayers in individual cases generally takes place for the purpose of national taxation. In the process of the collection of the information, it will not be understood automatically by the taxpayer that the collected data are intended for use in another country. What is more, after the collection, the tax authority still needs to decide whether it will actually disclose the information to the other country.

5. These rights, however, are not absolute in their nature. The Privacy Directive restricts the right to be informed, the right of access, and the right to rectify, if this serves the individual protection of data subjects, the rights and/or freedoms of others, or the public interests of states, such as security and 'important' economic and financial interests. The public interest of the states and the rights and freedoms of others may also restrict the right to object to disclosure, which for that matter exists only if there are *compelling* individual interests.

6. To improve the applicability of the Privacy Directive for the protection of the data provider in the exchange of information, and for the purpose of creating an equal level of protection in all states, I believe that the term 'important' financial interests of states in Article 13 should be described more clearly. To this end, the description could include serious suspicions of tax fraud in one or both states. For the explanation of the term 'compelling' individual interests (which justify an objection), a link should be sought with the interests of data providers selected from rules on the exchange of information between states in Chapter 7. On those

conditions the Directive in principle would be able to offer protection to both the taxpayer to whom the data relate and the person who supplies these data.

7. However, other elements of the Directive stand in the way of an application to the international exchange of information.

First of all, there is the provision regarding the disclosure of data to other states that may have an inadequate level of protection. The Preamble wrongly defines the interstate exchange of information as such a 'compelling public interest' that it should always prevail over the protection of data subjects. The guarantee of confidentiality protecting the data provider is a condition for this exchange, which is not subject to a weighing of interests.

8. But even more important is the conclusion that the definition of the term 'data subject' from the Privacy Directive excludes its application to the greatest part of the international exchange of data, that is, the taxpayer in the disclosing country, who has to supply the information. The reasons for this are:

- The description of the concept of 'data subject' as 'the person to whom the data relate' makes this concept unsuitable for the application of Article 10 of this Directive to trans-border *disclosure* of information, because it only establishes a right to be informed with regard to the *collection* of personal data, and not in respect of the *disclosure* of these data. The only possible benefit of this right to be informed could be that the notification of the purpose of the collection (in this case levying of tax in the other state) offers the data provider the chance to request inspection of the documents compiled by the tax authorities on the basis of 'freedom of information legislation', which could demonstrate any disclosure of data to another country.
- If the data are *not* collected directly (Article 11 of the Directive), the supplier of the data is not protected, but again only 'the person to whom the data relate'. In the cross-border context of international information exchange, the data collected in the one Member State usually 'relate' to a person in the other Member State. In those cases, I feel that Article 11 of the Privacy Directive cannot offer protection to the supplier of the data. Because this supplier in terms of the Directive is 'not the data subject', his interest is not acknowledged. As a result, the right to be informed, the right of access, and the right to rectify and object would not apply to him, although he certainly runs risks.

9. This means that presently, the implementation of the European Privacy Directive by the European Member States does not offer any guarantee that they can fulfil their legal duty toward their taxable suppliers of data when it comes to international exchange of data.

10. For the protection of the information supplier involved in the international exchange of data, an alternative data protection right must be established, which does not focus exclusively on personal privacy and the corresponding definition of the concept of 'data subject'. A link should be sought with the 'definition' proposed by the ECHR, of information as immaterial property, and with the

fundamental right for individuals to peacefully enjoy this property. This would offer protection to more informational interests than through privacy law, and it would protect more persons having legal rights, including the natural persons and legal persons involved in the exchange of information. The *instruments* of informational legal protection that were developed in the Privacy Directive could be embedded, in slightly altered form, in this legal system. For the application of these instruments, the general principles of sound administration, as these developed in states under rule of law and within the European law system, could be converted to general standards of sound data processing. The requirement of lawfulness of government action in our case refers to the material international rules on the exchange of information between states, while the requirement of due process in this relation implies that the data provider must be informed of decisions to disclose data. The data provider's interests also must be carefully weighed.

11. If administrative law cannot or does not offer or inadequately offers the opportunity to start proceedings regarding the international exchange of information, the civil court must bring relief. Based on the universal character of the legal principles, as shown in European administrative and liability law and the Draft Articles on interstate liability of the International Law Committee of the United Nations, it may be assumed that civil courts in the states test government actions largely along the same lines. The civil law, however, has the disadvantage that it in itself creates no right of publication. Because the taxpayer must be aware about the decision to disclose data from his own sources, interlocutory proceedings to prevent damage often are not a useful instrument.

Obtaining compensation afterwards (in my dictionary is correct) for loss suffered as a result of an unlawful action by one of the states, is often a difficult process for the taxpayer. After all, the loss is mostly inflicted in the other state. For this reason, it will be hard to proffer evidence of unlawfulness, damage, and a causal connection. What is more, OECD convention law lacks a regulation for discussing and determining any liability of states.

Among OECD convention partners, opening the 'mutual agreement procedure' could be a solution for establishing the liability for unlawful acts of states in violation with the OECD information provision.

In principle, intra-Community law does offer taxpayers the opportunity to hold the Member State receiving the data liable for acting in breach of its obligation of confidentiality. After all, this obligation also aims to protect the individual and can be derived from the relevant provision of Community law with sufficient clarity. However, the proceedings must be brought before the national court of that state. Again the trans-border character of the government action may form an extra obstacle for the requirement of causality.

12. The conclusion must be that the state disclosing information has the obligation to prevent damage for the data provider as much as possible. For this reason, data processing law in respect of the international exchange of information should be embedded in the administrative law system of the states, with the general standards requiring specification on some points. This choice results from the quality so characteristic for administrative law that it is aimed at having a dialogue

between the government and citizens. The obligation of publicizing government decisions and the weighing of interests are examples of this characteristic.

13. The national rules on the exchange of information between states should have the following elements:

- A notification of the taxpayer, before the disclosure of information, with regard to the purpose of the disclosure, the identity of the state receiving the information, and the data categories. In case of *important* interests of states, such as combating of fraud, notification may occur after or coincide with the moment of disclosure.
- A clear definition of the interested party: the taxpayer of the state disclosing information, whom the data originate from and/or who is the subject of the information.
- Specific grounds for objection and appeal. These grounds should be derived from the precepts and prohibitions of the international information exchange provisions and from the options for the supplying states, created in these provisions, to weigh the interests of the treaty partner against their own interests. This option also may be applied to weigh the interests of their data providers, which run along parallel lines. In this connection, a definition was given of the argument of inadequate confidentiality, the argument of public order, the argument of reciprocity, and the argument of the business secret. These should be considered as grounds for appeal for the data provider. Of these grounds for appeal, the arguments regarding the (extra) guarantee of confidentiality, the inviolability of the state's own laws, and the public order should be prohibitory in character. These pertain to the constitutionality of the government action as such. The international exhaustion rule does not affect the interests of the information supplier, in my opinion. Application thereof is left to the discretion of the state requesting the data, with respect to its effectiveness in a specific case. What is more, neither the state disclosing the data, nor the taxpayer supplying the information, can assess compliance with the standard.
- The arguments under international law, regarding the business secret and the reciprocity, should be formulated as optional. If these arguments were to have a mandatory character, the defence of the interests of the treaty partners, which after all is the aim of the exchange of information, would be restricted too much.

# Chapter 9
# Summary and Conclusions

The subject of this study was the legal position of the taxpayer in the exchange of tax-related information between states. It was triggered by the observation that states needing each other's assistance in assessing internal tax liabilities cannot obtain this assistance without involving taxpayers in the other state. The information to be exchanged must be gathered from them, assuming they possess it state. This may be the case because it concerns their own tax liability in that state or because they are an associated or business partner of the taxpayer being examined in the other state. In some cases, the gathering information can be limited to data bases, but these, too, were in fact 'fed' by the taxpayers in the requested state. In all cases, for providing tax-related information to a contracting state, the (coerced) cooperation of these persons in the supplying state is necessary.

Meanwhile, in constitutional states it is generally accepted that the taxpayer has rights and safeguards secured to him, and that his obligations toward the tax administration are exclusively based on the law. In case information must be supplied to a contracting state, this relationship of administrative law must be embedded in rules of international law between two contracting states. This gave rise to the question as to what the actual legal position of these taxpayers is. Would they not be 'crushed' or overlooked in the fulfilment of international obligations between states? This concern was deepened by the modifications of the OECD (OECD) Model Tax Convention, in which the discretionary powers of the states were limited, but also by the European Union (EU) legislation on the exchange of information. There, the possibility to weigh the interests of the supplying party was limited in favour of (supposed) requirements in the field of efficiency and effectiveness. These modifications also left their impact on the Dutch legislation and practice in mutual assistance. This study has grown out of this concern, and four main questions arose from it:

- When exchanging information, do states have a legal duty to protect the interests of their internal taxpayers/suppliers of information, apart from the obligation to protect the interests of the contracting states?

- If the answer is yes, can this duty be fulfilled under the current rules concerning the international exchange of information?
- Within this framework, what are the interests of states and taxpayers to be weighed?
- How can the legal protection of taxpayers supplying information be realized?

Why Mutual Administrative Assistance is Important

The questions described above appear of interest in the light of the ever-increasing importance attached to the international exchange of tax-related information during the last decades. In Chapter 1, it was concluded that, as a consequence of the increasing globalization of economies, a growing number of taxpayers generate income in states in which they are not a resident. Although the tax treaties developed since the 1940s have proved to be an adequate instrument to reasonably divide the taxation of these cross-border categories of income *between* the contracting states, fair taxation *in* the states themselves was not yet safeguarded. There is a high risk that these cross-border incomes will not become known to the states, which will lead to loss of tax and the corruption of what states consider to be the fairness of their tax assessment system. Therefore, all tax treaties appeared to contain a provision in which the contracting states were obligated to exchange foreseeably relevant information in tax matters. These international obligations were also laid down in EU legislation.

Why Tax-payers Need Legal Protection

To find an answer to the question whether this legal duty exists, it is necessary to examine its the general concept of legal protection. This was done in Chapter 2. To this end, the more abstract field of the philosophy of law had to be explored. There we discovered the inspiring concept of the free and autonomous individual 'as it appears to us in all its dignity', having an indefeasible right to freely develop its potential. This freedom, however, appeared to be defined differently in different periods of time. In the classic constitutional state, it was particularly envisaged as the absence of government interference, which made it possible for the individual to pursue its own goals. The state could interfere with the individual only to ensure that the individuals would not jeopardize the lives and freedom of others. In addition, the state had to ensure the safety and stability of the community. The acquired characteristics of the classic constitutional state most relevant for this study appeared to be the separation of powers in the legislative, the executive and the judicial power and its system of checks and balances, as well as the basic principle that every action of the state regarding its citizens must be based on the law. This principle of legality gave legislation an enormous prestige: it became the shield against abuse of power and arbitrariness, the protector of legal certainty and predictability, and thus also synonymous with the concept of law. Law and justice became one. In the nineteenth century, however, the concept that the state must maintain a distance from its citizens turned out to lead to social misery. Societies became increasingly more aware of the fact that self-realization is defined by contacts with other individuals and that the realization of one's potential is also determined by the position of the individual within society. The state was not to stand aside in these matters, but must protect less fortunate groups and further their emancipation. To this end, the state had to safeguard the access of all groups within society to the public debate on what was fair and desirable. In the democratic constitutional state that thus arose, the ideal of the autonomous individual appeared to be toned down in favour of a more relational concept of law. Rather than the dichotomy between the state and the individual that dominated the concept of law of the classical democratic state, the friction between the autonomous dignity of which it is the carrier, and the relationships with others on which it depends, had to be seen as the intrinsic hallmark of the 'condition humaine' of every individual. According to some twentieth-century philosophers of law, this gap, if it were to be bridged, involved a larger role for the general principles of law rather than fixed rules of law, with their concept of 'all or nothing at all'. These principles are not promulgated, but they are generally accepted notions and concepts about what is fair and just between people, which in law are like presumed. They are the guidelines to new rules of law in an ever-changing social reality. The principle of equality was considered to be the leading principle, because it could be the link between the *ideal* of individual freedom and autonomy and the *reality* of mutual dependences, and it could organize inter-human relationships in such a way that *all* individuals can freely develop themselves. In this context, equality is to be understood as the standard of 'equal concern and respect', as formulated by Dworkin. It means that one individual should never be reduced to a mere means to the ends of another, and that the participants in legal relationships should treat each other *as equals.* This holds the assignment to carefully weigh the interests of others within the goal of the legal relationship, applying first and foremost to the strongest party. Thus, a moral dimension is added to the concept of law. In the 'asymmetrical' relationships between governments and citizens, the government is the strongest party because it is able to enforce legal relationships on citizens on the basis of its responsibility to protect the general interest, as well as its democratic legitimacy. From the coherence between the relational concept of law, the evolution of the principle of equality, and the moral assignment to protect the weak in a democratic (constitutional) state, the notion was developed that the treatment of citizens by governments should be based not only on rules of law, but on rules of care as well. This duty of care implies that their interests are taken into account wherever possible, even if they are not yet codified. This naturally also must to be true for the relationship between tax authorities and taxpayers. To execute their official authority to assess tax liabilities, the authorities are able to enforce the taxpayer's cooperation. In the ongoing dialogue between governments and their taxpayers, the interests of the latter will have to be weighed to a reasonable extent. When applied to the exchange of information between states, this vision led to the conclusion that governments, in fulfilling their obligation to exchange information with contracting states, *also* have a legal duty to weigh the interests of the taxpayers supplying this information. This legal duty should, however, be embedded in rules of international law.

## 1. THE INTERNATIONAL FRAMEWORK OF THE EXCHANGE OF INFORMATION

The existence of an international framework made it necessary to discuss the general aspects of the law of treaties, and especially the OECD Model Tax Convention which, although in itself not 'binding', is an important source of law for the international exchange of information. This is the result of the continuous train of thought on this subject as maintained by the Committee on Fiscal Affairs, which is reflected in the different versions of the Model Tax Convention, in the official Commentaries and in international literature. On the one hand, these continuous dynamics, discussed in Chapter 3 cause the necessity to adapt the terms of tax treaties to new developments, but on the other they cause problems in interpreting those terms, as in practice apart from Model Tax Convention, the older tax treaties still apply. This situation is aggravated by the sometimes poor transparency of the proceedings of the Committee on Fiscal Affairs of the OECD. Desired changes are not always laid down in the Model Tax Convention, but rather in the Commentaries. This leaves the affected parties in legal uncertainty, giving rise to the question of whether existing provisions in tax treaties must be interpreted according to the more recent Commentaries (which are in fact the viewpoints of the Committee on Fiscal Affairs) or according to the older, but still applicable treaty. The solution of the Committee to interpret the old treaties according to the outcome of more recent notions appeared to be susceptible to criticism. In this respect, the question arises whether the OECD Commentaries can be considered part of the context of a treaty in the sense of Article 31 of the Vienna Convention on the Law of Treaties, because this was not stipulated by the parties at the time the individual tax treaties were drawn up. Besides this, in my opinion, rather artificial objection, particularly the lack of democratic legitimacy of the Commentaries turned out to be a point of discussion. That is because tax treaties are drawn up by tax officials and are presented to the Houses of Parliament only at the moment of their ratification. On the other hand, it is sometimes also crucial to interpret older treaties in a flexible way. The problem of legal uncertainty can be mitigated by limiting dynamic interpretation to situations in which the new Commentaries can be considered a clarification of the old. It was with this restriction that states generally accepted dynamic interpretation as presented by the Committee on Fiscal Affairs. However, the Committee should be closely monitored in this.

The interpretation of provisions in tax treaties against the background of rapidly changing domestic tax laws of the states appeared to be more problematic, because these developments could modify or undermine the interpretation of provisions in tax treaties. This problem arises from the obligation laid down in Article 3, paragraph 2 of the tax treaties to interpret undefined terms of treaties in the light of the meaning of these terms in the *domestic law* of the state applying the treaty in question, (unless the *context* requires otherwise). In the international discussion about static versus dynamic interpretation, triggered by the sensational Canadian Melford case, the majority of authors appeared to embrace dynamic interpretation: terms should be interpreted according to their meaning in the newer domestic law. The states should have taken the changeability of their domestic tax laws into account when accepting these as a frame of reference for the interpretation of the Treaty in Article 3, paragraph 2 of the OECD Model Tax Convention.

In its struggle to solve the problem of reaching a balance between safeguarding a 'firm ground' in the commitment between states on the one hand and respecting the changing notions about taxation on the other, the Committee on Fiscal Affairs has chosen dynamic interpretation and has thus sharpened Article 3, paragraph 2 of the Model Tax Convention. But, in the Commentaries, when determining the context, more emphasis was put on the intentions of the parties to the treaty 'when signing the Convention'. Thus, it remains unclear whether the interpretation must be based on either the old shared intentions or the newer domestic law. This friction between new domestic law and older international law proved difficult to resolve, caused by the fact that states, although tied by the provisions of the Vienna Convention, cannot be *forced* to stick to the original joint intentions. The mutual agreement procedure included in the treaties for matters of interpretation does not contain an obligation to come to a conclusion, nor does it contain an obligation to *implement* a possible conclusion in domestic law. Even today, OECD countries cannot even be obligated to recognize binding verdicts of an International Court of Justice about the interpretation of tax treaties and the way in which states are to comply with them. The only way to avoid problems of interpretation seemed to lie in the best possible autonomous description of what is meant by certain terms of the tax treaty. This discussion also played a dominant role in the international exchange of information within the OECD, because the information to be exchanged often concerns terms in a treaty. Besides, over the years, the Committee on Fiscal Affairs repeatedly modified the provision on the international exchange of information as well as the Commentaries thereof.

## 1.1. Ways to Protect Taxpayers in the International Exchange of Information

This analysis of the interpretation problems left the question unanswered whether the administrative duty of care of exchanging states, postulated in the second Chapter, could be *feasible* within the context of the existing rules on the international exchange of information. To answer this question, a further analysis of the contents of these rules proved necessary. These contents appeared in the tax treaties drafted by the OECD, mentioned above, but also in the multilateral Treaty of 1988 between the OECD and the Council of Europe (the so-called Strasbourg Convention), and in the OECD Agreement for the Exchange of Information on Tax Matters, concluded in 2002 between the Committee on Fiscal Affairs and some former tax havens. Also relevant are the European Council Directive concerning Mutual Assistance (European Directive 1977/79) and the European Council Regulation on Administrative Cooperation in the field of Value Added Tax (Regulation 1798/2003). A thematic treatment of the elements in these different sources of law required a division in three Chapters: in Chapter 4, besides the special position of the provision on the exchange of information in tax treaties, the prerequisite of an existing fiscal interest was discussed, as well as the objective scope and methods used. In Chapter 5, the obligations to secrecy in the use of information were discussed, and in Chapter 6 the restrictions stipulated with respect to this obligation. For all three subjects it appeared that, inasmuch as developments could be detected, these could especially be seen in the OECD rules, which happen to be the best-documented ones.

In Chapter 4, it became clear that these developments were concentrated in the scope of the obligation to exchange information and the information exchange methods. The number of taxes about which information was to be exchanged was extended in the OECD rules (including the Convention of Strassbourg) until basically all taxes were covered, including local ones. In 2003, a reform appeared to have taken place in EU law along the line of direct taxes on the one hand (in the European Directive as early as 1977) and along that of value added tax on the other. For the latter category, the obligations regarding mutual assistance were summed up in the Council Regulation 1798/2003. Moreover, in 1977 the restriction of the obligation regarding the exchange of information about *residents* as laid down in the OECD Model Tax Convention, was abolished as well. The mutual obligations of states became more and more onerous, modelled as they were on the Directive 1977/79 and the Convention on Mutual Administrative Assistance in Tax Matters. Methods such as the participation of officials of the requesting state in administrative enquiries and conducting simultaneous controls were eventually included in all sources of law as specific forms of the classic method of mutual assistance on request. All sources of law, except the OECD Agreement with the former tax havens, also contain spontaneous exchange of information as well as automatic exchange, in which periodical data flows are initiated. This development appeared to be furthered by the increasing possibilities for committing tax fraud as detected by states. For OECD countries, the campaign of the Committee on Fiscal Affairs against 'harmful tax competition' between states was also an incentive. On the one hand, the exchange of information appeared in this respect to be seen as a proof of international ethics, and on the other it appeared to be the only instrument to soften the sharp edges of this competition. These developments in the rules of the international exchange of information made it clear that they are first and foremost aimed at the interests of states.

In Chapter 5, the obligation to secrecy was discussed, which is a *conditio sine qua non* for the existence of an obligation to exchange information. It protects the interest of states to obtain and exchange information in a sequestered atmosphere. An element of uncertainty is that the secrecy of the information received appeared to be safeguarded according to the domestic laws of the requesting state. This in itself can lead to uncertainty, because the circle of bodies authorized to receive the information mentioned in the international provision may include different bodies in each country. Besides that, for the contracting state the relationship between both the national obligation to secrecy and the national obligation of transparency of government proceedings may not be clear from the beginning. This could lead to unwanted disclosure of the information itself and of the correspondence between states, which could harm essential interests. The Model Tax Convention turned out to contain since 2005 a rule of preference to minimize this risk.

In Chapter 6 an inquiry was made after the way in which the discretionary restrictions to the obligation to exchange information can be of influence to the protection of the interests of the taxpayer supplying the requested information. For the requested state, they appeared to offer the possibility to refuse or omit the exchange of information if, in the opinion of that state, one or more of the following situations occur:

- if the exchange of information would be contrary to the sovereignty of national laws or national administrative practice (the argument of sovereignty);
- if an equal availability of the requested information would not be safeguarded in the other state (the argument of reciprocity);
- if the exchange of information would be contrary to public order and the security of the state (the argument of public order) or to generally accepted principles of fair taxation;
- if the provision of information might lead to the disclosure of a commercial secret.

These arguments to refuse or omit the exchange of information protect the requested state against too heavy a claim by the requesting state and give it a wide berth to weigh its own political and economic interests against those of the requesting state.

At this stage the first two questions of this study were answered: on the one hand the supplying state did indeed appear to have an administrative duty of care – albeit an uncodified one – to protect its supplier of information, on the other hand the rules of the exchange of information appeared to offer the possibilities to fulfil this duty. It has to beadmitted though that these rules appeared to contain neither an *obligation* to, *nor a guarantee or incentive* in that direction. At that point the question still remained *which* interests of taxpayers are to be weighed in the international exchange of information and whether these interests balance out the interests of the states.

## 2. INTERESTS OF THE TAXPAYERS

In Chapter 7, these interests were examined. It appeared then that basically, they are not of a fiscal, but of an informational and a commercial nature. The supplier of information runs the risk that the information is not correct, that it will not be properly kept secret in the other state, or that it will not be used rightfully, which could lead to immaterial and material damages. If the other state is liable, suing for damages will be trying. Therefore, states must seriously scrutinize their powers of discretion before they decide to exchange the requested information. These discretionary powers not only play a role in the determination of the applicability of the grounds of exception, but also in the previous stage. They have to judge as carefully as possible the proceedings of the applicant state with regard to the conditions or safeguards in the exchange of information system. In this respect, the so-called rule of subsidiarity) and the guarantee of secrecy by the requesting state can play an important role. The rule of subsidiarity, on the ground of which the applicant state must first exhaust its usual instruments or sources before requesting information from another state, appeared however not to be a requirement of lawfulness, but an instrument enabling the requested state to protect itself (and its taxpayer/informant from unnecessary efforts. In the Convention on Mutual Administrative Assistance in Tax Matters and the European Directive 1977/79 (but, unfortunately, not in the OECD Model Tax Convention), this rule finds an exception in case the results of the examination in the applicant state would be jeopardized as a consequence of the subsidiarity rule. A taxpayer under examination in the applicant state could advise his associated or contract partner in the other state that he should make evidence disappear. The applicant state must therefore be able to opt against the application of the subsidiarity rule. In my opinion, this leads to the conclusion that this rule cannot be an argument in the hands of the taxpayer supplying the information in the requested state, because neither that state, nor he/, can prove or test non-compliance of this rule.

The duty of secrecy of the requesting state is a duty of care and as such of crucial importance to the taxpayer. However, the protection it offers the taxpayer in the supplying state appeared to be all but certain, because it must be fulfilled partly by the requesting state. The appeals procedure which, in the general opinion, is open to the taxpayer in the requesting state in case of breach of secrecy, hardly proved to offer him adequate protection. For a start, there are the practical problems adherent to having to sue in a foreign country. Furthermore, there appeared to be no obligation for the states to enter into a mutual agreement procedure about liability in case of breach of secrecy or wrongful use of information in the requesting state. The only measure a requested state can take is to use the possibility from the European Directive 77/799 or the Strasbourg Convention to require extra measures in case serious doubt would arise about the level of protection in the requesting state. The taxpayer supplying the information should be able to enforce its application. The fact that the secrecy of the information exchanged is subject to the secrecy legislation in the requesting state and the fact that states are not obligated to enter into a mutual agreement procedure about the question of liability turned out to be shortcomings in the rules on mutual administrative assistance. This also applies to the OECD Model Tax Convention, which does not enable parties to require extra measures of secrecy in case of doubt.

These shortcomings have led to the recommendation that the OECD insert these terms in the Model Tax Convention, creating an obligation to agree (e.g., within the framework of the mutual agreement procedure of Article 25 of the

Model Tax Convention) on liabilities in case of breach of secrecy in the other state. Moreover, it was recommended that the legal position of the supplier of information be enhanced by the most autonomous description of the secrecy rule and that an obligation for states is created to establish a right of information for the benefit of this taxpayer, so that he is at least informed of the exchange of information. In case the OECD fails to take this initiative, states should at least provide for the latter themselves.

The obligation to supply information is, however, not an absolute one, and for that reason all provisions on the exchange of information contain grounds on which the exchange of information can be declined or omitted. It became clear that the grounds of exception designated to states may also be used by taxpayers. The argument of sovereignty protects their legal certainty, and the argument of reciprocity protects their market position against taxpayers in other states. However, the arguments concerning public order and general principles of taxation represent more general interests, so that it is not clear whether they are sufficiently direct and personal for individuals to be invoked. According to the OECD Commentary and the Commentaries on the Strasbourg Convention and the OECD Agreement, in fact, only the argument concerning the possible disclosure of a business secret is specifically meant for the taxpayer.

This analysis of the demands of lawfulness and effectiveness with regard to the obligation to exchange information and the discretionary grounds of exception could lead to the conclusion that the supplying states do in fact have the possibility to weigh certain interests of their taxpayers against their own or those of the other state. To secure that this in effect takes place, the taxpayer also should be able to invoke these arguments in an appeals procedure.

## 2.1. Ways to Protect Interests

Having reached the point described above, a fourth question remained to be answered, namely, how to realize the protection of the interests of the taxpayer supplying the information on a national level. Linked to this is the question of which system of standards is most suitable to this end. These questions were answered in Chapter 8.

Because of the informational nature of the risks, it seemed logical to link onto the system of standards on data processing, as developed step by step since the 1970s. In the beginning of what is called 'the information era' standards of legitimate data processing were developed, as a reaction to the ever-growing role the possession of information played in the mutual relationships of legal subjects and the increasing inequality this might give rise to. This was done by the OECD (Guidelines on the Protection of Privacy and Transborder Flow of Personal Data), and the European Community (European Convention on the protection of individuals with regard to the automatic processing of personal data). These were partly reflected in an OECD report about the practice of the exchange of information. Some countries created legislation on the informational self-determination.

These standards were finally incorporated in the European Privacy Directive. They aim to ensure that data processing meets the demands of 'fairness' and lawfulness. Processing appeared to be lawful on the condition of the consent of the affected party, or the existence of a general interest the protection of which is appointed to the responsible party. The 'fairness' of it depends on the condition that the processing serves a justified purpose defined beforehand and demands that the data subject affected is informed about the processing. Besides, the data subject must be able to correct the information, or to lodge an appeal against the collection, transmission, or use of this information. Especially the data subject's right of information and appeal laid down in the European Privacy Directive seemed to be applicable to the situation in which the government as the party responsible collects information and transmits it to other states. On the other hand, especially the 'essential economic interests of states' also appeared to be a reason to limit information rights.

However, a setback for the applicability of the European Privacy Directive is the concept of the 'data subject'. In a further analysis of the rights of information in the processing of direct and indirect information, a 'data subject' turned out to have been exclusively defined as the party 'to whom the data are related to'. If these data are obtained from a third party, then this is not 'the data subject'. Moreover, this definition was limited to natural persons. These facts proved the European Privacy Directive to be unfit as such for the protection of the taxpayer in the supplying state in the many cases that he supplies information concerning a third person, resident of the applicant state.

After this conclusion, a different legal framework had to be found not so much aimed at the protection of privacy, but linked onto the notion of information as an object of the right to undisturbed property. Here, not only the interests of the affected party, but also those of the supplier of information appeared to be potentially recognized and protected. In that case, the instruments of legal protection in the European Privacy Directive could be maintained.

Besides this, it turned out that administrative law, if adapted to the specific situation and interests of the taxpayers supplying the information, could offer adequate protection as well. The reason for this is that the party responsible for the exchange of information is an administrative authority, so that the relationship is one of administrative law. Moreover, it is typical for administrative law that decisions made by government bodies must be made known *before their execution*. This creates a basis for a dialogue with the affected citizen, in which the interests of the latter are considered.

The protection in civil law of the taxpayer involved in the exchange of information appeared not quite adequate. Certainly the civil court will be able to determine the lawfulness (including the carefulness) of government proceedings mainly along the same lines as the administrative court does. The problem is, however that, if there is no (inter)national obligation to inform the taxpayer on forehand of the actual exchange of his information, the protection of the civil court will be given too late. In that case, the taxpayer/informant runs the risk that the other state uses the information unlawfully, and that damage has already occurred. The taxpayer then will have to sue in the other state. The conclusion was that the best option for states to avoid damage for (and therefore their duty) is to create a set of rules for data processing that is embedded in the administrative legal system. This set of rules should contain the following elements:

- A government duty to inform the tax-payer about a decision to exchange in formation, basically before the execution of that decision.
- A clear definition of the notion of 'the affected party' as the party supplying the information in the requested state.
- Specific grounds of appeal, derived from the requirements of lawfulness in the international rules on the exchange of information, and from the grounds of exception with regard to the obligation to exchange information, which are to be considered as interests of the tax-payers supplying the information.
- Last but not least there should be an efficient process of notification with terms which can reasonably serve the legal position of the taxpayer/informant as well as the need for information of the other state. Therefore states could consider to introduce different proceedings for cases in which fraud seems obvious, and the information is urgently needed by the other state.

This will enable the states and the taxpayer to start a dialogue, so that both parties can defend their interests, and in which the supplying state has to take care that the interests of the treaty partner are balanced properly.

# List of References


Ault, H.G. 'The Role of the OECD-Commentaries in the Interpretation of Tax Treaties'. *Intertax* 22, no. 4 (1994).

Avery Jones, J.F. 'The Interpretation of Tax Treaties with Reference to Article 3(2) of the OECD'. *British Tax Review* 2 (1984a).

Avery Jones, J.F. 'The "One True Meaning" of a Tax Treaty, Tax Treaty Monitor'. *IBFD Bulletin* (June 2001).

Avery Jones, J.F. 'The Effect of Changes in the OECD-Commentaries after a Treaty Is Concluded'. *IBDF Bulletin* 56, nr. 3 (March 2002).

Bakker, A.J. 'Verbetering Van de Mutual Agreement: Procedure noodzakelijk?'. *Weekblad voor Fiscaal Recht (WFR) 132* (2003): 6547, 537-1544.

Barents, R. & L.J. Brinkhorst. *Grondlijnen van Europees Recht*. Alphen aan de Rijn: Samson H.D. Tjeenk Willink, 1996.

Barnard, J.C. 'Voormalige belastingparadijzen bereid tot doorbreking van bankgeheim'. *Weekblad voor Fiscaal Recht (WFR)* 131 (2002): 6490.

Becker, H. 'Limits on Exchange of Information in Connection with Tax Audit Practice'. *Intertax* 10, no. 2 (1982).

Bentley, D. (ed.). *Taxpayers' Rights: An International Perspective*. Australia: Gold Coast, 1998.

Blok, P.H. 'De grondslagen van het gegevensbeschermingsrecht herzien'. *Rechtsgeleerd Magazijn Themis* 163, no. 1 (February 2002a): 17-19.

Blok, P.H. *Het recht op privacy* (diss.). Tilburg, 2002b.

Boer, P. den. 'Het Multilaterale bijstandsverdrag'. *Maandblad voor Belasting Beschouwingen (MBB)* nr. 3 (March 1988): 82-86.

Bomer, A. H. 'Internationale bijstandsverlening bij de heffing van accijnzen enomzetbelasting'. *Weekblad voor Fiscaal Recht (WFR)* 122 (1993): 6068.

Bont, G.J.M.E. 'Tax Treaty Interpretation in the Netherlands'. In *Tax Treaty Interpretation*, edited by M. Lang. Deventer: Kluwer, 2001.

Bricker, M.P. 'Arbitration Procedures in Tax Treaties'. *Intertax* 26, no. 3 (1998).

Brodersen, C. 'Limits on the International Exchange of Tax Information'. *European Taxation* (June 1987).

Brouwer, P.W. 'Rechtsbeginselen en rechtspositivisme'. *Ars Aequi* 40, no. 10 (1991).

Bruggen, E. van der. 'State Responsibility under Customary International Law in Matters of Taxation and Tax Competition'. *Intertax* 29, no. 4 (2001).

Bruggen, E. van der. ' "Unless the Vienna Convention Otherwise Requires": Notes on the Relationship between Article 3(2) of the OECD Model Tax Convention and Articles 31 en 32 of the Vienna Convention on the Law of Treaties'. *European Taxation* (May 2003).

de Bruin, K. 'Verbroken evenwicht, Een verslag van het derde symposium NOB/VI/VAI'. *Weekblad voor Fiscaal Recht* 120 (1991): 5963.

Brunschot, F. van & J.M. Ellis. 'The Judiciary and the OECD Model Tax Convention Commentaries'. *IBFD Bulletin* (January 2005).

Bunders, E. & J.A.C. Overgaauw. 'Terugblik op een eeuw Nederlandse belastingverdragen. Wat zal de nieuwe eeuw brengen?'. *Maandblad voor Belasting Beschouwingen (MBB)* (January 2000).

Burg, F.H. van der. *Gemeenschapsrecht in de Nederlandse rechtsorde.* Deventer: W.J. Tjeenk Willink, 1998.

Burgers, I.J.J., R. Betten, & H.M. Bierlaagh. *Wegwijs in het Internationaal en Europees Belastingrecht.* 5[e] druk. Amersfoort: SDU, 2007.

Burger I.J.J. & F.A. Engelen. 'Interpretation of Tax Treaties under International Law'. *Weekblad voor Fiscaal Recht (WFR)* 134 (2005): 6644 (book review).

Burns, T. & R. Turner. 'Confidentiality of Taxpayer Information'. *International Transfer Pricing Journal* 7 (March 2000).

Calderon, J.M. 'Taxpayer Protection within the Exchange of Information Procedure between State Tax Administrations'. *Intertax* 28, no. 12 (2000).

Calderon, J.M. 'The Taxpayer's Right to Set the "Mutual Agreement Procedure" in Motion: The Spanish Tax Courts' Approach'. *Intertax* 29, no. 11 (2001).

Casley, A. & J. Henshall. 'Confidentiality of Taxpayer Information (United Kingdom)'. *International Transfer Pricing Journal* (January 2000).

Christiaanse, J.H. 'Terugwerkende kracht op fiscaal terrein'. *Weeklad voor Fiscaal Recht (WFR)* 129 (1990): 5936.

Christian, J. 'National Report Denmark'. *Cahiers de Droit Fiscal International.* Vol. LXXV. Deventer: Kluwer, 1991.

Cohler, A.M., B.C. Miller & H. Stone (eds). *Montesquieu, The Spirit of Laws.* Cambridge, UK: Cambridge University Press, 1989 [1748].

Cuijpers, C. *Privacyrecht of privaatrecht* (diss.). Gouda, 2004.

Curtin, D.M. ' "Citizens" Fundamental Rights of Access to EU-Information'. *Common Market Law Review* nr. 37 (2000).

Daniels, A.H.M. 'Het wetsvoorstel inzake de bijstandsverlening bij de heffing van belastingen', *FED* 45 nr. 303 (June 1985): 1079-1082.

Daniels, A.H.M. '*De grensoverschrijdende gegevensuitwisseling door belasting administraties*'. Fiscale brochures FED. Deventer: Kluwer, 1987.

Daniels, A.H.M. 'Fiscale Informatie-uitwisseling over de grenzen'. *Preadvies NOB*. Nederlandse Orde van Belastingadviseures, 1990.
Daniels, A.H.M. 'Sovereign Affairs'. *Intertax* 29, no. 1 (2000).
Davis, K.C. *Discretionary Justice: A Preliminary Inquiry*. Baton Rouge, 1969.
D'Agostino, F. The State under the Rule of Law. In: *European Democratic Culture*, edited by A.M. Rieu & G. Duprat. London, 1995.
Debatin, H. 'Neue Entwicklungen imsteuerlichen Auskunftverkehr'. *Der Betrieb* (1977): 2065.
Dijck, J.E.A.M. van. 'Een rechtspersoonlijke levenssfeer'. *Weekblad voor Fiscaal Recht (WFR)* 128 (1999): 6339.
Distaso, M. 'Confidentiality of Taxpayer Information (Italy)'. *International Transfer Pricing Journal* (March/April 2000).
Docclo, C. 'Exchange of Information: Belgium'. *European Taxation* (August 1999).
Douvier, P.J. 'Confidentiality of Taxpayer Information'. *International Transfer Pricing Journal* (January 2000).
Dworkin, R. *Taking Rights Seriously*. London, 1977.
Dworkin, R. 'Equality of Welfare, Part 1: What Is Equality?'. *Philosophy of Public Affairs* nr. 10 (1981).
Dworkin, R. *A Matter of Principle*. Cambridge, Mass: Harvard University Press, 1985.
Dworkin, R. *Law's Empire*. Cambridge, Mass: Harvard University Press, 1986.
Easson, A. 'Harmful Tax Competition: An Evaluation of the OECD-Initiative'. *Tax Notes International* (7 June 2004): 1037-1071.
Edward, D. 'Private Law Principles'. In *The Action for Damages in Community Law*, edited by T. Heukels & A. McDonnell. The Hague, 1996.
Ellis, M.J. *Waar blijft de tijd* (Oratie Rotterdam). Deventer: Kluwer, 1995.
Ellis, M.J. 'Enkele kanttekeningen bij het ontwerp van de Wet Inkomstenbelasting 2001'. *Maandblad voor Belasting Beschouwingen (MBB)* (November 1999).
Ellis, M. 'Enkele internationale kanttekeningen bij het ontwerp van de Wet Inkomstenbelasting 2001'. *Maandblad voor Belasting Beschouwingen (MBB)* (October/November 2001).
Ellis, J.M. 'Het veranderde internationale landschap voor ondernemers'. *Weekblad voor Fiscaal Recht* 125 (1996): 6186.
Engelen, P.B. 'Internationale inlichtingenuitwisseling: Kan spontaan verplicht zijn?'. *Weekblad voor Fiscaal Recht* (1991): 5954.
Engelen, F.A. *Interpretation of Tax Treaties under International Law*. Amsterdam: IBFD Doctoral Series, IBFD 2004.
Engelen, F.A. 'Some Observations on the Legal Status of the Commentaries on the OECD Model'. *IBFD Bulletin* (March 2006).
Engelen, F.A. & F.P.G. Pötgens. 'Zijn interpretatieve en legislatieve mutual agreements bindend?'. *Maandblad voor Belasting Beschouwingen (MBB)* (February 2000).
Engelen, F.A. & F.P.G. Pötgens. 'The Application of the OECD-Model Tax Convention to Partnerships, en de interpretatie van belastingverdragen, deel 1'. *Weekblad voor Fiscaal Recht (WFR)* 129 (2000): 6394.

Engelen, F.A. & F.PG. Pötgens. 'The Application of the OECD-Model Tax Convention to Partnerships en, de interpretatie van belastingverdragen, deel 2'. *Weekblad voor Fiscaal Recht (WFR)* (2000): 6395.

Erp, J.M.M. *Contract als rechtsbetrekking: Een rechtsvergelijkende studie.* Zwolle: W.E.J. Tjeenk Willink, 1990.

Eijsden, J.A.R. van. 'Rechtsbescherming tegen de controlehandelingen van de fiscus'. *Weekblad voor Fiscaal Recht (WFR) 135* (2006): 6687.

Feteris, M.W.C. 'Belastingen en mensenrechten'. *Maandblad voor Belasting Beschouwingen (MBB)* (March 2006).

Finaly, R.A.R.S. 'Privacy van rechtspersonen'. *Nederlands Juridisch Comite voor de Mensenrechten (NJCM) Bulletin* 23 (1998).

Fines, F. A 'General Analytical Perspective on Community Liability'. In *The Action for Damages in Community Law*, edited by T. Heukels & A. McDonnell. The Hague: Kluwer Law International, 1996.

Foqué, R. 'De noodzakelijke verwevenheid van recht en ethiek'. *Ars Aequi* 47 nr. 1 (1998).

Fuller, L.L. *The Morality of Law*. New Haven: Conn.: Yale University Press, 1977.

Gangemi, B. 'General Report IFA Conference on International Mutual Assistance through Exchange of Information'. *Cahiers de Droit Fiscal International.* Deventer: Kluwer, 1990, LXXVb.

Gerven, van. W. 'Creatieve rechtspraak'. *Tijdschrift voor Privaatrecht* nr. 1 (1997).

Glastra van Loon, J.F. 'Rules and Commands'. *Mind* (October 1958): 514-521.

Glastra van Loon, J.F. 'Regels en bevelen in: De eenheid van het handelen'. *Opstellen over recht en filosofie.* Amsterdam/Meppel, 1980.

de Graaf, A.C.G.A.C. *De invloed van het EG-recht op het internationaal belastingrecht: beleids en marktintegratie* (diss.). Deventer: Kluwer, 2004.

de Graaf, A.C.G.A.C. 'Oplossing conflict tussen belastingverdrag en gemeenschapsbepaling'. *Maandblad voor Belasting Beschouwingen (MBB)* nr. 5 (2000).

Geppaart, Ch.A. 'De invloed van artikel 6 EVRM op de fiscale boete'. *Weekblad voor Fiscaal Recht (WFR)* 123 (1994): 6122.

Gribnau, J.L.M. 'De wederkerige rechtsbetrekking als nieuw paradigma?'. *Nederlands Tijdschrift voor Rechtsfilosofie en Rechtstheorie (R&R)* nr. 2 (1993).

Gribnau, J.L.M. *Rechtsbetrekking en rechtsbeginselen in het belastingrecht* (diss.). Arnhem: Gouda Quint, 1998.

Gribnau, J.L.M. 'General Introduction'. In *The Principle of Equality in European Taxation*, edited by G.T.K. Meussen. The Hague: Kluwer Law International, 1999.

Gribnau, J.L.M. 'Soft Law and Taxation: The Case of The Netherlands'. *Legisprudence* I, no. 3 (2007): 295.

Gribnau, J.L.M. & G.T.K. Meussen. ' "Rechtszekerheid en de Wet" IB 2001 (1)'. *Maandblad voor Belasting Beschouwingen (MBB)* (October 2002).

Guest, S. R. Dworkin. Edinburgh, 1992.

Gyönghi Végh, P. 'Towards a Better Exchange of Information'. *European Taxation* (September 2002).

Happé, R.H. 'Artikel 26 BUPO-verdrag, ofwel hoe het belastingrecht de maat wordt genomen'. *Weekblad voor Fiscaal Recht (WFR)* 119 (1990): 5907.

Happé, R.H. *Drie beginselen van fiscale rechtsbescherming* (diss.). Deventer: Kluwer, 1996.

Happé, R.H. 'Fiscaal Compromis. Op de grens van publiek: en privaatrecht'. In *Contractsvrijheid*, edited by P. Wattel, J.L.M. Gribnau & R.H. Happé. Deventer: Kluwer, 1999.

Happé, R.H. 'Fiscale discriminatie en de kunst van het wetgeven'. *Weekblad voor Fiscaal Recht (WFR)* 132 (2002): 6477.

Happé, R.H., P.M.F. van Loon & J.P.F Slijpen. Algemeen fiscaal bestuursrecht. 2[e] druk. Deventer: Kluwer, 2005.

Hart, H.L.A. *The Concept of Law*. Oxford: Clarendon Press, 1961.

Hartlief, T. 'Het recht op eigendom onder het EVRM'. *Jaar EVRM*, Special Edition NJCM Bulletin (Nederlands Juridisch Comité voor de Mensenrechten 45 (1995): 129-146.

Hartogh, G.A. 'De Fiscale moraal en de moraal van de fiscus'. *Weekblad voor Fiscaal Recht (WFR)* 116 (1987): 5772.

Hay, R.J. 'OECD Level Playing Field Report Released: Consensus or Conflict?'. *Tax Planning International Review* (June 2006): BNA 3-10.

Heinrich, J. & H. Moritz. 'Interpretation of Tax Treaties'. *European Taxation* (April 2000).

Heithuis, E.W. 'Europees belastingrecht in relatie tot de bilaterale belastingverdragen vanuit Nederlands perspectief'. *Weekblad voor Fiscaal Recht (WFR)* 122 (1993): 6077.

Helfrich-Laubrock, J. 'Critical Review of the OECD/Council of Europe Multilateral (Draft) Convention on Mutual Administrative Assistance in Tax Matters'. *IBDF Bulletin* (August 1987).

Hertoghs, J.J.M. & G.M.J.E. de Bont. 'De WIB, de Awb en de rechtsbescherming'. *Maandblad voor Belasting Beschouwingen (MBB)* (March 1994): 195-204.

Hirsch Ballin, E.H.M. 'Wederkerig bestuursrecht'. *Rechtsgeleerd Magazijn Themis*, 1989.

Hirsch Ballin, E.H.M. 'Het Grondrecht op vrijheid en de wet'. In *Rechtsstaat & Beleid*, edited by E.J.M. Hirsch Ballin. Zwolle: W.E.J. Tjeenk Willink, 1991.

Hirsch Ballin, E.H.M. 'Waarop is beleid gericht?'. In *Rechtsstaat & Beleid*, edited by E.J.M. Hirsch Ballin. Zwolle: W.E.J. Tjeenk Willink, 1991a.

Hirsch Ballin, E.H.M. 'Het rechtspositivisme achterhaald'. In *Rechtsstaat & Beleid*, edited by E.J.M. Hirsch Ballin. Zwolle: W.E.J. Tjeenk Willink, 1991b.

Hirsch Ballin, E.H.M. 'De mens in de sociale rechtsstaat'. In *Rechtsstaat & Beleid*, edited by E.H.M. Hirsch Ballin. Zwolle: W.E.J. Tjeenk Willink, 1991c.

Hirsch Ballin, E.H.M. 'Hoe komt beleid tot ontwikkeling'. In *Rechtsstaat & Beleid*, edited by E.H.M. Hirsch Ballin. Zwolle: W.E.J. Tjeenk Willink, 1991d.

Hirsch Ballin, E.M.H. 'Een grondrecht op behoorlijk bestuur'. *Nederlands Tijdschrift voor Bestuursrecht (NTB)* nr. 10 (2000).

Houte, C.P.M. van. 'De Belastingdienst op "fishing expedition" '. *Weekblad voor Fiscaal Recht (WFR)* 134 (2005): 6634.

Hurk, H.T.P.M. van den. 'De bevoegdheid van lidstaten om belastingverdragen te sluiten aan de ketting?'. *Maandblad voor Belasting Beschouwingen (MBB)* (May 2003).

Jacobs, F.C.L.M. 'Lon Fuller'. In *Rechtsfilosofen van de twintigste eeuw*, edited by P.B. Cliteur & M.A. Loth. Arnhem: Gouda Quint, 1992, 137-138.

Juch, D. 'Internationaal fiscaal (verdragen) recht'. *Maandblad voor Belasting Beschouwingen (MBB)* (March 1999).

Keen, M. & J. Ligthart. 'Information Sharing and International Taxation'. *International Tax and Public Finance* 13 (2006).

Kemmeren, E.C.C. *Principle of Origin in Tax Conventions: A Rethinking of Models* (diss.). Tiburg, 2001. Private edition.

Kimman, E. 'Naar meer of minder gelijke fiscale behandeling?'. In *Belastingrecht en ethiek in debat*, edited by H.L.M. Gribnau. Deventer: Kluwer, 1999.

Klein Sprokkelhorst, A.K.H. *Overeenkomsten met de fiscus*. Deventer: Kluwer, 1999.

Kooijmans, P.H. *Internationaal publiekrecht in vogelvlucht*. Deventer: Kluwer, 2000.

Koopmans, T. 'De rol van de wetgever'. In *Honderd jaar rechtsleven*. Zwolle: W.E.J. Tjeenk Willink, 1970.

T. Koopmans. *Vergelijkend publiekrecht*. Deventer: Kluwer, 1986.

Lambooij, M.V. 'De uitwisseling van fiscale gegevens: rechtsbescherming in de praktijk'. In *Fiscale informatie-uitwisseling over de grenzen*. Preadvies NOB, 1990 (NederlandseOrde van Bellastingadviseurs. Private edition.

Lang, M. (ed.). *Tax Treaty Interpretation*. The Hague: Wien, 2001.

Lang, M. 'Later Commentaries of the OECD Committee on Fiscal Affairs, Not to Affect the Interpretation on Previously Concluded Tax treaties'. *Intertax* 25, no. 1 (1997).

Langbein, V. 'The Overriding of Tax Treaties by National Legislation or the Melford-Case Revisited. A German View'. *Intertax* 15, no. 1 (1987).

Langereis, C.J. 'Redelijkheid en billijkheid in het belastingrecht'. In *Geppaart-bundel, Beschouwingen over grondslagen*. Deventer: Kluwer, 1996.

Lauwaars R.H. & C.W.A. Timmermans. *Europees gemeenschapsrecht in kort bestek*. Groningen: Wolters-Noordhoff, 1997.

Lenaerts, K. 'Fundamental Rights to be Included in a Community Catalogue'. *European Law Review* 367, no. 5 (1991).

MacCormick, N. *H.L.A. Hart*. Stanford, 1981, 103-120.

Makhlouf, G. 'Transparency in Tax Systems: Keeping Pace with the Information Age'. *Intertax* 28, no. 2 (2000): 64-66.

Malherbe, J. 'General Report IFA-Conference on Protection of Confidential Information in Tax Matters'. *Cahiers de Droit Fiscal International*. Deventer: Kluwer, 1991, LXXXVI.

McLure, Ch.E. Jr. 'Globalization, Tax Rules and National Sovereignty'. *IBFD Bulletin* (August 2001).

McLure, Ch.E. Jr. 'Will the OECD Initiative on Harmful Tax Competition Help Developing and Transition Countries?'. *IBFD Bulletin* (March 2005).

Menck, Th. 'Internationale Amtshilfe in Steuersachen', *Deutsche Steuer Zeitung* (1971): 57.

de Moor-van Vugt, A. *Algemene beginselen van behoorlijk bestuur en buitenlandse equivalenten.* Zwolle: W.E.J. Tjeenk Willink, 1987.

de Moor-van Vugt, A. *Europees Bestuursrecht.* Deventer: Kluwer, 1998.

Musgrave, R.A. & P.B. Musgrave. 'Inter-Nation Equity'. In *Modern Fiscal Issues: Essays in Honor of Carl S. Shoup.* Toronto, Buffalo: University of Toronto Press, 1972.

Musgrave, R.A. & P.B. Musgrave. *Public Finance in Theory and Practice.* New York: McGraw-Hill, 1989.

Nationale Ombudsman, Rapport, nr. 92/906, *Vakstudie Nieuws*, 1993.

Niessen, R.E.C.M. 'Over de legitimatie van de belastingheffing'. In *Redelijkheid en billijkheid in het belastingrecht.* Deventer: Kluwer, 1996 (Geppaart-bundel).

Nieuwenhuis, J.H. 'Vechten met de beer'. *Rechtsgeleerd Magazijn Themis*, 1997, nr. 9.

Nieuwenhuis, J.H. 'Op gespannen voet, Een evenwichtstheorie over de betrekkingen tussen het publieke en het burgerlijke recht'. *Nederlands Juristen Bblad* 73, nr. 1 (1998).

Oberson, X. 'The OECD Model Agreement on Exchange of Information: A Shift to the Applicant State?'. *IBFD Bulletin* (January 2003): 14.

OESO-Rapport. Taxpayers' Rights and Obligations. A Survey of the Legal Situation in OECD Countries. Paris, 1990.

OESO-Rapport. Tax Information Exchange between OECD-Member Countries. A Survey of Current Practices. Paris, 1994.

OESO-Rapport. Harmful Tax Competition. An Emerging Global Issue. Paris, 1998.

Oliver, J.B. 'Exchange of Information and the OECD Model Treaty'. *Intertax* 23, no. 3 (1995).

Owens, J. 'The OECD's Work on Dispute Settlements in Tax Matters: A Progress Report'. *Tax Notes International* (27 March 2006): 1057.

Pijl, H. 'Uitwisseling van inlichtingen'. *Maandblad voor Belasting Beschouwingen* (MBB) (October 1998).

Pijl, H. 'Aantekeningen bij de lex-fori-bepaling in belastingverdragen'. *Weekblad voor Fiscaal Recht (WFR)* (1995): 6164.

Pijl, H. 'The Theory of the Interpretation of Tax Treaties, with Reference to Dutch Practice'. *IBFD Bulletin* (December 1997).

Pires, M. 'Quo Vadis International Tax Law'. *Intertax* 29, no. 12 (2001): 394-395.

Polak, J.E.M. *Burgerlijke rechter of bestuursrechter* (diss.). Deventer: Kluwer, 1999.

Prast, H. 'Terugwerkende kracht op het gebied van belastingwetgeving'. *Geschriften voor de Vereniging voor Belastingwetenschap*, nr. 150 (1978).

Prokisch, R. 'The Bank Secrecy and Its Implications on Tax Evasion'. *Tijdschrift voor Formeel Belastingrecht (TFB)* nr. 8 (December 2004).

Raad, C. van. 'Interpretatie van belastingverdragen'. *Maandblad voor Belasting Beschouwingen (MBB)* (February/March 1978).

Raad, C. van. 'Het nationale recht bij de uitlegging van belastingverdragen'. In *Van wet naar recht, Scheltens-bundel*. Deventer: Kluwer, 1984.

Raad, C. van. 'Internationale samenwerking bij heffing en invordering van belastingen'. *Leids Fiscaal Jaarboek* (1990).

Raad, C. van. 'Additions to Articles 3 (2) (Interpretation) and 24 (Anti discrimination) of the 1992 OECD Model and Commentary'. *Intertax* 12 (1992): 671.

Raad, C. van. 'Uitlegging en toepassing van belastingverdragen door de belastingrechter'. *FED Fiscaal Tijdschrift* (1996): 415.

Raad, C. van. 'International Coördination of Tax Treaty Interpretation and Application'. *Intertax* 29, nos 6-7 (2001).

Raz, J. 'The Rule of Law and Its Virtue'. *Law Quarterly Review* 93 (1977): 195.

Raz, J. *The Morality of Freedom*. Oxford: Clarendon Press, 1986.

Reimer, E. 'Interpretation of Tax Treaties'. *European Taxation* 39, no. 12 (December 1999): 512-521.

Reuter, H.P. 'Praktische Überlegungen zur Internationalen Steuerauskunft'. *Steuerberaterjahrbuch*, 1975-1976.

Runge, B.R. 'The German View on the Prevention and Settlement of International Disputes on Tax Law'. *Intertax* 25, no. 1 (1997): 4.

Schaumburg, H. *Internationales Steuerrecht*. Köln/London: Auflage, 1998.

Schaumburg, H. & S. Schlossmacher. 'Article 26 of the OECD-Model Convention in the Light of the Right to Informational Self-Determination'. *IBFD Bulletin* (October 2000).

Scheltens, D.F. 'De beginselen van het recht'. *Nederlands Tijdschrift voor Rechtsfilosofie en Rechtstheorie (R&R)* 5 (1976): 85-105.

Schenk-Geers, A.C.M. 'De rechtsbescherming van de Awb en de internationale bijstandsverlening'. *Weekblad voor Fiscaal Recht (WFR)* (1996): 6220, 1640-1648.

Schenk-Geers, A.C.M. 'Uitwisseling van inlichtingen in Europa'. *Tijdschrift voor Formeel Belastingrecht (TFB)* nr. 2 (March 2006).

Schenk-Geers, A.C.M. 'Rechtsplichten van de staat in de internationale uitwisseling van inlichtingen'. *Tijdschrift voor Fiscaal Ondernemen (TFO)* 85 (2006): 98-208.

Schenk-Geers, A.C.M. *Internationale fiscale gegevensuitwisseling en de rechtsbescherming van belastingplichtigen*. Deventer: Kluwer, 2007.

Schick, P. 'Confidentiality of Taxpayer Information'. *International Transfer Pricing Journal* 7 (January 2000).

Scholten, P. (ed.). 'Rechtsbeginselen'. In *Verzamelde geschriften*. Deel I. Zwolle: W.E.J. Tjeenk Willink, 1980 [1935].

Schuyt, C.J.M. 'Sturing in het recht'. In *Het schip van staat, Beschouwingen over recht, staat en sturing*, edited by M.A.P. Bovens et al. Zwolle: Tjeenk Willink, 1985.

Sentrop, J.W. 'De informationele privacy bedreigd'. *Ars Aequi* (1973): 207-222.

Soest, J. van. *Vrijheid in het belastingrecht* (Speech). Amsterdam, 1961.

Soeteman, A. 'Hercules aan het werk'. *Ars Aequi* (1991): 744.

Soeteman, A. 'Ronald Dworkin'. In *Rechtsfilosofen in de twintigste eeuw*, edited by P.B. Cliteur & M.A. Loth. Arnhem: Gouda Quint, 1992.

Strien, A.L.J., van. 'Rechtspersonen en mensenrechten'. *Rechtsgeleerd Magazijn Themis* (1996): 1.

Tieskens, R.W. 'De betekenis van het OESO-Modelverdrag voor de interpretatie van belastingverdragen'. *Weekblad voor Fiscaal Recht (WFR)* (1999): 6368.

Tillinghast, D.R. 'Issues in the Implementation of the Arbitration of Disputes Arising under Income Tax Treaties'. *IBFD Bulletin* (March 2002): 56.

Urtz, C. 'Confidentiality of Taxpayer Information'. *International Transfer Pricing Journal* 7, no. 2 (March/April 2000).

Velthuizen, H. 'Arbitrage in de Nederlandse Belastingverdragen'. *Weekblad voor Fiscaal Recht (WFR)* (2002): 6474.

Van de Ven M.P.M. Interregionale, Internationale en Supranationale Regelingen. *Pre-advies Nederlandse Orde van Belastingadviseurs (NOB)*. Deventer, 1990a.

Ven, M.P.M. van de. 'Fiscale informatie-uitwisseling over de grenzen'. *Pre-advies Nederlandse Orde van Belastingadviseurs (NOB)*. Deventer, 1990b.

Verstijlen, F.M.J. 'De rechtsbescherming in de Wet internationale bijstandsverlening bij de heffing van belastingen en de (buitenlandse) belanghebbende'. *Weekblad voor Fiscaal Recht (WFR)* (1993): 6077.

Vogel, K. 'Worldwide vs. Source Taxation of Income'. *Intertax* 16, no. 11 (1988).

Vogel, K. 'Changes to the OECD-Model Treaty'. *European Taxation* (December 1997).

Vogel, K. 'Tax Treaty News'. *European Taxation* (January 2000).

Vogel, K. 'Tax Treaty News'. *IBFD Bulletin* (March 2000a).

Vogel, K. 'Tax Treaty News'. *IBFD Bulletin* (December 2001).

Vogel, K. *Doppelbesteuerungsabkommen, Kommentar*. 4th edn. Beck: München, 2003.

Vogel, K. 'New Europe Bids Farewell to Treaty Override'. *IBFD Bulletin* (January 2004).

Vogel, K. & G. Prokisch. 'General Report of the IFA-Congress 1993, Interpretation of Double Taxation Conventions'. *Cahiers de Droit Fiscal International*. Deventer: Kluwer, 1993, LXXVIIIa.

Vogel, S. 'National Report Sweden'. *Cahiers de Droit Fiscal International*. Deventer: Kluwer, 1991, LXXV.

Waelbroeck, D.F. 'Liability of Member States'. In *The Action for Damages in Community Law*, edited by T. Heukels & A. McDonnell. The Hague: Kluwer, 1996.

Ward, D.A. 'The Role of the Commentaries on the OECD Model in the Tax Treaty Interpretation Process'. *IBFD Bulletin* (March 2006).

Wattel, P.J. 'Bespreking van A.H.M. Daniels: De grensoverschrijdende gegevensuitwisseling door belastingadministraties'. *FED* Fiscaal Tijdschrift 24, no. 3 (1988).

Wattel, P.J. 'Het spectaculaire trio Emmot, Frankovich, & Bonifaci'. *Weekblad voor Fiscaal Recht (WFR)* (1992): 626.

Wattel, P.J. & O. Marres. 'The Legal Status of the OECD Commentary and Static or Ambulatory Interpretation of Tax Treaties'. *European Taxation* (July/August 2003).

Weeghel, S. van. 'Fraus legis in internationaal verband'. *Tijdschrift voor Formeel Belastingrecht (TFB)* (2002): 1-12.

Westin, A.F. *Privacy and Freedom.* New York: Atheneum, 1967.

Wijk, van. H.D., W. Konijnenbelt & R.M. Van Male. *Hoofdstukken van bestuursrecht.* 12^e^ druk, Den Haag: Kluwer Law International, 2002.

Wijk, van, H.D. *Voortgaande terugtred.* Samsom: Alphen aan de Rijn, 1959.

Winkler, S.A. Aushöhlung der Individualrechte für fiskalische Zwecke (diss.). Frankfurt am Main: Bern, 2006.

Wisselink, M.A. 'Internationale uitwisseling van fiscale informatie tussen belastingadministraties'. *Maandblad voor Belasting Beschouwingen (MBB)* (February/March 1978).

Wisselink, M.A. 'Belgische heffingssystemen en fiscale informatieplichten. Internationale informatie-uitwisseling. Situatie tot 1992'. *Maandblad voor Belasting Beschouwingen (MBB)* (December 1993).

Wisselink, M.A. *Fiscale informatie-uitwisseling tussen Europese en andere landen.* Deventer: Kluwer, 1996.

Wisseling, M.A. 'International Exchange of Information between European and Other Countries'. *EC Tax Review* (1997): 2.

Wright, A.W. 'OECD Harmful Tax Competition Falls Short'. *Tax Notes International* (17 August 1998): 461.

Wright, D.R. 'Secrecy of Advance Pricing Agreements in the United States'. *International Transfer Pricing Journal* 7 (March/April 2000).

Woude, M.H. van der. 'Liability for Administrative Acts under Article 215(2) EC'. *The Action for Damages in Community Law*, edited by T. Huekels & A. McDonnell. The Hague, 1996.

# Table of Cases

**Netherlands Supreme Court**

| Date | BNB | Other sources | Paragraph |
|---|---|---|---|
| 21 November 1990 | 1991/132 | | 3.6.3 |
| 2 September 1992 | 1992/379 | | 3.5 |
| 4 November 1992 | 1993/38 | | 3.6.5.1 |
| 7 July 1993 | 1993/336 | | 6.3.2 |
| 25 May 1994 | 1994/219 | | 3.6.5.1 |
| 4 May 1994 | 1994/251 | | 2.3.4 |
| 29 June 1994 | 1994/294 | | 3.6.4 |
| 28 June 1995 | 1996/108 | | 3.6.3 |
| 19 September 1999 | 2000/16 | | 3.4.3, 3.6.1, 4.2 |
| 19 September 1999 | 2000/17 | | 3.4.3, 3.6.1, 4.2 |
| 21 February 2003 | 2003/178 | | 3.6.5 |
| 21 February 2003 | 2003/177 | | 3.6.5 |
| 5 September 2003 | 2003/379 | | 3.4.3 |
| 23 January 2004 | 2004/142 | | 3.4.3 |
| 19 November 2004 | 2005/77 | | 4.4.3.5 |
| 3 December 2004 | 2005/92 | | 3.4.3 |
| 10 December 2004 | 2005/195 | | 3.6.2, 4.2 |
| 23 September 2005 | | | 2.2.4 |

**Netherlands Council of State**

| | | | |
|---|---|---|---|
| 30 November 1990 | | R01.88. 3427 Infobulletin 1993/237 | 3.6.5.1 |
| 24 July1991 | | R01.89. 0881 V-N 1991/5 | 3.6.5.1 |
| 7 July 1995 | | H01.92 1869 Infobulletin 1995/785 | 4.4.2 |
| 20 October 1999 | | AWB 99/6917 | 7.3.1 |

**Netherlands High Courts**

| | | | |
|---|---|---|---|
| 22 Februari 1990 Hof den Haag | | 3083/ 88 V-N 18 juli 1990/12 | 2.3.4 |
| 6 September 2001 Hof Den Bosch | | 00/3486 V-N 2001/56.8 | 3.5 |

**Netherlands Courts**

| | | | |
|---|---|---|---|
| 12-September 2002 Rechtbank Amsterdam | | 13/120067 V-N 2002/45.7 | 4.4.6.1 |
| 16 October 2003 Rechtbank Groningen | | 18/07610-01 V-N 2003/56.4 | 4.4.6.2 |

**European Court of Justice**

| | | | |
|---|---|---|---|
| 5 februari 1963 | C -26/62 (*Van Gendt & Loos*) | ECR I 1963 | 4.4.3.2 |
| 15 juli 1964 | C -6/64 (*Costa Enel*) | ECR I 1255 | 4.4.3.2 |
| 17 December 1970 | C- 11/70 (*Internationale Handelsgesellschaft*) | ECR I 1135 | 4.4.3. 2 |
| 5 oktober 1977 | (*Tedeschi/Denkavit*) | ECR I 1555 | 8.4 |
| 9 maart 1978 | C- 106/77 (*Simmenthal*) | ECR I 629 | 4.3.2 |
| 24 juni 1986 | C- 53/85 (*Akzo*) | ECR I 1965 | 8.5.2 |
| 6 juni 1991 | C- 49/88 (*Al Jubail*) | ECR I 3187 | 8.53 |
| 19 November 1991 | C-6/90 & C9/90 (*Frankovich*) | ECR I 5357 | 8.5.3.4 |
| 27 June 1991 | C-49/88 (*Samad*) | ECR I 3187 | 8.5.3.4 |
| 12 April 1994 | C -1/93 (*Halliburton*) | ECR I 01137 | 4.2 |
| 5 March 1996 | C-46/93 (*Brasserie du Pêcheur*) | ECR I 1029 | 8.5.3.4 |

| | | | |
|---|---|---|---|
| 24 June 1986 | C- 53/85 (*Akzo*) | ECR I 1965 | 8.5.2 |
| 15 May 1997 | C -250/95 (*Futura*) | ECR I 2471 | 4.2 |
| 13 April 2000 | C -420/98 (*W.N.*) | ECR I 2847 | 4.4.5.7 |
| 26 September 2000 | C-478/98 (*Commission v. Belgium*) | ECR I 7587 | 4.2, 4.3 |
| 26 June 2003 | C-422/01 (*Skandia & Ramstedt*) | ECR I 6817 | 4.2, 4.3 |
| 4 March 2004 | C-334/02 (*Commission v. France*) | ECR I 2229 | 4.2 |
| 7 September 2004 | C-319/02 (*Manninen*) | ECR I 07477 | 6.3.1 |
| 10 March 2005 | C-39/04 (*Laboratoires Fournier*) | ECR I 02057 | 6. 3. 1 |
| 13 January 2005 | C-174/02 (*Streekgewest N. Br*) | ECR I 85 | 8.5.3.3 |
| 15 September 2005 | C- 495/03 (*Intermodal Transports*) | ECR I 08151 | 4.4.3.2 |
| 19 January 2006 | C -301/04 (*Carbon*) | ECR I 05915 | 4.3.2 |
| 30 January 2007 | C-150/4 (*Commission v. Denmark*) | ECR I 000 | 4.2, 6.3.1 |
| 12 September 2006 | C-196/4 (*Cadbury-Schweppes*) | ECR I 7995 | 4.2 |
| 14 December 2006 | C-170/05 (*Denkavit*) | ECR I 11949 | 4.4.3.2 |
| 24 May 2007 | C-157/05 (*Holböck*) | ECR I 0000 | 6.3.1 |
| 22 March 2007 | C- 383/05 (Talotta) | ECR I 02555 | 4.2 |
| 11 October 2008 | C-451/05 (*Elisa*) | ECR I 08251 | 4.4.3.2, 6.3.1 |
| 27 November 2008 | C- 418/07 (*Papillon*) | ECR I 000 | 4.4.3 |

**European Court on Human Rights**

| | | | |
|---|---|---|---|
| 30 March 1989 | (*Chappell*) | NJ 1991, 522 | 8.4.2.3 |
| 23 November 1992 | (*Niemietz*) | NJ 1993, 400 | 8.4.2.3 |
| 16 April 2002 | (*Colas Est*) | NJ 2003.452 | 8.5.2 |

**Other Courts**

| | | | |
|---|---|---|---|
| 15 Januari 1996 Court of Antwerp | | RGF6/7 Juin/ Juillet | 4.4.6.2 |
| 5 September 1980 Tribunal de Premier Instance Brussels | | European TAxation 198, p. 87 e.v. | 6.5.1 |

# Index


**A**

Acquiescence, 45
Adequate level of protection, 255, 256
Advance pricing Agreements (APA's), 4, 140
Asymmetrical legal relationships, 19, 20, 22, 24

**B**

Ban on self incrimination, 171, 184

**C**

Causality, 274, 275, 278, 279
Collection of taxes, 144
Committed jurisdictions, 90, 93, 97, 124, 125,192, 224
Consultation rights, 246

**D**

Draft Articles of State responsibility, 53, 272, 273, 275, 276
Diplomatic protection, 213
Discretionary powers, 162, 164
Dualistic system, 52-53
Duty of care, 18, 20,202
Dynamic interpretation, 48, 57-59

**E**

European Court of Human Rights, 66, 267
Estoppel, 45, 46
Equity, *See* Inter-nation equity
Equal concern and respect, 23, 29, 67, 73

**F**

Factual reciprocity, 182
Fair-play principle, 22, 268, 269
First Protocol ECHR, 267
Fishing expedition, 101
Freedom of information (legislation), 139, 214, 269

**G**

Generally accepted principles of taxation, 171
General principles
  of data processing, 201, 243
  of good governance, 244, 268
Grounds for exception, 82

**H**

Harmful tax competition, 68, 72
Human rights view (?) in treaty law, 65

**I**

Individual participation principle, 243, 245
Information rights, 170-171, 203, 224-226, 255, 258, 259
Informational interests, 10, 201-203, 206, 241-247, 268, 279
Information gathering powers, 165, 166, 169, 178, 220, 221, 233
Informational self determination, 25, 204, 242, 266-267
Inter-nation equity, 67
Intervention rights, 246

**L**

Lex fori clause, 50
Lex posteriori rule, 168

**M**

Monistic system, 51
Mutual agreement procedure, 52, 68, 140, 276

**N**

Night watcher state, 12
Nationality principle, 31
Normal course of administration, 105, 163, 166, 181
Normal procedure of tax administration, 105, 178
Notification rights, 246

**O**

Openness principle, 243

**P**

Personal data, 242, 243, 248
Privacy, 248-265, 266, 269-271
Positivist concept of law, 49
Principle of legality, 12, 80, 199, 233, 294
Principle of origin, 31
Principle of exclusive territorial jurisdiction, 110
Principle of territoriality, 31
Prior notification, 166, 203
Privacy protection and legal persons, 162
Prohibition on détournement de pouvoir (abuse of power), 167
Purpose specification requirement, 244

**R**

Reciprocity
  factual, 182
  juridical, 179
Recovery (use for), *See* Collection of taxes
Relativity requirement, 272
Retroactive effect, 90
Requirement of consent, 142, 147, 149, 153
Right of correction, 249, 262
Right of access (to data), 249, 262
Rule of law, 16, 63, 193
Rule of recognition, 15

**S**

Self- executiveness, 85
Separation of powers, 12
Solicitors' privilege, 189, 166, 172
State liability
  of the receiving state, 33, 205, 274
  of the supplying state, 272
State of law character, 206, 227, 255
Symmetric relationships, 19

**T**

Tax heavens, 123, 206
Technical Advisory Groups, 58
Treaty override, 38, 50
Trias politica, 12

**U**

Universality principle, 80

**W**

Wrongful act of the State, 272

EUCOTAX Series on European Taxation

(1) Peter HJ Essers, Guido JME de Bont & Eric CCM Kemmeren (eds), *The Compatibility of Anti-Abuse Provisions in Tax Treaties with EC Law*, 1998 (ISBN 90-411-9678-1).
(2) Gerard TK Meussen (ed.), *The Principle of Equality in European Taxation*, 1999 (ISBN 90-411-9693-5).
(3) Michael Lang (ed.), *Tax Treaty Interpretation*, 2001 (ISBN 90-411-9857-1).
(4) Pasquale Pistone, *The Impact of Community Law on Tax Treaties: Issues and Solutions*, 2002 (ISBN 90-411-9860-1).
(5) René Offermanns, *The Entrepreneurship Concept in a European Comparative Tax Law Perspective*, 2002 (ISBN 90-411-9887-3).
(6) Michael Lang & Mario Züger, *Settlement of Disputes in Tax Treaty Law*, 2002 (ISBN 90-411-9904-7).
(7) Carlo Pinto, *Tax Competition and EU Law*, 2003 (ISBN 90-411-9913-6).
(8) Michael Lang, Hans-Jörgen Aigner, Ulrich Scheuerle & Markus Stefaner, *CFC Legislation, Tax Treaties and EC Law*, 2004 (ISBN 90-411-2284-2).
(9) Mattias Dahlberg, *Direct Taxation in Relation to the Freedom of Establishment and the Free Movement of Capital*, 2005 (ISBN 90-411-2363-6).
(10) Michael Lang, Judith Herdin & Ines Hofbauer, *WTO and Direct Taxation*, 2005 (ISBN 90-411-2371-7).
(11) Dennis Weber, *Tax Avoidance and the EC Tray Freedoms: A Study of the Limitations under European Law for the Prevention of Tax Avoidance*, 2005 (ISBN 90-411-2402-0).
(12) Félix Alberto Vega Borrego, *Limitations on Benefits Clauses on Double Taxation Conventions*, 2005 (ISBN 90-411-2370-9).
(13) Michael Lang, Josef Schuch & Claus Staringer, *ECJ-Recent Developments in Direct Taxation*, 2006 (ISBN 90-411-2509-4).
(14) Reuven S. Avi-Yonah, James R. Hines Jr. & Michael Lang, *Comparative Fiscal Federalism. Comparing the European Court of Justice and the US Supreme Court's Tax Jurisprudence*, 2007 (ISBN 978-90-411-2552-1).
(15) Christiana HJI Panayi, *Double Taxation, Tax Treaties, Treaty-Shopping and the European Community*, 2007 (ISBN 978-90-411-2658-0).
(16) Dennis Weber, *The Influence of European Law on Direct Taxation: Recent and Future Developments*, 2007 (ISBN 978-90-411-2667-2).
(17) Michael Lang & Pasquale Pistone, *The EU and Third Countries: Direct Taxation*, 2007 (ISBN 978-90-411-2665-8).
(18) Oskar Henkow, *Financial Activities in European VAT: A Theoretical and Legal Research of the European VAT System and Preferred Treatment of Financial Activities*, 2007 (ISBN 978-90-411-2703-7).
(19) Michael Lang (ed.), *Tax Compliance Costs for Companies in an Enlarged European Community*, 2008 (ISBN 978-90-411-2666-5).

(20) Michael Lang (ed.), *Source versus Residence. Problems Arising from the Allocation of Taxing Rights in Tax Treaty Law and Possible Alternatives*, 2008 (ISBN 978-90-411-2763-1).

(21) Ioanna Mitroyanni, *Integration Approaches to Group Taxation in the European Internal Market*, 2008 (ISBN 978-90-411-2779-2).

(22) Rolf Eicke, *Tax Planning with Holding Companies. Repatriation of US Profits from Europe: Concepts, Strategies, Structures*, 2008 (ISBN 978-90-411-2794-5).

(23) Peter Essers et al. (ed.), *The Influence of IAS/IFRS on the CCCTB, Tax Accounting, Disclosure and Corporate Law Accounting Concepts: 'A Clash of Cultures'*, 2008 (ISBN 978-90-411-2819-5).

(24) Tonny Schenk-Geers, *International Exchange of Information and the Protection of Taxpayers*, 2009 (ISBN 978-90-411-3142-3).